A fascinating study of a politics that refuses
reading for anyone interested in the possibi
politics.

Matth...

Reading Univ...,

John Kelly has written the definitive guide to contemporary Trotskyism in England
and Wales. The analysis is sharp and clear, always taking its subject matter seriously,
probing every aspect of the phenomenon. It fulfils the author's intention to explain
the structure, influence and ambition of the movement utilising the techniques of
political science and a deep knowledge of the history of the far left.

John Callaghan, Professor of Politics and Contemporary History,
University of Salford, UK

Contemporary Trotskyism is a fascinating and well-researched excavation of a much
maligned and under-studied social movement. Mocked and feared in almost equal
measure, John Kelly's account provides a thorough overview of its highs and lows,
its persistence and challenges, as well as those moments Trotskyism influenced the
development of British politics as a whole.

Phil Burton-Cartledge, Lecturer in Sociology, University of Derby, UK

CONTEMPORARY TROTSKYISM

Almost 80 years after Leon Trotsky founded the Fourth International, there are now Trotskyist organizations in 57 countries, including most of Western Europe and Latin America. Yet no Trotskyist group has ever led a revolution or built an enduring mass, political party. *Contemporary Trotskyism* looks in detail at the influence, resilience and weaknesses of the British Trotskyist movement, from the 1970s to the present day.

The book argues that to understand and explain the development, resilience and influence of Trotskyist groups, we need to analyse them as bodies that comprise elements of three types of organization: the political party, the sect and the social movement. It is the properties of these three facets of organization and the interplay between them that gives rise to the most characteristic features of the Trotskyist movement: frenetic activity, rampant divisions, inter-organizational hostility, authoritarian and charismatic leadership, high membership turnover and ideological rigidity.

Trotskyist groups have been involved in a wide range of important social movements including trade unions, student unions, anti-war, anti-racist and anti-fascist groups. While their energy and activity in civil society have had some success, their influence has never been reflected in votes or seats at elections even after the financial crisis.

Drawing on extensive archival research, as well as interviews with many of the leading protagonists and activists within the Trotskyist milieu, this is essential reading for students, activists and researchers with an interest in the far left, social movements and contemporary British political history.

John Kelly teaches at the Department of Management, Birkbeck College, University of London. He has published widely on trade unions and the labour movement.

ROUTLEDGE STUDIES IN RADICAL HISTORY AND POLITICS

www.routledge.com/Routledge-Studies-in-Radical-History-and-Politics/book-series/RSRHP

Series editors:

Thomas Linehan, *Brunel University*, and John Roberts, *Brunel University*

The series *Routledge Studies in Radical History and Politics* has two areas of interest. Firstly, this series aims to publish books which focus on the history of movements of the radical left. 'Movement of the radical left' is here interpreted in its broadest sense as encompassing those past movements for radical change which operated in the mainstream political arena as with political parties, and past movements for change which operated more outside the mainstream as with millenarian movements, anarchist groups, utopian socialist communities, and trade unions. Secondly, this series aims to publish books which focus on more contemporary expressions of radical left-wing politics. Recent years have been witness to the emergence of a multitude of new radical movements adept at getting their voices in the public sphere. From those participating in the Arab Spring, the Occupy movement, community unionism, social media forums, independent media outlets, local voluntary organisations campaigning for progressive change, and so on, it seems to be the case that innovative networks of radicalism are being constructed in civil society that operate in different public forms.

The series very much welcomes titles with a British focus, but is not limited to any particular national context or region. The series will encourage scholars who contribute to this series to draw on perspectives and insights from other disciplines.

Titles include:

CONTEMPORARY TROTSKYISM

Parties, Sects and Social Movements in Britain

John Kelly

Routledge
Taylor & Francis Group

LONDON AND NEW YORK

First published 2018
by Routledge
2 Park Square, Milton Park, Abingdon, Oxon OX14 4RN

and by Routledge
711 Third Avenue, New York, NY 10017

Routledge is an imprint of the Taylor & Francis Group, an informa business

British Library Cataloguing-in-Publication Data
A catalogue record for this book is available from the British Library

Library of Congress Cataloging-in-Publication Data
Names: Kelly, John E., 1952- author.
Title: Contemporary Trotskyism : parties, sects and social movements in
    Britain / John Kelly.
Description: Abingdon, Oxon ; New York, NY : Routledge, 2018. |
    Series: Routledge studies in radical history and politics | Includes
    bibliographical references and index.
Identifiers: LCCN 2017052868 | ISBN 9781138943797 (hardback) | ISBN
    9781138943810 (pbk.) | ISBN 9781315671048 (ebook)
Subjects: LCSH: Communism—Great Britain—History. | Socialism—
    Great Britain—History. | Labor movement—Great Britain—History. |
    Social movements—Great Britain—History. | Political parties—Great
    Britain—History. | Great Britain—Politics and government—1945- |
    Trotsky, Leon, 1879-1940.
Classification: LCC HX243 .K45 2018 | DDC 324.241/0975—dc23
LC record available at https://lccn.loc.gov/2017052868

ISBN: 978-1-138-94379-7 (hbk)
ISBN: 978-1-138-94381-0 (pbk)
ISBN: 978-1-315-67104-8 (ebk)

Typeset in Bembo
by Swales & Willis Ltd, Exeter, Devon, UK
Printed and bound by CPI Group (UK) Ltd, Croydon, CR0 4YY

CONTENTS

FIGURES

TABLES

ABBREVIATIONS

AEU	Amalgamated Engineering Union
ANL	Anti-Nazi League
ATUA	All Trades Union Alliance
AUEW	Amalgamated Union of Engineering Workers
AWL	Alliance for Workers Liberty
CCRFI	Coordinating Committee for the Refoundation of the Fourth International
CND	Campaign for Nuclear Disarmament
CoR	Coalition of Resistance
CPSA	Civil and Public Services Association
CWI	Committee for a Workers International
CWU	Communication Workers Union
IBT	International Bolshevik Tendency
ICFI (SEP)	International Committee of the Fourth International (SEP)
ICFI (WRP)	International Committee of the Fourth International (WRP)
I-CL	International Communist League
ICL (FI)	International Communist League (Fourth Internationalist)
ICP	International Communist Party
ICU (T)	Internationalist Communist Union (Trotskyist)
ICWL	International Committee for Workers' Liberty
IMG	International Marxist Group
IMT	International Marxist Tendency
IS	International Socialists
IST	International Socialist Tendency
IWL-FI	International Workers League-Fourth International
IWU (FI)	International Workers Unity (Fourth International)

L4I	League for the Fourth International
L5I	League for the Fifth International
LCFI	Liaison Committee for the Fourth International
NALGO	National and Local Government Officers' Association
NRFM	National Rank and File Movement
NSSN	National Shop Stewards Network
NUT	National Union of Teachers
PRC	Permanent Revolution Collective
RCG	Revolutionary Communist Group
RCIT	Revolutionary Communist International Tendency
RCP	Revolutionary Communist Party (1977)
RMT	Rail, Maritime and Transport Union
rs21	revolutionary socialism in the 21st century
RSO	Revolutionary Socialist Organization
RtW	Right to Work Campaign
RWP	Revolutionary Workers' Party
SEP	Socialist Equality Party
SLL	Socialist Labour League
StW	Stop the War Coalition
SWP	Socialist Workers Party
SWP PT	Socialist Workers Party Pathfinder Tendency
TF-FI	Trotskyist Fraction–Fourth International
UAF	Unite Against Fascism
USFI	United Secretariat of the Fourth International
UtR	Unite the Resistance
VSC	Vietnam Solidarity Campaign
WIRFI	Workers International to Rebuild the Fourth International
WRP	Workers Revolutionary Party
WRP (NL)	Workers Revolutionary Party (News Line)
WRP (WP)	Workers Revolutionary Party (Workers Press)
WSL	Workers Socialist League

PREFACE AND ACKNOWLEDGEMENTS

I first encountered Trotskyist organizations as an undergraduate in the early 1970s and have followed their fortunes ever since, both as a member of the Communist Party in the 1980s and as an academic teaching trade union studies at the London School of Economics (LSE) and at Birkbeck. I critically examined Trotskyist writings on the labour movement in *Trade Unions and Socialist Politics* (Verso 1988) and re-examined the contributions of Marxist theory to the study of employment relations in *Rethinking Industrial Relations* (Routledge 1998). More recently, and in common with many others who share Marx' critical analysis of capitalism, I have been struck by the continuing divisions on the Trotskyist left and by its apparent inability to make significant gains during the economic crisis that began in 2008. In researching and writing this book I therefore set out to explore both the apparent resilience and the continuing weaknesses of the Trotskyist movement.

I would like to thank all those who agreed to be interviewed because without exception they were helpful and forthcoming. I would also like to thank the many colleagues who have deposited their extensive archives in Glasgow, London and Warwick; and the staff at the LSE Archives, the Modern Records Centre and the University of London Senate House Library. Particular thanks go to Terry Brotherstone and Hillary Horrocks for their access and help with the WRP archive at Glasgow Caledonian University and to John Callaghan, Gregor Gall and John McIlroy for kindly reading and commenting on the entire manuscript. The research was supported by a small grant from Birkbeck's School of Business. Parts of Chapter 7 first appeared in the *Journal of Political Ideologies*, 2016.

INTRODUCTION

In the centenary year of the Russian Revolution, the Trotskyist movement celebrated what its leaders and members regard as the greatest event in world history, the first successful revolutionary overthrow of a capitalist regime. The October Revolution continues to inspire contemporary Trotskyists whose admiration for its socialist ambition under the leadership of Lenin and Trotsky remains undimmed by its descent into Stalinist terror. Centenary exhibitions of revolutionary art and design in galleries and libraries have been augmented by a flood of Trotskyist lectures, conferences and books lauding the achievements of the Bolsheviks and seeking lessons that can help with the overthrow of British capitalism (for example Faulkner 2017; Miéville 2017; Sherry 2017; Vernadsky 2017). In pursuit of this goal the Trotskyist movement in Britain remains undaunted by the fact that no Trotskyist organization has led a revolutionary struggle anywhere in the world and none has ever built an enduring and influential mass political party.

Many people will dismiss the scenario of a British October Revolution as a fantasy and its Trotskyist proponents as an anachronistic irrelevance but the Trotskyist movement is far more significant than its small size and revolutionary politics would suggest. Several Trotskyist groups are active in the Labour Party, including the Alliance for Workers Liberty, Socialist Action and Socialist Appeal. Trotskyist newspapers and placards are an integral part of any large protest march or demonstration. There are Trotskyist-influenced groupings inside many major trade unions such as Grassroots Left in Unite and UCU Left in higher education. Almost every major university campus has at least one active Trotskyist group and the larger campuses such as Kings College London, Leeds and Manchester have two or three competing groups. The Trotskyist movement is also remarkably resilient despite the failure to achieve its overarching objective. The first British Trotskyists emerged in 1932 and the precursors of today's Socialist Party and Socialist Workers Party began in 1950 whilst the Workers Revolutionary Party can trace its origins to 1947. Groups in other countries with a major contemporary Trotskyist presence, such as Argentina, France and the USA, can also trace their lineage back to the 1930s (Alexander 1991a).

The main aims of this volume are therefore to describe and explain the structure, influence and resilience of the British Trotskyist movement, meaning the movement in England and Wales but excluding Northern Ireland and Scotland.[1] The Trotskyist group will be analysed as an organizational hybrid, a body comprising elements of the political party, the doctrinal sect and the social movement. As parties, many of them participate in elections, competing for votes and office, in order to implement their policies. Yet they are also unconventional parties, not only because of their commitment to revolutionary methods but because of their strong attachment to elements of Trotskyist doctrine. The salience of doctrine and doctrinal orthodoxy and the differentiation from rival groups are all hallmarks of the sect. Finally however Trotskyist organizations occasionally seek to build broad coalitions of social forces around a specific issue or demand and to that extent they function as social movements. The characteristics and the dynamics of Trotskyist groups are shaped by the interactions between these three facets and their competing organizational logics.

The main focus of the book is contemporary British Trotskyism, from the 1970s to the present day, and the evidence to be presented and discussed is taken from a variety of sources: from 30 archives in four separate locations (listed in the Bibliography), interviews with 26 leading members of the Trotskyist movement, publications including books, pamphlets and newspapers, Trotskyist websites and observations at meetings, conferences and demonstrations. The academic literature on Trotskyism is surprisingly limited and there are only three contemporary academic studies, Smith and Worley's (2014) edited collection which also covers anarchism and mainstream communism, Birchall's (2011) extremely detailed biography of SWP founder Tony Cliff and the short monograph by Callinicos (1990a) (and both Birchall and Callinicos were leading members of the SWP at the time of writing). Callaghan (1984 and 1987) published two path-breaking studies of British Trotskyism but these are now dated as is Widgery's (1976) collection of original material from the 1950s and 1960s.[2] There are some older critiques of Trotskyism by left but non-Trotskyist writers, for example Hodgson (1975) and Jenkins (1977). The development of the world Trotskyist movement is extensively chronicled in Alexander's (1991a) huge reference book and the history of the British movement prior to 1950 has been painstakingly described by Trotskyist historians Bornstein and Richardson (1986a, 1986b).[3] There are numerous books by Trotskyist activists about their own movement and its leaders but despite some useful detail these are predictably partisan, for example Bensaid (2013), Frank and Bensaid (2010), Taaffe (1995, 2017) and Woods (2013a). The collapse of communism has generated a substantial literature on the communist movement but this has devoted almost no attention to Trotskyism, for example Brown (2009), Smith (2014).

The plan of the present book is as follows: Chapter 1 sets out the main approaches required to understand the different facets of the Trotskyist organization, drawing first on the political science literature and the analysis of political parties as organizations seeking votes, office and policy implementation. Trotskyist parties, however, are also sects – a group of people who adhere to a particular doctrine based around certain core texts – and they are also social movements – they seek to mobilize people in civil society campaigns and protests around specific issues. Sects have been studied most extensively by both sociologists and economists of religion whilst the social movement literature has been developed primarily by sociologists and political scientists. Each sect bases itself on a particular interpretation of classical texts that eventually becomes enshrined as group orthodoxy, reinforced by charismatic leaders, yet the preservation of doctrine often conflicts with the tactical and strategic adjustments required to build broad-based social movements.

Chapter 2 describes the development of Trotsky's thought and political activity and its emergence from within Russian Bolshevism, avoiding the intense hostility of critics such as the Maoist Kostas Mavrakis (1976) or the Cold-War anticommunist Robert Service (2010a) and the hagiography of Trotskyists such as Richard Brenner (1996) and Ernest Mandel (1979, 1995a). The chapter covers his early clashes with Lenin, the growing rapprochement with the Bolsheviks during the First World War, his leadership role in the Russian Revolution and the factional struggle with Stalin and his supporters through the 1920s and 1930s, culminating in the creation of the Fourth International and its Transitional Programme in 1938. It charts the shifts in his political thinking as well as exploring its weaknesses, limitations and contradictions. The chapter also aims to establish the key elements of what would eventually become Trotskyist doctrine, some elements of which are shared by other communist currents, such as Maoism and Stalinism.

Chapter 3 begins with a discussion of the first comprehensive database of Trotskyist organizational membership and the remainder of Chapter 3 and Chapter 4 describe the evolution of British Trotskyism from 1950 to 2017. The argument is that it can be divided into four discrete phases, each of which is characterized *inter alia* by significantly different rates of growth and decline.[4] At the same time, the Trotskyist movement has become increasingly fragmented and the chapters also chart the emergence of seven discrete families of Trotskyism, divided from each other on doctrinal lines. Chapter 5 charts the doctrines of the different Trotskyist organizations and families and documents the ways in which they are defended, particularly through the creation and deployment of a rich language of 'deviations' against internal and external critics. The chapter then explores the role and impact of 'charismatic' or 'transformational' leadership and its many dysfunctional consequences, whilst the final section looks briefly at the ways in which Trotskyist organizations have used the centenary of the Russian Revolution to reinforce their existing doctrines.

Chapter 6 explores in detail the shifting loci of recruitment since the 1950s, particularly in light of the sharp decline in trade union membership since 1979. The final section of the chapter recuperates the discussion on doctrine and sectarianism in order to throw light on the obstacles to recruitment into the Trotskyist milieu. An appendix to this chapter assembles what little information we have on membership of the Trotskyist movement elsewhere in Western Europe. Chapter 7 considers elections and electoral performance from 1974, the first time Trotskyist candidates participated in a British general election, up to 2017. In order to gauge the impact of the majoritarian ('first past the post') electoral system on votes and vote shares it also discusses the results of elections held under some form of proportional representation, that is those for the European Parliament, Greater London Assembly, Welsh Assembly and various mayoralties. For comparison, an analysis of recent election results in Western Europe demonstrates they are as poor as those in the UK. Such dismal results pose a serious challenge for Trotskyist groups claiming to be the sole guardians of working-class interests and the chapter therefore explores the ways in which Trotskyist groups have rationalized their poor performance.

Chapter 8 straddles the party and social movement faces of Trotskyist groups by analysing four types of resources they can acquire and mobilize in campaigns. Human resources comprise members and their willingness to work for the organization; finance is raised in a variety of ways from members; social-organizational resources consist of the large staff numbers employed by Trotskyist groups and the organizational structures designed to organize and motivate members, to formulate policies and to decide on forms of collective action; and cultural resources include publications such as newspapers or magazines but also comprise books, online publications and websites.

Chapter 9 turns to trade union activity at the workplace, regarded by almost all Trotskyists as the nucleus of class warfare and the crucible of revolutionary class consciousness. The chapter describes the many forms of involvement over the years, noting the differences between Trotskyist families as well as the changed forms of engagement since the great strike wave that began in the late 1960s and came to a definitive end with the 1984–1985 miners' strike. After charting the current strength of the Trotskyist groups in the unions, the chapter then explores the perennial tensions between the competitive logic of party building at the expense of one's rivals and the cooperative logic of working as a social movement.

Chapter 10 explores a wide range of social movements built by Trotskyists in a series of domains such as anti-racism, anti-austerity and anti-war. It describes five of the most successful bodies, including the Anti-Nazi League and the Anti-Poll Tax Federation before looking in turn at those which have proved less successful and those in which Trotskyists have exerted relatively little influence. The chapter then seeks to establish the conditions conducive to success and uses the analysis to throw light on the serious problems faced by Trotskyist groups in their engagement with gender and sexual politics.

Chapter 11 turns to the international plane starting with the formation of Trotsky's Fourth International in 1938 and noting that almost 80 years later there are now 23 international Trotskyist organizations. The chapter begins with a discussion of what constitutes an 'International' and then deploys the analysis of doctrine, sects and Trotskyist families to chart the evolution of competing Fourth Internationals. Chapter 12 concludes with an appraisal of the achievements, limitations and weaknesses of the Trotskyist movement. Apart from the maintenance and dissemination of a Marxist tradition, it is the creation of a series of successful social movements that constitutes the most striking achievement of contemporary Trotskyism. Yet that success has been achieved by downplaying its *raison d'être*, the core elements of revolutionary socialist doctrine and the scenario of a British October Revolution. The chapter concludes with a summation of the fundamental flaws in Trotskyist doctrine that together explain why it has never led a revolution or built an influential mass party anywhere in the world and probably never will.

Notes

1 The political traditions, party and electoral systems and political institutions of both places are sufficiently different from the rest of the United Kingdom that separate studies would be required to do them justice.

2 There is also an older journalistic literature varying from relatively dispassionate, for example Shipley (1976, 1983), to extremely hostile, both from the right, for example Baker (1981), Tomlinson (1981), and from the communist left, for example Reid (1969), Walker (1985).

3 There is also interesting material in Croucher (1982), the special issue of *Revolutionary History* dealing with Britain (Vol. 6(2/3), 1996) and memoirs such as Hunter (1998), Ratner (1994) and Wicks (1992).

4 The year 1950 has been chosen as the start date because the two largest contemporary organizations, the SWP and the Socialist Party, came into existence that year. Although they both originated in the Revolutionary Communist Party, the first unified Trotskyist group created in 1944, the pre-1950 period has been well covered in Bornstein and Richardson (1986b).

1

THEORETICAL PERSPECTIVES

Trotskyists often describe their own organizations as revolutionary vanguard parties built on the principles of 'democratic centralism' whose political aim is the destruction of the capitalist state and the capitalist mode of production. Does this self-description imply they can be analysed as political parties using the same frameworks that have been applied by political scientists to social democratic and Christian democratic parties? Or are Trotskyist organizations qualitatively distinct from mainstream parties because of their revolutionary goals and disdain for elections and perhaps more akin to communist parties? This chapter begins with political science accounts of parties in order to establish there are points of similarity between Trotskyist organizations and their mainstream rivals. What will also become clear, however, is that there are fundamental differences whose analysis requires the deployment of a distinct set of conceptual tools. In the first place many Trotskyist organizations can also be analysed as sects, groups of people who strongly adhere to a worldview or doctrine based around certain core texts and which they seek to defend against heterodox rivals. There is an additional layer of complexity to be considered because Trotskyist organizations also seek to mobilize people in civil society campaigns and protests around specific issues and they can therefore be examined through the lens of social movement theory. Some of their social movement activity has involved the creation of new organizations, such as the Anti-Nazi League, but Trotskyist groups have also operated inside existing social movements such as trade unions. Some of these features of Trotskyist organizations are shared with their far left rivals, the communist parties, and it is therefore important to review the sparse academic literature on the British Communist Party.

The chapter will discuss the attributes of parties, sects and social movements respectively before then considering some of the interactions between these different facets of organization. For example, effective work in trade unions is likely to require building alliances with people holding very diverse political views and it may also entail compromises on bargaining demands and on the language in which they are 'framed'. In other words the logic of effective social movement action may clash with the logic of maintaining doctrinal orthodoxy. One consequence of this tension is factional disputes inside Trotskyist organizations which in turn can lead to organizational splits.

Political parties

One of the most influential frameworks used to analyse political parties argues they are best understood as organizations that pursue three broad goals, votes, office and policy, but they 'rarely have the opportunity to realize all of their goals simultaneously' (Strøm and Müller 1999: 9).[1] Depending on the influence of party structures, electoral systems and governmental and legislative institutions, party leaders frequently face trade-offs between different goals: for example, some conference policies may be unpopular with the electorate and their promotion during election campaigns may hinder the acquisition of votes. The votes/office/policy seeking framework has been used extensively, and fruitfully, to analyse dilemmas faced by a variety of West European socialist and communist parties since the 1970s including the Spanish Socialist Workers Party, the Dutch Labour Party and the Italian Communist Party (Müller and Strøm 1999). Hildebrand and Irwin (1999) for example show how the Dutch Labour Party responded to a series of electoral defeats in the 1980s by shifting economic policy rightwards in order to facilitate office-seeking through coalition with their highly successful Christian democratic rival. The framework has also been used to examine the incidence of factional breakaways from political parties. Ceron's (2015) research on Italy found that such splits were more likely in proportional electoral systems, because even low vote shares for small breakaway parties could still secure parliamentary seats. Under less proportional systems where small parties obtain very few seats, factional splits were far less common.

The votes/office/policy framework has also been expanded by several researchers to incorporate the importance of party membership and organization as key resources that can facilitate the acquisition of votes but can also act as potential constraints on the power of party leaders (Webb 2002). Trends in political party membership have been the subject of much research and some controversy. In the first place the absence of reliable public data has forced many researchers to use political parties' own accounts as their principal source of data. Whilst it is easy to enumerate the problems of relying on such partisan and biased sources it has proved almost impossible to circumvent them. On the basis of available evidence it appears that mainstream party membership has been falling across Western Europe for at least three decades (Mair and van Biezen 2001; van Biezen et al. 2012). However the rising membership (and votes) in some countries of 'challenger' parties, such as far right and Green parties, appear to have bucked this trend, undermining the idea of a general alienation of citizens from parties and raising interesting questions about the trajectories and prospects of Trotskyist party membership (Häusermann and Kriesi 2015).

The significance of elections for mainstream parties has also generated a literature on the factors that shape party responses to electoral setbacks. According to Mair et al. (2004) party leaders typically respond in at least one of five ways: changing policies, altering party organizational structures in order to enhance leadership power in relation to activists, campaigning to amend electoral institutions, altering their target electoral constituencies and shifting their relations with other parties, for example by accommodating to the policies of more successful rivals. This framework assumes that party leaderships will acknowledge electoral setbacks; attempt to engage in a rational process of decision-making; and will select appropriate responses to their electoral problems, notwithstanding the constraints on decision-makers, whether from party groups with opposing views or from a 'traditional mode of thinking' that inhibits rational appraisal of, and response to, evidence.

To what extent are these frameworks likely to prove useful in the analysis of Trotskyist organizations? In regard to electoral activity, the first point to note is that Trotskyist groups have contested every UK general election since February 1974. In the 2010 election no less than eight groups stood candidates and in 2015 there were six Trotskyist challengers (Kelly 2016). All Trotskyist groups have policies on a wide range of issues and seek political power, albeit by revolutionary rather than electoral means. Like mainstream parties, they debate major policies, occasionally undertake major shifts in direction and seek to recruit and build membership, yet there are also three ways in which they differ from mainstream parties. First, whereas mainstream parties often seek to pursue the policy preferences of the median voter and adapt to voter opinion, Trotskyist parties base themselves on the Leninist model of the vanguard party. The purpose of this type of party is the revolutionary overthrow of capitalism, the 'historic interests of the working class' (Mandel 1995a: 87), a goal reflected in its composition and structure. The Leninist party is a centralized organization, focused on the destruction of the capitalist state and led by professional revolutionaries, drawn from the ranks of the most class-conscious workers (Harding 1983: 155 ff.). Because the working class is normally heterogeneous in composition and often influenced by reformist ideas, open, mass recruitment risks diluting the party's revolutionary cohesion and intransigence and therefore the party membership is often described as the 'vanguard' of the class (Birchall 2011: 224–25).

Second, Trotskyist parties often operate as secret factions within other parties so in the 1970s for example, the International Marxist Group (IMG), Revolutionary Socialist League, Socialist Organiser (now the Alliance for Workers Liberty, AWL) and Workers Power all operated inside the Labour Party, aiming to recruit members to their respective groups. This approach was gradually abandoned in the late 1990s and 2000s when Labour was led by Tony Blair and his supporters but resumed by a number of groups (AWL and Workers Power) after Jeremy Corbyn's accession to the leadership in 2015. Third, it could be argued that whilst some Trotskyist parties contest elections they do not, fundamentally, take them seriously as a means of achieving political power. In other words, they expect to obtain political power primarily through revolution and are therefore indifferent to votes and office (or at least, in the conventional route to office). Indeed they often deride parliament as nothing more than a branch of the state that is necessarily subordinate to capitalist class interests: 'power does not lie in parliament [but with] . . . unelected bosses and bankers' (Choonara and Kimber 2011: 39).

However, there is a more nuanced view which suggests that Trotskyist parties *do* anticipate some increase in mass support when people 'find the conditions under which they live and work intolerable' (Choonara and Kimber 2011: 57–58). On this criterion, the period of prolonged and profound economic austerity that began in 2008 has generated discontent with government policies, as evidenced in very large protests and demonstrations against British government austerity policy (in March 2011 and October 2012) and against the 200 per cent rise in university tuition fees (November 2010). Consequently it would be reasonable to expect that voter hostility to austerity policies would translate into support for candidates of the far left, particularly amongst younger people, interested in politics but critical of mainstream parties (Henn et al. 2005). According to the SWP, 'the number of votes . . . provides an expression of how large numbers of people feel, and this in turn affects their willingness to fight for a better society' (Harman 2001). Consequently poor electoral performance may well be taken seriously, for as one senior party official observed, 'Elections are cruel . . . if you get a really bad vote, it's very crushing' (Charlie Kimber interview). Overall therefore it can be argued that vote-seeking does comprise one element of the portfolio of Trotskyist party activity and it is therefore legitimate and useful to assess the electoral performance of Trotskyist parties. It also goes without saying that as the capacity of political parties to implement their policies is strongly influenced by their resources, principally membership and income, then we also need to examine these two aspects of Trotskyist parties.

Doctrine, sects and sectarianism

One of the limitations of the votes/office/policy seeking framework is that it is silent on the issue of party ideology. For Trotskyist organizations the promotion of the revolutionary ideas of Marx, Engels, Lenin and Trotsky is essential because 'without revolutionary theory there can be no revolutionary movement' (AWL Constitution, Preamble). In the case of Trotskyist groups, doctrine is a more accurate term than theory because it denotes a body of incontrovertible propositions and associated texts. Its importance is underlined by the key role it has played in debates and conflict between Trotskyist groups. For example, in 1974–1975 the Workers Revolutionary Party (WRP) published six volumes of correspondence, resolutions and reports emerging out of disputes within the world Trotskyist movement under the tendentious title of *Trotskyism versus Revisionism* (Slaughter 1974, 1975). For the WRP leadership the purpose of these volumes was to denigrate a variety of organizations and individuals by 'exposing' their heretical departures from Trotskyist orthodoxy. If 'revisionism' was the WRP's preferred term of abuse, 'centrism', vacillation between reformist and revolutionary politics, was the cardinal offence detected by Workers Power (Workers Power and Irish Workers Group 1983) in its hyper-critical history of international Trotskyism. These few examples – and many more will be presented in subsequent chapters – are sufficient to suggest that a deep attachment to doctrine, or 'doctrinarism', is a key attribute of Trotskyist organizations.

Disputes over doctrine are most commonly associated with religious organizations and their study is the subject of a substantial literature on 'sects' and 'sectarianism' (for example Barrett 1996; Hunt 2003; Wilson 1970, 1990).[2] According to the eminent sociologist of religion Bryan Wilson, the sect can be defined in terms of the following six attributes: a voluntary organization with its own set of beliefs, or what Tourish (2011: 216) describes as a 'compelling vision', often rooted in key classical texts; a claim to possess either a 'monopoly of the truth' or 'superior beliefs' to those of non-members; membership comprising an elect group which is vetted and then 'converted' to the organization's world view through internal education (Lofland 1977); an expectation that members will display high levels of commitment and participation; penalties for dissent including suspension and expulsion; and hostility towards rival organizations (Wilson 1990: 106; and see also Hunt 2003: 35). It is important to note that non-Trotskyist organizations also display some of these attributes: the Maoist left and the far right, for instance, are both highly fragmented (Barberis et al. 2000). Moreover, the Labour Party expelled several hundred supporters of the Militant Tendency in the 1980s because they belonged to its secret faction – the Revolutionary Socialist League (RSL) – and were therefore in breach of party rules (Crick 2016: 312). But in contrast to the sect, the Labour Party does not have a well-developed body of doctrine that is promoted through party education programmes and which members are expected fully to endorse.

There is some dispute in the literature as to whether a sect is necessarily controlled by a charismatic leader, understood as somebody who inspires and motivates followers with a group vision, builds personal relations with them and seeks to enhance their commitment to the organization (Bird 1993; Haslam et al. 2011). Lalich (2004) used her case studies of a religious cult and a Californian revolutionary socialist group to argue the affirmative whereas Wilson (1990: 109) offers the more persuasive claim that whilst charismatic leaders are common in religious sects they are not ubiquitous. Moreover such leaders are not unique to sects and the mainstream organizational literature provides many examples of charismatic leaders in business firms (Bryman 1992). There is also disagreement in the literature over the scale and significance of what Conger (1990) calls the 'dark side' of charismatic leadership, for instance the mutation of a strong vision into dysfunctional obsession or the conversion of dynamic and inspiring leadership into authoritarian command and control (see also Wilson 1970: 37–40).

Some of these attributes of sects also help explain the attractions of group membership. The existence of an over-arching doctrine supposedly capable of explaining a wide range of phenomena arguably appeals to the deep-seated human desire to construct meaning. Insofar as doctrines also provide guidance to members on desirable (and undesirable) forms of behaviour they may also help structure key elements of people's daily lives, providing a degree of emotional security. The existence of a probation period during which members undergo various forms of testing and initiation may lead recruits to attribute a high value to such exclusive group membership. It also selects out those unwilling to provide the desired levels of commitment and participation, indirectly reinforcing group cohesion (Berman 2009; Iannaccone 1994). Cohesive groups built around a shared doctrine and high levels of member commitment also facilitate effective social control, both by leaders and through social networks. Control and commitment in turn are likely to induce high levels of participation in organizational life. Early studies of religious sects anticipated that high entry standards and rigorous selection methods would ensure that sects were typically small and exclusive organizations with rates of recruitment, turnover and growth well below those of their mainstream rivals. In fact more recent and more systematic evidence has shown that sects often display remarkably high growth rates although the reasons for this are unclear (Wilson 1990).

The properties of sects that generate many positive outcomes, such as a clear doctrine and charismatic leadership, are simultaneously responsible for a series of well-documented problems, paramount among which is the proliferation of organizational splits. Many of these are rooted in disputes over the interpretation of doctrine and more specifically in challenges to the prevailing orthodoxy of the organization. Over time they give rise to a multiplicity of doctrinal 'families', differing from each other in one or more aspects of doctrine and each claiming to be the sole representative of 'orthodoxy' or 'truth' (Barrett 1996). Just as there are discrete families of Christian religion, such as Roman Catholicism, Anglicanism and Methodism, so too there are distinct families of Trotskyism that have gradually emerged over time (see Chapter 3). Splits in the religious world have been extensively studied and almost invariably turn on doctrinal disagreements. According to Wilson (1990) successful sects gradually shed some of their sectarian traits in order to accommodate new members holding less orthodox beliefs. Doctrinal relaxation or amendment often then triggers a reaction from more orthodox members and the call for a 'return to orthodoxy' can sometimes be the prelude to a fresh split. The sixteenth-century revolt by Martin Luther against the Roman Catholic Church, leading to the formation of Protestantism, is probably the most well-known example.

The death of a charismatic leader may also precipitate a split because such leaders typically neglect succession planning and their demise leads to a power struggle between rival contenders. After the assassination in 1844 of Joseph Smith, Founder of the Mormon Church, the organization rapidly spilt in two with each group claiming the mantle of true succession (Barrett 1996: 64). Even during their reign, however, charismatic leaders typically generate a variety of problems. High levels of membership loyalty can reinforce the leader's sense of personal power and a belief in their indispensability. These attributes are often associated with a lack of accountability leading to 'excesses and poor judgements' (Wilson 1990: 231–35). Finally it is important to note that hostility between sectarian organizations is not a constant but can fluctuate over time. Issues that once bitterly divided organizations may decline in importance even to the point where erstwhile opponents engage in merger (Wilson 1990: 120).

The relationship between sectarianism and membership growth has already been mentioned as it has proved to be a contentious issue not least among economists who have deployed the concepts of supply and demand curves and the framework of competition analysis in the study of religion (McCleary 2011). Viewed as an 'industry', religion has low 'barriers to entry' which means that new organizations can be established at very low cost and quickly pose a threat to existing organizations. The proliferation of new churches, often through splits and divisions, increases the supply of religious services but the impact on the level of demand is unclear. Theoretically, if demand is unaffected by supply then new, sectarian organizations will simply increase their own memberships at the expense of mainstream and sectarian rivals; on the other hand, the appearance of new organizations may generate increased demand from previously unrepresented constituencies so that no churches end up worse off despite increased competition (Olson 2011).

Many Trotskyist militants would strongly object to the idea that their organizations can usefully be compared to religious groups. After all they are atheists who have no time for the superstitious claims of religion and many would resent the idea that their organizations can even be mentioned in the same breath as sectarian religious groups. However, the claim being made in this chapter is that Trotskyist groups *share* many features in common with religious sects, not that they *are* religious sects. In other words the relationship being posited is one of similarity not identity. Trotskyist groups do adhere to a well-established body of doctrine, either in the form of a declaration of principles, for example the SWP's weekly 'What We Stand For' column in *Socialist Worker*, or a programme, such as those issued by the International Communist League (1998) and Workers Power (2014). Most groups regard themselves and their members as the 'vanguard' of the working class, a term as elitist in meaning as the religious notion of the 'elect'. Many operate probationary periods of membership and extensive education programmes; expulsions are not uncommon as later chapters will demonstrate; and there have been, and still are, many charismatic Trotskyist leaders, past and present, most notably Tariq Ali, Tony Cliff and Gerry Healy.

We shall therefore explore the degree to which the attributes of sects can be found within the Trotskyist movement, noting variations between organizations and over time and exploring the ways in which doctrinal disputes have generated distinct Trotskyist 'families'. We shall also explore the vexed question of the consequences of doctrinarism and sectarianism for the membership levels of the movement as a whole.

Social movements

There are many definitions of social movements in the literature but the one to be used here combines detail with parsimony and emanates from a group of the world's leading social movement scholars. A social movement, they write, has at least three of the following five attributes: 'collective or joint action; change-oriented goals or claims; some extra- or non-institutional collective action; some degree of organization; and some degree of temporal continuity' (Snow et al. 2004: 6).

Social movements are distinct from political parties because they do not contest elections or seek government office and because their agenda is typically focused around a discrete set of issues rather than covering the full range of social, economic and political concerns. They are also distinct from interest groups because they are typically less integrated into political decision-making structures and tend to rely more on direct action than on lobbying or negotiation. One consequence of these distinctions is that trade unions, one of the main arenas for Trotskyist activity, are hybrid organizations, comprising elements of both social movements and interest groups.[3]

The study of social movements has passed through a number of phases, starting with the resource mobilization perspective of the 1970s (Edwards and McCarthy 2004). Its core argument began from the observation that whilst numerous groups in society held grievances about their social or economic conditions only a few engaged in social movement activity to redress them. The critical factor offered to explain differential degrees of activity was the capacity of groups to acquire and deploy resources, particularly personnel and finance.[4] Subsequently, mobilization theory argued that whilst effective social movements clearly needed resources, the *sine qua non* of collective action was a sense of shared grievance, the belief that a group's situation was unjust or unfair (Tilly 1978). Mobilization theorists have therefore sought to explore the ways in which individuals come to acquire a sense of grievance and to identify targets for collective action in the form of those held responsible for their plight (Kelly 1998). Increasingly social movement researchers focused on language as a key resource through which activists 'framed' arguments and demands. Following the path-breaking work of Snow and Benford in the 1980s, the study of linguistic 'frames' has become a major component of social movement research, blending into the earlier foci on resources and grievances (Snow 2004).

The years of economic crisis and austerity, beginning in 2008, have helped place a fresh issue onto the social movement research agenda, that of the link between political identity and class politics (for example Della Porta 2015). Protests and demonstrations against austerity have brought together older, class-based social movements, such as trade unions, with newer movements, such as anti-globalization campaigns. In some social movement literature the newer movements have been analysed in terms of social identities linked to issues such as the environment, war and sexuality. In relation to organizational structure, some of the new anti-austerity movements, like Occupy in the US and the UK, appear to have drawn more inspiration from anarchism than Marxism, opting for open assemblies and participatory democracy over the traditional forms of delegate representation. Tensions between different modes of organizing became evident in the pro-Corbyn organization Momentum not long after its formation. On one side were Trotskyists and others arguing that decisions be reached through delegate conferences, in which activists are likely to wield more influence; on the other side was the Momentum leadership, keen to promote referenda and open assemblies in order to empower rank and file members and disempower Trotskyist militants.[5]

These debates have some resonance in Britain because Trotskyist groups appear to display many of the features of social movements: they engage in various forms of non-institutional collective action, such as demonstrations and pickets; they seek radical changes in economic and social policy; they have organizational structures and are enduring not ephemeral bodies. It does not follow that Trotskyist organizations are simply one variety of social movement, for they also display some of the attributes of political parties and of sects. The core argument of the book is that Trotskyist groups are hybrid organizations, combining the attributes of political parties, sects and social movements with the balance between these elements varying from one group to another and from one time period to another

A brief note on the British Communist Party

The academic literature on British communism provides a set of rich, descriptive accounts of its evolution and radical policy shifts, its wide range of activities and interventions and its numerous tensions and contradictions from which we can draw three main conclusions that might have a bearing on the fortunes of the Trotskyist movement. First, and for all its proclamations of the need for an independent revolutionary party, the CPGB always operated in the shadow of the Labour Party and acknowledged that a transition to socialism would require Labour to play a key role. That is why the CP sought affiliation to Labour in the 1920s, 1936, 1943 and finally in 1946 only to be rebuffed each time (Branson 1985: 17–23, 115–17; Callaghan 2003: 305). Second, Fishman's (1995) detailed study of the 1930s and 1940s suggests the CP forged a policy of 'revolutionary pragmatism', combining trade union loyalty and rank and file militancy that was successful in building its substantial trade union base. Yet CP involvement in the trade unions also involved a profound tension between building workplace organization to conduct struggles on terms and conditions of employment and the overarching project of building revolutionary class consciousness and a revolutionary party. Critical observers of the CP's heroic efforts to politicize economic struggles have noted its repeated relapse into 'workerist militancy' (Samuel 2006) or 'militant labourism' (Andrews 2004) as they 'built shop steward committees not Little Moscows' (McIlroy 1999b: 247). Third, the CP was active for many years in a range of social movements, such as CND and the Movement for Colonial Freedom, in which it exercised a substantial influence. Through the 1970s and 1980s, however, it experienced significant frictions in its relations with the 'new social movements' of women and gays (Andrews 2004; Andrews et al. 1995). For many Trotskyist writers, as we shall see, the failings and weaknesses of the CP derived from its Stalinist policies, its subservience to the Soviet leadership and its uncritical admiration for the failed socialist experiment of the USSR. Freed from these constraints,

Trotskyist leaders believed their organizations would be able to register significantly different experiences of party political work, trade union activity and social movement involvement.

Conclusions

The remainder of this book will explore the ways in which the attributes of parties, sects and social movements generate organizational logics that are mutually reinforcing or contradictory and examples of the latter are not hard to find. In the electoral arena Trotskyist parties may not share the mainstream party concern with vote maximization but they are presumably keen to avoid electoral annihilation. One way of doing so might be to pool their resources and enter the electoral arena as a far left coalition, rather like Antarsya in Greece. Such coalitions have occurred in Britain in the 1970s (Socialist Unity), and again from the 1990s (Socialist Alliance, Respect and the Trade Unionist and Socialist Coalition). Yet as we shall see, all of these endeavours have created enormous tensions and have resulted in a series of divisions and splits as the sectarian logic of building one's own party, and differentiating it from rival Trotskyist groups, clashes with the coalitional requirement to compromise for the sake of reaching agreement. Or again, in the 2017 General Secretary election in the trade union Unite some groups backed the pro-Corbyn incumbent Len McCluskey (for example the AWL, Counterfire and the Socialist Party) whilst others backed the independent left candidate Ian Allinson (for example rs21, Socialist Fight and the SWP).

A similar tension emerges in the construction of social movements, of which the Anti-Nazi League is one of the best examples (to be discussed in more detail in Chapter 10). It was initiated by SWP activists who faced a strategic choice in their design: to build a campaign around revolutionary Marxist analysis and slogans, linking racism and immigration to capitalism and imperialism; or to construct a more narrowly based campaign, treating the rise of the far right as a discrete single issue. The former choice would uphold Trotskyist orthodoxy but arguably have limited appeal; the latter would have far wider appeal, embracing a range of views from liberal to Marxist but downplaying Trotskyist analyses and revolutionary slogans. It would also lead to the accusation from more sectarian Trotskyists of building a despised, cross-class 'Popular Front' instead of a more radical United Front (for example Sewell 2017a: 23). The construction of broad social movements throws up other dilemmas: is it better to work in cooperation with other Trotskyist groups even if one's own group holds a minority position on leading committees or is it better to be in control of one's own organization even at the price of Trotskyist disunity? This issue will be examined later when we consider the existence of three anti-austerity organizations, each controlled by a separate Trotskyist group. In order to proceed with the analysis of sects and doctrine we must first outline the development of Trotsky's thought over the course of his political career.

Notes

1 Older accounts of political parties often defined them exclusively in terms of elections, for example the influential study by Sartori (2005: 56).
2 There is also a literature on 'political religion' that explores the ways in which totalitarian regimes can be analysed through the lens of religious rituals, goals and values, for example Griffin (2004). These ideas have mainly been deployed in the study of fascism rather than communism and its variants (see for example Smith 2014).
3 Compare Allan Flanders' distinction between the union as 'sword of justice' and the union as 'vested interest' (Kelly 2010: 76–77).
4 Resource mobilization theorists, as they became known, rightly rejected the prevailing Olsonian wisdom that the obvious costs and the uncertain benefits of collective action would lead rational individuals to 'free ride' and decline to participate in such action (see Kelly 1998: 66–82).
5 For details of the changes proposed by the current Momentum leadership see www.peoplesmomentum.com/constitution, accessed 18 January 2017. A related debate centred on Momentum's identity: should it continue as a pro-Labour social movement or should it seek affiliation to the Labour Party and therefore exclude its Trotskyist backers such as the AWL and Workers Power?

2

TROTSKY AND THE ORIGINS OF TROTSKYISM

Trotskyist groups and their leaders self-evidently locate themselves in a body of thought emanating from Leon Trotsky, yet are also keen to stress that 'Trotskyism' should be regarded as the contemporary form of Leninism or Bolshevism and sharply differentiated from 'official' or Stalinist communism. However, isolating the main elements of Trotsky's thought is difficult not least because he shifted his views on several major issues over his lifetime. Before the Russian Revolution he was critical of Lenin's insistence on the vital role of the party but came round to this position in 1917; he supported the ban on factions in 1921 but several years later was engaged (as was Stalin) in openly factional activity; until 1933 he regarded himself as a member of the Communist International but in summer 1933 wrote its obituary and commenced preparations for a new International. Even where his views remained seemingly unchanged, as with the theory of permanent revolution for example, their lack of precision rendered them amenable to different inter-pretations and evaluations (Radice and Dunn 2006). It is also true that Trotsky's political thought and writings are so wide-ranging, spanning history, contemporary politics, literature, culture and morality, it would be almost impossible to offer a concise yet comprehensive summary in the space available here (for example Trotsky 1923, 1929a, 1931–1933, 1936, 1939a, 1970).

Nevertheless by drawing on a variety of sources it is possible to set out the core elements of what we can call 'Trotskyist doctrine', a set of incontrovertible propositions that structure the world views of Trotskyist organizations. Alexander (1991b: 5–12) lists five defining features: the theory of permanent revolution, the theory of combined and uneven development, transitional demands, the united front tactic and the idea of the USSR as a workers' state. Bensaid (2009: 22–28) lists four key features: permanent revolution, transitional demands, the nature of Stalinism and the need for a revolutionary party and International.

Hallas' (1979) account is organized under the headings of permanent revolution, Stalinism, strategy and tactics, and party and class. From these and other sources (for example Mandel 1975b, 1979, 1995a), it will be argued that 'Trotskyism' embraces nine core elements (Table 2.1 below). It goes without saying that not all groups and individuals will endorse all of the propositions below and there is ample scope for disagreement about the meaning and the applicability of key terms. Nor is there any presumption that all of the elements below are equally important. It is also true that some of what now passes for 'Trotskyism' consists of propositions shared by many Marxists, for example that capitalism is an exploitative economic system and that the working class is the only social force that can destroy it. Moreover, some propositions adhered to by Trotskyists originated with Lenin or emerged from the Bolshevik Party and the Communist International, for example the necessity for a democratic centralist, vanguard party, which is why Trotsky and his supporters initially described themselves as Bolshevik-Leninists. 'Trotskyism' therefore represents just one of the ideological currents that crystallized after the Russian Revolution and others include official or Stalinist communism and Maoism (Alexander 2001). Some readers may judge this exercise in summation so fraught with problems as to be worthless, but that would be a mistake. Debates about doctrine, revisionism and orthodoxy have dogged the Trotskyist movement from its inception. Without some attempt to specify the key elements of Trotskyist doctrine, however difficult and problematic, it is impossible to make any sense of these disputes.

This chapter will describe each of the core elements of Trotskyist doctrine followed by critical commentary, exploring some of the problems and contradictions inevitably implicated in the construction of Trotsky's world view. The significance of this exercise lies in the fact that many Trotskyist activists have constructed an idealized and sanitized account of Trotsky, suppressing or significantly downplaying many of the profound problems with his political views and actions (for example Brenner 1996; Choonara 2007; and Woods and Grant 1976). That said,

TABLE 2.1 The core elements of 'Trotskyism'

1	Theory of permanent revolution (vs stages theory and 'socialism in one country')
2	United front tactic (vs popular front)
3	Transitional demands (vs minimum and maximum demands)
4	Critical analysis of the Stalinist states (vs USSR as socialist)
5	Necessity for a new revolutionary, Fourth International (vs communist, social democratic and reformist labour movement leaders)
6	Necessity for a democratic centralist, revolutionary vanguard party
7	Necessity to build a rank and file movement against the trade union bureaucracy
8	Revolution as seizure of power and the creation of proletarian dictatorship (vs parliamentarism and reformism)
9	Imperialist epoch as one of wars and revolutions (vs capitalist stability)

Source: Author.

two writers from the SWP have written far more critical and useful accounts of Trotsky, namely Hallas' short (1979) introduction and Cliff's four-volume biography. This chapter does not purport to offer new archival material on Trotsky but draws on existing biographies and studies such as Deutscher (1954, 1959, 1963), Knei-Paz (1978), Le Blanc (2015) and Swain (2006) and secondary sources on the Russian Revolution such as Cohen (1985), Figes (1996) and Fitzpatrick (2008) as well as Trotsky's own history (1931–1933).

Trotsky and Trotskyism

Permanent revolution

Conventional wisdom amongst Russian social democrats in the early twentieth century was that increased political freedoms coupled with land reform and economic growth would eventually create an advanced capitalist economy and only then would socialist revolution become a possibility. In *Results and Prospects* (1906), written shortly after the 1905 revolution and again in *The Permanent Revolution* (1929), Trotsky advanced a radically different prognosis, the theory of permanent revolution. In essence he argued that within the globalized world economy individual countries comprised both backward sectors such as subsistence farming and highly advanced sectors, such as large manufacturing plants employing modern technology and often owned by foreign capital. This process of 'combined and uneven development' gave rise in Russia to a local bourgeoisie with limited economic power (because of the size and foreign ownership of the industrial sector) and little political power (because of the Tsarist autocracy). Consequently, said Trotsky, it would be unable to lead a democratic revolution and that task would fall to the working class. Yet such a revolution would not stop at the stage of democratic reforms because the power and demands of the working class would push it in the direction of a socialist revolution: one revolution would thus flow inexorably and uninterruptedly into the other in a process of 'permanent revolution'. Moreover, in the context of an inter-connected global capitalist economy, a socialist revolution in one country, particularly a backward country like Russia, would trigger similar events elsewhere. Indeed, a socialist revolution in backward Russia could only survive and flourish if there were revolutions elsewhere; 'socialism in one country' was an illusion.

The theory was used to argue that revolutionaries in less developed countries should not rest content with 'democratic revolutions', as in the Arab world 2010–2011, but should seek to push developments in the direction of socialist revolution. There is some debate as to whether Lenin adhered to this theory before 1917 and if not, whether he then moved closer to Trotsky's position as argued by Howard and King (1989: 255–56) and Knei-Paz (1978: 146, 174), whether he adopted Trotsky's theory wholesale (Roberts 2007) or whether his different arguments in 1905 and 1917 were each right at the time (Michail 1977).

The primary significance of the debates around permanent revolution, then and now, is that they reflect an attempt to unite Lenin and Trotsky as intellectual co-thinkers in opposition to Stalin and to reinforce the legitimacy of Trotsky with the authority of Lenin. It is therefore important to note that the debate between Stalin's 'socialism in one country' and Trotsky's 'permanent revolution' was needlessly polarized by both sides (Johnstone 1968: 24–28; Krasso 1967: 79–80). At critical junctures, such as early 1918 and again in 1921 with the stabilization of world capitalism, Lenin argued that the defence and consolidation of Soviet power was the most effective method of strengthening the forces of international revolution whilst Trotsky was instrumental in normalizing relations with Germany through the Treaty of Rapallo (Harding 1983: 249–55; Deutscher 1959: 56–58). Moreover the debates did not turn simply on matters of doctrine or theory, but also involved differing estimates of the policies required to ameliorate the demoralization caused by revolutionary defeats in other countries and the ensuing isolation of the Soviet Union.

Although Trotsky first constructed his theory on the basis of the 1905 Russian Revolution he believed it was vindicated by the two revolutions in 1917 and the events in China in the 1920s and Spain in the 1930s. The leading American Trotskyist, Felix Morrow (1976), argued forcefully that the Spanish Civil War between democrats and fascists would only succeed if it followed the path of permanent revolution, moving beyond 'defence of the Republic' to socialist revolution. Morrow's contemporary account, reprinted many times since 1938, has been highly influential within the Trotskyist movement and widely regarded as an exemplary illustration of the theory of permanent revolution. Yet the view of Spain as a revolutionary opportunity squandered by the Stalinist commitment to a purely democratic struggle did not go unchallenged even in the 1930s. Two contemporaries of Trotsky, both of whom fought in Spain, castigated his sectarian hostility to the most substantial leftist group, the Workers Party of Marxist Unification (POUM); noted that his own organization had an insignificant number of supporters and was therefore in no position to promote revolution; and criticized his tendency to view Spanish events through the lens of Russia 1917, overlooking the many significant differences in domestic and international class forces between the two countries (Senex 2013; Solano and Iglesias 2013).

It also important to note that since Trotsky's lifetime there have been numerous exceptions to his schema of permanent revolution, all of which have posed challenges for those anxious to preserve ideological orthodoxy: the independence struggle in India, the communist and peasant-led revolution in China, the revolutions in Algeria, Bolivia, Ethiopia and Vietnam, and the Cuban revolution led by armed sections of the intelligentsia (Anderson 1984: 118–19; Howard and King 1989: 237; Mavrakis 1976). The editors of a centenary collection of essays on permanent revolution acknowledged that Trotsky's generalization of his theory beyond the bounds of Russia was 'less conspicuously successful', yet ended their overview chapter with the vague and unconvincing claim that 'Read critically,

Trotsky's insights of 1906 can still inform our understanding of the world and our struggles to change it. They can provide the basis for a rejuvenated, anti-determinist Marxism' (Radice and Dunn 2006: 9).

The united front

As the post-1917 revolutionary wave abated in 1920–1921, the newly formed communist parties often found themselves leading a minority of workers in opposition to the majority social democrats, and were forced to re-appraise their strategy and tactics. Trotsky and other Comintern leaders developed the idea of the 'united front', an agreement between communists and social democrats to engage in joint struggle around specific, immediate issues. By promoting unity in action and maintaining their freedom to criticize social democracy, communists sought to win recruits and gain influence (Trotsky 1922). After 1928 the Comintern abandoned the policy, declaring that social democrats were now the main enemy of the revolutionary movement. In Germany this disastrous policy split the labour movement, facilitating the Nazi rise to power and two years later the Comintern executed a radical *volte face* calling for an anti-fascist 'Popular Front' of all progressive forces, including bourgeois political parties. For Trotsky the popular front signified the abandonment of revolutionary socialism in the interests of defending liberal democracy against fascism. During the Spanish Civil War of 1936–1939 for example the Comintern argued for a popular front to defeat the fascist forces led by Franco whilst Trotsky called for a united front and permanent revolution (Morrow 1976).

Trotsky's antagonism to popular fronts actually had three foundations: the idea of the contemporary period as an epoch of wars and revolutions (see below); the theory of permanent revolution (see above); and the class character of parliamentary democracy. His view of parliamentary systems, at least until the early 1930s, does not appear to have differed in any way from Lenin's dismissive (and ill-informed) claim that parliamentary elections merely allow workers, 'To decide once every few years which member of the ruling class is to repress and crush the people through parliament – this is the real essence of bourgeois parliamentarism' (1916: 56). As Lenin wrote in *The State and Revolution*, parliament should be considered as a branch of the capitalist state which is *necessarily* an instrument of class rule, consisting at its core of 'special bodies of armed men, prisons etc.'. After the Comintern adopted the policy of the popular front, Trotsky wrote: 'the conciliatory politics practiced by the "People's Front" dooms the working class to impotence and clears the road for fascism' (1938: 6).

As a new world war approached Trotsky was equally scathing about the idea of taking sides in a 'struggle against fascism', a proposal described as no more than 'lame phraseology' (1938: 22). Yet this was something of a shift in Trotsky's position because in his major essay on Germany, *What Next?*, published in 1932, he had argued that it was vital to distinguish democratic and fascist political systems and to defend the freedoms available to the working class in liberal democracies (1932: 123–33; and see also Anderson 1984: 119–20; Johnstone 1977: 15; Johnstone 1991). One common strand that links these radically differing judgements was antagonism to the policies of Stalin and the Comintern: in 1932 the latter had downplayed the differences between fascism and liberal democracy (and in response Trotsky strongly emphasized them) but from 1935 as the Comintern came to attach great significance to the differences between political regimes so Trotsky downplayed them. As Perry Anderson perceptively wrote in 1977:

> No single phenomenon in the contemporary world has been so central a barrier to socialist revolution, and yet so little engaged or explored by Marxist theory, as the bourgeois–democratic state. The paradox of stable rule by capital combined with universal right of suffrage was unknown in the epoch of Marx; still incomplete or peripheral in the world of Lenin; apparently in regression during the exile of Trotsky and the imprisonment of Gramsci. Yet since 1945, bourgeois democracy has become the normal and general form of state system throughout the advanced capitalist countries.
>
> *(Anderson cited in Thompson 2007: 82)*

Transitional demands

Trotsky promoted in the 1938 programme of the Fourth International the concept of a 'transitional demand': 'stemming from today's conditions and from today's consciousness of wide layers of the working class and unalterably leading to one final conclusion: the conquest of power by the proletariat' (Trotsky 1938: 7). These were counter-posed to 'minimum' demands that were affordable and would not therefore undermine capitalism and 'maximum' or revolutionary demands that could only be realized under socialism. One of the most popular examples of a transitional demand is the 'sliding scale of wages', designed simultaneously to protect workers against rising inflation and falling profits and to question the logic of capitalist profit-making. In the course of struggling for such demands, and under the leadership of a revolutionary party, Trotsky believed that workers' class consciousness would be significantly enhanced.

If Trotsky's inadequate grasp of parliamentary democracy was one problem in his strategic political thought, the contradictions and limitations of working-class consciousness were to provide another. In its declaration that the chief problem facing revolutionaries was a 'crisis of leadership' the Transitional Programme clearly implied that a lack of class consciousness and the grip of reformist ideas were less serious problems. In this scenario, where the 'objective conditions' for revolution already exist, it is the 'subjective factor', the party and its programme of transitional demands, that become decisive (Beilharz 1987: 75–76). One significant element in Trotsky's thinking is that worker support for social democracy was rapidly being eroded because, 'in an epoch of decaying capitalism . . . in general, there can be no discussion of systematic social reforms and the raising of the masses' living standards'

(Trotsky 1938: 7). Consequently his claim that 'The multimillioned masses again and again enter the road of revolution' only to be restrained by reformist and Stalinist leaderships is consistent with this view of a mass revolutionary, or at least radical, consciousness (Trotsky 1938: 5). Nor is the idea a specific product of the 1930s conjuncture – the French Popular Front, the Spanish Civil War and the sit-down strikes in the USA – because a similar theme can be found in his major works on the 1905 and 1917 revolutions: *Results and Prospects* (1906) and *The History of the Russian Revolution* (1931–1933) (Knei-Paz 1978: 171–72, 243; Krasso 1967: 67–68).

The Bolshevik Party is presented throughout the *History* as the embodiment of revolutionary working-class consciousness, a prominent theme in Trotsky's writings from 1917. Four years after the revolution, as Moscow and other cities were rocked by strikes and the Kronstadt sailors called for free and open elections to Soviets, Trotsky attacked their supporters in the Workers Opposition group. Speaking at the Russian Communists' Tenth Party Congress he declared,

> They have made a fetish of democratic principles. They have placed the workers' right to elect representatives above the Party. As if the Party were not entitled to assert its dictatorship even if that dictatorship temporarily clashed with the passing moods of the workers' democracy!
>
> *(Trotsky cited in Brinton 1970: 78)*

In other words, the actual consciousness of workers could be ignored if it conflicted with the views of the party vanguard, particularly if the former could be attributed to anti-Bolshevik class influences. For example, Trotsky knew enough of the realities of Russian labour movement politics to appreciate that in 1917 many of the most powerful trade unions in Russia, in rail, postal services and printing, were strong supporters of the Mensheviks (Keep 1976). In *The New Course*, he reiterated the claim that anti-Bolshevik ideas reflected alien, not working-class, influences both from the petit bourgeoisie and from the ranks of state, party and trade union bureaucrats whose numbers now significantly outweighed those of factory workers (Trotsky 1924a: 20; and see also Pirani 2008: 167 for further discussion of this theme). Yet these arguments were never fully integrated into his later thinking about transitional demands and the mechanisms through which they would develop class consciousness, although a passage in the Transitional Programme provides an important clue:

> If capitalism is incapable of satisfying the demands inevitably arising from the calamities generated by itself, then let it perish. "Realizability" or "unrealizability" is in the given instance a question of the relationship of forces, which can be decided only by the struggle. By means of this struggle, no matter what its immediate practical successes may be, the workers will best come to understand the necessity of liquidating capitalism.
>
> *(Trotsky 1938: 9)*

Class consciousness develops through struggle, a familiar theme in socialist thought as far back as Marx, although Trotsky offers the counter-intuitive suggestion that the *outcome* of the struggle has no bearing on this dynamic. In other words, the cost of any defeat is likely to be outweighed by the gains in class consciousness. Yet it remains wholly unclear precisely how and under what conditions workers would come to abandon support for social democracy, reformist trade unionism and parliamentary democracy. Moreover since he makes the implausible claim that it is impossible to establish the balance of power in advance of any struggle then it becomes clear that Trotsky has bequeathed to his supporters a powerful motivation for calling strikes whenever possible in order to test the balance of power and enhance class consciousness.

Stalinism and the workers' state

Trotsky always insisted that so long as the means of production were owned by the state rather than capitalist firms then the USSR was a workers' state. Yet the rise to power of a violent, despotic, bureaucratic caste, led by Stalin, with the accompanying restrictions on workers' rights and political activity led him to label it more precisely as a 'degenerated workers' state', a theme most clearly expressed in *The Revolution Betrayed*. Trotsky drew a sharp distinction between the economic base and the political superstructure and was consequently able to claim that the USSR was characterized by the co-existence of a socialist economic base and a parasitic, anti-Bolshevik bureaucratic caste in charge of its state apparatus (Trotsky 1937). The former claim rested on the simplistic assumption that state vs private ownership was the only decisive criterion in gauging a mode of production; the actual relations of production, between workers and managers for instance, were of no analytical consequence (Howard and King 1992: 55). The latter claim rested primarily on the thesis that the bureaucracy did not own means of production and could not therefore pass them onto their children but this is only one of a number of criteria for establishing the existence of a social class and ignores the role of the Stalinist state in organizing both the domination and exploitation of Soviet workers (Wright 2015). It followed, so Trotsky believed, that the Stalinist regime had nothing in common with the genuine workers' state established by the Bolshevik revolution in 1917. This argument is complex and Trotsky's own position was never entirely consistent not least because of the difficulty in establishing 'At precisely which point the revolutionary dictatorship of Lenin gave way to the totalitarianism of Stalin' (Howe 1978: 82; and see also Cohen 1985: 38–70).

The entrenched character of the Stalinist bureaucracy eventually led Trotsky to the view that reform of the Soviet political system was impossible and that only a working-class political revolution, led by Trotskyists, could overthrow the Stalinist tyranny (Trotsky 1937). Trotsky's analysis of Stalinism and the rise of Stalin evolved significantly over time although it is unclear whether he ever arrived at a satisfactory and convincing account. Deutscher for instance suggested his unfinished biography of Stalin would almost certainly have proved to be his weakest book (1963: 451) and its index entries for 'Stalin' are revealing of Trotsky's understanding of leadership qualities: 'Stalin: not a writer', 'Stalin: not an orator' (unlike Trotsky who was both a gifted writer and speaker) (Trotsky 1947; and see also Beilharz 1985). His difficulty in understanding Stalin was equally apparent in his autobiography when he offered the definitive statement that 'Stalin is the outstanding mediocrity in the party' (Trotsky 1930: 534). The fact that this 'mediocrity' could rise through the ranks of the Party to become General Secretary and defeat a variety of opposition groups led by Bolshevik luminaries such as Trotsky, Bukharin and Zinoviev suggests Stalin possessed political and administrative skills that Trotsky never grasped (Service 2010b: 8–10).

At different times Trotsky mentioned a variety of factors behind the rise of Stalin: the isolation of the Revolution, Russia's cultural backwardness, its tradition of autocracy, the economic destruction wrought by the Civil War, the corrosive effects of the New Economic Policy, the associated growth of private enterprise, the fragmentation of the industrial working class and the political struggle between the Stalin, Bukharin and Left Opposition factions (see for instance his essays on culture in *Problems of Everyday Life* 1923). On the other hand he appears to have given little weight to an obvious psychological explanation for the popularity of the Stalinist slogan 'socialism in one country', namely that it offered some hope and optimism to demoralized party activists and workers in a country ravaged by years of war and deprivation (Cox 1992: 93–94; Kolakowski 1978: 24). What is quite unclear from Trotsky's voluminous writings is whether Stalin's victory was determined largely by structural factors or whether agency, the activity of the Left Opposition, could have made a significant difference (Kolakowski 1978: 193–94; Knei-Paz 1978: 381–85, 429–30).

Trotsky's account of the Soviet bureaucracy is equally elusive, as the definitive study of Twiss (2010) has made clear. Initially he understood the Stalin group to be a relatively weak political force, hovering between the working class (represented by the Left Opposition) and the petit bourgeoisie (represented by Bukharin). In *The New Course* he therefore called on the Party to organize an influx of factory workers into its ranks but when this policy was enacted in 1924 – the so-called Lenin Levy – it boosted the Stalinist leadership, not the Opposition (Trotsky 1924a; Krasso 1967: 77–78). Later he shifted to the view that the bureaucracy was the product of alien class forces but after the first Five Year Plan and the collectivization programme – initially, and wrongly, dismissed as a 'left zig zag' (Swain 2006: 184–86) – he concluded that the bureaucracy had become an independent and contradictory social force, committed to defending socialist public property whilst simultaneously pursuing its own specific caste, not class, interests. Underpinning all of his different formulations, however, was a crude, pejorative view of 'bureaucracy' as an inefficient, self-serving, parasitic body; there is no trace of the Weberian idea of bureaucracy as a *modern* development in organizational structure and functioning (Beilharz 1987: 64).

In the international sphere, Trotsky often argued that the Stalinist bureaucracy was a purely counter-revolutionary force, protecting the USSR by betraying revolutions in other countries such as Spain. But when the Soviet Union invaded both Poland and Finland in late 1939, he appeared to abandon the logic of his own argument, claiming these were progressive, revolutionary actions (Anderson 1983b: 56–57; Howard and King 1992: 57). The Red Army was expropriating big landlords in both Poland and Finland and the Finnish Communist Party was calling for a workers and peasants' uprising (the Polish Communist Party had been dissolved by Stalin in 1938 and most of its leaders executed; Medvedev 1976: 219–20) (Trotsky 1940: 168–69). Max Shachtman, James Burnham and others in the American SWP initially queried whether a policy of unconditional defence of the USSR against attack necessarily entailed support for *offensive* actions by the Red Army but the dispute soon spread into differing assessments of the USSR itself: was the Stalinist group a ruling caste in a degenerated workers' state or should it be analysed as a new ruling class? And was the Soviet Union a socialist economy because a 'workers' state' owned the means of production or was it in fact a different, non-socialist mode of production – bureaucratic collectivism or state capitalism (Trotsky 1939b; and see Matgamna 1998, 2015; van der Linden 2009: 69–98)? If there was merit in any of these alternative analyses, then revolutionary socialists would be relieved of their duty of unconditional defence of the USSR (and would in turn have to construct a plausible account of the timing and mechanics of the counter-revolution). Out of this dispute, focused on just one of the core elements of Trotskyism, there began to emerge a current of opinion that would eventually be described as 'Third Camp Trotskyism'.

The Fourth International

In his 1935 diary in exile Trotsky wrote that the building of the Fourth International, 'despite its extremely insufficient and fragmentary nature, is the most important work of my life – more important than 1917, more important than the Civil War' (Brotherstone 1992: 237). At first glance, it is tempting to discount this claim as self-evident hyperbole but it is worth recalling that Trotsky was a late convert to Bolshevism and his party loyalty was often questioned by some of his critics, not least Stalin (Service 2010b: 213–14). His insistence on the salience of the Fourth International may have reflected both tactical and strategic considerations as well as an awareness of his own fraught relations with the Bolshevik Party in pre-revolutionary years. Trotskyist forces in the early 1930s were hardly numerous: the first Trotskyists in Britain – the Balham Group – numbered just 13 people and throughout the 1930s Trotsky had to consider the most appropriate tactics for his small groups of followers (Groves 1974: 94). The emergence of leftist parties, such as the Independent Labour Party in the UK or the left-moving Socialist Party in France, led to the creation of the entry tactic or 'entrism'. As originally formulated in the so-called 'French Turn', small groups of Trotskyists would enter a left-moving party, disseminate their own propaganda, criticize the policies of their party host and aim to recruit people to their group. The tactic was a short-term measure because sooner rather than later either the Trotskyists would be expelled or they would resign en masse, having exhausted the recruitment opportunities in the larger organization (Trotsky 1934).

By the late 1930s Trotsky had already launched the Fourth International with its bold, opening declaration: 'The world political situation as a whole is chiefly characterized by a historical crisis of the leadership of the proletariat' (Trotsky 1938: 4). The conclusion followed from Trotsky's view that the 'objective pre-requisites' for socialist revolution had already matured as the capitalist mode of production had exhausted its economic potential. Yet his understanding of 'leadership' was never developed theoretically and not surprisingly he was unable to transcend the limitations of the conventional wisdom of the inter-war years. In this view, leaders were 'born not made' and the successful leader was a 'great man' (women rarely appeared in these discussions), distinguished from others by their intelligence, self-confidence and knowledge (Bryman 1992: 2–3). That Trotsky adhered to this type of thinking is clear from the following extraordinary claim in his 1935 diary in exile:

> Had I not been present in 1917 in Petersburg, the October Revolution would still have taken place – *on the condition that Lenin was present and in command* . . . If Lenin had not been in Petersburg, I doubt whether I could have managed to overcome the resistance of the Bolshevik leaders.
>
> *(Trotsky cited in Brotherstone 1992: 237, italics in original;*
> *and see Dunn 1989: 40, 46 for a similar view)*

His *History of the Russian Revolution* had adopted a slightly more nuanced view, that without Lenin the 'party might have let slip the revolutionary opportunity for many years', but revolutionary success still turned on the actions and influence of one person (Trotsky 1931–1933: 348).

Trotsky's own experiences in party-building were somewhat mixed. During his lengthy period of opposition to both Bolsheviks and Mensheviks he had helped build an organization, the Inter-District Group, which eventually reached a membership of around 4,000 by July 1917.[1] Yet this was paltry in comparison with the Bolsheviks whose membership rose dramatically, from 24,000 in February 1917 to 100,000 by April, reaching 375,000 by October 1917 (Fitzpatrick 2008: 52). Throughout his period of opposition, from roughly 1923 onwards, he sought to build leftist factions inside the CPSU and the Comintern and eventually independent parties as his supporters were expelled from a succession of national communist parties. Trotsky's experiences in party-building outside the USSR proved successful up to a point but also frustrating. By 1938 there were Trotskyist groups in 31 countries, a remarkable achievement for a tendency subject to such intense hostility and vilification, although the only large section was the American SWP, which claimed 2,500 members (1,000 according to other sources) (Alexander 1991a: 270; Deutscher 1963: 420). On the other hand, the movement was already displaying the fissiparous tendencies for which it would become notorious (and which are considered below): nine countries had two Trotskyist groups, including

Great Britain, whilst three countries had already managed multiple splits and contained *three* Trotskyist groups – Argentina, Austria and the USA (Alexander 1991a).

The revolutionary vanguard party

The case for a revolutionary vanguard party was clearly argued in the Transitional Programme but it was a view Trotsky had held as long ago as 1906 and throughout his life (Knei-Paz 1978: 142, 316). From 1917 he had come to believe that revolutionary leadership would be embodied in a militant, Bolshevik-type party that comprised the most advanced class-conscious workers, organized on the principle of democratic centralism. Stated in its simplest terms democratic centralism entails free discussion and a free vote on party policy but unity in action under the direction of the party central committee once policy has been decided. Prior to 1917 he had taken a rather different view and during the 1903 dispute amongst Russian social democrats he had expressed strong criticism of Lenin's (1902, 1904) call for a centralized, disciplined party whose members worked under the direction of its leading committees. 'Lenin's iron hand' he claimed, would lead, 'to the Party organization substituting itself for the Party, the Central Committee substituting itself for the Party organization, and finally the dictator substituting himself for the Central Committee' (1904: 77; and Trotsky 1903). These ominous words turned out to be prescient but they would also come back to haunt Trotsky in his battles with Stalin over the legacy of Lenin on the nature and role of the party. Is the working class likely to be represented by several revolutionary parties, as it was in Russia until the end of the Civil War or by just one? In the early-mid 1920s Trotsky seemed wholly content with the Bolshevik monopoly of power and hostile to the idea of rival parties, declaring in *The Platform of the Joint Opposition* (1927) that,

> We, the Opposition, unqualifiedly condemn every attempt whatsoever to create a second party . . . We will struggle with all our force against the formation of two parties, for the dictatorship of the proletariat demands as its very core a single proletarian party.
>
> *(Trotsky 1927: 113)*

By the time of the Transitional Programme his position had shifted somewhat, because that document mentioned 'the legalization of soviet parties', subject to the approval of 'workers and peasants'. On the other hand, the caveat would certainly permit an autocratic 'workers and peasants' movement to outlaw all non-ruling parties (Trotsky 1938: 39–40).

The discussion on political pluralism was intimately connected to the debates on factions and splits. It has sometimes been argued that the tendency towards splits reflects the immense pressures on small, isolated groups of revolutionaries operating in a hostile climate, but this hardly constitutes a satisfactory explanation. In the first place, the same conditions could just as easily be said to create powerful incentives for group cohesion and unity, both of which are rare attributes of the Trotskyist movement, although not unknown. Schismatic tendencies are ultimately rooted in the defence of doctrine but they have been reinforced by two specific aspects of Trotsky's own thought, the first of which was his deeply ambivalent attitude to party loyalty and party unity. He supported the ban on factions in 1921; declared in 1923 in his first major critique of the Stalinist leadership – *The New Course* – that there could only be one party in the USSR (Trotsky 1924a: 27); and at the 13th Communist Party Congress in May 1924 he boldly affirmed,

> none of us wishes to or can be right against the party. In the last instance the party is always right, because it is the only historic instrument which the working class possesses for the solution of its fundamental tasks.
>
> *(Trotsky cited in Deutscher 1959: 139)*

The ban on factions at the 1921 Bolshevik Party Congress was moved by Lenin, but supported by many leading Bolsheviks including Trotsky both at the time and in his 1930 autobiography, although by 1937 he had shifted ground, claiming it was a purely temporary measure (Trotsky 1930: 485; Trotsky 1937: 96). Yet the reasoning behind Lenin's resolutions points to enduring not transient problems. They were drafted against the background of Russian isolation, peasant revolts, the Kronstadt mutiny and industrial unrest. There were widespread strike waves in 1920 and 1921 and Moscow was placed under martial law in February 1921 (Figes 1996: 759). The resolutions cited 'syndicalist and anarchist deviations' and referred more generally to 'inevitable petit-bourgeois vacillations . . . and relapses of narrow craft unionism' that could generate factionalism and its misuse for 'counter-revolutionary purposes'. The aim of these resolutions was therefore to protect the Bolshevik monopoly of power against longstanding internal and external critics (Lenin 1921a, 1921b; and see also Lih 2011: 171).

As late as 1928 Trotsky still maintained a steadfast loyalty to the party, refusing to support the latest opposition grouping, the Democratic Centralist faction or the wave of strikes called to protest at wage reductions and work intensification (Marot 2006: 196–97). How can such protestations of loyalty be reconciled with the reality of factional struggles inside the party from late 1923 onwards? Trotsky argued quite rightly that if the ban on factions was taken to prohibit any 'grouping' of party members sharing a view on a contentious issue then inner-party debate would be extinguished. Meaningful debate implies differences of opinion which in turn can lead to factions; in *The New Course* he struggled with this conundrum but was unable to resolve it. Elsewhere in the same book he repeatedly warned of the danger of 'bureaucratism', clearly implying that a section of the party leadership was acting as a faction. A less charitable interpretation is that Trotsky believed in loyalty only to a *truly* Bolshevik party led by revolutionary Marxists such as himself. Once he had convinced himself the Russian Communist Party leadership no longer satisfied this criterion then the normal Bolshevik obligation of party loyalty was rendered nugatory.

The tendency towards splits also emerged from Trotsky's sectarianism and from his own view of their benefits, which fluctuated between the sanguine and the euphoric. His calls in the early 1930s for an anti-Nazi united front of communists and social democrats are rightly famous (Trotsky 1975). Less well-known are his virulent criticisms of a variety of German left groups: he refused to work with the KPO (Communist Party Opposition) because its leader, Heinrich Brandler, had supported Stalin in the 1928 factional struggle inside the USSR and he was dismissive of the SAPD (Socialist Workers Party of Germany) because of its 'sectarian' refusal to work inside the German Communist Party (KPD) (Marot 2006). On the topic of splits, he wrote in 1931 to the Communist League in France, one of the most important centres of Left Oppositional activity, about its ongoing factional battles and the prospect of a split: 'at times a split is a lesser evil. An organization that is smaller but more unanimous can have enormous success with a correct policy, while an organization which is torn by internal strife is condemned to rot' (Trotsky 1931). Two years later in the immediate aftermath of the decision to break with the Comintern and form a new International, he wrote to the League at more length and with real enthusiasm about the benefits of a split:

> The League is passing through a first crisis under the banner of great and clear revolutionary criteria. Under these conditions, a splitting off of a part of the League will be a great step forward. It will reject all that is unhealthy, crippled and incapacitated; it will give a lesson to the vacillating and irresolute elements; it will harden the better sections of the youth; it will improve the inner atmosphere; it will open up before the League new, great possibilities. What will be lost – partly only temporarily – will be regained a hundredfold already at the next stage.
>
> *(Trotsky 1933b)*

It would be difficult to find a more wholehearted endorsement of the enormous gains, and the minimal losses, that arise from organizational splits.

Rank and file organization against the trade union bureaucracy

Trotsky's analysis of trade union leadership was consistent with the arguments of Lenin and Luxemburg on its class collaborationist role but he always placed more stress on its negative role, even going so far as to claim that 'The bureaucracy of the trade unions is the backbone of British imperialism' (Trotsky 1929c: 59). This theme was set out even more starkly in the Transitional Programme with its pivotal assertion of the 'historical crisis of the leadership of the proletariat' (Trotsky 1938: 4). His scattered writings on trade unions sketched out several other themes that have underpinned almost all post-Trotsky analyses of trade unionism, beginning with the need for revolutionaries to work inside trade unions, however right-wing their leaderships (Trotsky 1938: 10). This argument repeats Lenin's formulation from *Left Wing Communism* (1920), but Trotsky was also at pains to stress that revolutionaries have no time for the 'fetish of trade union unity' because trade unions 'are not ends in themselves' (Trotsky 1929b: 44; Trotsky 1938: 11).

In terms of policy, Trotsky mapped out a series of options, arguing that, 'revolutionaries should strive not only to renew the top leadership of the trade unions . . . but also to create in all possible instances independent militant organizations' (Trotsky 1938: 11). Yet he also argued that revolutionaries should not hesitate to split trade unions, and form breakaway organizations, if their leaderships proved to be an insuperable hindrance to revolutionary struggle or if the unions become subordinated to the state (Trotsky 1938: 11). Trotsky stressed the necessity to challenge union officialdom as a whole, including both right-wing leaders such as Walter Citrine and Jimmy Thomas as well as 'left-wing' officials like coal miners' General Secretary A.J. Cook. Whilst Trotsky was eloquent in his denunciations of British union officials and Labour leaders and their moderate, reformist politics, he wrote almost nothing about the underlying, material and social causes of their behaviour, a theme that would be addressed by post-Trotskyists (Trotsky 1972 and 1974a, 1974b).

Revolution and the dictatorship of the proletariat

Trotsky adhered to the Bolshevik argument that the main task of the party was to launch a revolutionary seizure of power and establish the 'dictatorship of the proletariat'. By this he meant, following Lenin's *The State and Revolution* (1916), a state apparatus based not on parliament but organized through soviets or workers councils. These working-class bodies would be elected in workplaces or neighbourhoods and their delegates subject to regular recall by their constituents. The 'dictatorship' of the proletariat would be a repressive organization, directed at counter-revolutionary forces and parties. For Trotsky and his followers there is a clear and fundamental divide between the revolutionary phase of Bolshevism from 1917 until 1923 under the leadership of Lenin and Trotsky and the degeneration of the revolution from 1923 under Stalin. It is easy enough to refute the proposition that the early Bolshevik regime inevitably led to Stalinism, the gulags and the Great Terror. The 1927 Joint Opposition was a powerful force that included many leading veteran Bolsheviks such as Kamenev and Zinoviev and had it recognized Stalin rather than Bukharin as the main enemy, an anti-Stalinist alliance might also have produced a different outcome, a proposition argued many years ago by Bukharin's biographer (Cohen 1975; and see also Cox 1992: 91; Krasso 1967: 76).

Nonetheless the fact there were several possible political trajectories after Lenin's death does not prove the complete absence of any common features between pre- and post- Lenin Bolshevism. The most striking commonalities are the restriction of political pluralism, authoritarianism and coercion, the willingness to use violence against political opponents, and it is clear that Trotsky wholeheartedly subscribed to all of them. The restriction of political pluralism proceeded through a variety of specific decisions: the rapid transfer of powers in October 1917 from the multi-party Soviet Central Executive Committee to the Bolshevik-dominated

Council of Peoples Commissars (with Trotsky as Commissar of Foreign Affairs) (Fitzpatrick 2008: 65–66); the outlawing of the Constitutional Democratic Party (Cadets) and the first arrests of Menshevik and Left Social Revolutionary leaders in November 1917 (Figes 1996: 509–10; Rubinstein 2011: 103); the creation of the Cheka (Extraordinary Commission for Struggle Against Counter-Revolution, Sabotage and Speculation, forerunner of the GPU and the NKVD) in December 1917 with its wide-ranging powers of arrest, interrogation, prosecution, conviction and execution (Fitzpatrick 2008: 76); and the dispersal of the Constituent Assembly in January 1918, a body dominated by the Social Revolutionaries not the Bolsheviks (Thatcher 2003: 95).

When Karl Kautsky (1964) criticized these measures Lenin (1918) did not hesitate to denounce him as a 'renegade' and two years later Trotsky was equally scathing in *Terrorism and Communism*, a vitriolic and authoritarian polemic directed against Karl Kautsky's (1920) book of the same title (Trotsky 1920).[2] The critique issued by the Bolshevik ally Rosa Luxemburg, written the same year (1918) but published only in 1922, was more challenging as she asserted that 'Freedom only for the supporters of the government, only for the members of one party – however numerous they may be – is no freedom at all' (Luxemburg 1961: 69). She then proceeded, with unerring prescience, to map out the trajectory of the authoritarian road:

> with the repression of political life in the land as a whole, life in the soviets must also become more and more crippled. Without general elections, without unrestricted freedom of press and assembly, without a free struggle of opinion, life dies out in every public institution, becomes a mere semblance of life, in which only the bureaucracy remains as the active element. Public life gradually falls asleep, a few dozen party leaders of inexhaustible energy and boundless experience direct and rule . . . a dictatorship, to be sure, not the dictatorship of the proletariat, however, but only the dictatorship of a handful of politicians.
>
> *(Luxemburg 1961: 71–72)*

As for political violence, one of the most significant challenges to Bolshevik rule was the Kronstadt rebellion, about which Trotsky (1930) said almost nothing in his autobiography, only responding when pressed by critics in the late 1930s. He was scathing about what he dismissively referred to as the 'hue and cry' surrounding Kronstadt and merely reiterated the party line from 1921, that the Kronstadt sailors were no longer the vanguard of the October Revolution's working class but a self-interested, declassed, anti-communist social force objectively assisting counter-revolution (Mutnick 1979). In fact, as subsequent research has shown, many Kronstadt sailors in 1921 were long serving, not recent peasant recruits, and their 15-point programme for political reform was supported by Menshevik, Social Revolutionary and Bolshevik members alike at the Kronstadt base (Getzler 1983: 207–26). Some of the factory strikes in the mid-late 1920s also echoed the

Kronstadt calls for free elections to multi-party soviets (Murphy 2007: 106–11). Yet Trotsky, like Lenin, was now wholeheartedly committed to the Bolshevik monopoly of power, with its inevitable corollary, the repression of anti-Bolshevik forces on the grounds they were 'objectively' counter-revolutionary.

On the broader issue of the morality of violence Trotsky's limited grasp of the issues involved in means-ends debates led him, unwittingly, to offer *de facto* a blank cheque for widespread coercion and violence. In *Their Morals and Ours*, a series of essays written towards the end of his life, he repeatedly dismissed the idea of absolute or universal standards of morality, claiming instead, 'the end is justified if it leads to increasing the power of humanity over nature and to the abolition of the power of one person over another' (Trotsky 1939a: 48). Yet in the context of everything Trotsky wrote about revolutionary socialism, this is incoherent as it would justify Stalinist industrialization and collectivization and downplay the *immediate* negative consequences, such as injury, suffering and death (Kline 1992). He then posed the question as to whether actions such as 'frame-ups, betrayal and murder' were acceptable means to revolutionary ends.

> Permissible and obligatory are those and only those means, we answer, which unite the revolutionary proletariat, fill their hearts with irreconcilable hostility to oppression, teach them contempt for official morality and its democratic ethos, imbue them with consciousness of their own historic mission, raise their courage and spirit of self-sacrifice in the struggle.
>
> *(Trotsky 1939a: 49)*

These criteria are so vague and imprecise as to justify almost any action by a revolutionary government, however brutal and capricious.

The imperialist epoch

Trotsky shared the view of Lenin and most other leading Bolsheviks that since the early twentieth century world capitalism had entered a new era. Speaking in 1921 for instance to the third Comintern Congress, his main report opened with the ringing declaration that 'With the imperialist war, we entered the epoch of revolution' (Trotsky 1921: 226). Trotsky also presented the 21 conditions of admission to the Communist International which included a commitment to support anti-imperialist struggle (Hessel 1980a: 94). That said, it is unclear whether Trotsky's somewhat catastrophist assessment remained fairly constant throughout the post-1917 period, as Hodgson (1975) maintains, or whether his views shifted from a more nuanced to a more dogmatic position between the 1920s and 1930s, as Ticktin (1992) suggests. It is clear in hindsight that in the 30 years after the Second World War the world capitalist system enjoyed the most sustained period of economic growth in its entire history, described by some writers as 'the Golden Age of Capitalism' (Marglin and Schor 1990). Continuing adherence to Trotsky's apocalyptic vision of 1930s capitalism would create problems in the analysis of post-war economies whilst a critical engagement with the evidence of the post-war boom would require the abandonment of some part of Trotsky's perspective (Hodgson 1975).

Finally, it is worth commenting briefly on Trotsky's own personality because of the heroic stature he has acquired within the Trotskyist movement, particularly when contrasted with his murderous and tyrannical rival Stalin. His positive attributes are well known and widely recognized: he was, without doubt, an extremely gifted orator, a cultured and cosmopolitan intellectual and a stylish writer of powerful and compelling prose: *The History of the Russian Revolution*, for all its theoretical problems and limitations, is a majestic piece of literature. He was repeatedly re-elected to the Bolshevik Central Committee, at least until his expulsion at the hands of Stalin and during the early years of the revolution was entrusted with some of the most important offices of state, including foreign affairs and war. But there is another side to Trotsky's character which goes some way to explaining his problems in building a constituency both inside and outside the Bolshevik Party in the 1920s. According to the independent leftist Victor Serge, who worked in the Soviet Union from 1919 until his arrest in 1933, 'we had much admiration for him, but no real love' (Serge 1967: 141). According to Swain, Trotsky was 'not used to working in a team' because in the years before 1917 he had become used to editing his own newspaper, working as a freelance journalist and running his own small organization (2006: 211). Krasso (1967: 73) argued that whilst Trotsky could move crowds with emotion he was not an organizer who could patiently persuade. Relations with Bolshevik colleagues were not helped by his disdainful attitude to the endless round of party committee meetings, for according to Deutscher, 'he used to appear dutifully at the sessions of the Central Committee, take his seat, open a book – most often a French novel – and become so engrossed as to take no notice of the deliberations' (1959: 249–50). The idea that such matters were beneath him hints at a conceit that is even captured in his autobiography. Writing of the social life of his party colleagues – visits to each other's homes, drinking sessions and trips to the ballet – he wrote, 'If I took no part in the amusements that were becoming more and more common in the lives of the new governing stratum, it was not for moral reasons, but because I hated to inflict such boredom on myself' (Trotsky 1930: 525). Trotsky's response to criticism – on issues such as Kronstadt or the creation of the Cheka, for example – was often arrogant and dismissive. When Victor Serge raised these matters in the late 1930s, Trotsky imperiously dismissed his remarks as 'an exhibition of petty-bourgeois demoralization' (cited in Sege 1967: 349).

Conclusions

That Trotsky was a brilliant writer, an inspiring political leader and an exceptional orator is beyond question. He was a fierce opponent of the Stalinist leadership and its draconian policies, including the Great Terror and paid for his opposition with his life. Yet he was also a key protagonist of Bolshevik authoritarianism, fully behind the harassment and repression of rival parties, the ban on factions, and the suppression of strikes and other forms of worker and peasant unrest. It is therefore ironic that a leading member of the newly emerging one-party state should end up as a heroic, revolutionary critic of Stalinist bureaucracy and authoritarianism. At the very least it should be clear that his political legacy is complex and contradictory and that the relationship between Leninism, Trotskyism and Stalinism cannot be reduced to a crude contraposition of an heroic Bolshevism and a Stalinist tyranny that have nothing in common. Trotsky's theoretical legacy, the various ideas that can be said to constitute Trotskyist doctrine, can be summarized as follows: the theory of permanent revolution, the united front tactic, transitional demands, critical analysis of the Soviet state, the necessity for a new, Fourth International, the necessity to build revolutionary, democratic centralist, vanguard parties, the necessity to build militant organizations to challenge trade union bureaucracy, the insistence on revolution not reform and the characterization of the imperialist epoch. Some of these themes are unique to Trotskyism whilst others are shared with the official communist tradition from which Trotskyism emerged in the 1920s.

All of these themes are contentious and problematic: what is the status of the theory of permanent revolution in light of the numerous revolutions led by non-working-class forces that have overthrown autocracies? What is the value of a united front between revolutionary and social democratic forces when the former are tiny and divided and the latter have succumbed to various forms of neo-liberal ideology and policy? Can working-class politics really be reduced to a 'crisis of leadership'? How are we to understand the 'crisis of working-class leadership' in a world where political party systems are immeasurably more complex than the 1920s and 1930s and where trade union membership has plummeted around the advanced capitalist world? These issues will be explored in the next three chapters where we describe the development of the Trotskyist movement in Britain and then turn to the role of doctrine.

Notes

1 On the Inter-District Group see www.marxists.org/glossary/orgs/i/n.htm, accessed 6 February 2017.
2 Mandel (1995a: 83) rightly asserted that it was 'certainly his worst book'.

3

DEVELOPMENT OF THE TROTSKYIST MOVEMENT IN BRITAIN, PART 1: 1950–1985

The aims of Chapters 3 and 4 are threefold: first, to assess trends in the membership of the Trotskyist movement over time; second, to describe the development of the Trotskyist movement in Britain through a series of distinct phases; and third, to chart the emergence of discrete organizations linked to particular families of Trotskyist doctrine where a family is understood as a set of organizations, both national and international, that share most of the core elements of Trotskyism (see Chapter 2) but diverge on one or two key issues.[1]

Defining Trotskyist organizations and measuring organizational membership

Material on the period since 1970 has been drawn from archives, interviews, newspapers and magazines whilst material for the pre-1970 period has been taken mainly from secondary sources, for example Alexander (1991a) and Callaghan (1984). There is some dispute over where to draw the boundaries of the Trotskyist movement and the approach taken here is to include all those organizations that self-identify as 'Trotskyist' or which locate themselves 'in the Trotskyist tradition', irrespective of whether rival groups dispute such claims. The category therefore includes a range of organizations with somewhat differing ideologies and a variety of labels such as Party, League, Network and Tendency (see Table 3.1). A small number of organizations gradually abandoned their Trotskyist heritage such as the Revolutionary Communist Group (RCG) which evolved into an anti-imperialist, pro-Cuba and non-Trotskyist body.[2] For organizations such as this I have included membership figures only for their early years (see note to Figure 3.1 below). Radical left parties like the Socialist Labour Party (SLP) and Left Unity and libertarian socialist groups such as Big Flame have been excluded as non-Trotskyist despite the presence of Trotskyist factions within them.[3]

TABLE 3.1 The 22 contemporary British Trotskyist organizations 2017

Organization	Year founded	2016 membership
Socialist Workers Party*	1950	5,936
Socialist Party	1950	c. 2,000
Counterfire	2010	300
Socialist Appeal	1992	300
revolutionary socialism in the 21st Century	2014	250
Alliance for Workers Liberty**	1966	140
Workers Revolutionary Party***	1947	120
Socialist Resistance****	1987	95
Socialist Equality Party	1986	50
Marxist World	2014	35
Workers Power/Red Flag	1975	30
Socialist Action*****	1962	30
Independent Socialist Network	2011	20
Communist League	1988	15
International Socialist League	1988	12
Socialist Fight	2009	10
Spartacist League/Britain	1975	10
Workers Fight	1987	10
International Bolshevik Tendency	1985	5
Workers International to Rebuild the Fourth International	1990	5
Fourth International (Lambertist)	1970	2
Revolutionary Communist International Tendency in Britain	2015	2

Sources: See Appendix 2.

* Began 1950 as the Socialist Review Group.
** Began 1966 as Workers Fight, formerly a faction inside the Revolutionary Socialist League.
*** Began 1947 as a faction inside the Revolutionary Communist Party.
**** Began 1987 as the International Socialist Group.
***** Began 1962 as the International Group, official British section of the Fourth International.

Data on political party membership, even for mainstream parties, is problematic because there is no legal requirement to collect, publish or audit membership figures, either in Britain or elsewhere in Western Europe. In principle there are four grounds on which an individual could be designated a member of a Trotskyist group. The loosest definition is anyone who has completed a membership application form, but that raises the question of precisely what is signified by such an action. In organizations such as the WRP there was tremendous pressure on activists to sell the party's daily newspaper through door-to-door canvasses and simultaneously encourage buyers to complete a membership application form. The signed sheets were duly returned to Head Office and quickly appeared in internal WRP reports of membership figures. Attempts to transform paper members into card-carrying, dues-paying members, however, sometimes came unstuck, as one ex-WRP interviewee recalled:

> We were following up on one of these canvassing things in a desperate hous-
> ing estate, in one of these great big blocks of flats right on the Mersey, we
> knocked on the door and this guy looked at us, and we said who we were.
> "Wait a minute", he said, and he came back with his docker's hook and said,
> "now fuck off!" So it was unreal.
>
> *(Bob Archer interview)*

A second definition therefore includes only those people issued with a membership card, yet this definition too might be problematic because people may hold
a party card without paying regular membership dues. One aim of the SWP's
2016 recruitment and subs drive was to 'increase the number of people who pay
a regular sub' (clearly implying that some pay irregularly or not at all) (SWP Party
Notes 18 January 2016). Financial contribution to the organization provides a
more demanding test of membership but that in turn means counting people who
only pay money and are otherwise inactive. Participation in party activities such as
branch meetings, paper sales and demonstrations constitutes the strictest criterion
for membership but suffers from a chronic lack of reliable time-series data. In short,
we are driven, out of necessity, to follow the political science practice of using the
self-reported membership figures of political parties, despite their known limitations and likely biases (cf. Keen and Audickas 2016; van Biezen et al. 2012).

In the case of Trotskyist groups the problem of data unreliability is compounded
by two further issues: the widespread reluctance to publish membership figures,
most likely, as we shall see, because they are embarrassingly small; and complex
classifications of membership. Fortunately the absence of public data is mitigated
by an abundance of private, internal data usually in the form of reports to national
party committees. The figures in these reports should be regarded as upper estimates because they include non-dues payers, people who are inactive as well as
people who have left the organization but have yet to be struck off the membership records (Charlie Kimber interview). In other cases it has been possible to
draw on data from interviews or memoirs as well as estimates from informed third
parties. The only strict pre-requisites for membership of larger organizations are
the completion of an application form and the issuance of a membership card (this
is true for instance of the Socialist Party and the SWP). Smaller groups, however,
often categorize interested applicants as probationary members, pending the outcome of interviews and successful completion of an induction programme, for
example the Alliance for Workers Liberty (AWL) and Workers Power.

Some organizations deploy the category of 'sympathisers'; others refer to a
'periphery' of supporters which might or might not be included in overall membership figures; and some recruit students into separate units of the organization.
Numbers in these three categories can be quite substantial. For instance, the
Revolutionary Communist Party (RCP) claimed a membership in 1995 of 380
but a periphery of 'around 1,100–1,200 close contacts'.[4] There are no reliable
data on student members so they are excluded from the figures presented in the

chapter although we do know which universities have registered Trotskyist societies (see Chapter 6). Where possible, probationer members have been included
in the membership count as they pay dues and participate in the group's political
activities but 'sympathizers', 'supporters' or those attached to a 'periphery' have
been excluded because they do not hold a membership card. The absence of public, consistent time series data means there are inevitably significant gaps in the
membership record and these have been filled by interpolation, assuming a linear progression between the two figures either side of a gap (for more details on
sources and methods see Appendix 2). Finally, the figures cover England, Wales
and Scotland but exclude Northern Ireland.

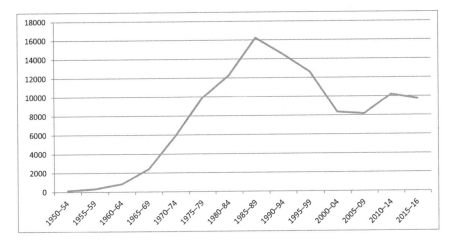

FIGURE 3.1   UK Trotskyist organizations, total membership 1950–2016

Sources: See Appendix 2.

Note: Membership data is for the current groups listed in Table 3.1 and for the following defunct groups:
Anti-Capitalist Initiative (2012–2014), Communist Forum (1986–1988), International Socialist Alliance
(1978–1979), International Socialist Group (Scotland) (2011–2015), International Socialist Movement
(Scotland) (1992–2015), International Socialist Network (2013–2015), Intervention Collective
(1976–1980), League for Socialist Action (1975–1982), Marxist Party (1987–2004), Marxist Worker
Group (1976–1982), Permanent Revolution Group (2006–2013), Revolutionary Communist Party
(1976–1996), Revolutionary Internationalist League (1988–1994), Revolutionary Marxist Current
(1975–1979), Revolutionary Workers' Party (1963–2011), Socialist Current (1957–1988), Socialist
Labour Group (1975–1990), Socialist Union (Internationalist) (1974–1981), Spartacus League
(1970–1971), Workers International League (1983–1984), Workers International League (1987–2006),
Workers International Review Group (1984–1985), Workers League (1976–1978), Workers News
Group (1981–82), Workers Revolutionary Party (Workers Press) (1986–2000) and Workers Socialist
League (1974–1987). Figures have also been included for the dates shown for several groups that evolved
away from Trotskyism, viz. A World to Win (1990–2004), Red Action (1981–1984), Revolutionary
Communist Group (1974–1976), Revolutionary Communist League/Chartist Group (1969–1980),
Revolutionary Democratic Group (1983–1996) and the Workers Party (later the Economic and
Philosophic Science Review) (1979–1980).

Overall membership trends are shown in Figure 3.1 and we can divide the period since 1950 into four phases. The time from 1950 to the mid-1960s, the 'Bleak Years', was marked by membership levels counted in the hundreds and very modest rates of annual growth. In 1950 the Trotskyist movement comprised three organizations with a grand total of just 124 members and by the end of the decade it had grown to 475 in four organizations. It was from the mid-1960s that Trotskyist membership growth really took off. From a little over 1,500 members in 1965 the movement grew rapidly over the next 20 years, reaching almost 4,000 by 1970, nearly 10,000 by 1980 and peaking at over 20,000 in 1985. This 'Golden Age' of Trotskyism came crashing to a halt with the disintegration of the WRP and the Socialist League in 1985 and the collapse and split in the Militant Tendency in 1992. The WRP claimed a membership of almost 10,000 in 1985 but several years later its various fragments probably comprised no more than about 700–800.[5] Although the SWP briefly bucked the trend of decline in the 1990s, hitting a membership peak of 10,000, it too succumbed to membership contraction so that by 2004 the entire Trotskyist movement had shrunk to 6,500 members, less than one-third of its 1985 peak. The period since the early 2000s has witnessed a very limited recovery of membership but after years of right-wing Labour and Conservative governments and a deep and prolonged economic crisis, overall Trotskyist membership in 2016 was only 9,500. Figure 3.2 depicts membership trends for the four largest groups, the International Marxist Group (IMG) and its successors, the Militant Tendency/Socialist Party, the Socialist Workers Party (SWP) and the Workers Revolutionary Party (WRP). Although peak membership for the movement as a whole occurred towards the end of the Golden Age, two

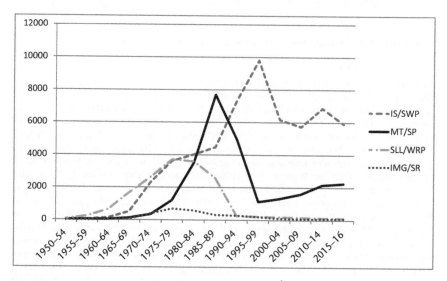

FIGURE 3.2 Membership of individual UK Trotskyist organizations 1950–2016

Sources: See Appendix 2.

TABLE 3.2 The development of the Trotskyist movement in Britain 1932–2017

1932–1949	Formation: growth and decline of independent organizations
1950–1965	The Bleak Years: limited growth inside the Labour Party
1966–1985	The Golden Age: rapid and substantial growth
1985–2004	Disintegration: organizational turmoil and membership decline
2005–2017	Stasis: limited and uneven recovery in the neoliberal era

Source: Author.

of the major groups actually recorded their highest membership totals in the late 1980s (Militant) and the mid-1990s (SWP).

Table 3.2 summarizes these trends, including the pre-1950 period of formation. The appellations for each period are intended to be useful summaries of a number of trends but they are approximations, in two respects: first, the turning points between periods are rarely confined to a single year but often span several years; second, the diversity of the Trotskyist movement means that during periods of overall growth, there are a few organizations that decline and conversely during periods of retrenchment, some organizations have defied the downward trend.

1950–1965 The Bleak Years: limited growth inside the Labour Party

In December 1950 the Trotskyist movement comprised a little over 100 members in three organizations, all of which were engaged in Labour Party entrism: Tony Cliff's Socialist Review Group and Ted Grant's Marxist Tendency were separate organizations following their expulsions from the Club, the main Trotskyist group in Britain, which was under the firm control of Gerry Healy. Cliff's group belonged to a distinct branch of the Trotskyist tradition that would later come to be labelled Third Camp Marxism, and which traced its origins to the disputes in 1939–1940 over the class nature of the Soviet Union following the Russian invasions of Poland and Finland. It was into this ongoing debate that Cliff launched his book *State Capitalism in Russia* (1974). First published in 1948, the key message was summed up in its title and was largely grounded in two claims: workers were exploited within the USSR by a ruling class; and these relations of production arose from military and economic competition between the USSR and the capitalist world. The emergence of Stalinist regimes in Eastern Europe from 1946 permitted Cliff to add a political dimension to the argument, namely that a socialist society could only be created 'from below', by the working class itself; it could not be installed 'from above' by a Stalinist party or its Red Army (Hallas 1971). Ted Grant (1989a) wrote a lengthy rebuttal which claimed *inter alia* that Cliff had departed from both orthodox Marxism and Trotskyism, for downplaying the progressive character of the Soviet system in developing the productive forces (for details of the argument see Birchall 2011: 110–19 and for more general discussion of state capitalist theories see Mandel 1990; van der Linden 2009: 91–98, 119–22, 153–58). With the outbreak of the Korean War in 1950, Cliff drew the logical political conclusion from his analysis, encapsulated in his group's famous slogan, 'Neither Washington nor Moscow'. If both sides were exploitative, class societies then Trotskyists should remain neutral, a position radically at odds with the Trotskyist mainstream which backed socialist China and North Korea against the imperialist USA. Cliff and his supporters were duly expelled from the Club but so too were Grant and his few supporters as Healy sought to consolidate his power (Birchall 2011: 129–30).

The emergence of orthodoxy

Internationally, the Club was the British section of the mainstream Fourth International but developments in the early 1950s led to a major split in that organization, a process in which Healy played a key role. Trotskyist Internationals will be examined more fully in Chapter 11 so for the moment it is sufficient to note that in the post-war period the world Trotskyist movement and its Fourth International was faced with a daunting set of challenges arising from the fact that the contemporary world bore little resemblance to the scenarios mapped out by Trotsky in the late 1930s: Stalinism in the USSR had survived and spread into Eastern Europe; social democratic and communist parties were still strong; Trotskyist forces were extremely weak; and the world capitalist economy had not sunk into a new depression but was in the early stages of what would prove to be a prolonged period of growth.

Under the leadership of Michel Pablo, the International gradually developed a new set of analyses and policies, first clearly enunciated in 1951 at the Third World Congress and in a subsequent report the following year.[6] He departed from Trotsky's argument that the current period represented an unstable, imperialist epoch of wars and revolutions claiming instead that the Stalinist states and the communist parties might survive for centuries. He also modified the idea of Stalinism as an irrevocably counter-revolutionary force, arguing that the Eastern European countries liberated by the Red Army were not capitalist states but 'deformed workers' states'. In this new scenario of what Pablo called 'War-Revolution' he questioned whether the immediate, strategic priority for Trotskyists should be the construction of independent, revolutionary parties, proposing instead that the optimal strategy was to pursue long-term entry into social democratic or communist parties (depending on their respective national strengths). Originally envisaged by Trotsky in the 1930s as a short-term tactic, entrism had now been re-imagined by Pablo as a long-term strategy, *entrism sui generis* (Frank and Bensaid 2010: 60–77; Trotsky 1934). This set of analyses marked the emergence of what would become a hallmark of the *Mainstream Trotskyist* family, namely a high degree of ideological flexibility and a willingness to modify or even abandon core elements of Trotskyist doctrine.

Pablo's ideas gave rise to a heated struggle in which the leaders of the British, French and American sections of the International sought to re-establish and preserve *Orthodox Trotskyism*, the programme and analyses developed by Trotsky in the 1930s (Callinicos 1990a: 39–54). In particular they branded his opposition to the necessity of building mass, revolutionary, Trotskyist parties as 'liquidation-ism' and his willingness to work inside communist and social democratic parties as 'opportunism'. Yet the dispute was not initially framed as a matter of *doctrine*: throughout 1952 and 1953 the French section was involved in a *tactical* disagree-ment over whether to practise deep entry into the Communist Party (the Fourth International position) or the Socialist Party (the French Trotskyist position). As the International moved to assert its authority over the French party, and later that year over the American and British parties, these varied disputes soon coalesced into a battle over *organizational power* as the national sections fought to protect their autonomy. Adding fuel to the conflict were the strong *personalities* of the key protagonists: Michel Pablo and Ernest Mandel on the one side; Pierre Lambert (France), James Cannon (USA) and Gerry Healy (UK) on the other (Alexander 1991a: 322; Frank and Bensaid 2010: 78–79; Workers Power and Irish Workers Group 1983: 31–36). Following Cannon's 'Open Letter' of November 1953 denouncing 'Pablo's revisionism', the guardians of orthodoxy now regrouped in an International Committee of the Fourth International (ICFI) in which Healy was to play a leading role (National Committee of the SWP 1953).

A few years later the political environment of British Trotskyism became slightly more favourable when Nikita Khrushchev delivered his famous 1956 speech to a closed session of the Soviet Communist Party congress denouncing Stalin's crimes and his abuse of power. The speech, coupled with the Soviet invasion of Hungary to crush a worker and student uprising, triggered a crisis inside the British Communist Party leading to an exodus of between 9,000 and 10,000 members over the next few years (Callaghan 2003: 76; Thompson 1992: 112). Healy was quick to see the potential for Trotskyist growth and his organization recruited between 100 and 200 disillusioned CP members including leading intellectuals and writers such as Peter Fryer, Tom Kemp, Brian Pearce and Cliff Slaughter.[7] He also recruited trade union militants, mainly in London buses, the docks, railways and the building industry including the rank and file building activist Brian Behan (An Anonymous Author 1996: 199). In 1959 the Club changed its name to the Socialist Labour League (SLL) but the growth of the organization and of genuine debate amongst its diverse membership came into conflict with its highly authoritarian internal regime and with Healy's intolerance of dissent. One consequence was a string of resigna-tions as many of the trade union recruits left and joined the Labour Party whilst Behan was expelled for factional activity (An Anonymous Author 1996: 200; Pitt 2002: Chapter 5). One of the most high-profile quits was the journalist Peter Fryer whose 1959 resignation letter described the internal regime of the League as 'the rule of . . . the general secretary's personal clique' and complained of its tendency to 'lies, bullying and blackmail'.[8]

In 1963 the SLL suffered another blow when the US Socialist Workers Party chose to reunite with the mainstream Fourth International, a decision based in part on a shared admiration and sympathy for the 1959 Cuban Revolution. Whilst the SLL defended Castro's Cuba against US aggression, it strongly objected to the heterodox claim that a guerrilla army could lead a socialist revolution in a colonial country and create a 'workers' state' because this contradicted Trotsky's theory of permanent revolution (North 1988: 347–60, 375–90; Pitt 2002: Chapter 6). Moreover the British and French parties insisted unity could only proceed on the basis of a wholehearted repudiation of the 'heresy' of Pabloism.[9] Healy, along with Pierre Lambert's group in France, therefore remained outside the newly formed United Secretariat of the Fourth International (USFI). Personalities were again important in the dispute: the mainstream Fourth International leader Ernest Mandel held an extremely low opinion of Healy and had repeatedly clashed with Lambert (Germain 1974; Stutje 2009: 100–01, 120).[10] Notwithstanding these problems, the SLL continued to grow, reaching 1,000 members by 1964 and allowing Healy to respond to escalating hostility from the Labour Party leadership by abandoning entry work and operating as an open revolutionary organization.

The Socialist Review Group, the Revolutionary Socialist League and others

In contrast, Cliff's group (renamed the International Socialism Group in 1962) expanded only very slowly so that by 1965 it had no more than 230 members (Callaghan 1987: 79). Both the IS and SLL were producing regular newspapers and magazines, the monthly *Labour Worker* and quarterly *International Socialism* from IS and the weekly *Newsletter* and quarterly *Fourth International* from the SLL. Recruitment into IS picked up in the early 1960s, partly from the Campaign for Nuclear Disarmament but mainly from the Labour Party Young Socialists where IS and Ted Grant's group briefly cooperated in producing a joint paper called *Young Guard* (Birchall 2011: 201–07).

Grant's organization meanwhile had become the Revolutionary Socialist League (RSL) in 1957 and its tiny membership of a few dozen remained loosely attached to the mainstream Fourth International (Woods 2013a: 124). In 1964 it launched the first issue of its monthly newspaper, *Militant*, and was determined to continue operating inside the Labour Party despite the SLL withdrawal. In 1959 Grant wrote what would turn out to be a seminal article in which he revised Trotsky's notion of entrism as a short-run tactic, replacing it with the idea of entrism as a long-term strategy. The core reasoning was summed up in one sentence: 'All history demonstrates that, at the first stages of revolutionary upsurge, the masses turn to the mass organisations to try and find a solution for their problems' (Grant 1959). In light of this alleged fact, Trotskyists should seek, slowly and patiently, to build a Marxist current inside the Labour Party in readiness for the upsurge of class struggle that would provide a receptive audience for Marxist ideas. In this scenario, the growing strength of the left would split the party, leaving Marxists in control. In effect, Grant defended the Pabloite policy of *entrism sui generis* but for reasons that were rooted in what he claimed to be labour movement traditions and institutions. His second departure from orthodoxy was the claim that with sufficient support inside and outside parliament, a socialist government could effect 'an entirely peaceful transformation of society' without having to build new state institutions such as soviets (Militant 1981a: 25), a theme that persists in the Socialist Party, one of Militant's successors (Socialist Party 2008: 27). The commitment to the institutions of the Labour Party and of parliament represents such a significant departure from two of the core elements of Trotskyism that it merits the designation of a new and distinct family, which for want of a better term we can label *Institutional Trotskyism*.

By 1965 a movement comprising the three original Trotskyist groups – IS, RSL and SLL – had also been joined by three tiny organizations of which only the International Group, soon to become the IMG, would prove to be of any significance. The first of these groups broke away from Grant's organization in 1956 and began publishing a monthly journal, *Socialist Current*. It survived until 1988 but its influence and significance never matched its longevity (Woods 2013a: 126).[11] A second group emerged in 1962, composed mainly of Latin American Trotskyists led by the Argentinian Juan Posadas. Described by Mandel as 'one of the nastiest schismatics the movement had ever known' (Studtje 2009: 120), he broke away from the Fourth International (and from fellow Argentinian leader Nahuel Moreno), complaining about its domination by European and American activists. Posadas' main claim to fame was his idiosyncratic thesis that a nuclear war was inevitable yet should be welcomed by revolutionaries as it would constitute the prelude to a new socialist civilization (Alexander 1991a: 663–64). He and his supporters began vigorous efforts to expand their new International, both in Latin America and Europe, including the creation in 1963 of a British section, the Revolutionary Workers' Party. The hallmark of its newspaper *Red Flag* was the domination of its few pages by lengthy articles and speeches of Posadas (Alexander 1991a: 499, 663–64).[12] Doctrinally, there was little to distinguish Posadist Trotskyism from the mainstream, apart from its geographical origins, but his organization would prove to be the first of many that would insist on the specificity of a nebulous *Latin American* family of Trotskyism. Finally, there was the equally small International Group, founded in 1961 by Pat Jordan and Ken Coates (the future Labour MEP) and also affiliated to the mainstream Fourth International. It published a succession of magazines the most famous of which was *The Week* edited from its first issue in January 1964 by Coates and a young researcher Robin Blackburn (Tate 2014: 24–28).

The long-post war boom coupled with the expansion of the world communist movement and the survival of social democratic parties had thrown the Trotskyist movement completely off-balance. For a long period it was forced to survive in a world that was both unexpected and unfamiliar as steady economic growth challenged the perspective of imminent slump. There were contemporary efforts to explain the post-war boom: Tony Cliff's collaborator Michael Kidron (1961, 1967) argued that rising armaments expenditure, fuelled by competition between Western capitalism and Soviet state capitalism had helped counteract the falling tendency of the rate of profit. Ted Grant, on the other hand, opened his 1960 essay in thoroughly orthodox fashion by swearing fidelity to the 'laws underlying the development of capitalist society . . . worked out and explained by Marx'. He then proceeded to list a series of specific, *ad hoc* factors underpinning the post-war boom, whilst declaring the impending arrival of a 'catastrophic downswing'

(Grant 1989b: 393, 412).[13] The claim was hyperbole but there were signs in the early-mid 1960s that the Bleak Years were coming to an end and in this new conjuncture the Trotskyist movement was about to enter a period of unprecedented advance.

1966–1985 The Golden Age: rapid and substantial growth

From the mid-1960s Britain experienced a dramatic rise in the numbers of strikes, as workers sought to protect earnings against rising inflation despite the restrictions of the new Labour government's state incomes policy (Lyddon 2007). Student protests started in France in 1968 and quickly spread to Britain, often merging with international solidarity protests, against the Vietnam War, South African apartheid and the entry of British troops into Northern Ireland in 1969. The Conservative election victory in 1970 escalated the ongoing strike wave as workers rebelled against a new state incomes policy and protested against the legal restrictions on trade unions in the Industrial Relations Act (1971) (Darlington and Lyddon 2001). In response Labour developed a relatively left-wing programme and secured re-election in February 1974 (and again in October the same year) before its defeat in 1979 at the hands of the Conservatives, now led by Margaret Thatcher.

Together these developments ushered in and nurtured the Golden Age of British Trotskyism, a period of unusually rapid growth that would last until the miners' strike of 1984–1985. Membership of the International Socialists reached 1,000 in 1971, 4,000 in 1977 and stabilized at that figure for the next ten years (Birchall 2011: 299, 372, 457). The SLL grew unevenly throughout the 1970s and early 1980s, reaching 4,000 by 1976 and claiming over 9,000 a few months after the end of the miners' strike. The RSL was officially transformed into the Militant Tendency in 1964 but beneath the veneer of a group of newspaper readers and supporters it continued to exist as a democratic centralist organization and it too began to expand, less from the upturn in industrial struggle and more from the growing ferment inside the Labour Party at the time of the 1974–1979 Social Contract (Meredith 2008). By 1975 it was claiming around 770 members yet by 1985 it had grown astronomically to approximately 7,000 (Crick 2016: 340). The overall growth of the Trotskyist movement throughout this period is impressive by any standards. In 1966 its total membership of less than 2,000 was dwarfed by the 33,734 communists of the CP. In 1985, the position was reversed as the Trotskyist movement reached its zenith, with a combined membership of almost 20,000 in the SWP, WRP and RSL alone, whilst the Communist Party had slumped to just 12,711 and was entering a terminal crisis (Thompson 1992: Chapter 8; and Figures 3.1 and 3.2).

Two of the larger groups transformed themselves into parties: the SLL became the WRP in 1973 whilst IS became the SWP in 1977 (and one of their smaller rivals, the International Group became the IMG in 1967). Weekly newspapers were now a regular feature of the movement and by 1975 there were no less than six: *Militant* (RSL), *Red Flag* (Revolutionary Workers' Party), *Red Weekly* (IMG), *Socialist Press* (Workers Socialist League, a group expelled from the WRP in 1974), *Socialist Worker* (IS) and *Workers Fight* (the ex-IS faction Workers Fight).

In addition there was the world's first Trotskyist daily newspaper, *Workers Press*, a broadsheet launched in September 1969 by the SLL and re-launched as a more popular tabloid in 1976 as *The News Line*. Finally, the most notable feature of the Trotskyist organizations of this period is a remarkable degree of leadership stability, despite rapid and substantial membership turnover. In 1950 the three main Trotskyist groups were led by Tony Cliff (IS), Ted Grant (RSL) and Gerry Healy (SLL) respectively; 35 years later, in 1985, these three men still led their organizations (and in terms of longevity one could add Sean Matgamna, leader of Workers Fight and its various successor organizations).

The International Socialists

In the mid-1960s IS still operated a loose federal structure; it was active in the Labour Party; and its social composition was predominantly 'middle class' and student-based. By the mid-1970s, and in response to the dramatic strike wave of the period, it had formally adopted a democratic centralist structure, abandoned Labour Party work (both decisions were taken in 1968), and had acquired a small but significant base in a wide range of trade unions as it sought to promote industrial militancy, the precursor, so it was believed, of a more radical and ultimately revolutionary class consciousness (Birchall 2011: 290–92, 300–01):[14] 'Every struggle of the working class, however limited it may be, by increasing its self-confidence and education, undermines Reformism' (Cliff cited in Birchall 2011: 169).

By the mid-late 1970s the IS/SWP had built groups of supporters in many of the large unions, both public and private sector, including AUEW, CPSA, NALGO, NUT and the TGWU (see Chapter 9 for more detail).[15] The group's ambitions rose in line with the level of industrial militancy: in 1973 it launched a National Rank and File Movement, an ostensible rival to the main left-wing trade union body, the Communist Party-led Liaison Committee for the Defence of Trade Unions, and two years later, as unemployment began to rise, it launched the first of a series of National Right to Work marches. As militancy waned under the impact of the Labour government's Social Contract, the IS detected the first signs of a 'downturn' in class struggle and the 'bureaucratization' of the shop steward committees in which it had once placed so many hopes. By 1982 with unemployment heading towards three million and trade union membership beginning its long decline, the SWP closed down its rank and file groups and settled in for a long period of slow and modest party-building (Callinicos 1982). Perhaps its best known achievement of this period was the launch in 1977 of the single-issue campaigning body, the Anti-Nazi League (ANL), designed to counter the growing influence of the far-right party, the National Front (see Chapter 10). In terms of doctrine, the group steadfastly maintained its state capitalist view of the Soviet Union and extended the analysis to the East European communist regimes (Harman 1969, 1974).

In 1976, repelled by the sectarianism of Healy's International and the support of the USFI for guerrilla struggles in Latin America (a position effectively repudiated at the 1979 Congress; Alexander 1991a: 757–58), the IS decided in 1976 to issue an International Bulletin and shortly afterwards to create a loose international structure, the International Socialist Tendency (IST), through which other 'state capitalist' groups could exchange ideas. From 1984 the Tendency began to hold annual meetings of its six affiliates, in Australia, Canada, Ireland, West Germany, the UK and the USA (Birchall 1981: 29; Cliff 2000: 205).

The Socialist Labour League

The other major Trotskyist group, the Socialist Labour League, also became increasingly active in the trade union movement. In 1968 it created an industrial organization, the All Trades Unions Alliance, which held national annual rallies, often attended by several thousand party members and trade union militants.[16] This was not an IS-type rank and file organization, with workplace and union groups and rank and file papers; rather it operated primarily as a transmission belt for the dissemination of SLL/WRP policies and as a mechanism for recruitment into the party (Lotz and Feldman 1994: 251). By the early 1970s its two industrial strongholds were in the car industry, particularly the Oxford Cowley plant, and in the actors' union Equity where its star recruits were Corin and Vanessa Redgrave (Informal conversation with Terry Brotherstone).

As a thoroughly orthodox Trotskyist group, the SLL took to heart Trotsky's insistence that capitalism was in deep crisis and that the role of Trotskyists was to build the party that would lead the revolutionary struggle for state power. A 1967 letter to members claimed that rising prices and wages signalled 'The end of the post war boom' and 'still deeper crisis for British capitalism, a crisis in which all the class compromises are smashed and in which the issue of power is posed'. Two years later, in response to the Labour government's proposals for greater legal regulation of trade unions (*In Place of Strife*), an SLL leaflet spelled out its apocalyptic meaning: '*EITHER the dictatorship of Wilson and, after him, a right-wing semi-fascist dictatorship of Tories, OR a workers government based on workers' councils and trade unions with a socialist home and foreign policy.* This is the choice' (Emphasis in original).[17] By 1980 the WRP's paranoia and perceived self-importance had mushroomed, leading to the following apocalyptic claim at a Central Committee meeting:

> the Tories have been preparing, training and equipping the forces of the capitalist state for mass violence and mass repression . . . The Party . . . must actively prepare for semi-legality and possible illegality. *Semi-legality* means building a secret apparatus in the party which runs parallel with its public work . . . *Illegality* would arise in a Tory State of Emergency when the Privy Council would abolish basic political rights, outlaw the party, shut its newspaper and force the party to go underground and wage clandestine revolutionary struggle. Preparations for this situation must start forthwith.[18]

At the 7th WRP Congress, meeting in December 1984 as the miners' strike was disintegrating, the WRP leadership detected 'unmistakeable signs of a pre-revolutionary period developing rapidly into socialist revolution' but warned of an impending danger that the ruling class will 'attempt to transform the Bonapartist dictatorship [the Thatcher government] into an open military police dictatorship' (Workers Revolutionary Party 1984b: 52, 70). The proper response, then as now, was to build the WRP, call a general strike and seize power (Workers Revolutionary Party 1984a, 1985a).

Four of the other hallmarks of the SLL/WRP were its daily paper, seen as one of the key means for winning recruits (and for raising money), its large youth organization, the Young Socialists (YS), its stress on Marxist education and training and its emphasis on the baleful role of Stalinism. Despite repeated claims about the historic significance of the world's first Trotskyist daily paper, *The News Line* increasingly proved to be a millstone, as we shall see in Chapter 8, so from April 1976 the WRP began cultivating friendly relations with a variety of Middle Eastern dictators, in particular Libya's Muammar Gaddafi. In exchange for favourable coverage in the party's daily press, the WRP received substantial sums of money.[19] In contrast, the party's youth organization was highly resilient: it numbered several thousand in the early 1960s and by March 1985 the YS could still attract 2,000 people to its annual conference (*Young Socialist* 23 March 1985). The organization also became the first Trotskyist group in Britain to open its own training centre, the College of Marxist Education, at which it offered both introductory and advanced training. One of the regular tutors was party leader Gerry Healy, who (mistakenly) believed that his reading of Lenin's *Philosophical Notebooks* had transformed him into a leading expert in dialectical materialism.[20] Healy had insisted as far back as the 1960s that the party had to train its members 'as dialectical materialists in the struggle to build the revolutionary party'.[21] As for Stalinism, one measure of the party's belief in its major counter-revolutionary role was the publication of a 440-page exposé of 'Stalinism in Britain' in response to a 56-page CP pamphlet on 'ultra-leftism' (Black 1970; Reid 1969).

At about this time, Healy's International, the ICFI, began to splinter and by 1971 its two main components, the SLL and Lambert's OCI, had irrevocably parted company. The ostensible issue in dispute was the relevance of dialectical materialism in cadre training but there were also tactical disagreements over the importance of the Transitional Programme, an issue more salient for Lambert than for Healy (Alexander 1991a: 543–44).[22] The ICFI met seven times between the early 1970s and 1985 but never acquired more than 10–12 national affiliates (see various issues of *Fourth International*).

The Militant Tendency and the International Marxist Group

Meanwhile the Militant Tendency continued with its policy of working to establish control of Labour Party wards and to shape Labour policy through the election of delegates to its annual conference and the passage of Militant-sponsored motions. Factional groupings had now emerged on both the left and right of the Labour Party and Tony Benn MP was starting to emerge as one of the leading figures in Labour's left wing, eventually challenging Denis Healy for the Deputy Leadership position in 1980. In this febrile atmosphere, Militant as one of the oldest and most tightly organized factions was able to make considerable headway and its growth was also helped by the absence from the Labour Party of the other major Trotskyist groups, IMG, IS/SWP and SLL/WRP. That said, a succession of very small groups did begin to work in the Labour Party throughout this period, starting with the Socialist Charter group in the early 1970s, the International-Communist League and the Workers Socialist League from the mid-late 1970s and both the IMG and Workers Power from the early 1980s.[23] In addition, the WRP began a collaboration in 1981 with the Labour leftists Ken Livingstone (then Leader of the Greater London Council), Ted Knight and Mathew Warburton, publishing a weekly newspaper, the *Labour Herald*. Although Livingstone and his colleagues were the ostensible editors, the paper was actually edited, printed and financed by the WRP although it is unclear whether the venture provided either greater influence or more recruits for the party (Hosken 2008: 126–37; Mitchell 2011: 393–99). None of these organizations, however, was able to prevent either Militant's growing influence or the backlash that it provoked from the Labour right. Following several investigations in the late 1970s and early 1980s the five editors of its weekly paper – including the late Ted Grant and current Socialist Party General Secretary Peter Taaffe – were expelled from the Labour Party in 1983. Within the trade unions, Militant began building organized groups of Militant supporters from around 1975 and as it gradually acquired a critical mass of supporters it launched its own trade union organization, the Broad Left Organizing Committee in 1984 (Mullins 2014).[24] One other key development in the 1970s was Militant's decision to begin the construction of an international organization and in 1974 it launched the Committee for a Workers International (CWI), a body with fewer than 1,000 members of whom 500 were in Britain.[25]

In addition to these three organizations the membership and influence of the IMG began to grow significantly through its key role in establishing and organizing the Vietnam Solidarity Campaign, helped by the flamboyance of one of its leading activists, Tariq Ali (1987).[26] The IMG always had a strong orientation towards anti-imperialist work and a few years later it initiated the Troops Out Movement, directed at the violent conflict in the north of Ireland between the IRA and the British state. After the 1968 student revolts in Paris and as part of the mainstream Fourth International, it developed an equally strong orientation towards the student movement in the belief that universities could function as 'red bases' that would link up with and help intensify other anti-capitalist struggles (Callaghan 1984: 133–43). In 1967 the group could claim no more than about 50 members but it grew to a peak of just over 750 by 1978 before commencing a long decline (Tate 2014: 201; Callaghan 1984: 154; Figure 3.2).

Fragmentation of the Trotskyist movement

The growth of the Trotskyist movement in the 1970s and 1980s is particularly remarkable when we consider the number of organizational splits that occurred throughout this period. Of the major groups, the IS/SWP suffered seven splits (wholesale expulsions or a mixture of expulsions followed by resignations) and the IMG and the WRP three each (Table 3.3). The fragmentation of the Trotskyist movement will be considered later (Chapter 5) but it is worth noting that these splits typically combine both substantive issues and procedural conflicts over how disagreements should be discussed and resolved. Substantive disagreements within the IS/SWP were extremely varied including attitudes to troops in Ireland and to the EU, then known as the Common Market (the Workers Fight split), the lack of a party programme and transitional demands (Workers Power) and the analysis of the causes of capitalist crisis (Revolutionary Communist Group). Both these and other factions also became embroiled in arguments about the alleged authoritarianism of the IS leadership (Birchall 2011: Chapter 9; Higgins 1997: Chapter 13; Shaw 1978).

One of the more significant splits involved the 1974 expulsion from the WRP of Alan Thornett and much of the industrial base of the party in and around the Cowley car plant. The main issues in dispute were both substantive and procedural: Thornett was convinced the WRP had abandoned the pursuit of transitional demands in favour of 'maximum', revolutionary demands but it is equally apparent that Thornett and Healy were engaged in a power struggle involving the WRP's Trade Union Committee – led by Thornett – and the Central Committee – controlled by Healy (Thornett 1979).[27] The loss of 200 members, including many industrial workers,

TABLE 3.3 Major organizational splits during the 'Golden Age' 1966–1985

Year	Host organizations		
	IS/SWP	*IMG*	*SLL/WRP*
1969		Revolutionary Communist League	
1971	Workers Fight		
1973	Revolutionary Communist Group		
1974			Socialist Labour Group Workers Socialist League
1975	Workers Power	League for Socialist Action Revolutionary Marxist Current	
1976	Workers League		
1978	International Socialist Alliance		
1979			Workers Party
1981	Red Action		
1983	Revolutionary Democratic Group		

Sources: Alexander (1991a: 479, 485–86, 496–99); Birchall (2011: Chapter 8); Burton-Cartledge (2014: 84); Callaghan (1984: Chapters 4 and 6); Craig, D. 'RDG to Rejoin SWP?' *Weekly Worker*, 5 July 2000; Episodes in Big Flame History, Nos. 22 and 25, https://bigflameuk.wordpress.com/2009/12/10/international-socialist-alliance-isa-groups-who-joined-big-flame-or-in-this-case-didn%E2%80%99t-no3/, accessed 20 May 2017; Hayes (2014); *Workers Party Bulletins*, Alan Clinton Papers, Warwick, File 539/3/9.

significantly weakened the WRP and resulted in a prolonged period of bitter inter-necine warfare between the WRP and Thornett's new organization, the Workers Socialist League (WSL).

Another significant split involved the Revolutionary Communist Group (RCG), formed in 1974 after David Yaffe and others were expelled from the International Socialists the previous year. After criticizing IS for its lack of a for-mal programme and its excessive faith in trade union militancy ('Economism'), the RCG set out with the ambitious aims of reconstructing the Marxist tradition in Britain and drafting a revolutionary programme.[28] Over the next few years it gradually shed its Trotskyist origins and metamorphosed into an anti-imperialist, anti-racist and pro-Cuba solidarity group, in the course of which it expelled Frank Richards (pseudonym of Frank Furedi) and his fellow critics of this trajectory (Revolutionary Communist Group 1984).[29] In 1977 the expellees created the Revolutionary Communist Tendency (from 1981, the Revolutionary Communist Party, RCP). Thanks to a combination of lively publications, particularly its weekly newspaper *the next step*, popular anti-racist campaigning and extensive recruitment on university campuses, the RCP grew steadily into the 1980s and beyond. Its supreme confidence was captured in a 1981 statement in its magazine: 'Two forces are growing on the left in Britain today. One is the Labour Party. The other is the *Revolutionary Communist Party*' (emphasis in original).

In terms of doctrine, the other significant development in this period emerged from Workers Power, a small faction expelled from the IS in 1974. Nine years later it published a hyper-critical monograph, *The Death Agony of the Fourth International and the Tasks of Trotskyists Today*, which rewrote the history of the Trotskyist movement (Workers Power and Irish Workers Group 1983). For the orthodox Trotskyists of the WRP and the Spartacist League, the Fourth International was a healthy organization from its foundation in 1938 until the Pabloite policies of the early 1950s. Workers Power, in contrast, argued the mainstream Fourth International had begun to degenerate as early as 1940 and that in the intervening years all of its members had succumbed to various forms of deviation from Marxist orthodoxy and had lost sight of the need for a revolutionary programme. As they summed up,

> The so-called "world Trotskyist movement" is, in our view a centrist swamp. A revolutionary International cannot be "reconstructed", "reunified" or rebuilt out of its existing fragments . . . A Leninist-Trotskyist International has to be founded on a completely new programmatic basis.
>
> *(Workers Power and Irish Workers Group 1983: 97)*[30]

This document marked the appearance within the world movement of *Radical Trotskyism*, a family that shared the commitment of the WRP and others to Orthodoxy but rejected their claims to that title by tracing the roots of ideologi-cal degeneration back to 1940. In 1984 the group therefore announced that it was creating a Movement for a Revolutionary Communist International, later to be known under its current title as the League for the Fifth International (Workers Power 1984a).

One new organization, the Spartacist League, was created from scratch in this period by US Spartacist Tendency militants. The tendency was an 'Orthodox' breakaway from the US SWP but personal animosity between its leader James Robertson and the British guardian of orthodoxy, Gerry Healy, as well as concerns about the latter's authoritarianism, left them outside the Healyite International Committee of the Fourth International (Wohlforth 1994: 135–39). The Spartacists sought to build their organization from 1975 by vigorous interventions at the meetings of other Trotskyist groups, an approach candidly described in a 1981 internal report:

> We have expended much effort on trying to split Workers Power in the last period . . . IMG . . . we must try and capture more of their members . . . Socialist Organiser Alliance remains a pole of attraction for rightward-moving ostensible Trotskyists and raw youth entering left politics. That alone demands we pay it attention with the aim of sterilising such growth . . . RCT (P) combines a deeply rightist sterile academicism with a frenetic social worker activism . . . We must seek to sterilise and destroy any presence it has (eg Warwick University) where we compete.[31]

Spartacist League orthodoxy was expressed not only in hostility to rival groups but in its uncompromising defence of the 'degenerated and deformed workers' states' of the USSR and its allies. When the Soviet Union invaded Afghanistan in December 1979, provoking widespread condemnation on the left, the League's British newspaper headline was clear and uncompromising: 'Hail Red Army!' (*Spartacist Britain* February 1980). The denunciations of rival groups undoubtedly alienated many people, but the League did succeed in winning small factions from the WSL and the IMG in the 1970s and early 1980s, boosting its membership to around 50. In 1979, after acquiring supporters in Australia and New Zealand, the group announced it was forming a new Fourth International, the International Communist League (Fourth Internationalist). One further hallmark of its orthodoxy was a strict adherence to international democratic centralism: 'our comrades consider themselves to be members of the International Communist League . . . they're national sections of the League' (Len Michelson and Mick Connor interview).[32] When the ICL (FI) was launched in 1979 it had just five national sections, rising to nine by the mid-1980s.

In general, the departure of a faction from a major organization was often the prelude to fresh disagreements and splits within the new grouping, a fate that befell not only the RCG but also Workers Fight, the Workers Party, Workers Power and the WSL. More commonly, expulsion was the prelude to dissolution: of the 21 groups expelled in this period ten disappeared completely, four joined other organizations and only seven still survive.[33] By 1979 there were 21 Trotskyist groups in Britain, falling back to 15 in 1985 (see Appendix 1).[34]

Innovations: unity initiatives and electoral participation

This period was also marked by a series of unity initiatives, only two of which came to fruition and even they were short-lived. In December 1975 there was a fusion of two groups expelled from IS, Workers Fight and Workers Power, to form the International-Communist League (I-CL). As the new grouping moved towards a policy of entry work inside the Labour Party, many of the ex-Workers Power members refused to accept the policy and quit, restarting their former organization.[35] Just a few years later, in 1981, I-CL leader Sean Matgamna was involved in another unsuccessful fusion, this time with the depleted forces of Alan Thornett's WSL. The new group had barely reached its third anniversary before the two halves of the fusion resumed their separate existences in a welter of bitterness and acrimony. The event that triggered the breakup was the 1982 Falklands War as the two components of the new group adopted radically different positions: most of Thornett's group called for victory to semi-colonial Argentina against imperialist Britain whilst Matgamna's group refused to support either the military dictatorship in Argentina or the imperialist rulers of Britain.[36] There were many other short-lived unity initiatives but all of them quickly floundered, including a proposal from IS to the IMG (1967), Workers Fight and the IMG (1971–1972), the IMG and the Workers League (1976–1977), the WSL to IMG (1982) as well as general calls for unity issued by Workers Fight (1974) and the IMG (1978).[37]

One other interesting development in this period of growth and confidence was the decision by several groups to challenge the electoral hegemony of the Labour and Communist Parties. Electoral performance will be considered in detail in Chapter 7 but the first wave of Trotskyist electoral participation began with the February 1974 general election when the WRP and the IMG stood eight and two candidates respectively. Two years later IS launched its first electoral foray, at by-elections in Newcastle and Walsall, November 1976, and followed this up with five more by-election contests until it abandoned electoral participation in spring 1978. IMG meantime issued a call for a joint Trotskyist electoral platform but its Socialist Unity initiative only attracted the support of the libertarian socialist group Big Flame, although it did contest several by-elections as well as the 1979 general election. The initiative did little for either organization as both incurred steady membership losses in subsequent years and Big Flame expired in 1984.

The flourishing of the Trotskyist movement did not go unnoticed by the state and in 1971 the Joint Intelligence Committee (the heads of the various agencies and relevant civil servants) commissioned a detailed report from the domestic intelligence service MI5 on the revolutionary left and the far right (reproduced in Hennessy 2010: 127–52). Covering the IMG, IS, RSL and the SLL, as well as their youth groups, the report provided accurate summaries of their objectives, membership levels, activities and international links. Some of the information was taken from public sources but the state also engaged in surveillance and infiltration. Telephones at the national and the Liverpool offices of the Militant Tendency were tapped and its mail was intercepted (Andrew 2009: 661); telephones at the SWP Head Office were also tapped, along with those of its leader Tony Cliff (from 1951 until 1991) and its Industrial Organizer John Deason; and there were telephone taps on the RCP (Hollingsworth and Fielding 2000: 79). Intelligence agents also infiltrated Trotskyist groups and Trotskyist-led organizations including the Anti-Nazi League and the IMG in the 1970s and the SWP in the 1980s (Evans and Lewis 2013: 18, 23, 117; Hennessy 2010: 106; Hollingsworth and Fielding 2000: 61). Between the 1960s and the 1990s state agencies persuaded approximately 30 members of Militant to act as paid informers and after the Militant Tendency split (see below) state agents were active in Militant Labour's Youth Against Racism in Europe (Evans and Lewis 2013: 121, 147). There was a highly placed 'mole' in the WRP in the 1970s and 1980s and around 25 agents and informers inside the SWP (Hollingsworth and Fielding 2000: 61, 86–87). Unfortunately it is impossible to gauge the impact of the information obtained in assisting the state to curb Trotskyist influence.

Conclusions

The 20-year period from the mid-1960s to the mid-1980s represented the Golden Age of British Trotskyism: total membership rose from less than 2,000 to approximately 20,000, overtaking the British Communist Party, now in long-term decline. Many groups broke out of their student milieux and began to sink roots in the trade union movement, building rank and file organizations and challenging the hegemony of the Communist and Labour Parties. Trotskyists launched two well-supported and successful social movements, the Vietnam Solidarity Campaign in the 1960s and the Anti-Nazi League in the 1970s (see Chapter 10). Both Trotskyist individuals and organizations began to acquire public recognition, whether it was through the speeches of Tariq Ali, the growing influence of the Militant Tendency at Labour Party conferences or the presence of IS/SWP activists at trade union conferences and rallies. Trotskyist newspapers such as *Militant*, *Socialist Worker* and *Workers Press* became a familiar sight at labour movement events. On the other hand, although the Trotskyist movement was significantly larger by the mid-1980s than in 1950 it was also more divided with its membership now spread over 15 organizations. Towards the end of this period there were already signs of the turbulence to come: the acrimonious split in the WSL; the mounting hysteria in the WRP over the alleged imminence of fascism; and the first signs of a fightback by the Labour leadership against the Militant Tendency.

Notes

1 In the other domain marked by the saliency of doctrine, namely religion, the Christian Church has also evolved competing ideas about core doctrine. These have crystallized over many centuries into competing families, or churches, such as Catholicism, Protestantism, Congregationalism, Methodism and Presbyterianism (Barrett 1996: 37–53).

2 Other groups in this category are Red Action (1981–1984), Revolutionary Communist League/Chartist Group (1969–1980), Revolutionary Democratic Group (1983–1996) and the Workers Party (later the Economic and Philosophic Science Review) (1979–1980). On Red Action see Hayes (2014) and Renton (2014).

3 The following organizations were never Trotskyist groups: Left Unity (formed in 2013 by Ken Loach and others), Peace and Progress Party (formed in 2004 by the Redgraves), Socialist Labour Party (formed in 1996 by Arthur Scargill) and the United Socialist Party (formed in 2004 by Liverpool dockers).

4 Furedi, F., email correspondence, 9 April 2014.

5 The WRP (News Line) still exists in 2017 and has never published membership figures but its network of branches has shrunk significantly. A stable branch network tells us little about membership as it can co-exist with rising, constant or falling numbers, but a declining number of branches almost certainly signifies declining membership. In 1984 *The News Line* reported meetings on the miners' strike at 181 different branches; in 1986 there were meetings on the Wapping printers' dispute at 73 branches; but by 1989 the paper reported public meetings at just 35 branches, a trend that suggests a rapid and dramatic loss of membership. Some portion of the apparent collapse of membership from 1985 is doubtless due to the unreality of the 1985 figure, but it is also true that bitter splits do propel significant numbers into political quiescence.

6 Pablo, M., *Where Are We Going?*, 1951, available at www.marxists.org/archive/pablo/1951/01/where.html, and Pablo, M., *The Building of the Revolutionary Party: Report to the Tenth Plenum of the International Executive Committee*, 1952, available at www.marxists.org/archive/pablo/1952/02/revparty.html, both accessed 28 November 2016. Neither document was ever reprinted by the WRP in its official six-volume history of the struggle against 'Pabloism' (Slaughter 1974, 1975).

7 Pearce subsequently published several influential essays on the history of British communism (see Woodhouse and Pearce 1975).

8 www.marxistsfr.org/archive/fryer/1959/11/resignation.html, accessed 21 February 2017.

9 Ironically, Pablo himself was soon expelled from the USFI because of differing assessments of the significance of Maoism and of Khrushchev which Pablo made public, allegedly violating norms of democratic centralism (Alexander 1991a: 545). He launched his own International Revolutionary Marxist Tendency in 1965 but it achieved little and rejoined the USFI in 1995.

10 Ernest Germain was one of three pseudonyms under which Mandel wrote at various times (Stutje 2009: 386).

11 The journal is available at both the LSE Library and the British Library.

12 Digitized copies of *Red Flag* from issue 1 in 1963 to the final issue in 2000 are available on the Posadism Today website: http://quatrieme-internationale-posadiste.org/EN/collections-12-red-flag.php, accessed 1 December 2016.

13 Like most Trotskyist predictions of imminent slump, recession or collapse the argument is never located in a time-frame so whether a recession follows 20 months or 20 years later it will be taken as vindication of the theory.

14 Students comprised 27 per cent of IS membership in 1965 but just 18 per cent in 1974 (Minutes of IS Executive Committee, 24 July 1965, Colin Barker Papers, File 152/1/1/1; IS Internal Bulletin Pre-Conference Issue, n.d. c. July 1974, Alastair Mutch Papers, File 284/1/1/1). Much of the following material on IS and the SWP can be found in Birchall (2011: Chapters 7–10) and Callaghan (1984: Chapter 5).

15 Recruitment and Composition of Present Membership, n.d., probably 1976, Stirling Smith Papers, File 205/1/6.

16 For example 2,000 attended an ATUA rally in October 1968 and attendance figures for the May 1973 and February 1985 ATUA conferences were reported as 2,200 and 'over 2,000' respectively (Thornett 1987: 118; *Workers Press* 14 May 1973; *Young Socialist* 9 February 1985).

17 Letter on the Devaluation of the Pound 1967 and leaflet, Against in Place of Strife, 15 April 1969 both in Alan Clinton Papers, Warwick, File MS 539/1/5. Similar predictions were routinely made throughout the late 1950s with regular warnings of an imminent 'full-scale offensive' (1957), 'great clashes between capital and Labour' (1958) and 'struggles on a scale quite unprecedented in Britain' (1959) (cited in An Anonymous Author 1996: 208).

18　WRP Central Committee Special Meeting, 24 August 1980, WRP Papers, Box 376. The minutes were marked: SECRET Not for discussion outside the CC.

19　WRP (Workers Press) International Committee Commission Interim Report, 16 December 1985, WRP Papers, Box 97.

20　The manifest falsity of this claim is apparent from even the most cursory reading of his collected lectures in Healy (1990). To take just one example from hundreds: 'The *unity* of this antithesis of *negative* IDENTITY into a *POSITIVE* image on the *negative* of *difference* which contains contradiction is *Essence*' (Healy 1990: 12, emphasis and uppercase in original). This type of obscurantist prose was also inserted into conference resolutions as in the following example: 'Congress . . . *resolutions* are always the *negative of the immediate moments of time* when we are actually *making* the report. This is what is meant by "OTHER OF THE FIRST" becoming 'the negative of the *immediate*' (Workers Revolutionary Party 1983: iii, emphasis and uppercase in original). For the most part Healy's method of exposition was to quote Lenin, occasionally Engels, Marx or Trotsky and follow up with a clumsy paraphrase which strongly suggested little or no understanding of the philosophical concepts and arguments. His collected lectures make no reference to original sources but rely almost exclusively on Lenin.

21　Letter from G. Healy, Towards the Seventh National Conference of the S.L.L., 28 May 1965, Bob Purdie Papers, File 1/4/1 and see the biography of SLL/WRP activist Bob Shaw, written at the time, which repeatedly emphasizes his own theoretical and philosophical limitations (Shaw 1983).

22　Shortly afterwards Lambert and the French OCI launched a new International which seems to have consisted almost entirely of the French section until the late 1970s (Alexander 1991a: 388). It was relaunched as the Fourth International (Lambertist) in 1993.

23　The views of Socialist Charter are clearly set out in their 1976 conference document: Political Report. Perspectives for British Revolution, Chris Bambery Papers, Modern Records Centre, File 1/5. By the late 1980s the group had become a democratic socialist current (*Chartist*, 121, July/August 1988). On the I-CL see: Summary Balance Sheet on the Election, I-CL Political Committee, 4 April 1979, AWL Papers, File AWL/1/9. On the WSL see: WSL Pre-Conference Discussion, 1980, Alan Clinton Papers, Warwick, File 539/2/1/4. On the IMG see: Our Attitude to Other Left Wing Newspapers, January 1983, International Marxist Group Papers, LSE, File 212. On Workers Power see: George Binette interview.

24　Militant Internal Bulletin, December 1975, Socialist Party Papers, File 601/C/5/1/6.

25　CWI Bulletin No. 1, July 1974, Tim Lewis Papers, File 341/3.

26　Another influential member of the IMG at this time was Robin Blackburn, a leading member of the editorial board of *New Left Review* (Thompson 2007: 55, 71).

27　The 'official' WRP version of the split can be found in Banda (1975) and *The News Line* (1980). The latter's subtitle – *The Case History of a Revisionist Provocation* – nicely captures two key elements in the WRP worldview: its orthodoxy and its paranoia. The split also involved a second organization, the Socialist Labour Group (SLG), one of whose leading members, Robin Blick, helped draft Thornett's critiques of the SLL/WRP (Pitt 2002: Chapter 9). Another member of the SLG was the veteran Trotskyist John Archer whose son Bob now runs the small WRP breakaway the Workers International to Rebuild the Fourth International (see below). On John Archer see www.revolutionary-history.co.uk/index.php/obits/2295-john-archer#memorial, accessed 1 December 2016.

28　See the RCG foundation document 'Our Tasks and Methods' and Richards (1975) for its critique of the IS, both in *Revolutionary Communist*, No. 1, January 1975.

29　The views of the two sides in the split can be found in the following: Editorial, *Revolutionary Communist*, No. 6, 1977; *Revolutionary Communist Papers*, No. 1, 1977.

30　Centrism, the tendency to oscillate between reformist and revolutionary perspectives, was the focus of numerous attacks by Trotsky in the 1930s so the Radical Trotskyist critique recapitulates this theme. See for example 'Centrism and the Fourth International', 'A Centrist Attack on Marxism', Once More on Centrism', in *Writings of Leon Trotsky 1933–34*, New York: Pathfinder Press, 1975.

31 Tasks and Perspectives, Spartacist League/Britain Internal Bulletin, No. 3 October 1981, IMG Papers, Warwick, File 221.

32 International Communist League (Fourth Internationalist), Declaration of Principles and Some Elements of Program, 1998, www.icl-fi.org/english/icldop/index.html, accessed 9 December 2016.

33 Those that disappeared are the International Socialist Alliance, Red Action, Revolutionary Democratic Group and the Workers League (all ex-IS/SWP); the Revolutionary Communist League (ex-IMG), the Revolutionary Communist Party (ex-RCG), Socialist Union Internationalist (ex-RWP, the Posadist group), the Workers International League (ex-WSL) as well as one of its offshoots the Workers International Review Group and the Workers News Group (a split from the Workers Party which itself was a split from the WRP). The League for Socialist Action (LSA), Marxist Worker Group and the Socialist Labour Group (SLG) all joined the IMG and successor organizations whilst the Revolutionary Marxist Current joined Big Flame, only a few years before the latter's dissolution. The Marxist Worker Group was a tiny splinter from Workers Power; the LSA split from IMG in 1976; and the SLG broke from the WRP in 1974 (Letter from League for Socialist Action to IMG, 18 December 1981, IMG Papers, Warwick, File 170; Report from Socialist Labour Group Conference 16 December 1989, ISG Pre-Conference Discussion Bulletin No. 13, 1990, Dani Ahrens Papers, File 401/3/9).

34 This period also witnessed the emergence of Big Flame, a libertarian and revolutionary socialist group, critical of the democratic centralist structures of most Trotskyist groups and their neglect of the women's and other autonomous social movements (Big Flame 1973; Thompson and Lewis 1977). The excellent Thompson-Lewis critique of Trotskyism has stood the test of time, but the same cannot be said for Big Flame, which dissolved itself in 1984 (Howell 1981).

35 Their fusion document can be found in the journal of the new organization, *International Communist*, No. 1, June 1976.

36 The intensity of the debate is clear from its scale: between January and April 1983 the organization published a staggering 35 Internal Bulletins, each one running to between 20 and 25 pages. Another set of Internal Bulletins preceded the expulsions and resignations that occurred in the first six months of 1984 (Richardson/Higgins Papers, Box 110, Files 1, 2 and 3).

37 IS, An Open Letter to the Comrades of 'The Week', n.d. 1968, Colin Barker Papers, File 152/1/1/2; Tate (2014: 273–78); Workers Fight, National Committee Minutes, 12 December 1971 and 16 January 1972, AWL Papers, File AWL/1/5; Proposals on Unity from the International Marxist Group to the Workers League, 7 March 1977, Chris Bambery Papers, File 1/5; WSL, National Committee Minutes, 8 January 1983 and 12 February 1983, AWL Papers, Files AWL/ 1/16 and AWL/1/17; Editorial Board of Workers Fight, Open Letter for a Revolutionary Regroupment, 1974, IMG Papers, Warwick, File 253; IMG, An Open Letter to Comrades of the SWP, 1 November 1978, IMG Papers, Warwick, File 169; The State of the Organisation, SWP Bulletin No. 7, December 1978, Nigel Clark Papers, File 489/8. A unity proposal in 1970 from IMG to the IS was narrowly defeated, 14 votes to 12 with Cliff, Harman and Birchall voting against (IS, National Committee Minutes 22 August 1970, Colin Barker Papers, File 152/1/1/4).

4

DEVELOPMENT OF THE TROTSKYIST MOVEMENT IN BRITAIN, PART 2: 1985–2017

1985–2004 Disintegration: organizational turmoil and membership decline

At the beginning of the 1984–1985 miners' strike, the upward trajectory of the Trotskyist movement looked set to continue as many of its constituent organizations threw themselves into the strike with the expectation of making fresh waves of recruits from this titanic class struggle. Groups such as the Spartacist League, Workers Power and the WRP even believed Britain was in a pre-revolutionary situation (George Binette interview; Len Michelson and Mick Connor interview). Events were to turn out very differently because the repercussions of the strike were largely negative as two significant groups disintegrated in its immediate aftermath – the WRP and the IMG. At about the same time – October 1985 – Labour leader Neil Kinnock launched a scathing attack on the Militant Tendency, opening the way for a purge of its members that would lead to a split in the organization in 1991, leaving a tiny rump inside the Labour Party whilst the majority decamped to form an independent organization, Militant Labour.[1] A few years later the RCP, already evolved from Trotskyism to a form of libertarianism, was bankrupted by a libel action and dissolved itself in 1997. All of these events resulted in a substantial haemorrhage of members although losses were offset for a few years by the rising fortunes of the SWP whose membership rose steadily towards a peak of around 10,000 in the mid-late 1990s before a precipitate fall to a little over 4,000 in 2004 (Birchall 2011: 517). Almost every other Trotskyist group lost members during this 'Disintegration' period so that by 2004 total membership had fallen dramatically, probably to around 6,500, which was back to the level of the early 1970s and just one-third of the figure achieved in 1985.

Disintegration of the Workers Revolutionary Party

The WRP had for many years been claiming that Britain's economic crisis was so severe that it could only be resolved in two ways: either the ruling class will begin, 'setting up the Bonapartist state whose logic leads inescapably to the growth of fascism and attempts to impose military-police dictatorship' or 'the organisation of the General Strike as the struggle for power led by the Workers Revolutionary Party' (Workers Revolutionary Party 1985b: 7, 10). This apocalyptic perspective was intensified throughout the months of the miners' strike yet the absence of either outcome was a shattering blow to the party membership whose expectations of a revolutionary rupture had been raised and then swiftly dashed, as national politics returned to its pre-strike rhythms (Workers Revolutionary Party 1984a, 1984b, 1985a; Clare Cowen interview). In this tense and volatile environment a letter from Aileen Jennings, Healy's long-serving personal assistant, precipitated the conflicts which effectively destroyed the organization as a major force on the Trotskyist left. She accused Healy of sexually abusing 26 party members, herself included, over a period of 19 years, allegations that were subsequently confirmed (Harding 2005: 248–50, 254–60). Several months later a report by Corin Redgrave accused Jennings and others of deliberately wrecking the finances of the party whilst concealing the details from its members.[2] The party leadership now rapidly divided: one group, led by Cliff Slaughter, pushed for Healy's expulsion whilst his supporters, including the Redgraves (and Ken Livingstone), absurdly dismissed the Jennings letter as an MI5 'provocation' (Redgrave 1991: 250; Livingstone in Lotz and Feldman 1994: vii). An organization once renowned for

TABLE 4.1 The disintegration of the Workers Revolutionary Party from 1985

Organization	Dates	Leading figures
Extant (N = 6)		
WRP (News Line)	1985–	Sheila Torrance
International Communist Party (now Socialist Equality Party)	1986–	Dave Hyland
International Socialist League	1988–	Bill Hunter
Workers International to Rebuild the Fourth International	1990–	Bob Archer
Communist League (now A World to Win*)	1991–	Paul Feldman, Corinna Lotz,
Socialist Fight	2009	Gerry Downing
Defunct (N = 5)		
WRP (Workers Press)	1985–2000	Cliff Slaughter
Communist Forum	1986–1988	Mike Banda
Marxist Party	1987–2004	Gerry Healy, the Redgraves
Workers International League	1987–2006	Richard Price, Bob Pitt
Revolutionary Internationalist League	1988–1995	Gerry Downing, Tony Gard

* 'A World to Win is not a Trotskyist group' (Corinna Lotz interview).

Sources: Communist League (1991), Downing (1991), Lotz and Feldman (1994), Pitt (2002).

its 'hard' Bolshevik culture, monolithic structure and implacable hostility to all rival groups, now rapidly disintegrated. Within five years it had fractured into ten small organizations, five of which still exist in 2017 although only two of them appear to have any significant membership, the WRP itself and the Socialist Equality Party (SEP) (Table 4.1).[3]

The former emerged as the faction led by Assistant General Secretary Sheila Torrance, Gerry Healy and the Redgraves, although Healy and others resigned in 1987 to form their own organization, the short-lived Marxist Party. The WRP still publishes a daily paper, *The News Line*, and largely repeats the annual cycle of activities established by the WRP back in the 1970s, such as the Young Socialist (YS) AGM in January, a May Day march and rally, a *News Line* anniversary rally in November and the occasional ATUA meeting. Its general political message is invariant and timeless:

> the working class in Britain is being driven along the road of socialist revolution, . . . by the historical crisis of world capitalism . . . The working class are faced with the task of taking hold of the state power through smashing the capitalist state, and overthrowing the capitalist class.
>
> *(Marxist Review 5(8): 11, September 1990)*

> Immediately on the agenda is a massive confrontation between a bankrupt capitalist class and a working class revolutionised by this crisis. The urgent issue today is the building of a new revolutionary leadership . . . that will lead the working class to power . . . through the victory of the socialist revolution.
>
> *(The News Line 23 February 2017)*

The other main fragment of the WRP was the International Communist Party (ICP, now the SEP) led by Dave Hyland in Britain (until his death in 2013) with the strong backing of David North, Healy's equivalent in the US Workers League. Loyal to the traditional politics of the SLL/WRP, in particular the struggle for 'Orthodoxy' against various forms of 'revisionism', the SEP argued that Healy (and by extension, the WRP) had undergone a process of: 'political and personal degeneration . . . into political opportunism . . . marked by unprincipled relations with bourgeois nationalist leaders and with trade union and Labour Party reformists in Britain' (North 1991: 102–03). The group quickly established its own International Committee of the Fourth International but for the next 30 years it comprised just five small groups, in Australia, Germany, Sri Lanka, the UK and the USA until the creation in 2016 of two new, tiny affiliates in France and New Zealand. The organization distinguishes itself from everyone else, dismissed as the 'pseudo-left', in two respects: it claims that in the era of globalized capitalism the trade unions have now become incorporated into the capitalist state and therefore, in the words of the Transitional Programme, revolutionaries should: 'create in all possible instances independent militant organizations corresponding more closely to the tasks of mass struggle against bourgeois society' (Trotsky 1938: 11; and also Socialist Equality

Party 2011: 114–15, 140–41). Second, it also makes the curious and rather cerebral claim that, '[the] most important instrument for the development of socialist consciousness within the working class is the World Socialist Web Site . . . With its daily analysis of world political and economic developments' (Socialist Equality Party 2011: 146).

In the wake of the crisis both North's International Committee and Hyland's ICP began to rewrite the history of the SLL/WRP in order to demarcate healthy from unhealthy traditions as a base from which to denounce all other WRP fragments as 'renegades' (International Committee of the Fourth International 1986a, 1986b; International Communist Party 1990; North 1988; Socialist Equality Party 2011). The hostility engendered during the 1985 split persisted for decades. Sometime in 2015 Bob Archer greeted a former WRP member whom he hadn't seen for many years only to be rebuffed and told, 'I don't talk to traitors, I don't talk to renegades' (Bob Archer interview).

Splits in the Socialist League and the Militant Tendency

The miners' strike also impacted on the Socialist League, formerly the IMG, although its membership on the threshold of the strike was already well below its late 1970s peak (Callaghan 1987: 160). In the aftermath of the strike its dominant leader John Ross argued the group should orient towards an emerging 'class struggle left wing', based around miners' leader Arthur Scargill, the Labour MP Tony Benn and Greater London Council leader Ken Livingstone.[4] Critics of this perspective and of what they took to be Ross' increasing authoritarianism left the League in 1986, eventually joining forces with Alan Thornett's Socialist Group, and later transforming themselves into Socialist Resistance, part of the mainstream Fourth International. In 1988 Ross' organization, now known as Socialist Action, was racked by a second major split as Brian Grogan and others decided to follow the strongly pro-Cuba line of the American SWP. Under the charismatic leadership of Jack Barnes the US SWP had come to believe the epicentre of world revolution now lay in Central America following the Cuban, Grenadian and Nicaraguan revolutions. He argued the leadership and development of these revolutions did not conform to Trotsky's theory of permanent revolution which should therefore be considered an over-generalization of the Russian experience (Barnes 1983). Having failed to convince the mainstream USFI of this perspective, Barnes and the SWP endeavoured to split Trotskyist parties around the world including Britain, creating national Communist Leagues, loyal to the US party and its international organization, generally known as the SWP Pathfinder Tendency (after its publishing company).[5]

The Militant Tendency also succumbed to a dramatic split when the overwhelming majority at its 1991 conference voted to reject the advice of its founder and guru Ted Grant and abandon 40 years of entry work in the Labour Party (Crick 2016: 312–19; Taaffe 1995: 433 ff.; and for the minority view see Woods 2013a: 189–225). The background to this decision was a growing hostility to the Tendency within the Labour Party, marked by the expulsion of Militant's editorial board in 1983 and party leader Neil Kinnock's 1985 denunciation of the Militant-dominated Liverpool City Council and District Labour Party. Over the next few years a small but growing number of Militant Tendency supporters were expelled and the climate for entry work became increasingly inhospitable. Meantime Militant had played a key role in organizing the national All Britain Anti-Poll Tax Federation, encouraging non-payment of the Conservative government's new property tax, the highly regressive Community Charge, more commonly known as the poll tax. Piloted in Scotland in 1989 and rolled out in England and Wales a year later, the national and local anti-poll tax groups soon comprised a mass social movement (Burns 1992: 30–34; and see Chapter 10). Scottish Militant leaders such as Tommy Sheridan became concerned the organization was not reaping the benefits of its pivotal role because 'it wasn't that easy to get people to join the Labour Party' (Sheridan cited in Gall 2012: 51). Convinced that a separate party would attract considerable support they created an open party in Scotland in 1991 and later that year, in the face of opposition from Ted Grant, the group decided overwhelmingly (93 per cent in favour) to turn its back on the Labour Party and come out as an open organization (Taaffe 1995: 441). This was initially called Militant Labour but in 1997 changed its name to the Socialist Party, a process that led to a number of small splits over the next few years (Burton-Cartledge 2014: 87; Taaffe 2017: 126–42). Having abandoned entry work, Militant Labour reworked its analysis of the Labour Party, concluding that it was no longer a 'bourgeois workers' party' but was rapidly becoming a purely bourgeois party (Taaffe 1995: 488; Taaffe 2017: 17–32). In 1995 it therefore launched a campaign for a new mass workers' party.

The emergence of Militant Labour as an open revolutionary party posed an immediate and ongoing challenge as to how it would differentiate itself from its rivals. The mainstream Socialist Resistance was also committed to the idea of 'a new party of the left' whilst disagreements with the SWP on its state capitalist analysis of the USSR had become less relevant after the Soviet disintegration in 1992. There are differences between the Socialist Party and the SWP over the role of parliament and of elections in the transition to socialism but the Socialist Party's lengthy 2008 critique of the SWP focused almost entirely on tactical not doctrinal disagreements (Taaffe 2008; and see MacGregor 1986 on Militant). Having jettisoned Labour Party entrism, one of the hallmarks of Institutional Trotskyism, the Socialist Party now occupies an uncertain and unstable position where it is difficult to discern its distinctive and defining features.

Meantime Militant's defeated minority, led by Grant, Alan Woods and Rob Sewell created a new organization called Socialist Appeal with a magazine of the same name. Grant and his supporters also moved quickly to re-establish their own international organization, the Committee for a Marxist International (which soon adopted its current name, the International Marxist Tendency, IMT). Despite its modest beginnings, the IMT has succeeded in creating sections in 26 countries and is now one of the largest of the many Fourth Internationals.[6] A few years before leaving the Labour Party, Militant claimed 8,000 members yet after ten years of open work its 2002 membership was just over 1,000 whilst Socialist Appeal probably numbered no more than 200 (Taaffe 2002). As in the case of the WRP, these numbers imply a dramatic collapse of membership in the aftermath of the split.

New Labour and the renaissance of electoral participation

Notwithstanding the escalating purge of Militant Tendency supporters in the Labour Party, other Trotskyist groups continued to operate there, including the Socialist Organiser Alliance (a group with many previous incarnations such as Workers Fight), Socialist Action and Workers Power. By the mid-late 1980s, Matgamna's Socialist Organizer group had begun to question elements of orthodox Trotskyism in three main areas: it abandoned the characterization of the USSR as a 'degenerated workers' state' and began to recuperate the positions of Trotsky's 'Third Camp' critics such as Max Shachtman who were both anti-capitalist *and* anti-Stalinist (Matgamna 1998, 2015; *Solidarity* 9 December 2016). It moved away from the idea that imperialism was always the principal enemy of the working-class movement and that any anti-imperialist forces were therefore objectively progressive, for example the Iranian clerics in 1979, the Taliban in Afghanistan and Hamas in Gaza. Finally, it rejected the traditional leftist call for the replacement of the Israeli state by a secular, democratic state embracing Israel and Palestine and moved instead to a two-state solution, acknowledging Israel's right to exist.[7] In the midst of this rethinking it created an 'International Committee for Workers Liberty' but this seems to have done no more than organize two ill-attended conferences, in 1987 and 2003.[8] Although Socialist Organiser was not the largest of the Labour Party entrist groups, it was the only one to be expelled and shortly afterwards relaunched itself as the Alliance for Workers Liberty (AWL). By the late 1990s only Socialist Appeal and Socialist Action were still operating inside the Labour Party but their small size means they proved no hindrance to the electoral success of Blair's New Labour whilst Socialist Action's powerbase was increasingly localized around Ken Livingstone, London mayor 2000–2008 (Hosken 2008: 256–57, 322–27).[9]

Tony Blair's election as Labour Party leader in 1994 was to have contradictory implications for the Trotskyist movement. On the one hand, it fuelled renewed optimism of a Labour victory after the crushing disappointment of the narrow defeat in 1992. The ruling Conservative Party was racked by divisions over membership of the European Union, its narrow majority had been eroded and its poll ratings had slumped in the run-up to the 1997 election despite GDP growth which resumed in 1992 and continued through to 2008. At the same time the Labour Party's high-profile recruitment campaign pushed its individual membership up from 266,000 in 1993 to 405,000 by 1997, further reducing the attractions of the small and deeply divided Trotskyist movement (McGuinness 2012). On the other hand, Blair's embrace of neoliberal policies, including privatization and outsourcing, and his fulsome support for the US invasion of Iraq in 2003 opened the way for both electoral and social movement challenges that would eventually end the period of Trotskyist disintegration and decline (Hay 1999). The Socialist Party in its first incarnation as Militant Labour fought three seats in the 1992 election and 21 in 1997 before the emergence in 1999 of an institution hitherto unknown on the Trotskyist left, a successful unity initiative embracing many of the major groups and focused on electoral activity. The Socialist Alliance was supported by organizations from a range of Trotskyist families including the SWP, the AWL, the Socialist Party, Workers Power and the International Socialist Group (now known as Socialist Resistance), although not of course by the WRP, which adhered to its consistent policy of shunning the rest of the Trotskyist left (Burton-Cartledge 2014: 88–91).

The birth of the Alliance reflected the continuing membership decline of the Trotskyist movement as the SWP fell from its 10,000 peak and the Socialist Party struggled to make headway. It was also a response to renewed competition on the left from the Socialist Labour Party, established in 1996 by the charismatic miners' leader Arthur Scargill and the failure of groups such as Workers Power to build factions inside the SLP (George Binette interview; Burton-Cartledge 2014: 88–89; Slaughter 1996). Finally, there were changes in 'opportunity structures' with the first elections to the new Welsh Assembly in 1999 and to the Greater London Assembly in 2000. The initial outings of the Socialist Alliance produced distinctly modest vote shares of between 1 and 3 per cent, even under various forms of pro-portional representation. Undeterred, the Alliance stood 98 candidates in the 2001 general election, the largest number of Trotskyist candidates ever to participate in a British election, and recorded a median vote share of just 1.25 per cent (see Chapter 7).[10] Unfortunately the continuing divisions on the Trotskyist left and the lack of trust between the main groups resulted in the breakup of the Alliance, with the Socialist Party withdrawing in 2001, concerned about SWP domination, followed in 2003 by the AWL and Workers Power in protest at the concessions to Islam being made by the SWP as it courted the Muslim Association of Britain (George Binette interview). Following the collapse of the Socialist Alliance, the SWP in conjunction with the expelled Labour MP George Galloway formed the Respect coalition in 2004 to fight the European Assembly elections that same year (Harman 2008).

Opposition to 'neo-liberal' economic policies also assumed a more dramatic form with the anti-globalization protests at the World Trade Organization meeting in Seattle 1999, the first of many such protests over the ensuing years. The SWP moved quickly to engage with the protests, launching a body called Globalize Resistance (now defunct) and setting out its critique of global capitalism (Callinicos 2003).[11] The case for critical engagement with the anti-globalization protests was set out in Callinicos (2003). In 2001 a number of Trotskyist groups, led by the SWP and including the AWL, Socialist Resistance and Workers Power, formed the Stop the War Coalition which in February 2003 organized one of the largest demonstrations in Britain to protest at Labour's preparations for the invasion of Iraq (Murray and German 2005: 163). Yet the capacity of Trotskyist groups to mobilize members and sympathizers on marches, and persuade protestors to buy their newspapers, consist-ently failed to translate either into votes in elections or into membership. During the first seven years of New Labour governments (1997–2004) the British Trotskyist movement halved in size, from approximately 12,500 to around 6,500 and remained highly fragmented because of splits and expulsions. Although some of the expelled groups quickly expired, many others survived so that a movement which comprised 15 organizations in 1985 had swelled to 19 organizations by 2004.[12] Nonetheless, the twin policies of electoral participation and social movement creation that emerged in this period laid the foundations for the main attributes of the Trotskyist movement after 2004.

Stasis: limited and uneven recovery in the neoliberal era 2005–2017

Although the Labour government secured a third successive election victory in 2005 its vote share fell to 35.2 per cent, compared to 43.2 per cent in 1997, whilst its seat total had slumped from 418 to 355. In 2010 its vote share fell once more to an historic low of 29.0 per cent (improving only slightly in 2015 to 30.4 per cent before rising dramatically in 2017 to 40.0 per cent). The long period of economic growth and falling unemployment that began in 1993 faltered from around 2005–2006 shortly before the banking collapses of 2008 ushered in one of the deepest and most prolonged economic crises in British history. The core austerity policies of bailing out the banks with state revenue and then cutting public expenditure and welfare benefits to pay for it was begun by Labour in 2008 and maintained by both the Conservative-Liberal Democrat coalition (2010–2015) and the Conservative government elected in 2015. Some of these policies produced huge protests, in particular the 2010 decision to allow universities to increase domestic undergraduate tuition fees by 200 per cent, taking them to £9,000 per annum; the attacks on public sector pensions from 2011; and the junior doctors' dispute 2015–2016. Strikes and demonstrations on these issues were followed up with large anti-austerity demonstrations in June 2015 and April 2016 and a pro-NHS demonstration in March 2017.

The combination of Labour decline, right-wing government, economic recession and savage cuts to public spending should have proved auspicious for the Trotskyist movement but events were to prove otherwise. Overall Trotskyist membership did begin to recover from its 2004 nadir and by 2008 had climbed from below 7,000 to around 8,500, yet over the next eight years of recession, austerity and protests, the movement increased its total membership by less than 1,000, a paltry achievement under the circumstances. The two largest groups – the SWP and the Socialist Party – both recorded some growth and the latter's international body, the Committee for a Workers International, steadily expanded and is now the largest of the many Fourth Internationals with sections in 30 countries (see Chapter 11). Two new organizations also increased their membership – Counterfire and rs21 (see below) – but elsewhere on the Trotskyist left some long-standing organizations have either remained very small, for example Socialist Resistance, or have declined in the aftermath of damaging splits, for example Workers Power (see below). The Spartacist League for example had around 40–50 members in the mid-1980s in three branches but by 2017 had shrunk to just one small branch in London whilst its international organization, the ICL (FI) has only one more national section in 2017 compared to the mid-1980s.[13] In international policy, it still adheres to the view that a 'workers' state' should *always* be defended against capitalist and imperialist opponents, for example North Korea (*Workers Vanguard* 23 September 2016). Remarkably the WRP continues to publish a daily paper, *The News Line*, the weekly *Young Socialist* and a bi-monthly magazine *Marxist Review* and to repeat the same injunction it has been pushing for the past 44 years: build the WRP!

One significant factor in the limited renaissance of the Trotskyist left is the continuing decline of the labour movement. Union membership fell by almost 6 million between 1980 and 2015 and trade union density, the proportion of workers belonging to a trade union, slumped from over 50 per cent to less than 25 per cent. Strike activity has also declined, whether measured by numbers of stoppages or working days lost, despite a small increase in recent years owing to large public sector disputes over pensions and wages. Throughout the 1970s there were never less than 2,000 strikes per year; by the early 2000s there were fewer than 200 strikes per year (Lyddon 2007: 365). As Callinicos observed in relation to the SWP, the party came through the strike downturn of the early 1980s anticipating the upturn to come:

> 'Preparing for the upturn we saw was a kind of active process, being involved in strikes and struggles, building rank and file groups and so on. But of course the upturn never came. And to some extent we're still debating why it hasn't come.'
>
> *(Alex Callinicos interview)*

It would be tempting, but misleading, to attribute the weakness of contemporary Trotskyism to an additional factor, the persistence of deep divisions within its own ranks. These had already become apparent in the electoral arena when the Socialist Alliance fell apart in 2003 and in 2008 when the same fate overtook the Respect Coalition (Harman 2008; Leplat 2008). In contrast the Trade Unionist and Socialist Coalition (TUSC) formed in 2010 between the Socialist Party, the SWP and Socialist Resistance, along with the RMT union, has managed to survive two general elections although it chose not to contest the 2017 general election, opting instead to throw its support behind Corbyn's Labour Party. There have also been splits *within* organizations and the SWP has been particularly hard hit, with four splits in five years.[14] In 2010 a dispute over its involvement in the Respect and Stop the War coalitions led to the resignation of John Rees and Lindsey German (two of the chief organizers of the Stop the War Coalition). According to Rees, the SWP leadership was concerned about the slow rate of recruitment from social movements into the SWP whereas Rees believed the movements were essential to party building (John Rees interview).[15] That said, the SWP has devoted considerable resources to the creation of a range of social movements in this period, maintaining its role in the Stop the War Coalition (launched in 2001), building Unite Against Fascism (from 2003) to counter the British National Party and English Defence League and most recently promoting Stand up to Racism (from 2011). Nonetheless John Rees and others went on to form Counterfire and to establish an anti-austerity movement, the Coalition of Resistance (2010, now the People's Assembly) and in the process pushing its membership up from an initial 40 to around 300 six years later (John Rees interview). It also became the first Trotskyist group to turn its occasional, eponymous newspaper into a free publication.

Another split led to the creation of the International Socialist Group in Scotland (now defunct) but it was the fallout from the investigation in 2012 of sexual assault and rape allegations against a senior member of the party that led to an upsurge of bitter factional struggle over several years and the creation of two more splinter groups, the International Socialist Network in 2013 (now defunct) and rs21 (revolutionary socialism in the 21st century) in 2014.[16] rs21 was relatively open-minded, less concerned with disseminating party lines on a variety of issues and more concerned with 'exploring what it means to be revolutionary socialists in the 21st century' (*rs21* No. 1 Summer 2014, Editorial) and 'what kind of organization socialists need' (*rs21* No. 9 Winter 2017, p. 39; and Birchall 2014). As one of the leading figures in rs21 remarked, 'We would see ourselves as Cliffite in the tradition of the early IS and Socialist Review Group in the post-war period, reinventing Trotskyism perhaps by questioning some of the fundamental tenets' (Anindya Bhattacharyya interview).[17] Other divisions have appeared in the realm of social movements: there are three anti-austerity bodies each controlled by a separate organization – the National Shop Stewards Network (Socialist Party, dating from 2007), the People's Assembly (Counterfire, started in 2010) and Unite the Resistance (launched by the SWP in 2011). Anti-racist activity is now dominated by the SWP's Stand up to Racism but the older Socialist Party organization Youth Against Racism in Europe is now in its twenty-fifth year whilst on university campuses there is intense rivalry between the student branches of the different groups, in particular the AWL, Counterfire, rs21, Socialist Appeal, Socialist Party and the SWP.

However, the link between membership growth and organization splits is complex, a fact that emerges from analysis of the fortunes of the IS/SWP. Its membership grew in the early 1970s (despite splits in 1971 and 1973) and again in 2010 and 2011 despite the splits in those years. In contrast the larger splits of the mid-1970s and in 2013–2014 were associated with net membership losses. Nevertheless some smaller organizations were sufficiently concerned about disunity on the left to launch a formal process of 'revolutionary regroupment' in April 2014 involving Socialist Resistance, Workers Power, Anti-Capitalist Initiative (ACI, a 2012 split from Workers Power) and two SWP splinter groups, the International Socialist Network (ISN) and rs21. ACI and ISN soon collapsed; rs21 lost interest; and the mainstream Socialist Resistance was hostile to the radical Trotskyism of Workers Power so the talks quickly petered out.[18] Whatever the contribution made by organizational splits and divisions to the limited gains of the Trotskyist left since 2008, another perhaps more significant factor is external competition. The Green Party has gradually re-positioned itself as a mainstream radical left party and experienced significant growth. In 2008 its membership was approximately 7,000 but rose to 12,800 in 2010 and to a remarkable 55,000 by July 2016 (Keen and Audickas 2016: 10). Campaigning organizations such as UK Uncut, started up in 2010 to protest against tax avoidance, have attracted significant numbers of young protestors but it was the creation of a new left party and the leftward shift of the Labour Party that created the most significant opportunities, and threats, for the Trotskyist movement.

Left Unity and Corbyn's Labour Party

In November 2013 the film director Ken Loach and others launched a new, radical left party, Left Unity which quickly grew to around 2,000 members. Less than two years later, the veteran left-wing Labour MP Jeremy Corbyn contested, and won, the Labour leadership contest and in the course of his campaign (and its successor in 2016) several hundred thousand people joined (or rejoined) the party (Keen and Audickas 2016: 9).These developments may well have hindered the growth of the Trotskyist left but they have also contributed to a resurgence of the entry tactic.

The formation of Left Unity attracted an organized presence from two Trotskyist groups, Workers Power and Socialist Resistance. Workers Power was famous for its critical study of the world Trotskyist movement but the unremitting negativity of the critique perhaps explains why the radical call for a new, Fifth International never attracted more than tiny handfuls of supporters (Workers Power and Irish Workers Group 1983). Its founding congress in 1989 was attended by delegates from just six countries: Austria, France, Germany, Ireland, Peru and the UK (League for a Revolutionary Communist International 1989). Over the ensuing years three of these groups disappeared although a handful of French and Peruvian Trotskyists founded their own Radical Trotskyist International, the Permanent Revolution Collective in 2002. In addition to these international setbacks, the membership of Workers Power was depleted by three further splits, in 2006 (the Permanent Revolution group), 2011 (the Revolutionary Communist International Tendency) and 2012 (Anti-Capitalist Initiative).[19] Against this background, Left Unity seemed to offer a potential new audience for its radical critique of the Trotskyist tradition. Socialist Resistance, British section of the mainstream Fourth International, had long been committed to the latter's 1991 project of building broad left parties such as Die Linke in Germany and Left Bloc in Portugal and also shared the eco-socialist orientation of the Fourth International, adopted in 2010 (Bensaid et al. 2011: 10–11; Frank and Bensaid 2010: 148–62). Sadly for Left Unity and Socialist Resistance their prospects were quickly overshadowed by Corbyn's victory in the Labour leadership contest (and his re-election in September 2016) an outcome that led 600 members of Left Unity to quit and join Labour by the end of 2015 (Alan Thornett interview).

Socialist Resistance opted to stay with Left Unity although one of its most senior leaders observed in 2016 this was a tactical decision that did not preclude refocusing on the Labour Party at some future date: 'If Corbyn continues to be successful, and if he gets big policy changes through, like Trident, and if he starts to democratise the party, there comes a time when existence outside will make no sense' (Alan Thornett interview).[20] Workers Power, in contrast, having achieved little from its involvement in Left Unity, took a radical strategic decision in September 2015 to dissolve itself and join the Labour Party en bloc.

> 200,000 people decide that they want to be in the Labour Party, they're going to want some action and they want to see some results, they obviously want to discuss where to go and what to do. Corbyn is a prisoner of the right, and there's a referendum coming up, and there's going to be class struggles coming up, and . . . that is the place to be.
>
> *(Workers Power interview)*

Its small membership now operates as a faction with a newspaper *The Red Flag*, campaigning for 'revolutionary socialist change'.

The AWL also opted for the entry tactic and instructed all of its 140 or so members to join the Labour Party (and a similar decision was taken in December 2015 by the small Independent Socialist Network).[21] It also chose to de-register with the Electoral Commission as an independent political party in order to avoid Labour disciplinary measures but unlike Workers Power, the group decided to maintain its own independent organization, newspaper and website. Its adoption of the entry tactic was partly a product of the AWL's traditional orientation to the Labour Party but may have reflected the failure of its new international initiative. In 2013 the group launched an international journal, *Marxist Revival*, with co-thinkers in Iran, immodestly claiming in its first issue that 'There are almost no other such journals of international Marxist discussion'. Only two subsequent issues have appeared (in the summer of 2014 and the spring of 2015) so the initiative appears stillborn.

The Socialist Party was clearly wrong-footed by Corbyn's victory, having previously written off the Labour Party as a significant political arena:

> In the past Labour was a workers' party at bottom even though it had a pro-capitalist leadership. Today New Labour is capitalist to the core of its being . . . The Socialist Party has initiated the Campaign for a New Workers Party.
>
> *(Socialist Party 2008: 26)*[22]

It is true Taaffe and colleagues had occasionally noted the theoretical possibility of Labour moving to the left, but this was a minor qualification to its mainstream position. By early 2016 its Congress had executed a U-turn, declaring that Labour was now 'two parties – a capitalist party and a potential workers party – within one' (*Socialism Today* April 2016, pp. 11, 12). Emboldened by Corbyn's second election victory in September 2016, it called (unsuccessfully) for the re-admission of 75 'expelled socialists' whose number included the leading cadres of the Socialist Party (and formerly of the Militant Tendency) such as Peter Taaffe, Keith Dickinson, Clare Doyle, Clive Heemskerk, Hannah Sell, Lynn Walsh and many others.[23] It also decided that TUSC would operate a more selective challenge to Labour in the 2017 local elections and a month later announced it would not mount any challenge to Labour in the snap general election of June 2017 (*The Socialist* 16–22 March, 18–24 May 2017). Whilst the SWP concurred with this decision and backed Corbyn against his critics, it has also maintained its traditional view that Trotskyists must remain outside Labour and continue the construction of a revolutionary vanguard party (Kimber 2016).

Corbyn's first election victory was quickly followed by the creation of a supportive social movement Momentum that was led by his campaign manager and veteran left-wing Labour activist Jon Lansman. It soon achieved a membership of around 20,000 comprising a mixture of Labour and non-Labour members and appeared to provide fertile territory for Trotskyist activists such as the AWL's Jill Mountford, elected to its steering committee in 2016. It is too early to say what impact, if any, these Labour Party developments will have on Trotskyist recruitment although we know that Left Unity lost around 600 members to Labour in 2015 and the Socialist Party may have lost a similar number in 2016. We also know that a small number of activists were expelled from the Labour Party in 2016 because of their Trotskyist affiliations including 15 from Socialist Appeal and seven from the AWL.[24] This hostility to Trotskyism is not confined to the traditional Labour right because early in 2017 Momentum leader Jon Lansman, with Corbyn's support, pushed through a new constitution that would largely supplant delegate meetings with one member, one vote; require all new members to belong to the Labour Party; and encourage existing non-members to join Labour. Expelled members such as the AWL's Mountford would, at a stroke, be removed from Momentum, placing a significant question mark over the utility of the entry tactic.[25]

Conclusions

Despite splits, expulsions and increased fragmentation, the Trotskyist movement in 1985 was close to its membership peak and had already eclipsed its Communist Party rival, in terms of total numbers, influence in the Labour Party and, possibly, influence within the trade unions (see Chapter 9). What followed was a 20-year period of organizational disintegration and membership decline: three large groups – the WRP, the Socialist League and the Militant Tendency – underwent acrimonious splits that fragmented the movement and significantly depleted its membership. The SWP was the only large organization that both avoided such splits and grew substantially but by the late 1990s it too began haemorrhaging members. The result was that the Trotskyist movement in 2004 was a shadow of its former self, with a membership reduced by two-thirds from its mid-1980s peak. Since then its fortunes have stabilized but with total membership only a little higher in 2016 than on the eve of the Great Recession in 2008.

The movement has also become more differentiated. In 1950 Britain's three Trotskyist groups were divided between the Mainstream (Healy and Grant's groupings) and the Third Camp (Cliff's state capitalist group). By the late 1980s there were representatives of all seven Trotskyist families in Britain (see Table 4.2). The Mainstream has always been marked by a significant degree of ideological flexibility, whether on the role of students, guerrilla armies and workers or on the nature of the Cuban regime. The Orthodox family, as the term implies, has been characterized by a strict adherence to the core elements of Trotskyism but the complexity of Trotsky's thought and the sheer volume and range of his writings allow ample scope for doctrinal disputes between its key members, the WRP, the SEP and the Spartacists (see Chapter 5). Third Camp Trotskyism is also quite heterogeneous with considerable animosity between its two main British representatives, the SWP and the AWL. The project of building independent revolutionary parties was downplayed by the Institutional family but once the Socialist Party had abandoned entrism its proposal to build a new, mass workers' party bore a striking resemblance to the Mainstream project of building 'new parties of the left' (Videt 2011: 10). That said, the ascendancy of Corbyn in the Labour Party has significantly increased the number of Trotskyist organizations engaged in the entry tactic, including the Radical Trotskyists of Workers Power.

The fragmentation of the Trotskyist movement clearly reflects doctrinal differences but it is clear from the numerous organizational splits that other factors have also come into play: personality differences, disagreements over tactics and allegations of authoritarianism and abuse of organizational power have almost invariably featured in the most significant organizational splits.

Finally, it should be noted the present state of the movement does *not* reflect the absence of tactical and strategic variety and innovation. Trotskyist groups have

TABLE 4.2 The seven families of Trotskyism

Family	British members
Mainstream	Socialist Resistance, Communist League
Third Camp	Socialist Workers Party, Alliance for Workers Liberty, Counterfire, rs21
Orthodox	Workers Revolutionary Party, Spartacist League/Britain, International Bolshevik Tendency, Socialist Equality Party, Socialist Fight, Fourth International (Lambertist)
Institutional	Socialist Party, Socialist Action, Socialist Appeal, Independent Socialist Network, Marxist World
Radical	Workers Power, Workers International to Rebuild the Fourth International, Revolutionary Communist International Tendency (Britain)
Latin American	International Socialist League
Workerist	Workers Fight

operated both inside the Labour Party (in the 1950s and early 1960s, the late 1970s and 1980s and from 2015) and outside Labour (most groups in the 1970s and from the 1990s until 2015). Electoral participation has displayed similar fluctuations, from the enthusiasm of the late 1970s through abstention in the 1980s and 1990s and back to renewed participation through electoral coalitions since 2000 and virtual abstention in 2017. The construction of social movements peaked in the late 1960s and 1970s with the Vietnam Solidarity Campaign and the Anti-Nazi League, waned in the 1980s and 1990s but resumed in the 2000s with the Stop the War Coalition. Yet despite the recent favourable context of economic recession, right-wing governments and savage austerity policies, Trotskyist campaigning, electoral participation and social movement activity has failed to achieve the growth and influence anticipated by its leaders.

Notes

1 There was a fourth split in this period, also in 1985, as members of the Spartacist League's international body, the ICL (FI), disillusioned with the authoritarianism and power of its leader James Robertson, created a new organization, the International Bolshevik Tendency (IBT). There is no record of activity of the British section of the IBT until it emerged as a faction within Arthur Scargill's Socialist Labour Party in 1997, publishing the *Marxist Bulletin*. Since then its handful of supporters do little more than sell its annual journal *1917* and distribute the occasional leaflet at national demonstrations: www.bolshevik.org/, accessed 27 February 2017. The American Spartacist League expelled its newspaper editor Jan Nordern in 1998 who then started his own League for the Fourth International (with small pockets of members in five countries); and it expelled another faction in 2016 who decamped to Nordern's group. All three groups have many similar positions and slogans, for example defend North Korea against imperialist aggression, and not surprisingly in light of their origins spend much of their time engaged in internecine warfare.

2 Redgrave, C., Financial Report, 8 October 1985, WRP Papers, Box 97.

3 The other surviving organizations and their fates are as follows: the ISL split from the WRP with around 12 people in 1988 and quickly affiliated to the International Workers League – Fourth International, an organization founded by the Argentinian Nahuel Moreno and one of the main representatives of an ill-defined Latin American Trotskyism. The ISL was led by Bill Hunter until his death in 2015 and publishes an occasional 12-page magazine *Socialist Voice* as well as contesting local elections in Liverpool.

The Workers International to Rebuild the Fourth International, launched in 1990, is effectively a handful of British activists led by Bob Archer, publishing an online journal in solidarity with the Namibian WRP, a group of some significance in that country. Its critical re-assessment of the various Fourth Internationals places it in the family of Radical Trotskyism: see Draft Resolution for Third Congress 1999, http://workersinternational.info/?s=draft+resolution+for+third+congress, accessed 14 March 2017 (Bob Archer interview; Vodslon 2016).

Socialist Fight began in 2009 and consists of Gerry Downing and a handful of supporters who have published prolifically – 25 issues of *Socialist Fight* magazine 2009–2017 and 22 issues of *In Defence of Trotskyism* magazine 2009–2017. One of their key principles is the idea that 'US-led imperialism' is 'the main enemy of humanity' (Gerry Downing interview). The group helped start the small Liaison Committee for the Fourth International, by a process that illustrates the power of the internet in connecting like-minded thinkers. Finding himself isolated in his critical stance towards the anti-Gaddafi opposition in Libya, Downing reported that:

I had nobody at this stage and I put out a kind of an international statement to every Left group that I knew who would take this position . . . And then . . . a Republican Sinn Fein man in Austria . . . sent me an email and he said there's this group in Brazil who would agree with this line that you're taking.

(Gerry Downing interview)

Finally, A World to Win is a small group expelled from Healy's Marxist Party, whose key members, Corinna Lotz and Paul Feldman, are best known for their glowing biography of Healy in which the charges of sexual abuse are simply dismissed as 'poisonous allegations' orchestrated by MI5 as part of an anti-WRP plot (Lotz and Feldman 1994: 300–01; see also Communist League 1991; Redgrave 1991: 250–51). A World to Win now focuses on the creation of participatory democracy and 'is not a Trotskyist group' (Corinna Lotz interview).

4 Socialist League Central Committee, Party or Sect – Tasks for our Organisation, Report to 1985 Conference, IMG Papers, Warwick, File 234.

5 I consider the Communist League to be part of Mainstream Trotskyism despite its rejection of the theory of permanent revolution. It still adheres to the other core elements of Trotskyism and moreover other Mainstream organizations (for example Socialist Resistance) have also questioned core Trotskyist ideas such as proletarian dictatorship. Nonetheless the League's attitude to permanent revolution does raise a legitimate question: how many elements of core doctrine can be rejected before you cease to be a Trotskyist?

6 'A Brief History of the International Marxist Tendency', 2006 www.marxist.com/history-marxist-tendency.htm, accessed 12 June 2017.

7 '10 Reasons You Should Join Workers' Liberty', www.workersliberty.org/ten, accessed 6 March 2017.

8 On its Australian co-thinkers see Socialist Organiser, Executive Committee Minutes, 12 September 1985 and 26–27 September 1985, AWL Papers, File AWL/1/25; National Editorial Board Minutes, 30–31 August 1986, AWL Papers, File AWL/1/29/1; AWL, National Committee Minutes, 3 April 1992, AWL Papers, File AWL/1/32. On the 1987 and 2003 conferences see AWL, National Committee Minutes, 28 September 2003, AWL Papers, File AWL/1/45/1. The International Committee's work as of 2002 was described by the AWL leadership as 'haphazard': AWL, National Committee Minutes, 19 January 2002, AWL Papers, File AWL/1/44/2.

9 The Socialist Action website provides no means of joining or even contacting the organization, making it the most secretive organization on the Trotskyist left.

10 Adding in the six WRP candidates as well as four others gives a grand total of 108 Trotskyist candidates in the election.

11 However its American counterpart in the International Socialist Tendency, the International Socialist Organisation, refused to engage with the newly emerging anti-globalization protests and on those grounds, in addition to its attempt at splitting the Greek IST affiliate, it was expelled from the IST (Alex Callinicos interview). Clearly by the late 1990s the IST had devised an international structure because the expulsion was moved and implemented in 2001 by the IST Executive Committee. See International Socialist Tendency Resolution, 5 July 2001, http://weeklyworker.co.uk/worker/393/swp-seals-expulsion-of-us-organisation/, accessed 9 December 2016.

12 The ranks of the Trotskyist movement were swelled in 1987 with the appearance in Britain of Workers Fight, a small group affiliated with the French organization Lutte Ouvrière (Workers Struggle) and its international body the Internationalist Communist Union (see Chapter 10). Workers Fight believes that socialism will come through struggles at the workplace and so its activity centres on the production of workplace bulletins as well as a monthly newssheet *Workers Fight* and a quarterly magazine *Class Struggle* (Anna Hunt interview). The ICU considers itself to be a Trotskyist organization but its near total focus on the workplace means that it constitutes a distinctive

family, *Workerist Trotskyism*, a current recently joined by a tiny Vienna-based organization called the Revolutionary Socialist Organization and its supporters in Austria and Peru. For a while, 2011–2012, this group even managed to produce a journal in the UK called *Revolutionary Socialist*: see www.sozialismus.net/, accessed 6 December 2016. Clearly both groups have some affinities with revolutionary syndicalism (see Darlington 2013).

13 The ICL's only sizeable affiliate is the American organization which publishes a bi-weekly newspaper but the November 2016 reduction in its size, from 12 to 8 pages, suggests an organization in decline. The other national sections that produce a newspaper can manage only three to four issues per year, a reliable indicator of organizational weakness, viz. Australia, Canada, France, Germany, Mexico and the UK. Information from the ICL (FI) website www.icl-fi.org/directory/index.html, accessed 9 December 2016.

14 Unusually, the Socialist Party experienced a small split in 2014 following a dispute over economic theory. Critics charged that its analysis of capitalist crisis was a form of 'underconsumptionism' in which economic growth was restrained by low wages and inadequate demand, implying that Keynesian demand management policies could boost economic growth. In contrast, the organizers of the new group, Marxist World, located the causes of crisis in the tendency of the rate of profit to decline for which the only solution is a socialist economy: see 'Editorial Introduction' and 'Overcoming Capitalist Crisis', both in *Marxist World*, No.1, Spring 2016. How far Marxist World disagrees with other elements of the Socialist Party programme and perspectives remains unclear although they note 'there is still much that is positive to be reclaimed from that tradition' (see *Marxist World*, No.1, Spring 2016, 'Editorial Introduction').

15 Ian Birchall also stated that the SWP's main leader at the time, Chris Harman, was more focused on directly building the party (Ian Birchall interview).

16 A near-verbatim report of the Disputes Committee presentation and discussion at the SWP 2013 conference can be found at: http://socialistunity.com/swp-conference-transcript-disputes-committee-report/, accessed 10 March 2017. The first split was led by Richard Seymour in 2013 and formed the International Socialist Network, a grouping that dissolved two years later and became a faction within Left Unity.

17 The two previous organizations that split from the IS/SWP on organizational issues but vowed to maintain the 'IS tradition' – the Workers League (1976) and the International Socialist Alliance (1978) – both disappeared within a few years and the same fate may await rs21.

18 For contributions to the pre-conference discussion see the three Regroupment Conference April 26 Bulletins: http://cpgb.org.uk/pages/news/76/regroupment-conference-april-26-bulletin-no-1/ and http://cpgb.org.uk/pages/news/73/regroupment-conference-bulletins-2-3/, accessed 1 March 2017. On the ISN dissolution in April 2015 see http://internationalsocialistnetwork.org/, accessed 1 March 2017; on the ACI see http://anticapitalists.org/, accessed 1 March 2017. Some members of Workers Power's international group, the League for the Fifth International, were so alarmed at what they believed to be concessions to non-revolutionary forces in the quest for left unity that they quit and formed their own, new International, the Revolutionary Communist International Tendency, which now has one or two members in Britain; see Pröbsting (2012) and Chapter 11.

19 Two of these organizations were short-lived: the Permanent Revolution group, led by Stuart King, a founder member of Workers Power, published 24 issues of a well-produced journal before dissolving itself in March 2013. The group disputed the idea of an imminent economic crisis and a pre-revolutionary situation and whilst, in hindsight, it was far too sanguine about the contemporary state of world capitalism, the Workers Power majority was equally at fault in its over-estimation of the anti-globalization movement. The dissolution statement is available at www.permanentrevolution.net/, accessed 1 December 2016. The key figures in Anti-Capitalist Initiative (2012–2014) were Luke Cooper and Simon Hardy whose main goal was to develop a more participatory, grassroots and democratic revolutionary left, free from the constraints of democratic centralism (see Cooper

and Hardy 2012; and http://anticapitalists.org/, accessed 1 December 2016). Hardy subsequently joined Left Unity and stood as its parliamentary candidate in Vauxhall at the 2015 general election. The RCIT has subsequently acquired small pockets of supporters in eight countries, including a few in Britain, but as some of these have been poached from the diminutive sections of the old Fifth International, it seems unlikely their numbers are any more impressive than those of their old rival. Like other small groups it is dominated by one individual, the activist and prolific writer Michael Pröbsting.

20 Thornett was not alone in voicing this sentiment because late in 2016 Andrew Murray, Unite Chief of Staff and longstanding member of the Communist Party resigned from the CPB and joined the Labour Party.

21 For details see http://independentsocialistnetwork.tumblr.com/, accessed 1 March 2017. ISN (not to be confused with the International Socialist Network 2013–2015) was formed in 2011 to facilitate participation in the Trade Unionist and Socialist Coalition (TUSC) by revolutionary socialists who did not belong to any of its three constituent Trotskyist groups, the Socialist Party, Socialist Resistance and the SWP. One of its leading members was Nick Wrack, former Socialist Party member and brother of Matt Wrack, General Secretary of the Fire Brigades Union. Its involvement in the Socialist Party-dominated TUSC and the former affiliation of Matt Wrack suggests it belongs to the Institutional family of Trotskyism, although this remains unclear. In 2015 a militant from the French Independent Workers Party, Benoit Lahouze, became active in the British Labour Party, publishing an occasional bulletin *Labour News*. The POI belongs to an orthodox Fourth International led for many years by Pierre Lambert, a former collaborator of Gerry Healy. Lambert's version of orthodoxy and its associated Fourth International (see Chapter 11) attracted a number of British adherents through the 1970s, notably Robin Blick and John Archer (see above, note 14), but disappeared in the late 1990s.

22 A similar argument was made by the WRP (Workers Press): see Slaughter (1996).

23 'Readmit Expelled Socialists', November 2016, available at: www.socialistparty.org.uk/main/readmit_expelled_socialists, accessed 28 February 2017.

24 https://stopthelabourpurge.wordpress.com/, accessed 6 September 2016.

25 At the time of writing, June 2017, several hundred left activists including the AWL, have held meetings under the banner of 'Grassroots Momentum' but it is unclear if this is a faction of Momentum or the prelude to a split.

5

DOCTRINE, ORTHODOXY AND SECTARIANISM

Chapter 1 noted two of the main features of sects were the existence of a 'compelling vision' often linked to the doctrines derived from classical texts and a belief in the superiority of one's own views. The attachment to doctrine – doctrinairism – and the belief in its superiority compared to rival viewpoints – sectarianism – will often be intimately and positively connected. Trotskyist doctrine embraces the theory of permanent revolution, the united front tactic, transitional demands, a critical analysis of the Stalinist states, the necessity for a new revolutionary Fourth International, hostile to social democracy and Stalinism, the necessity for a democratic centralist, revolutionary vanguard party, the need to build rank and file organization against trade union bureaucracy, the idea of revolution as a seizure of state power and the notion of the imperialist epoch (see Chapter 2). Other ideas often associated with Trotskyism, such as the revolutionary potential of the working class, are shared by almost all Marxists and are not unique to Trotskyism. However the various elements of Trotskyist doctrine are subject to a variety of interpretations and it is the evolution of these differences that has generated competing 'families of Trotskyism', overlapping bodies of doctrine that have much in common but which diverge on one or two key issues (Table 4.2).[1] The corollary of strict doctrine is a series of rival views and beliefs that are deemed unacceptable. In the world of religion they would be labelled as heresies whilst in the Marxist world, both Trotskyist and non-Trotskyist alike, they are more commonly referred to as deviations from orthodoxy. Table 5.1 sets out the most common deviations to be found in Trotskyist discourse with very brief definitions of each one and many of them will be illustrated and discussed in the body of the chapter.

A strong attachment to doctrinal orthodoxy will manifest itself in a variety of ways: positive references to the concept of orthodoxy; claims for historical

TABLE 5.1 Main deviations from Trotskyist orthodoxy

Adventurism	Policies that are militant but inappropriate or doomed to fail.
Bourgeois/ Petty-bourgeois	Policies that reflect the interests of anti-working-class social forces.
Centrism	Vacillation between reformist and revolutionary policies and strategy.
Economism	Belief that class consciousness will be developed through participation in economic struggles such as strikes.
Empiricism/ Empirical Impressionism	Analysis of phenomena based on facts and evidence with little or no regard for Marxist theoretical categories.
Factionalism	Policies or practices that prioritize the rights and interests of a faction above those of the party.
Guerrillaism	The doctrine that socialist revolution can be achieved by a guerrilla army with little or no working-class involvement (a.k.a. Castroism).
Idealism	The doctrine that consciousness (ideas and beliefs) determines the social relations of production and not vice versa.
Liquidationism	Policies or practices that call into question the rationale or necessity for an independent revolutionary vanguard party.
Nationalism	Attaching excessive importance to purely national issues at the expense of international solidarity; favouring national party policymaking and thereby undermining the authority of international leadership.
Opportunism	Adaptation to current working-class moods or views, downplaying revolutionary policies and slogans, in order to gain popularity.
Pabloism	The policy of deep entry into social democratic and communist parties associated with Fourth International leader Michel Pablo (q.v. liquidationism).
Parliamentarism	Belief that socialism can be achieved through parliament (aka Kautskyism).
Popular Frontism	Creation of coalitions or alliances with non-working-class forces.
Propagandism	Belief that class consciousness can be created through the dissemination of socialist ideas, downplaying its emergence through involvement in class struggles.
Rank and fileism	Policies and practices that adapt to the existing trade union consciousness of working-class militants.
Reformism / Left Reformism	Belief that socialism can be achieved incrementally through a series of reforms.
Revisionism	Significant modifications of classical Marxist, Leninist or Trotskyist theories or doctrines.
Sectarianism	Policies or practices that place the interests of one's own revolutionary organization above the interests of the working class as a whole.
Social Imperialism	Policies or practices that use socialist language to conceal an adaptation to imperialist interests.
Stageism	Belief that the democratic and socialist revolutions represent distinct stages of political development rather than overlapping phases of a 'permanent revolution' (aka Menshevism).

Substitutionism	Replacement of the working class as the agent of revolutionary change with another agency, such as the party or the intelligentsia.
Syndicalism/ Anarcho-syndicalism	Belief that socialism can be achieved through class struggle against the employer, involving direct workplace actions up to and including general strikes.
Third Campism	Policies associated with critics of orthodox Trotskyism such as Shachtman and Burnham.
Ultra-leftism	Policies or slogans that sound 'leftist' but which are unrealistic and ineffective.
Workerism	The belief that socialism will come through class struggle and that conflicts over gender, ethnicity and so on are of secondary importance.

Source: Author.

continuity with Trotsky, the Fourth International and the Transitional Programme; claims that the analyses of one's own group alone have been vindicated by evidence and events; critiques framed through the language of deviations; hostility to other groups and individuals; and a bias towards classical Marxist and exegetical publications at the expense of original and contemporary social science.[2] The next section of the chapter charts the doctrines of the different Trotskyist organizations and families, the ways in which they are reproduced and the treatment of rival viewpoints. We start with the Orthodox Trotskyist family because it illustrates with particular clarity the key role of doctrine. In order of their emergence, the major families can be labelled Mainstream, Third Camp and Institutional whilst the other families – Radical, Workerist and Latin American – will be discussed only briefly. The final sections explore the role of charismatic leadership and its many dysfunctional consequences, as well as the role of membership education and control before brief comments on Trotskyist commemorations of the centenary of 1917.

Doctrine and sectarianism in the Orthodox Trotskyist family

According to the 1981 constitution of the WRP, a longstanding guardian of orthodoxy,

> (1) (a) The aim of the Party is to prepare and mobilize the working class for the overthrow of capitalism, the establishment of working class power and the building of a socialist society.
>
> (b) This Party bases its policy on the theory of Marxism as developed by Lenin and Trotsky, the decisions of the first four Congresses of the Communist International and the Founding Programme of the Fourth International (1938).[3]

As discussed in Chapters 3 and 4, the SLL/WRP leader Gerry Healy developed a general perspective in the late 1940s from which he never deviated. Like Trotsky he believed that the world was marked by: 'impending economic collapse, the erosion of parliamentary democracy, a drive towards right-wing dictatorship, and imminent revolutionary struggles' (Pitt 2002: Chapter 2). The SLL has always believed it is *the* revolutionary party:

> the Socialist Labour League is the only authentic voice of revolutionary Marxism in Britain today.
>
> *(1972 cited in North 1991: 114)*

> to win the most advanced layers of the working class to revolution . . . is the immediate and necessary task that history has placed on the agenda for the inheritors of Lenin and the Bolshevik Party, the International Committee of the Fourth International and the Workers Revolutionary Party.
>
> *(Wiltshire 1995: 73)*

This faith in the exclusive mission of the SLL/WRP was conveyed to *Workers Press* editor Alex Mitchell shortly after he joined the SLL in 1969:

> I once asked Healy whether it would be worthwhile holding a reunification conference to bring the splinter groups together. He gave me a pained look and said, "We don't need to have a meeting with them, Alex – we need to destroy them. They are an obstacle to the revolution".
>
> *(Mitchell 2011: 215)*[4]

Not surprisingly, the SLL/WRP has an unblemished record of non-cooperation with other Trotskyist groups and organizations and for a period in the 1970s even arranged for one of its members to join the IMG as an SLL spy.[5]

One key aspect of doctrine is that it remains largely impervious to empirical refutation or significant amendment and party leaders invariably conclude that events and evidence have vindicated their analyses:

> The unprecedented crisis of the world capitalist system is before anything else a vindication of Marxism. Every opportunist and revisionist has been left high and dry (1968).[6]

> The bankruptcy of the lefts and revisionists confirms that as the social revolution erupts in Britain the Workers Revolutionary Party is right out in front giving revolutionary leadership on a daily basis (1990).[7]

The corollary of the WRP being the sole guardian of Trotskyist orthodoxy is that all of its rivals have deviated from Trotskyism and their transgressions have been frequently and vigorously denounced. The IS/SWP was guilty *inter alia* of 'economism', 'rank and fileism', and 'syndicalism'; the IMG (now Socialist Resistance) was charged with 'centrism', liquidationism' and 'opportunism'; the RSL/Militant Tendency was guilty of 'Pabloism' and 'reformism' (Athow 2010; Banda 1971, 1972; Jeffries 1973; Slaughter 1971, 1972; Workers Revolutionary Party 1983).[8] The most vitriolic attacks, however, were reserved for Alan Thornett and his supporters following their expulsion from the WRP in 1974. His arguments were derived from a 'subjectivist dung-heap' and he subsequently underwent 'complete ideological degeneration' (Banda 1975: vii; News Line 1980: 7).[9] The pinnacle of WRP hostility towards its rivals was achieved in 1974 and 1975 with the publication of six volumes of correspondence, resolutions and minutes under the generic title of 'Trotskyism versus Revisionism', much of it directed against the policies of Mainstream leader Michel Pablo, architect of the deviation known as 'Pabloism'. In the world view of the doctrinaire, the most damning statement that can be made about an opponent is not that his/her policy has proved ineffective or unpopular but that it has deviated from orthodoxy.

For Trotskyist leaders such as Gerry Healy (and Ted Grant), their superior insights into political economy and class struggle were rooted in the *scientific* character of Marxism, a property it possessed owing to its dialectical materialist core: 'Without a conscious and uninterrupted struggle . . . for a dialectical materialist practice of cognition, there can be no revolutionary party and no building of the Fourth International' (Workers Revolutionary Party 1983: 30). Political opponents could therefore be attacked by searching out philosophical tendencies that departed from dialectical materialism such as Pierre Lambert's 'empiricism' or Alan Thornett's 'subjective idealism' (Banda 1975; International Committee of the Fourth International 1973). However, the WRP understanding of dialectical materialism was rudimentary, being derived mainly from Engels *Dialectics of Nature* and Lenin's *Philosophical Notebooks*, regurgitated by Healy at the WRP's College of Marxist Education (Lotz and Feldman 1994: 29; and see Healy 1990).[10]

The publications of the WRP fully reflected its faith in the writings of Marx, Engels, Lenin and Trotsky and their WRP interpreters and commentators with 38 books and pamphlets by Trotsky. The only contemporary titles were by WRP leaders such as Mike Banda, Tom Kemp and Cliff Slaughter. The current publishing arm of the WRP, Revolution Books, has a similar, if much shorter, list: 22 of its 47 titles are by Trotsky, a further 15 are by Marx, Engels and Lenin and in the category of 'Modern Marxists' there are just three titles, all by WRP leader Dave Wiltshire. The theoretical knowledge required to be a WRP militant can therefore be derived almost entirely from the Marxist classics; there is no need to study contemporary non-WRP Marxists, let alone contemporary non-Marxist social science.

The largest splinter group from the WRP implosion is the equally orthodox SEP, which declared in the first issue of its newspaper that, 'the *International Worker* . . . will be the only paper in Britain fighting for an international Trotskyist analysis' (*International Worker* No. 1, July–August 1986). Over 30 years later its website repeated the same refrain: 'The ICFI is the sole political tendency on the face of the planet that sets as its aim the revolutionary mobilisation of the working class against imperialism and the drive to war in the fight for international socialism'.[11]

It followed that all other 'Trotskyist' groupings had succumbed to one deviation or another, precluding them from playing any revolutionary role. The pre-1986 WRP was now declared to have been guilty of 'centrism', 'idealism', 'opportunism' and 'ultra-leftism' whilst the other fragments of the WRP were simply dismissed as 'renegades' who had become 'craven apologists for Stalinism' (International Committee of the Fourth International 1986a; International Communist Party 1990). More recent SEP pronouncements have gone even further, labelling all other Trotskyist groups as the 'pseudo-left . . . a professional *anti-Trotskyist* detachment of the petty-bourgeoisie . . . which promotes the socioeconomic interests of privileged and affluent strata of the middle class' (Socialist Equality Party 2016: 20, italics in original). The range of titles from the SEP publishing house, Mehring Books, is suitably narrow: 37 by Trotsky, 14 by Marx, Engels and Lenin but 24 by the ICFI Chair David North.

The other well-known member of the Orthodox family is the Spartacist League/ Britain, a section of the International Communist League (Fourth Internationalist), whose main focus has been the preservation of 'programmatic clarity', a perspective it shares with Workers Power (Len Michelson and Mick Connor interview). According to its 1998 programme,

> The International Communist League bases itself on Marxist historical, dialectical materialism . . . We seek in particular to carry forward the international working-class perspectives of Marxism as developed in theory and practice by V.I. Lenin and L.D. Trotsky, as embodied in the decisions of the first four Congresses of the Communist International and by the 1938 Transitional Program and other key documents of the Fourth International . . . These materials are the indispensable documentary codification of the communist movement internationally, and are fundamental to the revolutionary tasks of our organization.[12]

The remainder of the Declaration sets out all the core elements of Trotskyism discussed in Chapter 2, such as the theory of permanent revolution, the united front and transitional demands. In common with other members of the Orthodox family, the Spartacist League and its international parent organization have devoted enormous time and energy to debunking the revolutionary credentials of various rivals. In a series of 12 bulletins published in the 1990s under the eye-catching title 'Hate Trotskyism, Hate the Spartacist League', it reprinted material from rival organizations which it then assailed with its own vigorous critiques. Targets have included the mainstream United Secretariat of the Fourth International (USFI, whose British affiliate is Socialist Resistance), the Militant Tendency, the International Bolshevik Tendency (IBT) (an orthodox expellee from the Spartacist League) and the radical Trotskyists of Workers Power.[13] Critiques are mainly rooted in departures from orthodoxy, but are also rich in personal invective: Gerry Healy (WRP) was a 'revisionist and destroyer of the Trotskyist movement' whilst his arch-enemy Michel Pablo 'personally has done quite as much as any other living human being to destroy the Trotskyist movement from within and turn "Trotskyism" into a cesspool'.[14]

Perhaps one of the most distinctive features of orthodox Trotskyism is the vigour and consistency of its anti-imperialism, notwithstanding the fact that all Trotskyist groups are hostile to imperialism. Based on the claim that one of the greatest obstacles to socialist advance in the imperialist epoch is imperialism itself, Trotskyists have lent critical support to the degenerated workers' states and to any other social forces that come into conflict with imperialism and its allies. Hence the call by the Spartacist League/US to 'Defend North Korea!' (*Workers Vanguard* 23 September 2016) and the statement by Socialist Fight, an organization led by ex-WRP member Gerry Downing, that we 'defend the "Islamic State" in Syria and Iraq' (*Socialist Fight* No. 20 Autumn 2015, p. 3).[15]

Mainstream Trotskyism

The British section of the mainstream USFI only emerged in the late 1960s as the IMG (now Socialist Resistance)[16] and the 1971 Constitution proclaimed its commitment to 'revolutionary Marxism' whose principles are expressed in, 'the programme and perspectives of the Fourth International. Therefore the Group is based on the first four congresses of the Communist International and the World Congresses of the Fourth International'.[17] The Group operated a 'democratic centralist' structure and sought to achieve a 'democratic dictatorship of the working class', a phrase replaced by 'proletarian democracy' in its 1978 constitution.[18] By 2016 the group had abandoned the objective of building a Leninist vanguard party, in line with the new policy of the Fourth International: 'Socialist Resistance is an ecosocialist, feminist, internationalist and revolutionary organization with a central project of building a broad party of the radical left' (*Socialist Resistance* No. 81 Spring 2016, p. 2). Otherwise Socialist Resistance maintains its commitment to the core principles of Trotskyism such as the united front, transitional demands and the necessity for an international organization (Mostyn 2015).

In common with other Trotskyist groups it has often evinced a strong sense of the veracity of its own positions and a correspondingly negative view of its rivals. In 1973 its newspaper *Red Weekly* asserted that the IMG was, 'the only organization on the left with a clear understanding of the situation in which the working class now finds itself and with clear proposals as to how the movement can go forward' (cited in Roberts 1976b: 55). Throughout the 1980s and 1990s, the group repeatedly asserted the positive, sometimes critical, impact of its interventions: 'Our comrades have been central to important actions and mobilizations' (NHS dispute 1988); 'ISG now plays a key role' (Labour Party 1990).[19] Ten years later the historians of the USFI asserted that it has been, 'able to live and grow, because throughout all these years it alone represented the fundamental, historical interests of the world proletariat' (Frank and Bensaid 2010: 128).

The IMG has contributed its share of literature directed against Trotskyist rivals with critical publications on the IS (Mandel 1969), the Militant Tendency (Socialist Challenge 1977) and the SLL (Hansen 1974; Whelan 1970). Internal documents and correspondence from the 1960s and 1970s voiced complaints about the 'factionalism' of other groups and their 'inability . . . to work correctly in the mass movement', branding the Militant Tendency as 'centrist', the WRP as 'ultra-sectarian' and the SWP as 'centrist, syndicalist and sectarian'.[20] In 1989 a review of ISG student work described the SWP as 'resolutely ultraleft and manic', the Militant Tendency as 'narrowly sectarian' and the RCP as 'propagandist'.[21]

Yet unlike most Trotskyist groups the ISG was also capable of recognizing its opponents' strengths so in 1989 for example it noted that the SWP 'remains a dynamic and influential force' and the RCP leadership is 'skilled and flexible'.[22] Indeed its relations with other organizations were sometimes very cordial. An invitation to an IMG cadre school in 1980 listed the usual attractions with speakers, such as Tariq Ali, Robin Blackburn and Ernest Mandel, as well as movies and then continued, 'An event not to be missed is the Saturday afternoon cricket match between Socialist Challenge and Socialist Worker'.[23]

In similar vein, several USFI leaders were also willing to acknowledge problems with their world view, a rare occurrence on the Trotskyist left. Veteran leader Daniel Bensaid referred to events of the 1980s as representing: 'a theoretical crisis of Marxism, a strategic crisis of the revolutionary project, and a social crisis of the subject of universal emancipation' (2013: 198). Even Mandel, for all his alleged dogmatism, was eventually willing to criticize Bolshevik authoritarianism in the early 1920s, such as the outlawing of other parties and the ban on party factions: 'From 1920–21 the strategy of the Bolshevik leadership hindered rather than promoted the self-activity of the Russian workers. What is more, the theoretical justification and the generalization of this "substitution" made the situation even worse' (Mandel 1995a: 82).[24]

In terms of policy, the USFI and its British section have displayed an unusual degree of tactical and strategic flexibility, entertaining a wide range of alternative revolutionary subjects (a policy dismissed by Orthodox and other critics as 'substitutionism'). In the early 1950s Michel Pablo explored the conditions under which Stalinist parties might come to play a revolutionary role; in the early 1960s the USFI welcomed the Cuban revolution, led by armed sections of the intelligentsia; in the late 1960s the revolutionary potential of student actions and of guerrilla warfare were highlighted; and from the 1990s the project of building independent, revolutionary, vanguard parties was replaced in some countries by a policy of building revolutionary nuclei within broad workers' parties (Bensaid 2009; Frank and Bensaid 2010; Videt 2011). Vilified by some on the Trotskyist left for 'vacillation' and 'political instability', the USFI and its British section have at least been willing to rethink elements of Trotskyist doctrine in the light of evidence and events.

Finally, the IMG and its successors have devoted considerable time and energy to the creation of a unified revolutionary organization. Unity talks with the International Socialists began in 1968 but broke down after several years of discussion when the IS National Committee voted narrowly (14 to 12) for their termination.[25] After abortive talks with Workers Fight, the Socialist Charter group and the Workers League in 1972–1973, it eventually launched an ambitious Socialist Unity proposal but received declarations of interest from only a few small organizations and from a small faction within Big Flame.[26] Fresh overtures to the SWP ended acrimoniously in 1979 (Pennington 1977),[27] but in 1987 one fragment from the Socialist League breakup – the International Group – did eventually effect a merger with Alan Thornett's small Socialist Group.[28] In 2013–2014 Socialist Resistance was involved in another revolutionary unity initiative but like many of its predecessors the discussions petered out and failed to create a new organization (see Chapter 4). Meantime the emergence of Left Unity, founded as a radical left party in 2013, attracted Socialist Resistance, which chose to operate there as a faction.[29]

Third Camp Trotskyism

The IS/SWP

Historically the main exemplar of this family in Britain was the SWP because of its state capitalist analysis of the USSR and its refusal to take sides in the Korean War. Yet in 1968 IS backed the Vietnam Solidarity Campaign, along with the Mainstream Trotskyists of the IMG, shifting from its Third Camp slogan, 'Neither Washington nor Moscow'.[30] In contrast, the AWL only moved towards Third Camp Trotskyism in the late 1980s when it adopted the state capitalist analysis of the USSR. One might expect Third Camp Trotskyists to be quite heterodox and relatively free of doctrinairism but neither assumption entirely does justice to the complex positions and policies of these groups. As noted in Chapter 3, Cliff's *State Capitalism in Russia* was effectively the founding text of the Socialist Review Group (SRG) and marked a radical departure from the 'degenerated workers' state' orthodoxy. Moreover the argument about the relations of production within the USSR was strongly grounded in empirical evidence: the expanded 1955 edition contained 38 tables. It was also clearly heterodox, departing from the Marxist emphasis on the drive to accumulate through the extraction of surplus value within the capitalist firm and its realization within markets, and introducing the idea of military competition between states as the driving force of Soviet state capitalism (Howard and King 1992: 62–66; van der Linden 2009: 153–58). The other hallmark of the IS, Kidron's theory of the 'Permanent Arms Economy', identified arms expenditure as a means of counteracting the falling tendency of the rate of profit and thereby sustaining the post-war economic boom (Cliff 1999: 48–59). This was an equally innovative, albeit flawed idea: arms expenditure as a proportion of GDP in Britain fell between 1952 and 1970 yet the rate of profit in manufacturing remained stable until the late 1960s (Howard and King 1992: 158; Glyn 2006: 7; Mandel 1975a: Chapter 9).[31]

On the issue of organizational structure, Cliff's (1983) short book on Rosa Luxemburg, first published in 1959, presented a very positive appraisal of her ideas as against the more centralized party structure favoured by Lenin. So long as the SRG was a small organization he felt it did not require a democratic centralist structure but when IS entered a period of rapid growth, Cliff swung round to Lenin's argument for centralization. The 1969 reissue of the book no longer contained the sentence suggesting Western Marxists could learn more from Luxemburg than Lenin on organizational structure.[32] Fourth, Cliff and the SWP were always sceptical of the notion of transitional demands, arguing that classic examples such as 'a sliding scale of wages' made little sense in the post-war context of full employment and rising real wages (1993: 296). As for the Fourth International, Cliff maintained that whilst Trotsky was right in 1933 to declare the necessity for a new organization and to *start* its construction, he also believed the 1938 foundation conference was premature (Cliff 1993: 306).

Finally, it has been argued that one of Cliff's strengths was 'the way in which he combined adherence to basic principles with constant openness to new facts and changing realities' (Birchall 2011: 555). The IS/SWP launched a series of initiatives over many years, each designed to connect with, and exploit, a particular issue or development: the National Rank and File Movement (1974), the Right to Work Campaign (1975), the Anti-Nazi-League (1977 and relaunched 1992), the Stop the War Coalition (2001), Unite the Resistance and Stand up to Racism (both 2011). Many of these initiatives have been attacked by Orthodox and Radical Trotskyists for failing to advance a comprehensive, revolutionary socialist programme, for example Revolutionary Communist Group (1979), Workers Power (1978).[33] In the 1970s the SWP never dreamed of inviting senior trade union officials to any of its rank and file union events, whereas today every Unite the Resistance rally will feature a number of union general secretaries and presidents (for example Matt Wrack, Fire Brigades Union, November 2015, Ian Hodson, Bakers Union, November 2016).[34] In its defence, Darlington (2014) offered a subtle reformulation of the SWP's classical but crude analysis of the 'bureaucracy vs rank and file' thesis, noting that industrial action had always entailed an interplay between both groups and that the current, changed context of labour quiescence necessitated a change in tactics. As one interviewee said, the idea is 'we could have influence over the Mark Serwotkas and Bob Crows of this world' (Anindya Bhattacharyya interview). Radical and Orthodox critics have, not surprisingly, denounced Unite the Resistance as both sectarian – putting the interests of the SWP above other considerations – and opportunist – because of the close ties to union officials.[35]

Yet for all its ideological heterodoxy and tactical flexibility, the SWP remains a revolutionary organization committed wholeheartedly to many of the key tenets of Trotskyist doctrine. Under the strapline 'What We Stand For', displayed each week in *Socialist Worker*, are five headings: independent working-class action, revolution not reform, no parliamentary road, internationalism (meaning permanent revolution, state capitalism and anti-imperialism) and the need for a revolutionary party (see also Choonara and Kimber 2011).[36] The theory of permanent revolution is particularly interesting in this context because Cliff wrote an heretical essay on the subject in 1963 (Cliff 1963, 1999: 60–69). In the cases of China and Cuba he argued their bourgeoisies were too weak to lead national democratic revolutions but instead of the working class playing this role, as Trotsky's theory suggested, it was the peasantry and the intelligentsia respectively. An open-minded social scientist might have concluded that the theory was wrong on several counts yet Cliff's appraisal of the evidence was insufficient to produce any radical questioning of orthodoxy and he offered instead the convoluted and unconvincing idea that the 'permanent revolution' would still occur but had been 'deflected' from its predicted path.

A similar tension between theory and practice was evident in discussions around the character of the Stop the War Coalition, a broad movement launched in 2001 and embracing the SWP, Communist Party of Britain, the Green Party, left Labour MPs, the Liberal Democrats, CND and the Muslim Association of Britain (Murray and German 2005: 54–63, 163–67). Orthodox and Radical Trotskyists, as well as doctrinaire followers of Ted Grant, predictably attacked the Coalition as a collection of 'petty-bourgeois pacifists' building a reformist, cross-class 'popular front' that was doomed to fail (Socialist Equality Party 2011: 120; *Workers Hammer* Summer 2007; Sewell 2017a: 23) Some of the Coalition's SWP leaders struggled to fit the structure and broad composition of the movement into the classical framework of the united front, an alliance between revolutionaries and reformists around a specific objective. Writing about the electoral coalition Socialist Alliance, although his words could equally apply to the newly formed Stop the War Coalition, John Rees (2002) argued this was a 'united front of a special type'. Both this concept and the idea of 'deflected permanent revolution' seem primarily designed to resist charges of ideological deviation rather than to capture the dynamics of complex alliances involving multiple organizations and identities.

The complexities of SWP politics and the tensions between heterodoxy and orthodoxy also play out in their relations to other organizations and in their internal regime. The IS executive agreed in the 1960s then that it would avoid public attacks on other groups and would rebut accusations against IS only in its Internal Bulletin where it noted: 'the SLL was 'unable to break out of sectarian exclusiveness; the IMG represents a tradition without any stable practice . . . and the RSL remains immersed in the Labour Party acquiring meaningless resolutionary victories'.[37] Although it published a lengthy critique of the Militant Tendency in 1986, and a more peremptory critique two years later, neither work devoted much space to the identification of heresies and deviations (MacGregor 1986; Cliff and Gluckstein 1988: 361–65). Its lack of appetite for inter-organizational polemic derives from the viewpoint of its dominant and charismatic founder and leader, Tony Cliff: 'One rule I have always followed is not to read sectarian literature. I never read Healy's newspaper, nor that of the International Marxist Group' (Cliff 2000: 62).

Internally, the IS/SWP press has carried many debates, airing in public some of the divisions within the party over issues such as Ireland (in 1969), the Common Market (1971), the united front (2002) and more recently the EU referendum and levels of industrial militancy (2015–2016). Its main theoretical journal, *International Socialism*, has carried articles from a wide range of contributors in contrast to the journals of many rivals such as the SLL/WRP and Militant Tendency/RSL.[38] One explanation for these differences lies in the role of doctrine: for Orthodox parties such as the SLL/WRP and for doctrinaire individuals such as Ted Grant, the parameters of debate are configured by confrontation between the 'teachings' of the great Marxists and a variety of deviations. For the more heterodox SWP, the pull of orthodoxy is always present but less compelling. An additional factor behind the greater degree of internal debate in the IS/SWP derives from group composition because it is clear that Cliff's group has proved far more successful than any of its rivals in recruiting a substantial number of intellectuals. The SLL/WRP recruited a handful of ex-CP intellectuals in the 1950s as well as a few others over the next 20 years and the only well-known figures in the Militant Tendency were the economist Andrew Glyn and the industrial relations scholar Dave Beale.[39] In contrast, IS/SWP recruits, past and present, include many well-known academics: Colin Barker, Ian Birchall, Alex Callinicos, Ralph Darlington, Gregor Gall, James Hinton, Richard Hyman, Nigel Harris, Steve Jefferys, John McIlroy and Martin Upchurch. Moreover, a number of SWP (and ex-SWP) intellectuals have played key roles in the genesis and management of the independent Marxist journal *Historical Materialism*, including Paul Blackledge, Sebastian Budgen, Jim Kincaid, China Miéville and Richard Seymour.

Several groups that broke away from the SWP still adhere to many elements of its politics. Counterfire believes that in an era of capitalist crisis it is necessary to construct a revolutionary vanguard party to overthrow capitalism by leading the working class in struggle. Support for such a party will be built as people become involved in campaigns, often on immediate issues organized through united fronts, alliances between revolutionaries and reformists. Like the SWP, Counterfire makes little reference to transitional demands and its internationalism manifests itself as firm opposition to imperialist aggression (Rees 2010, 2014). Its two main leaders, John Rees and Lindsey German, continue to play leading roles in the Stop the War Coalition, and in common with the SWP, the theory of permanent revolution plays little part in discussions around tactics and strategy.[40] Stop the War is often held up as a model organization, by Counterfire and the SWP, because it involves a diverse range of social forces, it has mobilized large numbers of people and it is not confined to trade union struggles at the workplace (John Rees interview).[41] Counterfire is not affiliated to an international organization and appears to share the attitude of the IS/ early SWP that there is little value in trying to build such an organization 'from above' or to announce a new International because such a body can only emerge organically and 'from below' (Cliff 2000: 203). One of the distinctive features of Counterfire is the emphasis placed on building united fronts, such as Stop the War, Respect and the People's Assembly, because these organizations are thought to be critical in building a revolutionary socialist organization. Confident in its own political positions, Counterfire is unusual on the Trotskyist left in having devoted almost no space whatever to the policies and positions of its various rivals.

The Alliance for Workers Liberty

The other significant member of the Third Camp family is the AWL, an organization that has radically altered its politics and passed through more name changes than any other Trotskyist group (see Chapters 3 and 4).[42] Under its long-serving leader Sean Matgamna, it began life as a relatively orthodox Trotskyist group, declaring in 1969:

> Trotskyism is the . . . unfalsified Programme, method and experience of the Bolshevism of Lenin and Trotsky . . . It means reliance on the self-controlling activity of the working class, which it strives to mobilise on the Programme of Transitional demands as a bridge to the overthrow of capitalism and the attainment of workers' power . . . It is the Programme of the workers' revolution.[43]

A similar political orientation was set out eight years later (International-Communist League 1977) and since then the group has retained many classical Trotskyist positions: on the need for revolution and for a revolutionary party; on the role and value of the united front; the theory of permanent revolution; and the value of transitional demands (see the various articles in *Workers Liberty*, 3(2), 2006).[44]

In the 1980s, however, the organization became embroiled in a series of political disputes that led to its questioning key elements of Trotskyist doctrine. In the Falklands/Malvinas war Matgamna rejected the Orthodox line of support for Argentina against British imperialism and refused to support either side, a heterodox position that was soon applied to other conflicts, such as Northern Ireland and Israel. Instead of calling for the destruction of these states because of their creation by, and support for, British and American imperialism respectively, the AWL now committed itself to a federal solution, acknowledging the political rights of Irish Protestants and Israeli Jews alongside those of Nationalists and Palestinians.[45] In similar vein it has taken issue with conventional Trotskyist opposition to American and British involvement in North Africa and the Middle East, questioning the notion that any opponent of Western imperialism, however despotic and reactionary, should receive 'critical support' (Matgamna 2017).[46]

The late 1980s also witnessed the group's abandonment of the classical Trotskyist analysis of the USSR as a degenerated workers' state and its growing sympathy for Max Shachtman and his 'Third Camp' Trotskyism, reprinting many of his essays with extensive and sympathetic commentaries (Matgamna 1998, 2015). One final consequence of its firm identification with the heterodox Third Camp was that the AWL increasingly stressed the role of ideas and debate in the development of revolutionary politics (hence the name of its annual three-day meeting, 'Ideas for Freedom'). According to Matgamna (2006: 46), 'the AWL . . . is a vehicle for open, honest and free discussion'.[47] Yet the history of the AWL is replete with persistent hostility to other Trotskyist organizations. In a 1972 review it dismissed the SLL and the Militant Tendency (RSL) as 'sectarian and useless . . . reducing Trotskyism to an arid, often destructive and usually repellent dogma'.[48] A few years later it condemned the IMG because of its 'extreme political instability', claimed the WSL adhered to a 'religious conception of politics' and dismissed the RCG as a 'contemplative sect'.[49] In 1983 it agreed that it would not pursue unity discussions with the Socialist League (formerly IMG) because 'We are not at one with the SL, we are at war with them'.[50] In the early days of the electoral coalition Socialist Alliance, the AWL was wary about working with one of its dominant members, the Socialist Party, because, 'We are gearing up for war with the Socialist Party (SP). The SP have (sic) invited us to talks. OK. But we are still out to supplant and replace them'.[51] The Respect Coalition was denounced as an unsupportable 'Popular Front' and the AWL declared 'we must counterpose ourselves to it politically in a sharp way'.[52] The flipside of its hostility towards other Trotskyist groups was a willingness to undertake its own campaigns and initiatives, despite very limited resources: hence the Welfare State Network, launched in 1994 and the rank and file 'Unions Fightback' conference, launched in 2001 despite similar initiatives by other organizations.[53]

Although the AWL can be self-critical about its activities and campaigns, these reservations co-exist with an underlying certitude about its positions and policies: 'The I-CL alone has a clear and consistent record, and political positions worked out clearly and scientifically' (1976); 'We are . . . making a distinctive and invaluable contribution to building a real socialist party' (2009).[54]

Institutional Trotskyism

The hallmark of this family is a commitment to working within the institutions of the Labour Party and parliament, although the constitution of the secretive RSL (Militant Tendency) was very similar to those of its more Orthodox rivals:

> Basing itself on the principles embodied in the first four congresses of the Communist International and the founding world conference of the Fourth International, the R.S.L. strives to win the leadership of the working class for the establishment of a workers' government in Britain and in collaboration with the World working and toiling masses to abolish classes and build the World Socialist order of society.[55]

In the late 1970s the WRP was frequently ridiculed for its mechanical repetition of Trotsky's catastrophist prognosis of socialism or fascism but Militant leader Ted Grant took a very similar view, arguing in 1977:

> *The social crisis of Britain will be protracted.* It will end either in the greatest victory of the working class achieving power and the overthrow of the rule of capital, with the installation of workers' democracy, or a military police dictatorship which will destroy the labour movement . . . These are *long-term perspectives* over the coming period of 10–15 years.
>
> *(Grant 1989c: 501, italics in original)*[56]

Under Grant's leadership, Militant and its successor organization Socialist Appeal displayed levels of self-belief coupled with hostility and contempt towards other Trotskyist groups – 'the sects' – that were remarkably similar to those of the SLL/ WRP and its fellow adherents of Orthodoxy: 'only our tendency has stood the test of history' (1973);[57] 'Our perspectives have been brilliantly confirmed by the march of events' (International Marxist Tendency 2014: 22).[58] Shortly before he died in 2006 Grant summed up a world view that had barely altered since the 1940s:

> of the Fourth International . . . the ideas, methods, programme and traditions of Trotsky and the Left Opposition . . . you can only find these in our Tendency . . . *Socialist Appeal* . . . We have kept the banner flying . . . And we were the only ones to do so.
>
> *(Grant quoted in Woods 2013a: 275)*

The corollary of this self-belief was wholesale contempt for other Trotskyist groups and their, 'bogus "Fourth Internationals", all of which have soiled the banner of Trotskyism, [and] are now in process of disintegration'.[59]

In the 1970s Militant attacked all of its Trotskyist rivals, accusing the IS/SWP for example of 'infantile leftism' whilst the IMG was mired in 'reformist policies, ultra-left tactics and the whole petit-bourgeois atmosphere'.[60] Grant never abandoned his unreconstructed sectarianism and his view that Trotskyists must focus on the Labour Party and the class struggle, not on conflicts around racism or sexism. 'The sects have learned nothing. They have absorbed all the nonsense of the petty bourgeois – women's lib, gay lib, black nationalism, guerrillaism – you name it!' (Grant quoted in Woods 2013a: 275). Grant was equally enamoured of the 'scientific' claims of Marxism, writing in 1960 that, 'The laws underlying the development of capitalist society have been worked out and explained by Marx' (Grant 1989b: 393).[61] According to Woods, 'dialectical and historical materialism . . . alone provide us with the scientific tools necessary to analyse complex and contradictory processes' (1997: 37; see also Woods 1999: 18–22) and in a recent essay, he arrogantly dismissed almost 200 years of philosophical work, underlining his own deeply doctrinaire world view: 'In the period of its ascent the bourgeoisie was capable of producing great thinkers like Hegel and Kant. In the period of its senile decay it produces nothing of value' (Woods 2013b: 14).

Although the Militant Tendency abandoned entrism in 1991 it has retained the belief in a peaceful transition to socialism (Socialist Party 2008: 27; Socialist Party 2013: 25). Peter Taaffe, party leader since the 1991 split, was never as arrogant and sectarian as his former mentor Ted Grant but was equally prone to thinking that his own analyses were often confirmed by events:

> Since it was first published, we have not received a single example of an article or a review which challenged the main lines of this book [*Marxism in Today's World*] . . . this allows us to draw the conclusion that our analysis has been vindicated.
>
> *(Taaffe 2013: v)*

Under Taaffe's leadership the Socialist Party remained critical of other groups such as the SWP, although the tenor of their critiques was measured and the substance rooted more in evidence than in the language of deviation (for example Taaffe 2008).

The Socialist Party and its International were also more willing to engage in dialogue with other organizations such as the USFI although nothing substantial seemed to emerge from the talks (Taaffe 2004: 10).

The publications of these two groups are strikingly different. Socialist Appeal offers a narrow range of texts, mostly comprising classical Marxism (21 titles by Trotsky, 19 by Marx and Engels, 5 by Lenin) as well as books by the leading figures in the organization, Grant (six titles), Alan Woods (eight) and Rob Sewell (three). This is intentional because according to Alan Woods: 'the best source for rediscovering the history of Bolshevism is the writings of Lenin and Trotsky. They are an inexhaustible treasure-house of information and ideas' (Woods 1999: 18). The Socialist Party, in contrast offers a wide range of historical and contemporary literature by a variety of authors although a significant portion of its list comprises several hundred titles by Trotsky and other classical Marxists (as well as 17 by Peter Taaffe).

The other Trotskyist families

The Radical Trotskyist family, epitomised by Workers Power, is as strongly attached to the core elements of Trotskyism as its Orthodox rivals yet the key difference lies in its claim that *none* of the Trotskyist groups or their Internationals have remained faithful to Trotskyist verities. As we saw in the previous chapter the group's position finally emerged in its 1983 book *The Death Agony of the Fourth International* and much of its argument overlapped with the views of Orthodox Trotskyism. 'We stand in the tradition of the FI, founded by Trotsky. Its programme, the Transitional Programme, represented the culmination of the programmatic work of previous generations of revolutionary Marxists' (Workers Power and Irish Workers Group 1983: 12). In other words, Workers Power fully endorsed core themes such as the united front, the theory of permanent revolution and the necessity for a revolutionary International organization and insisted all these elements must be embodied in an updated revolutionary programme. The book was a thoroughgoing critique of the various strands of international Trotskyism and in similar vein to the proponents of orthodoxy the critique was couched in the language of deviation: the Fourth International under Pablo was 'revisionist' and 'opportunist' and whilst his British and French critics (Healy and Lambert) were right to berate him they were nonetheless guilty of 'nationalism'. The USFI in the 1960s succumbed to 'ultra-leftism' in its support for Latin American guerrillas (a policy also referred to as 'guerrillaism') whilst its critics, such as Healy's SLL, had become 'deeply sectarian'. More recently it has attacked the SWP-led electoral grouping Respect as 'opportunist' and accused both the Socialist Party and Socialist Appeal of adapting to imperialism (because neither calls for troop withdrawal from the north of Ireland) (Lloyd and Brenner 1994; Workers Power 1990).

All of these groups were charged with having abandoned Trotsky's crowning achievement, the Transitional Programme, and so the key task for revolutionaries was to reconstruct such a programme as the basis for a genuinely revolutionary party and a new International. Workers Power, under the banner of its various international organizations (see Chapter 11) duly issued a new Transitional Programme in 1989 with a shorter version in 2008 and a purely British 'Action Programme' in 2014 (League for a Revolutionary Communist International 1989; League for the Fifth International 2010; Workers Power 2014).

The leading exponent of Workerist Trotskyism in Britain is the tiny London-based group Workers Fight, which has long been critical of the Mainstream Fourth International because of its willingness to explore the role of social forces beyond the working class and because of its perceived domination by intellectuals (Internationalist Communist Union 1988). Although its orientation to workplace struggles is very similar to that of the IS/SWP, there remained disagreements over the analysis of the USSR (Workers Fight never accepted the 'state capitalist' analysis) and over the role of the union and Labour bureaucracies (Workers Fight has remained far more critical in recent years compared to the SWP).

Latin American Trotskyism is represented in Britain by the equally tiny ISL, a member of the International Workers League – Fourth International, but it is difficult to discern the doctrinal issues that separate this Trotskyist family from others, notwithstanding the grand claims made for the theoretical insights of the Argentinian Trotskyist leader Nahuel Moreno and his search for 'a path leading to the masses' (Hernandez 2012; Moreno 2014).[62]

Socialist Voice, the irregular magazine of the ISL, has occasionally carried criticism of other Trotskyist groups but they have focused almost entirely on tactical and strategic issues, for example the Socialist Party's positive appraisal of Corbyn and its decision not to contest the 2017 general election (*Socialist Voice* Nos. 25 and 26, September/October 2016, February/March 2017) and the SWP's handling of rape allegations against one of its senior officials (*Socialist Voice* No. 9, March 2013). Like many other groups it retains a faith in its own capacity and its future that bears no relation to its own size (around a dozen members in the Liverpool area):

> no variant of the Labour Party will lead the fight for socialism. That's why the ISL, with dozens of other parties on different continents, is building the IWL-FI, the largest and most dynamic revolutionary organization in the world! Come and join us!'
>
> *(Socialist Voice June/July 2016)*

Leadership and doctrine

One of the common features of sects is the presence of a charismatic or 'transformational' leader who can inspire and motivate followers with a persuasive vision. The Trotskyist movement has certainly thrown up its share of charismatic leaders: Tariq Ali (IMG) was a powerful, charismatic personality although the IMG was never as dominated by a single personality as some of its rivals (Tate 2014: 236–37). Tony Cliff (IS/SWP) was a dedicated and effective organizer who devoted considerable time to one-on-one meetings with new recruits and was also a charismatic and inspiring speaker (Birchall 2011: 207 ff.; Hughes 2012: 180). Gerry Healy

(SLL/WRP) was possessed of a clear and implacable world view and was capable of inspiring extraordinary loyalty amongst his followers as well as being an 'energetic' and 'exceptional organizer' (Wohlforth 1994: 198; McIlroy 2005: 145) and an outstanding orator (Lotz and Feldman 1994: 1; Thornett 1987: 74–75).[63] Although nobody would describe Ted Grant as charismatic he did build an organization whose membership reached approximately 8,000 at its peak and he played a major role in the life of the Militant Tendency (Tourish and Wohlforth 2000: 174). According to Woods' admittedly uncritical biography:

> All the political ideas came from Ted Grant, and most of the organizational ideas came from the same source. Our successes were the result of Ted's political guidance. He wrote all the perspectives documents and theses on national and international questions. He led off in the political sessions of the central committees, conferences and congresses.
>
> *(Woods 2013a: 201–02)*

Leadership positions once acquired are often held for many years, a fact explained partly by the 'recommended list' method of election and partly by the loyalty of followers (Haslam et al. 2011). In this procedure conference delegates are invited each year to vote for a full slate of candidates composed by the outgoing national committee; they cannot cast separate votes for individual candidates. Intended as a means for ensuring an effective, representative and democratically elected leadership, the recommended list actually reproduces an oligarchy, a stable, ruling elite that is almost impossible to dislodge from power. The stability and cohesion of the ruling elite are strengthened through the fact that many are also full-time employees of the organization (Crick 2016: 124). These facts explain the extraordinary longevity of Trotskyist organizational leadership from the early 1950s to the present day. Given the domination of public life at that time by men, it also explains why most of these organizations are generally led by older, white men.[64] Gerry Healy (1913–1989) led the SLL/WRP for 38 years until his expulsion in 1985 and for much of that period was assisted by Mike Banda (1930–2014), his younger brother Tony and Cliff Slaughter (b. 1928, who joined the SLL in 1957). Tony Cliff (1917–2000) led the Socialist Review Group/IS/SWP, for almost 50 years until a few months before his death in April 2000. He was succeeded by Chris Harman (1942–2009), who had held leading positions in the party since the 1970s and he in turn was succeeded after his death by Alex Callinicos (b. 1950) and Charlie Kimber (b. 1957), who have both occupied leadership positions since the 1980s. Ted Grant (1913–2006) was the key figure in the Militant Tendency, leading the organization for 41 years, until his expulsion in 1991. Of the two successor organizations, the Socialist Party is led by Peter Taaffe (b. 1942), the first editor of *The Militant* newspaper whilst Socialist Appeal is led by Alan Woods (b. 1944) and Rob Sewell who first joined Militant in the 1960s and early 1970s respectively.

The striking dominance by elderly white males is also replicated in the smaller and older organizations on the Trotskyist left: AWL (Sean Matgamna b. 1941 and

Martin Thomas, active in the group from the early 1970s); the Communist League (Jonathan Silberman b. 1951); Socialist Action (John Ross, an IMG activist from the early 1970s); and Socialist Resistance (Alan Thornett b. 1937). The various fragments of the WRP still in existence also have leaders who are in their sixties or seventies and have long records of activity in their respective organizations including the ISL (Martin Ralph), Socialist Fight (Gerry Downing), Workers International to Rebuild the Fourth International (Bob Archer) and the WRP itself (Sheila Torrance). Many of these organizations also have younger members in leading positions: for example, Joseph Choonara (b. 1977) is a member of the SWP Executive Committee and Hannah Sell (b. 1971) is the Deputy General Secretary of the Socialist Party, but nonetheless the rise of younger activists into positions of leadership has done little to disturb oligarchic rule.

One further element reinforcing leadership power and authority is the principle of 'democratic centralism', according to which an organization combines free debate and discussion on policy but then acts as a unified and centralized force once policy has been determined. In practice this seemingly innocuous combination is corroded by the fact that members of Trotskyist oligarchies will typically play a leading role in structuring debates through the submission of conference resolutions and perspectives documents, a practice that limits the scope for radical debate and increases the likelihood of criticism being framed as disloyalty to the long-serving leadership.

Membership education and control

An additional mechanism in the reproduction of doctrine in Trotskyist organizations, as in any sect, comprises the systems designed to create loyal followers, namely membership probation, education and control, all of which are far more extensive than in mainstream political parties. New Trotskyist recruits typically agree to comply with a series of far-reaching demands including attendance at branch meetings, participation in group activities and financial contributions:

> [M]embers are prepared to be active in carrying out the policies of the Group, and attend its meetings. We do not accept inactive members . . . members are prepared to make a regular financial contribution to the group, to indicate the level of their commitment.
>
> *(IMG 1971/72)*[65]

> Any person who accepts the programme, policy and constitution of the Party, agrees to work under the direction of its national bodies and of the appropriate local organisation and pays financial subscriptions, is eligible for membership.
>
> *(WRP 1981)*[66]

> The members of the AWL . . . are those who: Defend the basic aims of the AWL, in words and deeds; Engage in regular political activity under the discipline of the organisation; Are members of their appropriate trade union;

> Sell the literature of the AWL regularly; Pay regular money contributions
> to the AWL . . . Are loyal to the AWL at all times, and keep their links
> with other political groups under the supervision of the appropriate AWL
> committees; Educate themselves politically and attend structured education
> classes of the AWL (2016).[67]

Education is also a mechanism for increasing the commitment and effectiveness of
members as they engage in a variety of activities to promote and strengthen their
particular Trotskyist group. From its formation in 1971, Workers Fight (now the
AWL) insisted on a probationary period of membership during which new members
were required to make regular verbal reports to their cell (branch). In addition each
new member was assigned a mentor who would guide them through the group's
basic Marxist education programme.[68] The current AWL basic reading list for probationer members comprises the following items: Marx and Engels' *Communist
Manifesto*, Marx' *Wage Labour and Capital*, *Wages, Price, and Profit* and *Theses on
Feuerbach*, Engels' *Socialism Utopian and Scientific*, Lenin's *State and Revolution* and
Left-Wing Communism, Trotsky's *Revolution Betrayed* as well as four additional AWL
texts.[69] The IMG's New Members' Reading List in 1977 comprised 12 topics each
with essential and further readings and questions for discussion. The essential readings alone ran to nine pamphlets, two books and twenty book chapters.[70] The
Spartacist League also organizes an extensive education programme because, 'Our
purpose is to recruit and educate and train people who aspire to be lifetime cadres in
a revolutionary organization' (Len Michelson and Mick Connor interview).

The WRP education programme for new members stressed the importance
of Marxist method, dialectical materialism, and in the late 1970s comprised nine
pamphlets as well as attendance at a series of six lectures.[71] By 1981 the party was
trying to insist that all new members should register for a one-week training course
in Marxist theory at the party's College of Marxist Education in Derbyshire, an
impossible goal once membership began to grow quickly in the early 1980s.[72]
Two years earlier it had been decided that *all* congress delegates commit to a
one-week training course at the party's college (and approximately 80 delegates
duly complied including leading figures such as Bob Archer, Tony Banda, Gerry
Downing, Paul Feldman, Corinna Lotz and Dave Temple).[73] So keen was the
party's authoritarian leader Gerry Healy on dialectics that he instructed all members of the Political Committee to attend his weekly lectures on the subject and in
1980 obliged them to write a several hundred-word essay on three questions about
dialectics. It is indicative of his authority that almost all members of the PC duly
completed their 'homework', including Corin and Vanessa Redgrave.[74]

New recruits to the Militant Tendency would be engaged in lengthy political discussion over a period of months before a decision was made on whether to
introduce them to the Tendency's secret organization, the RSL.[75] Workers Power
operates a six-month probation period and then requires a decision on membership
by a vote of branch members (George Binette interview). In 2006 the organization expelled 25 members, over 40 per cent of its total, and the demographics of

the expellees underline the stability of this small group. Their tenure in Workers Power varied between two years and 31 years with a median figure of 20 years suggesting that stringent entry requirements may lead to high levels of membership commitment but low levels of recruitment and turnover.[76]

Small organizations with scarce resources have often sought to maximize their impact by redeploying members from one part of the country to another, treating them, in effect, as employees or conscripts, rather than volunteers, and the willingness of members to accept these demands is *prima facie* evidence of their commitment to the organization. In 1972 the IMG redeployed eight of its members to Liverpool in order to start up a branch in the city;[77] in 1980 the I-CL instructed one of its key members to remain in Coventry;[78] and in 1982 the WRP dispatched one of its activists to work in Scotland.[79] Decisions about holidays may also be subject to organizational control so in 1972 and 1975 for example the national committee of Workers Fight (now AWL) ruled on holiday times for several of its members and in 1981 Corin Redgrave formally wrote to the WRP General Secretary requesting a month's leave of absence to perform in a play.[80] In such cases it is clear that members accepted the legitimacy of a degree of organizational control over their personal lives. As an AWL leader wrote to a member in 1990, 'You can ask for a leave of absence, but you can't declare it unilaterally',[81] and the IMG took a similar view in the early 1970s.[82]

Rules on membership activity do appear to be regularly enforced, both against individuals and, in the case of factions, against groups of members. In Workers Power, a member whose activity level was declining, 'would be contacted by Branch organisers . . . sometimes it would just be a question of a quiet word, is it a political issue, is it a personal problem, would you like some time off?' (George Binette interview).

If informal approaches fail, then formal sanctions are deployed. The AWL and its predecessor organizations reprimanded and disciplined individual members for a variety of offences including refusal to attend a picket of Downing Street (1972), failing to attend a National Rally without adequate excuse (1981), moving overseas without the permission of the organization (1982), failing to attend NUS conference (2004) and refusal to attend annual Summer School (2006).[83] Membership sanctions are most apparent in the most doctrinaire organizations, such as the Orthodox WRP. Members of its Political Committee were often criticized by its leader Gerry Healy for a variety of philosophical and political 'deviations' and required to write and submit letters of recantation to the next PC meeting. One leading member (still active in the WRP) wrote in 1981 of her 'subjective idealism' and her 'mistakes that weakened the leadership and the Party' but pledged 'to analyse my weaknesses and overcome them'.[84] The following year another senior member apologized for 'the hollowness of my contribution' at a recent PC whilst a leading actor criticized his 'individualism' and his 'anti-Marxist approach'.[85]

Occasionally more severe penalties have been levied. An I-CL activist was suspended in 1979 for becoming too close to members of a rival organization, a pattern of behaviour that exposed him to alien and heretical views: 'The charge is:

relations with the Spartacist League not under the control of the leading committees of the organisation, contrary to section 5(xiii) of the constitution'.[86] Serious
offences can lead to expulsion as in the case of a WSL car worker who decided
in 1981 to accept voluntary redundancy, contrary to the policy of the organization, and was promptly expelled.[87] In another case a leading member of the
I-CL announced his resignation for 'personal reasons'. The decision to prioritize
personal life over political obligations so outraged the organization's leaders that
they voted to reject his letter of resignation and then promptly expelled him 'on
grounds of irresponsible behaviour'.[88] Sanctions of any kind are rare in Trotskyist
organizations but as in organizations more generally, their role is to clarify and
reinforce acceptable (and unacceptable) forms of behaviour.

Despite high levels of membership activity and commitment, one of the staple
and recurrent themes in leadership discussions is discontent with the membership
and the state of the organization. According to leaders of Workers Fight and its
successors, the organization was 'flabby' (1973), 'Labour Party work is in a bad
state' (1987), the union fractions 'perform very badly when it comes to recruiting' (1995) and 'branches are pretty sluggish' (2004).[89] Militant Tendency leaders
declared that branches need to 'throw off a routine approach' because they are 'just
not shaping up to meet the targets' (1975).[90] Similar complaints were made by the
WRP's Gerry Healy as he railed against 'routinism in branch work' (1963), even
though his organization was the largest on the Trotskyist left and was growing
quickly (from around 150 members in 1956 to almost 1,000 in 1963).[91] A report
on the WRP produced by the anti-Healy group shortly after the 1985 split found
that 'Most branches consisted of small groups of cadres and activists and the rest of
the members were inactive and uninvolved'.[92]

The biographies of the three major post-war leaders of British Trotskyism –
Cliff (IS/SWP), Grant (Militant Tendency/Socialist Appeal) and Healy (SLL/
WRP) – show that all three were absolutely single-minded and had practically no
life outside revolutionary politics (Birchall 2011; Woods 2013a; Lotz and Feldman
1994). Many members, in contrast, have demanding jobs, families and hobbies,
so that they are in effect part-time revolutionaries. These different life situations
generate a characteristic and predictable impatience on the part of Trotskyist leaderships with the perceived inadequacies of their memberships.

The dark side of charismatic leadership

Whilst high levels of membership commitment are clearly a positive feature
of Trotskyist groups, their structure, patterns of leadership and rootedness in
doctrine combine to produce authoritarian and hierarchical organizations that
generate a series of dysfunctional consequences. In the first place there is a tendency towards the creation of a leadership cult, in which the charismatic figure
at the head of the organization is imbued by the membership with extraordinary
powers, intellectual, organizational or both. In the case of the SLL/WRP, the
transformation of The Group into the SLL, the decision to quit the Labour Party,

the launch of the daily paper, the creation of the WRP, the link to Gaddafi and the underlying perspective of imminent revolution or fascism: all emanated from Gerry Healy. In the case of the IS/SWP, Cliff enjoyed extraordinary pre-eminence and was enormously influential in a range of key decisions, such as the adoption of a Leninist model of organization, the launch of the rank and file movement and the analysis of the 'downturn'. That said, he was occasionally challenged in the organization and did not always secure majority support for his views (Birchall 2011). Ted Grant was an even more dominant figure in the Militant Tendency and in the case of the SEP, it is the leader of its International Committee, David North, who has established himself as the organization's principal authority on matters of doctrine and whose many publications feature prominently in its publications catalogue. North is based in America and so too is another charismatic and increasingly authoritarian leader, Jack Barnes, National Secretary of the SWP since 1972 (its British affiliate is the tiny Communist League) (Sheppard 2012: 322–23).

The corollary of unwavering belief in the leader – by himself and his followers – is an intolerance of dissent and although this can be found in a variety of political parties, including the Labour Party with its expulsion of Militant Tendency members in the 1980s, it is a hallmark of Trotskyist organizations.[93] In theory many organizations formally permit dissenting members to organize and promote their views as minorities (for example RSL, WRP) or as factions (AWL, IMG, SWP, Spartacist League), but it is clear from the high incidence of group expulsions that Trotskyist leaderships tend to have a jaundiced view of factions. Healy had a long record of expulsions from his own organization which were always marked by an absence of debate and a refusal to learn from, or engage with his critics: the Grant and Cliff groups were expelled in 1950, the Cadogan group in 1959, Behan and his supporters in 1960, the WSL and the Socialist Labour Group in 1974 and the Workers' Party in 1979 (Pitt 2002). Ironically Healy himself was then expelled from the WRP in 1985 and just one year later split from his own supporters in the WRP (News Line). The IS/SWP expelled no less than five factions between 1971 and 1981 (see Table 3.3).

Organizations that exercise tight control over recruitment, induction and probation are likely to be ideologically more homogeneous than more open groups and consequently expulsions are rare, but are not unknown: the WSL expelled Alan Thornett and his supporters in 1984 and Workers Power expelled the Permanent Revolution group in 2006. Militant Tendency is somewhat unusual in having combined stable leadership, a low level of internal debate and mass recruitment but without factions or expulsions for many years. Nonetheless even Militant eventually succumbed to a major schism when founder Ted Grant and his followers were expelled in 1991 and the Socialist Party subsequently expelled several factions, in the 1990s and in 2014 (Marxist World) (Hearse 2000). Not surprisingly the absence of a powerful, charismatic leader coupled with greater tolerance for factions has generally been accompanied by fewer expulsions, as demonstrated by the IMG, which expelled only one organization during the 'Golden Age', the Revolutionary Communist League in 1969.

Another dysfunctional consequence of the pattern of leadership in Trotskyist organizations is aggressive behaviour by leaders towards those beneath them in the hierarchy, particularly where the leader in question has an abrasive and authoritarian personality. Gerry Healy was described as 'a very hard and aggressive man' (McShane and Smith 1978: 251) by those who knew him and reports of physical violence meted out on Healy's instructions are legion. Robin Blick, Stuart Carter, Dot Gibson, Aileen Jennings, Mark Jenkins, Tony Richardson and Ernest Tate (a member of the International Group) all suffered violent, physical assaults for challenging Healy (Harding 2005: 219–20; Pirani 2013; Tate 2014: 173–74; Thornett 1979: 94; Tourish and Wohlforth 2000: 165–67; Wohlforth 1994: 229–30; Clare Cowen interview). Healy was also guilty of sexual violence, an issue raised on several occasions throughout his life but exposed in June 1985 in a letter from his long-serving PA Aileen Jennings (see Chapter 4) and corroborated by others including Kate Blakeney, a West of England WRP organizer (Wohlforth 1994: 265–66). Symptomatic of the cult of loyalty to Healy, and of the moral degeneracy that afflicted the WRP, was the infamous comment by Corin Redgrave at a WRP meeting in Scotland. After listing Healy's many achievements, he proclaimed 'If this is the work of a rapist, let's recruit more rapists' (Pirani 2013).[94]

Sexual harassment is not, however, unique to the WRP because the conditions in which it flourished there – organizational hierarchy, a male-dominated leadership and women comprising a minority of the organization – are also found in other Trotskyist groups (McDonald 2012). In 2012 the SWP was rocked by an allegation of rape against one of its senior officials and as sometimes happens when one incident is reported, other women then felt emboldened to come forward with their own complaints.[95] Allegations have also been reported against at least one other senior member of the SWP dating back to the 1970s and 1980s (Anindya Bhattacharyya interview). The Spartacist League expelled one of its founder members, Bill Logan, in 1979 for sexual abuse (International Communist League (Fourth Internationalist) 1995). In 1983 the WSL Organizing Committee held a long and inconclusive discussion about how it should deal with an allegation of rape by one member against another whilst in 1999 the same organization (now the AWL) excluded a member from its London Tube fraction for one year because of his sexist behavior.[96] In the late 1970s the IMG dealt with two complaints of sexual harassment against one of its members but astonishingly decided 'these are not matters for discipline but for discussion in the branch about norms of behaviour'.[97] Finally in 2013 Socialist Party member and RMT Assistant General Secretary Steve Hedley faced charges of domestic violence, brought by his former partner, although both the police and the RMT decided not to proceed with the case.[98]

Bullying, violence and sexual harassment are widespread across many organizations and it is perhaps naïve to think that Trotskyist organizations can insulate themselves from the arrogant and misogynistic attitudes that underpin such behaviours. On the other hand Trotskyist organizations claim to have views about women's emancipation, freedom and equality which imply that their own standards of behaviour should be significantly higher than prevailing social norms.

The lessons of 1917

The centenary of the Russian Revolution has provided an ideal opportunity for Trotskyist organizations to reflect on the lessons of that monumental event and to consider its implications for contemporary socialist strategy. The publications issued to date (June 2017) suggest that the weight of core Trotskyist doctrine, crystallized over decades of ideological struggle, is overwhelming the capacity of most Trotskyist organizations to learn useful lessons from those distant events. In the case of Orthodox Trotskyist groups such as the WRP and the SEP, this is hardly surprising. Each bi-monthly issue of the WRP's journal *Marxist Review* is carrying an article on the events of 1917 that is descriptive, uncritical and based on extensive quotation from Lenin and Trotsky, aiming to show that 'The lessons of Lenin's struggle in 1917 are invaluable for the world working class' (Wiltshire 1995: 73). The SEP is providing two online lecture series, in March–May and September–November, that will aim to prove that Trotsky's theory of permanent revolution, Lenin's theory of the vanguard party and Trotsky's stress on revolutionary leadership are all correct and still relevant for today.[99]

Of the Third Camp Trotskyist groups, the SWP, Counterfire and the AWL are all promoting books by their respective members (Sherry 2017; Faulkner 2017; Vernadsky 2017). Despite the quantity and quality of the underlying research, they are conventional accounts which largely echo the arguments of Trotsky on permanent revolution and Lenin and Trotsky on the key leadership role of the revolutionary vanguard party. Bolshevik policy is largely exonerated by claiming it comprised measures that were both necessary and unavoidable, however tragic: the dispersal of the Constituent Assembly, the creation of the Cheka with its wide-ranging powers, the banning of all rival parties, the suppression of the Kronstadt rebellion and the ban on party factions all fall into this category.[100] In the late 1920s Russia succumbed to counter-revolution, a process generated by its isolation and war-induced devastation, but not, it seems, by serious mistakes in Bolshevik policy. Consequently all three volumes end with a similar upbeat message: 'The Bolsheviks have much to teach us' (Faulkner 2017: 253; and see also Choonara and Kimber 2011; Cliff 1990; Rees 1991).[101]

The Institutional Trotskyists in the Socialist Party and Socialist Appeal have been equally uncritical in their dedicated websites and publications.[102] On the ninetieth anniversary a Socialist Party pamphlet sought to rebut many of the criticisms raised by Figes (1996), concluding, 'The Bolshevik Party of Lenin and Trotsky in the Russian Revolution was separated by a river of blood from Stalinism. It was the most democratic party in history . . . Stalinism did not arise from Bolshevism' (Taaffe and Sell 2007: 39). Socialist Appeal's Rob Sewell noted that 2017 'is not merely a historical celebration but a preparation for new Octobers' (2017b: 3; and see also Woods 1999) whilst Grant's (1997) history of Russia, from 1917 to the early 1990s, is a wholly conventional and uncritical account.

In contrast, the Mainstream group Socialist Resistance re-issued a collection of essays including Mandel's (2016) thoughtful re-appraisal of the Russian Revolution and Le Blanc's (2016) reflective review of contemporary Marxist and non-Marxist literature on 1917. Unlike the majority of Trotskyists, Mandel (2016) was prepared to criticize the banning of non-Bolshevik parties, the ban on factions and the extraordinary powers granted to the Cheka as strategic choices that were both erroneous and avoidable. Moreover they were rooted not only in the isolation and poverty of Russia but in a particular conception of socialist democracy which downplayed the role of independent working-class organs and institutions. This was not a new theme in Mainstream literature but dates back to the 1970s and the United Secretariat's insistence on the need to rethink the concept of socialist democracy and reassert its value (United Secretariat of the Fourth International 1977; and see Ali 1978 for a similar viewpoint).

Conclusions

The core beliefs shared by almost all Trotskyist groups date back to the 1920s and 1930s and embody a set of ideas laid down by Trotsky including the theory of permanent revolution, the tactic of the united front and the vital leadership role of the revolutionary vanguard party. Both their longevity and their repeated defence against critics have confirmed their status as doctrine. For the Orthodox family, Trotskyist doctrine remains as relevant today as it was almost a century ago and a key role of the revolutionary party is therefore to defend orthodoxy against all forms of revisionism and deviation. The most striking corollary of orthodoxy is sectarianism, an intense hostility and antagonism towards other organizations, above all those belonging to rival Trotskyist families.[103] Within this world view, the most telling criticism of a rival group is not that its policies or practices are ineffective or unpopular but that they constitute a major deviation from orthodoxy. We also established that Trotskyist families which have openly abandoned one or other element of core Trotskyist doctrine do not necessarily become any more open-minded as a result. The Institutional Trotskyist groups led by Ted Grant (the Militant Tendency and Socialist Appeal) and the AWL and its predecessors have displayed levels of doctrinairism and hostility towards rival organizations that are strikingly similar to those displayed by guardians of orthodoxy such as the WRP.

Doctrinal disputes between Trotskyist organizations clearly run along family lines so that Orthodox and Radical Trotskyist groups have frequently attacked their Institutional, Mainstream and Third Camp rivals and vice versa. Yet there are also disputes *within* families so for example different organizations have quarrelled about how best to defend Orthodox Trotskyism. For the Spartacist League, the key requirement is a revolutionary programme; for the SEP it is the existence of a powerful International organization that can suppress nationalist tendencies; for Socialist Fight it is the adoption of a consistent anti-imperialist policy. Within Third Camp Trotskyism the AWL's widely derided policies on Israel/Palestine and Northern Ireland are clearly distinct from those of its Third Camp rival the

SWP, but are still rooted in the heterodox world view that gave rise to the theory of state capitalism.

A strong attachment to doctrine is intimately connected to a particular style of leadership and reinforced by leadership stability. Some major Trotskyist organizations were led for decades by strong charismatic leaders such as Cliff and Healy. The positive face of charismatic leadership is the high degree of loyalty generated amongst the membership, reinforced by systems of membership probation and education. Yet the downside is equally apparent: authoritarian rule, centralized control and occasional acts of sexual and physical violence. Trotskyist leaders stand at the apex of a stable oligarchy that is regularly returned to office through the recommended list system of election and which in the name of democratic centralism exercises enormous influence in the strategic direction and policies of the organization. Such entrenched leaderships are not conducive to theoretical or ideological innovation and generally reproduce the doctrine that is the hallmark of their particular organization, a tendency apparent in the uncritical publications marking the centenary of the Russian Revolution.

Notes

1 In the other domain marked by the saliency of doctrine, namely religion, the Christian Church has also evolved competing ideas about core doctrine. These have crystallized over many centuries into competing families, or churches, such as Catholicism, Protestantism, Congregationalism, Methodism, Presbyterianism, etc. (Barrett 1996).
2 Similar tendencies can be found in the Communist movement under Stalin as he sought to claim an unwavering link between contemporary policy and the views of Lenin whilst claiming at the same time that 'Trotskyism' had evolved from a dissident strand of the communist movement into a counter-revolutionary doctrine (McIlroy 2006).
3 Workers Revolutionary Party Constitution 1981, WRP Papers, Box 177.
4 During a brief period, 1958–1959, when the SLL was operating as a relatively open group with a relatively open journal it offered unity talks to the Socialist Review Group. They came to nothing once Healy made clear his journal would not publish an article by Tony Cliff setting out his state capitalist analysis of the USSR (Birchall 2011: 172).
5 Karen Blick Obituary, *Revolutionary History*, 5(4), 1995. Trotskyist groups have also infiltrated spies into the Communist Party: the RCP did so in the 1940s and the SLL in the 1960s (Redfern 2014: 346–47, 352).
6 Draft Resolution on Political Perspectives from the SLL Central Committee 12 April 1968 to 10th National Conference 1–3 June 1968, Richardson/Higgins Papers, Box 124, File 5.
7 'Workers Revolutionary Party 12th Congress July 1990 British Perspectives', *Marxist Review*, 5(8), September 1990, p. 16 and see also Banda (1975: viii) for a similar view.
8 See also SLL Political Letter, 23 November 1965, SLL Internal Bulletin, Alan Clinton Papers, Warwick, File MSS.539/1/1.
9 A few years earlier the SLL had declined to participate in the large 1968 anti-Vietnam war march on the grounds that it was 'a diversion from the role of Marxist theory and the building of the revolutionary party' led by 'phonies' and 'nondescript leaders whose record of struggle on behalf of the working class . . . is nil'. Leaflet issued by the SLL Political Committee, Why the Socialist Labour League Is Not Marching, 25 October 1968, Will Fancy Papers, Box 22/8.

10 Few other Trotskyist groups or writers have devoted as much attention to philosophy although the SWP's John Molyneux sought to defend dialectics with the illogical claim that because dialectics is based on the idea of constant change 'therefore capitalism is doomed to perish' (2012: 197).

11 SEP Russian Revolution Centenary Fund, http://socialequality.org.uk/donate/, accessed 2 May 2017.

12 Declaration of Principles and Some Elements of Program 1998, http://icl-fi.org/english/icldop/index.html, accessed 14 March 2017. Almost identical wording can be found in the 1986 founding statement of an equally orthodox breakaway from the Spartacists, the International Bolshevik Tendency: see 'Introducing *1917*: The Necessity of Revolutionary Organization', *1917* No. 1 Winter 1986.

13 In addition to the 12 Bulletins, see also Anonymous (1985) on the WRP, ICL (1994) on the Militant Tendency and ICL's 1990 pamphlet on Latin American Trotskyism, *Moreno Truth Kit*. The other organization that has matched the Spartacist League in its assiduous determination to expose deviations from Trotskyism is Socialist Fight. Its magazine *In Defence of Trotskyism* has attacked the Spartacist League and the International Bolshevik Tendency (Nos. 1 and 6), the Revolutionary Communist International Tendency (No. 9), the Socialist Party and Socialist Appeal (No. 8) and Workers Power (Nos. 3 and 7).

14 Leaflet, Joe Hansen is an Honest Revisionist, 14 January 1977, Spartacist League Papers, Warwick, File MSS 275/MISC 2.

15 The Mainstream organization Socialist Action as well as Counterfire and the SWP have all strenuously opposed Western intervention in the Middle East on the grounds that it is 'objectively counter-revolutionary' (Socialist Action 2013: 35).

16 Although the group's membership never reached four figures, and has hovered below 100 for the past 12 years (see Chapters 3 and 4), group leaders have often cited its affiliation with the Mainstream Fourth International as one of its defining and distinctive features. The IMG 'New Member's Introduction and Education Kit' (n.d. – probably 1977–1978) claimed that 'over 80 per cent of the world's Trotskyists are in the USFI', IMG Papers, Warwick, File 68. The following year IMG leading activist Phil Hearse asserted that 'Today, no one seriously disputes that the USFI *is* the Fourth International' (1978: 19). Publications by International figures such as Ernest Mandel and Pierre Frank have frequently been used and cited by Socialist Resistance and its predecessors and will therefore be cited here.

17 Constitution of IMG Adopted at 1971 Conference, IMG Papers, Warwick, File 103.

18 IMG Constitution 1978, IMG Papers, LSE, File 262. The successor organization, the International Group, adopted a very similar constitution: Constitution of the International Group, Dani Ahrens Papers, File 401/1/9/2.

19 International Socialism Group, National Mailing Trade Union edition, February 1988, Dani Ahrens Papers, File 401/3/5; ISG, Central Committee Minutes 26–27 May 1990 and 14 July 1990, Dani Ahrens Papers, File 401/1/1/3.

20 International Group Circular, 28 February 1962, Chris Arthur Papers, File 711/A/5/1; Relations with Trotskyist Organisations, or Groups Claiming to Be Trotskyist, Which Are Outside of the Fourth International, IMG International Internal Discussion Bulletin, 13(5), November 1976, Richardson/Higgins Papers, Box 94; An Open Letter to Comrades of the SWP 1978, IMG Papers, Warwick, File 169.

21 International Group National Mailing No. 14, 2 July 1986, Dani Ahrens Papers, File 401/3/4; ISG Student Perspectives 1989, Dani Ahrens Papers, File 401/1/1/3.

22 British Perspectives, ISG Central Committee Minutes, 8/9 July 1989, Dani Ahrens Papers, File 401/1/1/3.

23 Leaflet for 1980 IMG cadre school, IMG Papers, Warwick, File 217.

24 Compare Mandel's more equivocal assessment in his earlier study of Trotsky (1979: 61–62) and on his dogmatism see Bensaid (2013: 260).

25 IS, National Committee Minutes, 22 August 1970, Colin Barker Papers, File 152/1/1/4.

26 IMG, National Committee Minutes, 25/26 January 1973, Bob Purdie Papers, File 57; IMG, Political Committee Minutes, 5 February 1976, IMG Papers, Warwick, File 109; Balance Sheet of the IMG/SC Discussion on the FI, 1976, IMG Papers, Warwick, File 244; Proposals on Unity from the International Marxist Group to the Workers League, 7 March 1977, Chris Bambery Papers, File 1/5.

27 Founding Statement of the International Socialist Alliance, 17–18 June 1978, IMG Papers, File 55; Big Flame, Socialist Unity: A Critical Assessment, National Committee Meeting, July 1979, IMG Papers, Warwick, File 197; IMG, An Open Letter to Comrades of the SWP, IMG Papers, Warwick, Files 169 and 127.

28 International Group, Central Committee Minutes, 13–15 February 1987, Dani Ahrens Papers, File 1/1/1/. The WRP (Workers Press) led by Cliff Slaughter was also involved in discussions with the International and Socialist Groups but withdrew long before they came to fruition: International Group, National Mailing No. 20, October 1986, Dani Ahrens Papers, File 401/3/4.

29 Material on ACI can be found on their dormant website http://anticapitalists.org/, accessed 20 March 2017. The three regroupment conference bulletins can be found on the CPGB website: http://cpgb.org.uk/pages/news/76/regroupment-conference-april-26-bulletin-no-1/; http://cpgb.org.uk/pages/news/73/regroupment-conference-bulletins-2-3/, accessed 20 March 2017.

30 Birchall (2011: 273) denies any inconsistency by claiming (unconvincingly) the two wars were 'quite different'.

31 It is also interesting to note that Kidron (1977) himself later repudiated his own theory.

32 The SWP's Sally Campbell plays down Luxemburg's disagreements with Lenin and her criticisms of Bolshevik policy (2011: 20, 48–50).

33 In 2003 Alex Callinicos wrote a book entitled 'An Anti-Capitalist Manifesto' whose final chapter contained an 11-point 'Transitional Programme'. It was offered to the movement for discussion but few of its demands have made their way into introductory pamphlets on the SWP.

34 In 1966, when its membership numbered just 300, the IS was not quite so hostile to union officials because it invited leading CPGB member and engineering union official Reg Birch to write a Preface to its pamphlet on incomes policy (Cliff and Barker 1966).

35 See for instance Workers Power: Dewar, J. (2013) 'SWP Line in Unite the Resistance: Carry on Regardless', www.workerspower.co.uk/2013/01/swp-line-in-unite-the-resistance-carry-on-regardless/, accessed 10 March 2016.

36 Older SWP publications have laid out almost identical positions and policies, for example Foot (1990).

37 IS, Executive Committee Minutes, 19 December 1968, Colin Barker Papers, File 152/1//4; IS, Interim Political Report, October 1972, pp. 8–9, Colin Barker Papers, File 152/1/1/6; The Militant Grouping and the Labour Left, SWP Internal Bulletin June 1980, Nigel Clark Papers, File 489/10.

38 I wrote on one occasion for *International Socialism*, a reply in No. 42, Spring 1989 to a critical review of my book *Trade Unions and Socialist Politics* (1988) and also spoke at the SWP Marxism event on the same issue.

39 The IMG is more complex because although it was equally ineffectual in attracting significant numbers of academics or intellectuals in the UK – Norman Geras and Peter Gowan were amongst the few exceptions – its work was heavily influenced by the successful Belgian academic and Trotskyist Ernest Mandel. He was the author of numerous books including *The Formation of the Economic Thought of Karl Marx* (1971), *Late Capitalism* (1975a), *From Class Society to Communism* (1977b), *Trotsky* (1979) and *The Second Slump* (1980) and both these and other titles were translated into 40 languages (Stutje 2009: ix). Mandel's books comprised core elements in the IMG member education programme: IMG New Member's Introduction and Education Kit, n.d. – probably

1977–1978, IMG Papers, Warwick, File 68. Of the other Trotskyist groups, the sociologist Bob Fine was a member of Socialist Organiser and the journalist Paul Mason belonged to Workers Power (Common Cause 1985: 23).

40 There is the occasional discussion on the Counterfire website but with no linkage to contemporary political interventions, for example www.counterfire.org/articles/book-reviews/16301-in-defence-of-permanent-revolution, accessed 10 March 2017.

41 Many of these points can also be found in the Counterfire Constitution www.counterfire.org/constitution, accessed 10 March 2017.

42 AWL's leading figure, Sean Matgamna, has enjoyed a chequered political career. He first became active in the Militant Tendency, which he quit in 1966 to form Workers Fight. He and his group then joined the International Socialists in 1968, were expelled in 1971, fused with Workers Power in 1975, split apart in 1976 then fused with Alan Thornett's Workers Socialist League in 1981 only to split in 1984.

43 'Why We Joined I.S.', *Workers Fight*, 1(2), April 1969, Chris Arthur Papers, File 711/C/1/69.

44 See also '10 Reasons You Should Join Workers' Liberty', 2009, www.workersliberty.org/ten, accessed 13 March 2017.

45 AWL, Executive Committee Minutes 26 April 1993, AWL Papers, File AWL/1/32.

46 '10 Reasons You Should Join Workers' Liberty', 2009, www.workersliberty.org/ten, accessed 13 March 2017. These critical positions have led more orthodox Trotskyists to accuse the AWL of the heresy of 'social imperialism', for example *Socialist Fight* No. 1 Winter/Spring 2009, p. 6, No. 6, Spring/Summer 2011, p. 24.

47 Like its parent organization, the IS/SWP, the AWL has devoted relatively little time or energy to international discussion and organization (but see Chapter 11).

48 Matgamna, S. and Thomas, M., 'Workers Fight, The Left and the Crisis', October 1972, Chris Arthur Papers, File 711/C/4/28.

49 Founding of the I-CL, I-CL National Committee Minutes, 15 December 1975, AWL Papers, File AWL/1/4.

50 WSL, National Committee Minutes, 18–19 June 1983, AWL Papers, File AWL/1/17. And for a similarly-themed 1997 document see Fifth AWL Conference 29–30 November 1997, AWL Papers, File AWL/1/34/2. Sometimes the AWL referred to the 'kitsch-Trotskyism' of groups such as Workers Power: see 'Workers Power: Lessons for the Revolutionary Left', http://archive.workersliberty.org/publications/readings/trots/power.html, accessed 24 March 2017.

51 AWL, National Committee Minutes, 19 May 2011, AWL Papers, File AWL/1/43.

52 AWL, Report on Socialist Alliance, June 2003, AWL Papers, File AWL/1/45/3; AWL, Executive Committee Minutes, 11 March 2005, AWL Papers, File AWL1/47/1.

53 Proposal on Unions Fightback, AWL Executive Committee Minutes, 9 March 2001 and 20 March 2001, AWL Papers, File AWL/1/43. On the Welfare State Network see AWL, National Committee Minutes, 22 April 1995, AWL Papers, File AWL/1/41/1.

54 I-CL, National Committee Minutes, 9 May 1976, AWL Papers, File AWL/1/5; '10 Reasons You Should Join Workers' Liberty', 2009, www.workersliberty.org/ten, accessed 13 March 2017.

55 R.S.L. Constitution, Socialist Party Papers, File 601/C/1/1.

56 Grant had always been prone to apocalyptic prediction, writing as early as 1942 that 'Our untrained and untested organization [Workers International League] will, within a few years at most, be hurled into the turmoil of the revolution' (Grant 1989d: 56).

57 Militant Tendency, Internal Bulletin June 1973, p. 1, Socialist Party Papers, File 601/C/5/1/4.

58 See also Pickard (1989: xiii); Woods (1997: 38); Militant Tendency, World Perspectives Draft 1984, Socialist Party Papers, File 601/C/2/2/4.

59 Committee for a Workers International Bulletin No. 2, January 1975, AWL Papers, File 12/8.

60 Militant Tendency, Internal Bulletin July 1977, Socialist Party Papers, File 601/C/2/2/4; Internal Bulletin May 1976, Internal Bulletin September 1977 and Internal Bulletin March/April 1976 all in Socialist Party Papers, File 601C/5/1/6.

61 Some in Workers Power held a similar view, arguing that 'revolutionary socialism is . . . the application of science to politics and economics' (Workers Power interview).

62 Moreno fell out with the Mainstream Fourth International over tactical issues in the Nicaraguan revolution and created his own organization, the IWL-FI, in 1982. After his death in 1987 the organization succumbed to the normal fate of such bodies in the absence of a domineering, charismatic leader, and became locked in factional disputes (Sagra 2011: 12) (Chapter 11).

63 I have heard all three speak at public meetings and I'm happy to concur with this judgement.

64 Tariq Ali (IMG), Mike and Tony Banda (WRP) and Weyman Bennett (SWP) are the few exceptions to white Caucasian domination.

65 Lancaster IMG, What is the IMG?, n.d. – probably late 1971/early 1972, IMG Papers, Warwick, File 92.

66 Workers Revolutionary Party Constitution 1981, WRP Papers, Box 177.

67 The Alliance for Workers Liberty: Our Constitution, www.workersliberty.org/story/2006/04/15/join-awl#j4, accessed 18 August 2016. Workers Power has a similar set of requirements (George Binette interview 11 April 2014).

68 National Committee Minutes, 12 December 1971, AWL Papers, File AWL/1/1.

69 www.workersliberty.org/first6monthsreading, accessed 17 August 2016 and for details of required reading in the 1970s see: Notes on Reorganisation: Proposed Minimum Reading List for Members, n.d. – probably 1976, AWL Papers, File AWL/1/6 Pt 2.

70 IMG, New Members' Introduction and Education Kit, n.d. – probably 1977, IMG Papers, Warwick, File 68.

71 New Members' Course, n.d. – probably late 1970s, WRP Papers, Box 46.

72 National Recruitment Campaign, 26 February 1981, WRP Papers, Box 327.

73 WRP, College of Marxist Education, 1979, WRP Papers, Box 716.

74 WRP, Minutes of the Political Committee, 26 January 1985, WRP Papers, Box 244.

75 Organisation Report, Internal Bulletin July 1975, Socialist Party Papers, File 601/C/5/1/6.

76 The Split in the League for the Fifth International, May 2007, file:///F:/Trot. Workers%20Power/Permanent%20Revolution%20-%20The%20Split%20in%20the%20League%20for%20the%20Fifth%20International.htm, accessed 10 July 2016.

77 Workers Fight, Steering Committee Minutes, 28 August 1972, AWL Papers, File AWL/1/1.

78 I-CL, Steering Committee Minutes, 26 January 1980, AWL Papers, File AWL/1/9.

79 WRP, Minutes of Political Committee, 27 June 1982, WRP Papers, Box 660.

80 Workers Fight, Steering Committee Minutes, 13 August 1972, AWL Papers, File AWL/1/1; Workers Fight, Secretariat Minutes, 9 February 1975, AWL Papers, File AWL/1/3; Socialist Organiser Alliance, Executive Committee Minutes, 8 May 1988, AWL Papers, File AWL/1/36/5; Letter from C. Redgrave to G. Healy, 19 June 1981, WRP Papers, Box 348.

81 Letter from MT to AJ, 20 November 1990, AWL Papers, File AWL/1/30.

82 Lancaster IMG, What Is the IMG?, n.d. – probably late 1971/early 1972, IMG Papers Warwick, File 92.

83 Workers Fight, National Committee Minutes, 26 August 1972, AWL Papers, File AWL/1/1; I-CL, Secretariat Minutes, 11 November 1976, AWL Papers, File AWL/1/5; Workers Socialist League, Executive Committee Minutes, 11 October 1981, AWL Papers, File AWL/1/13; WSL, National Committee, 19 September 1982, AWL Papers, File AWL/2/13; AWL, Executive Committee Minutes 26 July 2003, AWL Papers, File AWL/1/45/3; AWL, Executive Committee Minutes, 8 April 2004, AWL Papers, File AWL/1/46/1-2; AWL, Executive Committee Minutes, 7 July 2006, AWL Papers, File AWL/1/48.

84 Statement made by Comrade ST, 7 July 1981, WRP Papers, Box 348.
85 Letter from G to Political Committee, 15 April 1982, WRP Papers, Box 248; Statement by CR to Political Committee, 27 September 1982, WRP Papers, Box 176; Statement by NH, 13 January 1982, WRP Papers, Box 345. See also Letter from AJ to the Political Committee, 4 May 1982, WRP Papers, Box 376.
86 Letter from I-CL to Cde Smith, Stoke, 24 June 1979, Richardson-Higgins Papers, Box 260, File 2.
87 WSL, National Committee Minutes, 17/18 October 1981, AWL Papers, File AWL/1/13. Interestingly an IMG member who took voluntary redundancy from the same plant in 1975 was simply suspended (IMG, Political Committee, 11 September 1975, IMG Papers, Warwick, File 109). The IMG was still heavily student-dominated in the mid-1970s with a very weak industrial base which it was reluctant to damage with expulsions.
88 Note for I-CL National Committee, 31 May 1980, AWL Papers, File AWL/1/9.
89 Workers Fight, National Committee Minutes, 15 December 1973, AWL Papers, File AWL/1/2; Socialist Organiser Alliance, Secretariat Report to Executive Committee, 27 April 1987, AWL Papers, File AWL/1/28; AWL, National Committee, 14 October 1995, AWL Papers, File AWL1/41/1; AWL, Executive Committee Minutes, 12 August 2004, AWL Papers, File AWL/1/46/1-2.
90 Militant Tendency Bulletin, January 1975, Tim Lewis Papers, File 341/7; Bulletin December 1975, Socialist Party Papers, File 601/C/5/1/6.
91 SLL, Internal Bulletin, Autumn 1963, David Spencer Papers, File 164/1/A/1. See also SLL, Political Letter to All Members, 28 December 1961, Richardson/Higgins Papers, Box 220, File 3 and SLL, Political Letter No. 3, 16 December 1962, David Spencer Papers, File 164/1/A/1.
92 WRP (Workers Press), Draft Resolution for London District Conference, 19 January 1986, WRP Papers, Box 610 and for similar problems in the WSL and SWP see Workers Socialist League, WSL: Problems and Tasks for 1979, Alan Clinton Papers Warwick, File 539/2/2/40; Perspectives SWP Conference 1984, Discussion Bulletin No. 1, Nigel Clark Papers, File 489/14.
93 Fissiparous organizations are not unique to the Trotskyist movement but can also be found in other political families marked by the presence of charismatic leaders and the saliency of doctrine, for example Maoism. Britain's first Maoist group emerged in 1963 but by 1976 there were already eight groups and even in 1999 there were still seven (Alexander 2001: 94; Barberis et al. 2000: 142–59). On charismatic and abusive leadership in a Maoist group see Lalich (2004).
94 Both Simon Pirani and Terry Brotherstone were present at the meeting and also described the uproar that followed Redgrave's remarks.
95 For details see http://socialistunity.com/swp-conference-transcript-disputes-committee-report/, accessed 2 April 2017.
96 WSL, Organizing Committee Minutes, 27 March 1983, AWL Papers, File AWL/1/17; AWL, Executive Committee Minutes, 25 February 1999, AWL Papers, File AWL1/35/4.
97 Report on Charges Laid Against Johns (Wolverhampton), n.d. – late 1970s, IMG Papers, Warwick, File 205.
98 On Steve Hedley, see: www.socialistparty.org.uk/keyword/Trade_union_figures/Steve_Hedley/16427/02-04-2013/rmt-concludes-steve-hedley-has-no-case-to-answer, accessed 2 April 2017.
99 www.wsws.org/en/special/1917/lectures.html#pk_campaign=sidebar&pk_kwd=imagelink-lectures, accessed 10 May 2017.
100 To his credit Vernadsky does at least dismiss the erroneous idea that the Kronstadt sailors in 1921 were largely new, peasant recruits with a low level of class consciousness (2017: 310).
101 Choonara's (2007) short booklet on Trotsky simply doesn't mention contentious issues such as the Constituent Assembly, the Cheka, the ban on factions or Kronstadt. It is also

worth noting that for some Trotskyist leaders Germany provides a more appropriate comparator than Russia because of its more highly developed parliamentary democracy (Alex Callinicos interview).

102 Socialist Party: http://1917revolution.org/; Socialist Appeal: www.socialist.net/in-defence-russian-revolution-1917.htm, accessed 10 April 2017.

103 It goes without saying that Trotskyists are opposed to other, non-Trotskyist radical world views, such as anarchism, Eurocommunism, Maoism and Stalinism; see for example Mandel (1978).

6

PARTY RECRUITMENT

For most of the twentieth century the two main political parties on the non–Trotskyist British left were the Labour Party and the Communist Party of Great Britain. British CP membership peaked at 56,000 in 1942 and declined relentlessly thereafter, falling to just over 30,000 in 1969 and to 20,599 in 1979. Following a split in the late 1980s, the main party dissolved itself in 1991 and the breakaway still exists but with a membership below 800 (Electoral Commission; Thompson 1992: 218). The Labour Party claimed to have just over 1 million individual members in 1953 and even prolonged decline throughout the postwar period still left it with a membership figure of a little over 665,000 in 1979 (McGuiness 2012: 11–12). The long-term erosion of its main leftist rivals should have provided a major opening for the Trotskyist movement, particularly in the 1970s and 1980s yet the fact remains that no Trotskyist organization in Britain has ever approached the membership levels of the Communist Party, let alone the Labour Party.[1]

Some Trotskyists like to claim that organizational size is far less important than the quality of the party cadres and that 'mass' social democratic parties often comprise substantial numbers of wholly inactive members. The latter observation is undoubtedly true as many surveys have shown but hardly proves the irrelevance of size. In the 1987 general election just 10 per cent of Labour members claimed to have engaged in telephone canvassing but that figure translates into an activist cadre force of 40,000 (Seyd and Whiteley 2004). Moreover the ostensible aim of almost every Trotskyist group, however tiny, is eventually to follow the trajectory of Lenin's Bolsheviks in 1917 and shift rapidly from being a relatively small, vanguard party to a mass party with significant political influence. Membership trends for the Trotskyist movement and for individual organizations were described in Chapter 3 so the present chapter looks first at the main sources of recruitment before turning to consider the many barriers that have prevented the emergence of any mass Trotskyist parties in Britain.

Sources of recruits

There are five main types of recruit into the Trotskyist movement and in no order of importance they are: trade unionists, students and young people, Labour Party activists, members of rival Trotskyist groups and social movement activists. Access to these groups is pursued mainly through the organization of public meetings, demonstrations and paper sales. Both the SWP and the Socialist Party for example, regularly suggest topical themes for public meetings in order to maximize attendance and their websites then report encouraging attendance and recruitment figures. For instance in spring and early summer 2016 the SWP ran a series of regional rallies on the theme 'Is Socialism Possible?' and subsequently noted that 120 had attended each of two events in Manchester and Birmingham yielding 16 recruits (SWP Party Notes 31 May 2016). On 19 March the SWP front organization Stand up to Racism mobilized 20,000 people on a march through London, 68 of whom either requested information about the SWP or asked to join (SWP Party Notes 21 March 2016).[2] And in the first week of March 15 people joined the SWP as a result of branch meetings, paper sales and a day school (SWP Party Notes 7 March 2016).

The street paper sale is perhaps the most common, regular method of trying to make recruits. Almost all Trotskyist groups produce a newspaper or magazine and in the absence of distribution through newsagents, member subscriptions and street stalls account for the majority of sales. Party branches are expected to organize weekend street sales in which all members are expected to participate although in practice only a minority does so (see Chapter 8). Street sales obviously generate revenue but their main purpose is to publicize the group and its activities and to obtain details of potential members. One common way of collecting such information is by inviting people to sign a petition on a topical issue and to leave contact details.

Trade union members

The revolutionary agency assigned to the working class means that unionized workplaces have always featured heavily as a focal point for Trotskyist activity and trade union work will therefore be examined more fully in Chapter 9. In the late 1960s the IS made a conscious turn to industry, seeking to capitalize on the rising tide of union militancy and to transform its largely student-based membership. The June 1968 Executive Committee noted there were too few industrial workers joining the group but by 1971 almost 30 per cent of its 1,635 members were manual workers and by 1976 this figure had risen to 33 per cent (and a further 31 per cent were classified as 'white collar' with only 21 per cent students) from a total membership of 2,994.[3] The IMG, in contrast, struggled to recruit trade unionists so that even by 1976 approximately 40 per cent of its 642 members were 'white collar' and just 14 per cent manual workers.[4] All the main groups have traditionally benefited from big industrial disputes so the IS/SWP for example claimed to have recruited 15–20 postal workers during their 1971 strike, 50 miners from the

1972 strike and an unspecified number from the 1984–1985 strike.[5] The Militant Tendency claimed in 1987 that 'since the last conference we have supplanted the CP as the Left opposition in the British trade union movement'.[6] Some indication of the continuing trade union base of the Trotskyist movement can be gleaned from their presence on union national executive committees (NECs) because a significant workplace base is often required to secure nomination and election, especially where elections are fought by rival factions. In 2015–2016 the SWP was particularly well represented on the UCU Executive (15 members) as well as Unison (4), the NUT (3) and PCS (3) whilst the Socialist Party was influential in PCS (7 on the NEC), Unison (6) and NUT (4) (Charlie Kimber interview; Clive Heemskerk interview).[7]

Groups with a high proportion of student members, such as the Socialist League (formerly IMG) and the I-CL (now AWL), sought to overcome their limited working-class base through a policy of 'colonization' in which student activists were advised or instructed to take jobs in strategic industries where they could engage in agitation and help recruit militants into the group.[8] The policy came to light in 1983 through press reports that the IMG had despatched no less than 29 of its activists to seek work at the BL Cowley factory, then a stronghold of Alan Thornett's Workers Socialist League (WSL).[9] Other targets for colonization identified by IMG's 1980 conference included BL Longbridge (also targeted by the Spartacist League of Britain), British Oxygen, British Rail, Fords Dagenham, the National Coal Board and the Post Office.[10] The AWL also has a long track record of colonization, dating back to 1975 and still in force today. Graduate student members were expected to follow the group's advice on job applications in order to secure influence in key industries and firms such as London buses, newspaper printing and Royal Mail.[11]

Students and young people

Trotskyist groups have long had a presence on university campuses. During the rapid Trotskyist growth in the 1970s it was the IS, IMG and, to a lesser extent, the SLL/WRP that were most prominent whilst in the 1980s the RCP acquired a significant presence. Student recruitment has now become critical for some organizations, particularly Socialist Appeal and the AWL. Asked about their main sources of recent recruitment an AWL interviewee said: 'To be honest I think it's still mostly students. One of the reasons for this is that large concentrations of young people today on university campuses . . . where it's relatively easy to hold meetings, to sell papers' (Martin Thomas interview).

Table 6.1 shows the number of Trotskyist organizations actually registered on English and Welsh university campuses over the four academic years between 2013 and 2017. The numbers do not always tally with the figures that appear on Trotskyist group websites but their claims about numbers of student societies are inflated. Registration as a student society does not necessarily entail political activity but it does appear, from websites at least, that many Trotskyist student groups do hold meetings.[12] Campus activity is currently dominated by three organizations, the Socialist Party, the SWP and Socialist Appeal; AWL student presence dramatically declined in 2015–2016. Trotskyist presence in the majority of campuses consists of just one group but in 40 per cent of cases there is competition between two or more groups. For example, in 2014–2015 Queen Mary College, London University, had five groups registered with its Student Union: Counterfire, Socialist Appeal, the Socialist Party, the SWP and Workers Power, although such intense competition is unusual. Data on student numbers from the Higher Education Statistics Agency (HESA) shows that over the past four years approximately 50 per cent of university students in England and Wales have potentially been exposed to Trotskyist literature and campaigns. It must therefore be a source of disappointment that total Trotskyist membership actually fell by almost 1,300 between 2013 and 2016.

Finally we should briefly mention direct attempts to recruit young people. Only the SLL/WRP has consistently maintained its own youth organization, the Young Socialists, a tradition dating back to the early 1960s (see Chapter 3). Unlike its rivals, the SLL deliberately sought to attract young people by appealing both to their leisure interests and to their political beliefs. Even today the YS membership form asks applicants to choose from a set of interests that includes 'meetings, marches and writing for the YS paper', as well as 'football, athletics, dances and bowling' (*Young Socialist* 22 February 2014). The SLL guide to building YS branches stressed the importance of mixing sport, discos and political meetings and two of the eight pages in its weekly paper are still devoted to sports.[13] At its

TABLE 6.1 Trotskyist groups in English and Welsh universities 2013/14–2016/17

Group (student group name)	2013/14	2014/15	2015/16	2016/17
AWL (Workers Liberty Students)	15	15	0	2
Counterfire (Counterfire)	6	5	4	1
rs21 (rs21)	n/a	3	4	3
Socialist Appeal (Marxist Students)	17	23	19	18
Socialist Equality Party (International Youth & Students for Social Equality)	6	0	1	0
Socialist Party (Socialist Students)	22	26	29	22
Socialist Workers Party (Socialist Worker Student Society)	29	30	19	18
Spartacist League/Britain (Spartacist League)	2	0	0	0
Workers Fight (Marxist Circle)	1	1	0	0
Workers Power (Revolutionary Socialists)	4	1	1	1
Workers Revolutionary Party (Young Socialists Students Society)	1	0	2	1
Total societies	103	94	79	66
Total universities	54	67	51	42

Sources: English and Welsh university student union websites 10 February 2014, 15 January 2015, 21 May 2016 and 29 November 2016.

height in 1985 the YS AGM was attended by 2,000 young people; by 2014 the AGM was attended by barely 100, a decline that reflects the disintegration of the parent organization, the WRP.[14] That said it is clear from recent issues of *Young Socialist* (2014–2016) that the WRP still retains a capacity to recruit young people, many in London, and to involve them in the traditional range of YS activities: sports, discos and street protests.

Labour Party activists

In the early 1970s only one major group, the Militant Tendency, was engaged in Labour Party entrism, although several small groups also operated inside the Labour Party.[15] For a brief period the policy was extraordinarily successful although Militant was always careful to enrol Labour members as newspaper supporters and only after a period of induction would they be introduced to the RSL, the organization behind the Tendency (Crick 2016). Militant grew from less than 1,000 members in 1975 to a peak of 8,000 members in the late 1980s and also had three MPs (Terry Fields, Dave Nellist and Pat Wall) and control of Liverpool City Council (Crick 2016; Taaffe 1995; Taaffe and Mulhearn 1988). Yet its success encouraged official opposition and in 1991 the Tendency abandoned Labour Party work following a wave of expulsions of its members. Grant and his 200 or so supporters remained inside the Labour Party and launched a new paper, *Socialist Appeal*. Almost 25 years later the group had made little headway, and has a membership of just 300 (Rob Sewell interview).

Not surprisingly Militant's success and the rise of the Bennite Labour left encouraged other Trotskyist groups to try the entry tactic, with varying degrees of commitment but far less success. The Socialist League (successor to the IMG) had always maintained some presence in the Labour Party but significantly increased its entry work in the early 1980s. It deployed the usual measures to avoid detection, such as removing reference to the organization in its new paper *Socialist Action*.[16] These efforts proved fruitless and as membership declined from over 700 in 1977 to less than 400 in early 1985, the League succumbed to the first of a series of destructive splits.[17] Other, smaller entrist groups included the Posadist Revolutionary Workers' Party from around 1978, the WSL from the mid-1970s and Workers Power from the 1970s until the late 1980s (George Binette interview).[18]

The most consistent exponent of some form of entry work is the AWL whose predecessor organization (I-CL) began in 1973 to encourage members to join and become active in local Labour Party branches.[19] In 1978 it launched an organization called Socialist Campaign for a Labour Victory, because of its well-founded fear that Labour was heading for defeat in the 1979 general election.[20] Its members had always been urged to conceal their real names to avoid expulsion and the group's concern with security intensified through the 1980s in line with Labour's desire to purge itself of Trotskyists.[21] But membership gains were poor, not least because the group's rank and file members displayed 'resistance' to the Labour entry tactic, often refusing its implementation.[22] The result was that an organization of 76 members in

1974 had reached only 160 in 1990. By 1999 it was reporting a mixture of secret and open Labour members but as a milieu for recruitment the Labour Party remained hostile territory: by 2012 AWL membership was around 140, a fraction lower than 20 years earlier.

In 2015 however Corbyn's victory led the group to a strategic reorientation and it *instructed* all its 140 or so members to join their local Labour Party (Martin Thomas interview). The regular column in its weekly paper is no longer titled 'What Is the Alliance for Workers' Liberty?' but 'Where We Stand' and it contains two new references, to the Labour Party and to Labour organizations. More radically still Workers Power announced its official dissolution in September 2015 and re-emerged inside the Labour Party as supporters of the monthly newspaper *The Red Flag*.[23] It is too early to say what impact, if any, these initiatives will have on recruitment although as of January 2017 ten AWL members had been expelled by Labour's Compliance Unit as well as seven from the long-standing entrist group Socialist Appeal.[24] In June 2017 AWL reported that new Labour Party members either saw no reason to join another organization such as the AWL, or if they did, then Momentum seemed more attractive.[25]

Other Trotskyist groups

Recruitment from mass labour movement organizations and university campuses requires a critical mass of activists and therefore poses a serious problem for small organizations. One perennial solution has been to intervene in the meetings of rival Trotskyist groups and offer a critique of the politics of the host organization coupled with an account of the superior politics of the raiding organization. This strategy has proven to be particularly attractive under two conditions: first, when a rival organization is in the throes of a bitter internal debate, for example IS/SWP in the early-mid 1970s and 2012–2014, IMG/SL in the mid-1970s and mid-1980s and the WRP in 1974 and 1985; second, in the aftermath of a split when the breakaway group is in a state of flux as members work out their broader political views and strategy beyond the issues that triggered the split, for example the WSL in the late 1970s and the WRP from 1985. Between 1970 and the mid-1980s the IS/SWP was embroiled in a succession of factional struggles which resulted in seven breakaway groups (Table 3.3). Needless to say this heightened internal debate attracted the attention of Trotskyist rivals including Workers Fight and the IMG, particularly in 1974–1975 and 1980. Workers Fight sold its paper at IS meetings in order to make recruits and the IMG analysed the 'crisis in the IS' at length and considered the potential benefits for the group.[26] Even the Militant Tendency overcame its general contempt for what it normally and dismissively referred to as 'the sects':

> the position of our tendency has always been that the future of IS will be one of splits, demoralisation and degeneration . . . c[omra]des should look out for possibilities to retrieve militant workers who are likely to be lost to the movement.[27]

The emergence of the WSL in 1974 also attracted the interest of Workers Fight/ I-CL as the former sought to define its political positions on a wide range of issues and to construct a party programme.[28] The 'organisational sectarianism' of the WRP led most groups to write them off as a source of recruits, a situation that changed significantly after the 1985 implosion.[29] At that point both Workers Power and Workers Fight, for example, attended meetings of the various WRP fragments in what proved to be a fairly fruitless search for recruits (they each made just one or two) (George Binette interview; Anna Hunt interview). Although the WRP itself was deeply and unremittingly hostile to every one of its rivals it did occasionally recognize recruitment potential there. In 1981, for example, its 5th Congress voted to: 'send small specially trained factions into the Labour Party Young Socialists to clarify the political issues by exposing the opportunist leadership of the "Militant" group, and win forces for the Revolutionary Young Socialists'.[30]

Whereas most Trotskyist groups have exploited factional struggles or splits in a reactive and opportunistic way, the small Spartacist League became the consummate exponent of 'splits and fusions' as core strategy.

> An authentic Trotskyist party – the indispensable instrument for the proletarian revolution – can be created only through a process of revolutionary re-groupment, that is through sharp political struggles to politically polarise and split centrist organisations such as the WSL and the IMG.[31]

The WSL was attractive because of its emergence from the WRP, a self-proclaimed defender of Orthodox Trotskyism whilst the IMG was interesting for a wholly different reason, namely that its unusually high tolerance of factions and inner-party debate provided the perfect arena for the Spartacist League to promote its 'intransigent Trotskyism' (*Spartacist Britain* May 1980). In 1978 the Spartacists achieved a significant breakthrough, successfully recruiting several dozen members of a Trotskyist Faction inside the WSL, a coup which led to the banner headline in the first edition of their paper, 'The Rebirth of British Trotskyism' (*Spartacist Britain* April 1978). Several years later they recruited another small group of disgruntled WSL members, the Leninist Faction and shortly afterwards picked up the Communist Faction, a group of dissidents from the IMG (*Spartacist Britain* May 1980 and October 1981).[32] However the capture of the IMG faction more or less ended the period of successful raids on other organizations although occasional recruits have been picked here and there, for example the Socialist Labour Party in 1999 (*Workers Hammer* May–June 1999). By the late 1990s the Spartacist League had seen much of its membership and all but one of its seven branches melt away so in the longer term its aggressive recruitment strategy really did not pay off.

There is, however, one downside to the policy of raiding other groups in order to detach some of their members, and that is the risk of 'reverse poaching'. Workers Fight, reported that its debates and arguments with other organizations had occasionally backfired, with some of its own members quitting the group and joining the target organization instead of vice versa, for example two of its members joined the IMG in 1973 and 1974 respectively.[33]

Social movements

Trotskyists have not only joined existing social movements, such as trade unions, but have from time to time created their own movements out of which they have sought to recruit members. The best examples are the Vietnam Solidarity Campaign (1967), the Anti-Nazi League (1977), the All Britain Poll Tax Federation (1989), the Stop the War Coalition (2001) and the People's Assembly. All these organizations will be considered in more depth in Chapter 10 but for now it is sufficient to note that whilst they do appear to have generated some recruits, the flow of new members has often proved insufficient to offset ongoing losses, resulting in net membership declines, for example for the SWP during the peak years of the ANL 1977–1979.

Problems of recruitment and retention

It is clear that despite sustained recruitment during the 'Golden Age' the Trotskyist movement has failed to produce organizations comparable in size to older left rivals, such as the Communist Party or the contemporary Green Party. Not surprisingly there is considerable discussion amongst leading Trotskyists about their recruitment difficulties although much of this occurs away from public view, in the internal bulletins that are restricted to group members. Nonetheless from a variety of public and archival sources and from interviews with leading activists it is possible to divide analyses of recruitment problems into three categories: re-descriptions of the problem; factors internal to the organization; and environmental factors that are probably beyond the control of the organization.

Re-describing the problem

Membership discussions within smaller organizations, such as Workers Fight/I-CL and Workers Power, often suggested their small size reflected a mode of recruitment based on attracting individual activists rather than large numbers (George Binette interview). Clearly the recruitment of one or two people each month is never going to build a mass party but this truism begs the question as to *why* recruitment proceeds at such a slow pace. Rapid turnover of membership has also been noted by many organizations as a perennial problem, vitiating the apparent success of recruitment campaigns. The SLL recruited 17 busworkers through its involvement in the 1958 London bus strike but six months later only one remained (An Anonymous Author 1996: 222–23). An I-CL recruitment campaign on Teesside in 1975 made some progress but the new recruits were quickly lost; the same organization in 1992 – now the AWL – was still suffering from a 'very high "instant drop-out" rate of new recruits' and four years later the group's leading committee was still complaining that, 'Over the last few years, the majority of people who have signed up as members have not in reality joined. Some we have literally never seen again'.[34]

Between January and March 1974 IS was recruiting at the rate of 150 per month, a figure implying annual membership growth of 1,320 yet IS net growth 1973–1974 was just 89, showing an astonishingly high rate of turnover and a low rate of retention. Nor does the position seem to have changed much in the intervening years. In 2009 the SWP recruited 1,041 people but made a net membership gain 2008–2009 of just 262 and in 2015 the same organization recruited over 600 new members for a net gain in membership of just 18 (Charlie Kimber interview).[35] Turnover rates among young recruits appear to be especially high: in 1966 the SLL was complaining that whilst several new Young Socialist (YS) branches had been established over the summer, 'most of these collapsed after a short time'.[36] Many years later the same problem was apparent: of the 32 YS branches active in 1995, no less than 23 had vanished by 2000 and of the 28 branches active in 2000 eight of them had disappeared by 2005.[37]

Complaints by Trotskyist leaders about the limited recruitment activity of their own members are commonplace. The AWL National Committee noted in 1995 that 'the group has not reaped the benefits expected from WSN (Welfare State Network) since its Oct 94 launch. Branches need to do more'.[38] Some years later a similar lament was being issued in relation to another of its front organizations, the anti-sweatshop group No Sweat whilst the creation of Socialist Organiser in the early 1980s yielded 'much less than it should have done'.[39] The IMG leadership noted in 1977 that whilst many trade union militants, 'will accept our positions, particularly on conjunctural issues . . . Nevertheless the branches are experiencing real difficulties in recruiting them to the IMG'.[40] At about the same time the WRP organized a series of cross-national, European marches to protest at youth unemployment. Although hailed at the time as a great success, a more impartial assessment conducted after the 1985 split concluded that: 'The long Euro marches never boosted our membership by significant numbers'.[41] Some years later Workers Power tried to access young people by creating a separate youth group called Revo, but despite its activity in a range of local anti-racist and other campaigns, it made very few recruits to the organization (George Binette interview).

Internal problems with recruitment and retention

One of the problems faced by small organizations is that significant groups of members will be located in relatively small branches, comprising just a handful of people. Consequently new recruits may be required to take on more work than they had anticipated or wanted; they are less likely to form enduring friendships, compared to entrants into larger branches with a more heterogeneous membership; and smaller branches are more vulnerable to collapse because of the departure of key individuals. For example between 1976 and 1986 the IMG/Socialist League lost a substantial number of branches whose recorded membership was no more than a handful of people in towns such as Bradford, Exeter, Hull, Norwich and Stoke.[42] Shortly before its 1981 merger with the WSL, I-CL's total membership of 74 was scattered amongst 16 branches, making the average branch size just under five![43]

Even in organizations whose branches, on paper, appear to be significantly larger it is clear that some Trotskyist groups record in their membership figures people who are rarely, if ever, active. In 1978 an internal assessment of the SWP noted that only around half the membership of 4,000 actually sold the weekly paper *Socialist Worker* despite this being obligatory for every member. In Bradford, for example, 50 copies of the average weekly paper sale of 80 were accounted for by just six of the branch's 43 members.[44] More recent evidence suggests the SWP is still 'carrying' a substantial number of inactive members on its books. During the factional struggle in 2013 around the handling of sexual harassment and rape allegations against a senior party figure, there were local aggregate meetings for which the competing factions mobilized extensively. One interviewee reported there were just 80 people at his north London aggregate despite party records suggesting total membership in the area was around 400 (Ian Birchall interview). In other organizations, there appears to be a similar phenomenon: a 1985 report on the WRP daily paper *The News Line* showed that the vast majority of sales were undertaken by a small minority of members.[45]

A third factor that has appeared in a number of documents and discussions is that heavy demands are often placed on new recruits to the organization, particularly in groups such as the AWL and Workers Power with strict membership requirements including compulsory attendance at new member education courses. Consequently, recruitment rates are often low although retention rates may be high. For example the median length of membership of the 24 people expelled from Workers Power in 2006 was 20 years.[46]

The final internal factor that helps explain the poor membership levels of the Trotskyist left is the aftermath of organizational splits because in the process of organizational division some members will simply drift away from Trotskyist politics leaving the combined membership of the splinter groups below that of the pre-fission organization. For example, between 1975 and 1976 the IS suffered two splits leading to new organizations with a combined membership of just under 200 (Workers Power took 40 in 1975 and the Workers League claimed 150 in 1976). Yet IS membership fell by approximately 700 from the pre-split period 1975 to the end of 1976. In 2014 two new breakaways from the SWP – International Socialist Network and rs21 – claimed a combined membership of approximately 260 yet total SWP membership 2013–2014 fell by 1,312 (Anindya Bhattacharyya and Alex Callinicos interviews). In 1974 the WRP expelled Alan Thornett and around 200 of his supporters (estimates vary) but over the next 12 months WRP membership fell by 500. The implosion of the WRP in late 1985 transformed an organization which claimed almost 9,000 members into four fragments which 12 months later probably included no more than 2,500 (see Chapter 3). Finally, the membership of the Militant Tendency immediately prior to the 1992 split was approximately 6,000 but within two years the combined membership of the two sides of the split had probably slumped to around 3,000.[47] It is possible that some portion of post-split reductions in membership may be more apparent than real, a reflection of bogus membership figures cleaned up in the course of

TABLE 6.2 The largest defunct Trotskyist groups since 1970

Group	Foundation and dissolution dates	Peak membership (year)
Revolutionary Communist Party	1977–1997	380 (1995)
Workers Revolutionary Party (Workers Press)	1986–2006	341 (1986)
International Socialist Alliance	1978–1979	202 (1978)
Workers League	1976–1978	150 (1976)
The Marxist Party	1987–2004	100 (1987)
International Socialist Network	2013–2015	60 (2013)

Sources: See Appendix 1.

a split, as happened in the SWP 2013–2014, but this is unlikely to be the whole story (Charlie Kimber interview).

The reasons why organizational splits depress total membership are unclear but there are several possibilities: members whose commitment to the organization has weakened already may take the opportunity to resign (or simply drift away); members who have become exhausted through frenetic activity and excessive demands on their time may also take the opportunity to leave; and some members may have become disillusioned because of the split and therefore quit. Moreover, an organization in the throes of a major split is likely to have resources diverted from recruitment into factional struggle and may also prove unattractive to potential members. Finally, many breakaway organizations have a very short life-span, resulting in a net loss of members as the new organization declines and then disappears (see Table 6.2).

External barriers to recruitment and retention

One obvious factor in Trotskyist party decline, although mentioned by only one interviewee, is the generalized decline in party membership across Western Europe since the final quarter of the twentieth century (Alex Callinicos interview). British Labour Party membership fell from a 1952 peak of just over one million and by 1993 had slumped to 266,000. It then rose briefly during Blair's early period as leader, peaking in 1997 before resuming its downward trajectory to around 190,000 in 2014 (Keen and Audickas 2016; McGuinness 2012). There were equally dramatic membership declines between the 1970s and the late 1990s for social democratic parties in Belgium, France, Germany, Italy and the Netherlands and for the communist parties of France, Italy and Spain (van Biezen et al. 2012). However, the conventional wisdom about party decline needs to be qualified: some social democratic parties have grown for significant periods since the early 1980s, in Australia, Ireland and Spain and, since 2015, in the UK; Green parties have grown since the 1990s in Belgium, Germany and the UK (Webb 2002); and newer leftist parties have also reported membership increases between 1990 and 2010 in Denmark (Red-Green Alliance), France (New Anti-Capitalist Party), Netherlands (Socialist Party) and Portugal (Left Bloc) (Videt 2011: 17). This mixed evidence suggests we cannot simply attribute the lack of attractiveness of British Trotskyist parties to a generalized antipathy towards political party membership.

A related theme is that whatever the merits or demerits of political parties, both anarchist groups and social movements have become far more attractive to activists, especially if they are young (Alex Callinicos and Corinna Lotz interviews). Ibrahim (2013) showed that the SWP faced stiff competition from anarchists in the early years of the anti-globalization movement; the Anti-Nazi League grew to a peak membership of 40,000–50,000 in just three years 1977–1979 (Renton 2006: 175); and the Stop the War Coalition grew quickly from 2002–2003 so that by 2016 its website reported 76 local groups in Great Britain (Murray and German 2005). Nor can we invoke the idea of a general 'shift to the right' amongst electorates, because some leftist parties have performed extremely well in recent elections and have also increased their memberships, for example Syriza in Greece and Podemos in Spain. Across Europe, a majority of radical left parties, a category including both new left groups such as Left Bloc as well as the old communist parties, significantly increased their vote share over the 1999–2010 decade (March 2011: 2–3). It is true that recent years have witnessed an even more dramatic rise in the vote shares of extreme right-wing parties, such as the French National Front and the Austrian Freedom Party but taking all these trends into account it would be more accurate to describe voting patterns as indicating polarization towards left and right rather than a rightwards shift.

Orthodox Trotskyist groups, such as the Spartacist League and the Institutional Trotskyist groups Socialist Appeal and the Socialist Party, argued that the disintegration of the Soviet Union and the 'deformed workers' states' of Eastern Europe represented an historic defeat for the working class, calling into question in the minds of many people the relevance of Marxist ideas and the feasibility of socialism (for example Grant 1997; International Communist League (Fourth Internationalist) 1998). In this harsh ideological climate 'genuine' Trotskyist organizations could expect to recruit in ones and twos and grow only slowly, if at all (Mick Connor and Len Michelson interview).

The difficulty with this proposition is that whilst some Trotskyist groups certainly did lose members in the early 1990s – Militant Labour, Socialist Resistance, Workers Power and the WRP (Workers Press) – the largest group on the British left recorded a dramatic *rise* in membership, reaching its highest ever membership total of approximately 10,000 some five years after the collapse of the Soviet regimes. This may have reflected the SWP's almost unique disdain for what it described as the 'state capitalist' regimes of Eastern Europe whose demise was cause for celebration not mourning. More likely is that growth stemmed from its prominence on the far left after the 1992 split in the Militant Tendency; its involvement in contemporary struggles around the poll tax and against the far right (it relaunched the Anti-Nazi League in 1992); and its willingness to accept recruits with minimal induction or vetting. Nevertheless the SWP boom was short-lived because its membership fell in the late 1990s almost as quickly as it had risen, so that by the early 2000s it had shrunk by around 50 per cent from its mid-1990s peak.

Perhaps one of the more prominent themes in the various explanations for recruitment failures is the declining level of working-class militancy (for example John Rees interview). The Golden Age of Trotskyism was rooted in the upsurge of strikes that began in the mid-1960s and ran through to the strike wave of 1978–1979 (Lyddon 2007). As strike totals rose and strike action spread into hitherto quiescent areas of the public sector, Trotskyist groups successfully recruited growing numbers of trade union militants (see Chapter 9). From the late 1960s it is clear that the IS/SWP and the WRP established pockets of membership within a wide range of unions as did the Militant Tendency in the 1980s. The decline of trade union membership and strike activity, driven in part by key strike defeats such as the miners in 1985 and the printers in 1986, is almost certainly one factor that has contributed to the shrinkage of the Trotskyist movement since the 1980s but the significance of this link should not be overstated, for two reasons. Even during the Golden Age of British Trotskyism no group succeeded in building a presence in the trade union movement even remotely comparable to that of the Communist Party at its peak, between about 1950 and 1970 (see Chapter 9). Second, whatever their success in persuading relatively small numbers of shop stewards to join a revolutionary organization, one of the themes of Trotskyist internal literature is the reluctance of many trade union militants even to contemplate joining such a group as indicated by two reports, in 1976 and 1995: 'TU militants [are] generally very wary of involvement with the revolutionary groups';[48] 'We have systematically failed to recruit out of trade union work'.[49] When the SWP closed down its 'rank and file' groups in 1982 it was noted that many had shrunk into small caucuses of SWP members that had increasingly come to substitute themselves for the actual rank and file of the union (Callinicos 1982: 33).

Conclusions

Trotskyist groups have recruited from a wide range of sources, beginning in the 1960s with students and young Labour activists before significantly expanding their industrial and trade union membership in the 1970s and early 1980s whilst continuing to recruit on university campuses and on demonstrations. At one time or another, groups within a range of Trotskyist families – Institutional, Orthodox and Third Camp – have built organizations of almost 10,000 members suggesting that doctrinairism and orthodoxy *per se* are not necessarily barriers to recruitment. But the lower membership entry standards required for large-scale recruitment have generated perennial problems of high turnover, hindering the capacity of these groups to achieve the status of mass organizations. Groups with strict periods of probation and member education, such as the Third Camp AWL or the Radical Trotskyists of Workers Power, have often avoided high turnover and built a cadre of committed activists, but at the price of remaining extremely small.

Overall, the Trotskyist movement today is significantly larger than in the 1950s but much smaller than in the Golden Age of the 1970s and early 1980s despite what would appear to have been propitious circumstances for growth: a rightward policy shift by the Labour Party, the economic crisis that began in 2008, the spread across Europe of neoliberal austerity policies and the rise of new, leftist parties such as Syriza and Podemos. On the other hand, the dramatic decline in trade union membership and strike activity since the 1970s has forced Trotskyist groups to seek out other sources of recruits: hence the considerable activity on university campuses and the efforts devoted to building social movements. But despite some highly impressive mobilizations, against the war in Iraq (15 February 2003), the Israeli aggression in Gaza (19 July and 9 August 2014) and austerity (20 June 2015 and 16 April 2016), the Trotskyist movement remains both small and divided. The renewed interest in Marxist ideas after the 2008 financial and economic crisis and the influx of Corbyn supporters into the Labour Party certainly demonstrate the existence of a widespread, leftist radicalism. Yet these developments have so far failed to generate a membership upsurge on the Trotskyist left.

Appendix: Trotskyist organizations in Western Europe

In 2017 there were Trotskyist organizations in every West European country[50] and the full list of the organizations and their international affiliations is provided in Appendix 3 whilst Figure 6.1 summarizes the number of current organizations in each country. A variety of sources and databases has been used to establish the existence of these organizations but they have only been included in Figure 6.1 (and the Appendix Table) once their website has been checked and confirmed as up to date. Because of the existence of some very small independent groups in the UK without international affiliations, for example Counterfire and rs21, it is possible that Figure 6.1 and Appendix 3 have missed some equally small, independent groups in other countries.

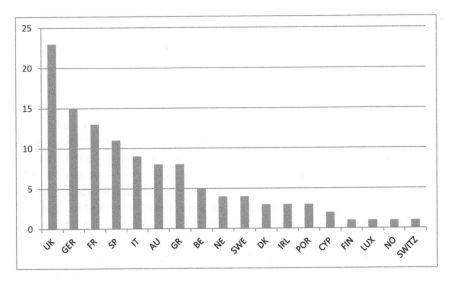

FIGURE 6.1 Numbers of Trotskyist organizations in West European countries May 2017

Sources: Fourth International websites, accessed 12 May 2017.

The first striking feature of the West European 'map' is that the UK situation of many different Trotskyist groups in each country is the norm. Only in the smaller countries of Finland, Luxembourg, Norway and Switzerland is there a single Trotskyist organization. In every other country there are multiple groups and the more populous the country, the more groups there are in existence as is clear from the numbers in Germany (15), France (13), Italy (8) and Spain (11). Consequently in the 18 countries of Western Europe, including the UK, there are currently (May 2017) 113 Trotskyist organizations. Second, the population of Trotskyist groups in Western Europe, as in Britain, displays a relatively high rate of births and deaths. During the past five years 18 organizations in ten different countries have ceased to function including the Que Faire? group (France), Fightback (Ireland) and the Revolutionary Socialism group (Portugal).[51] In contrast the number of new organizations has been far smaller – just seven – including three in Italy and one each in Austria, Belgium, France and Germany.[52] Third, almost all of the West European groups outside the UK – 82 out of 91 – are attached to a Fourth International, a factor that almost certainly consolidates divisions within and between countries. The proliferation of Trotskyist groups is not therefore a peculiarity of British politics but is the norm across Western Europe.

Membership of Trotskyist organizations in Western Europe

Reliable data on Trotskyist group membership around Western Europe is practically non-existent and the small quantity of available information is mostly out of date. European Trotskyist groups, like their British counterparts, rarely report membership figures and the Internationals to which they are affiliated are equally secretive. In the case of Germany, the domestic intelligence service Bundesamt für Verfassungsschutz gathers and reports data each year on the far left. In 2015 it estimated total Trotskyist membership at approximately 1,400 with 300 each in Marx 21 (part of the International Socialist Tendency) and Socialist Alternative (affiliated to the CWI). Two years earlier its estimate was 1,600 with 400 each in Marx 21 and Socialist Alternative.[53] The 2015 Socialist Alternative figure is consistent with a report of 200–300 in 2013 from two ex-Socialist Party interviewees who also added that Germany was the CWI's third largest section at that time implying all of its other West European affiliates were smaller, that is, those in France, Greece, Italy and Spain (Steve Dobbs and Toby Harris interview). The German movement has probably declined in recent years because Moreau (2008) estimated total Trotskyist membership in 2006 at approximately 1,800. Estimates for other times and other countries have also produced low membership figures: Denmark's Socialist Workers Party (part of the Fourth International 1938) had less than 200 members in 1982; the Norwegian Workers Power Group reportedly had 60–70 members in 1984; and the Swedish Socialist Party (part of the Fourth International 1938) comprised 700 members in 1981 (Alexander 1991a: 244, 633, 725). In contrast, membership levels in France were often significantly higher: the International Communist Party (part of the Lambertist Fourth International) reportedly had

7,000 members in 1982 whilst the Mainstream Fourth International's League for the Communist Revolution claimed 3,500 in 1977 (Alexander 1991a: 387, 717).

In the absence of other data it is impossible to tell whether these figures are accurate but there is an indirect method of estimating approximate group size. Trotskyist organizations almost invariably produce newspapers and journals and the larger the organization the greater the frequency of publication. Britain's two largest groups – the SWP and the Socialist Party – have each published a weekly paper for almost 50 years; the AWL, with fewer than 200 members, has also published a weekly since the early 2000s; and the WRP still produces a daily paper, first published in 1969. Smaller groups such as Socialist Resistance and Workers Power lack the personnel and financial capacity to produce and distribute weekly papers. We can therefore inspect the frequency of newspaper and magazine publication by the Trotskyist left in Western Europe as a proxy for group size. Evidence was obtained from the websites of individual Trotskyist groups and included all publications that were both hard copy and regular, but excluded publications that were purely online and/or irregular and the results are shown in Table 6.3.

Only four countries in Western Europe (in addition to the UK) have weekly Trotskyist papers, namely France, Greece, Spain and Sweden, whilst the remaining ten countries have a Trotskyist press that is unable to publish more frequently than once per month (or in the cases of Ireland and Portugal, bi-monthly, whilst Cypriot Trotskyists produce only a bi-annual journal). Three countries appear to have no Trotskyist press whatever: Finland, Luxembourg and Norway. The most extensive Trotskyist press,

TABLE 6.3 The Trotskyist press in Western Europe* December 2016

Country	Trotskyist groups	Weeklies	Monthlies	Bi-monthlies or less frequent	Total
Germany	15	0	4	8	12
France	13	4	3	4	11
Spain	11	1	6	4	11
Italy	9	0	4	2	6
Austria	8	0	4	1	5
Greece	8	1	3**	3	7
Belgium	5	0	2	2	4
Netherlands	4	0	1	1	2
Sweden	4	2	1	1	4
Denmark	3	0	1	1	2
Ireland	3	0	0	2	2
Portugal	3	0	0	2	2
Cyprus	2	0	0	1	1
Switzerland	1	0	1	0	1
UK	22	5	8	9	22

Sources: Individual organization websites, accessed 10 December 2016.

* I have been unable to locate any printed Trotskyist press in Finland, Luxembourg or Norway.

** Two of these papers are fortnightly.

measured by total number of publications, is to be found in Germany, whose 15 groups produce 12 newspapers and magazines, whilst the most extensive weekly press is in France, with four papers, published by the Anti-Capitalist Left, Communist League, New Anti-Capitalist Party and Workers Struggle (Lutte Ouvrière). If we recall that an official source estimated German Trotskyist membership at approximately 1,400 and assume a rough correlation between membership and press volume then a reasonable guess would be that only France, Germany and Spain have Trotskyist movements whose membership exceeds 1,000. The significantly smaller volume and frequency of publications elsewhere would suggest national Trotskyist movements in most other West European countries count their membership in the hundreds.

Notes

1 The Trotskyist movement certainly attracted famous names in arts, journalism and higher education including Paul Foot, Christopher Hitchens and Sheila Rowbotham (IS), Tariq Ali, Robin Blackburn and Hilary Wainwright (IMG), Jim Allen, Corin and Vanessa Redgrave and Frances de la Tour (WRP) (Ali 1987; Birchall 2011: 330; Harding 2005: 108–09, 191; Redgrave 1991; Rowbotham et al. 1979: 7).

2 For details of Stand up to Racism see its website www.standuptoracism.org.uk/, which can also be accessed from the SWP site www.swp.org.uk/, both accessed 3 March 2017.

3 EC Minutes, 1 June 1968, Colin Barker Papers, File 152/1/1/3; Membership report to National Committee, IS Bulletin, June 1971, Nigel Clark Papers, File 489/1; Recruitment and Composition of Present Membership, n.d. – July 1976?, Stirling Smith Papers, File 205/1/6.

4 April 1978 Conference, IMG Papers, Warwick, File 205.

5 National Committee Minutes, 27 March 1971, Colin Barker Papers, File 152/1/1/5; Industrial Sub-Committee Minutes, 13 February 1972, Colin Barker Papers, File 152/1/1/7; Perspectives SWP Conference 1984, Discussion Bulletin No. 1, Nigel Clark Papers, File 489/14.

6 Industrial Work – General Summary, 1987 Conference Report, Socialist Party Papers, File 601/C/3/2/5.

7 Some information was also obtained from the industrial sections of the SWP and Socialist Party websites.

8 The IS adopted a similar policy, though more sporadically, in the late 1960s and early 1970s: John McIlroy letter 1 July 2017.

9 Draft Statement for Political Committee: An Emergency Situation in the Socialist League, 17 February 1983, IMG Papers, Warwick, File 212. A smaller group of IMG members had also been sent into the car industry in the early 1970s: John McIlroy letter 1 July 2017.

10 IMG Political Bureau, Winter Tasks for the IMG, Internal Information Bulletin, October 1979, IMG Papers, LSE, File 1/19; National Conference Proceedings, Internal Information Bulletin No. 1, 1980, IMG Papers, Warwick, File 205. For the Spartacist League see their Central Committee Minutes, 4 June 1980, IMG Papers, Warwick, File 258.

11 Secretariat Minutes, 23 June 1975, AWL Papers, File AWL1/3; Secretariat Minutes, 12 May 1976, AWL Papers, File AWL 1/5; Executive Committee Minutes, 27 June 1991, AWL Papers, File AWL 1/31; National Committee Minutes, 18 June 2005, AWL Papers, File AWL 1/47/2; Secretariat Minutes, 24 May 2006, AWL Papers, File AWL1/47/1; National Committee Minutes, 25 February 2007, AWL Papers, File AWL 1/1/49.

12 It is of course possible to have Trotskyist activity on a university campus organized by the town branch of a group in the absence of a student society but this type of sporadic and *ad hoc* action is almost impossible to identify and record accurately.

13 Socialist Labour League, How to Build Young Socialists, n.d. – probably early 1970s, WRP Papers, Box 405.

14 Figures taken from various issues of *Young Socialist*, available at the British Library.

15 The smaller entrist groups were the Revolutionary Communist League which later evolved into the non-Trotskyist Socialist Charter Group, and Socialist Current, a small group based around an eponymous magazine. On the RCL, see Chris Taylor Papers, Files 406/1/1–5 and 406/2/1. The Socialist Labour League/Workers Revolutionary Party maintained a secret Labour Party fraction as late as 1981 as did its 1974 breakaway, Alan Thornett's Workers Socialist League. On the SLL/WRP see WRP, Letter to Branches, 16 November 1977, Alan Clinton Papers, Warwick, File 539/2/1/6; and Statement by Comrade S. Miller to Political Committee, 8 August 1981, WRP Papers, Box 376. On the WSL, see WSL, Pre Conference Discussion 1980 (4th annual conference 4–5/4/80), Alan Clinton Papers, Warwick, File 539/2/1/4.

16 On its 1970s entry work see Internal Information Bulletin, 1975 in IMG Papers, Warwick, File 4. On the 1980s see Proposals on re-organising the apparatus and leadership, n.d. – probably late 1983, IMG Papers, LSE, File 225.

17 The 'main' fragment emerging from the splits was Socialist Action, led by John Ross, which became a deep entry organization dedicated to exerting influence over Labour politicians such as Ken Livingstone even at the price of steadily losing members. On the split see articles in *Socialist Action* 7 February 1986 and the reply in *International*, No. 4, May/June 1986. On Socialist Action and John Ross, see Hosken (2008: Chapter 18). Uniquely on the Trotskyist left the organization's website makes no effort to recruit members.

18 On the Posadists, see Bulletin of the International Secretariat of the Posadist IV International, No. 1 August 1978, Posadist Tendency Papers, Box 13, File 1. On the WSL see the autobiography of the well-known Oxford academic Terry Eagleton (2001: 76–77) whose application was rejected.

19 Workers Fight, National Committee Minutes, 18–19 August 1973, AWL Papers, File AWL/1/2.

20 Resolution on SCLV/SO organisation, n.d. – probably November 1979, Richardson/Higgins Papers, Box 260, File 2.

21 Workers Fight, Steering Committee Minutes, 15 September 1975, AWL Papers, File AWL/1/3; WSL, Executive Committee Minutes, 13 November 1981 and Organization Committee Minutes, 17 December 1981, AWL Papers, File AWL1/14.

22 Socialist Organiser, National Committee Minutes, 6 June 1979, AWL Papers, File AWL/1/9.

23 The Workers Power website has not been updated since September 2015 in order to maintain the illusion of the group's disappearance, although the site of its international parent body, the League for the Fifth International continues to carry regular updates. *The Red Flag* has its own website at www.redflagonline.org//. Information on pseudonyms from Workers Power interviewee. Gerry Downing's tiny Socialist Fight group also entered the Labour Party and produces an irregular bulletin called *Socialist Labour*.

24 On the AWL see the 'Statement Against the Witchhunts' available at https://stopthela bourpurge.wordpress.com/no-witch-hunts/ and on the Socialist Appeal expulsions see 'End the Witch Hunt! Abolish the Compliance Unit! Defend Corbyn and Fight for Socialism', available at www.socialist.net/end-the-witch-hunt-abolish-the-compliance-unit-defend-corbyn-and-fight-for-socialism.htm, both accessed 24 June 2016. Expellees as of June 2016 included Sacha Ismail, Liam McNulty, Ed Maltby, Vicki Morris, Jill Mountford, Cathy Nugent and Daniel Randall (all AWL); Nick Wrack (Independent Socialist Network) and Gerry Downing (Socialist Fight): see *Socialist Fight* No. 22, Summer 2016, pp. 9–11. The small Socialist Party breakaway Marxist World is also active in the Labour Party (Steve Dobbs and Toby Harris interview).

25 Gregor Gall, email correspondence, 8 July 2017.

26 Workers Fight, Steering Committee Minutes, 5 May 1974, AWL Papers, File AWL/1/2; The Crisis Within the International Socialists, IMG Internal Information Bulletin, n.d. – probably 1974, Tony Whelan Papers, File 82.

27 Militant Internal Bulletin, February 1973, p. 20, Socialist Party Papers, File 601/C/5/1/4.
28 Workers Fight, Steering Committee Minutes, 30 June 1974, AWL Papers, File AWL/1/2.
29 The phrase comes from the foundation document of the I-CL: see I-CL, National Committee Minutes, 15 December 1975, AWL Papers, File AWL/1/4.
30 WRP Pre-Congress Report, Youth Perspectives 1980, WRP Papers, Box 29.
31 Spartacist League Leaflet, The CDLM [Campaign for a Democratic Labour Movement] Comes to Scotland, 25 June 1977, Spartacist League Papers, File MISC 2.
32 See also Documents of the Communist Faction of the IMG Part 11: Purge in IMG, London: Communist Faction, May 1981, Alan Clinton Papers, Warwick, File 539/3/1.
33 Pat Longman, 'Why I Am Leaving Workers' Fight and Joining the IMG', 9 January 1973, Richardson/Higgins Papers, Box 28, File 3; Workers Fight, Steering Committee Minutes, 8 December 1974, AWL Papers, File AWL/1/2.
34 Workers Fight, Secretariat Minutes, 4 August 1975, AWL Papers, File AWL/1/3; AWL, Secretariat Minutes, 31 January 1992, AWL Papers, File AWL/1/32; AWL, National Committee Minutes, 9–10 March 1996, AWL Papers, File AWL/1/41/2.
35 2009 data from SWP Internal Bulletin November 2009.
36 SLL, Internal Document, n.d. – probably 1966 for London Area Conference, Clinton Papers, Warwick, File 539/1/1.
37 Information on YS branches was obtained by checking branch listings and advertised meetings in all issues of Young Socialist, the weekly YS newspaper, for the years 1995, 2000 and 2005.
38 AWL, National Committee Minutes, 22 April 1995, AWL Papers, File AWL/1/41/1.
39 Perspectives for AWL student work, n.d. – probably August 2003, AWL Papers, File AWL/1/45/3; Socialist Organiser, Resolution to August EC 1984, AWL Papers, File AWL/1/9.
40 Building the IMG, Party Builder Bulletin, No. 1, January 1977, p. 4, Chris Bambery Papers, File 1/3.
41 J. Ralph, 'WRP (WP) The Young Socialists – A Critical Summary', WRP (Workers Press) Internal Bulletin No. 19, November 1986, WRP Papers, Box 77.
42 Branch Census November 1976, IMG Papers, Warwick, File 216; Appendix to Organisation Report 1978 National Conference, IMG Papers, Warwick, File 59; Facts 1981 Conference, Membership Figures 1985, IMG Papers, Warwick, File 228; Socialist Action, Finance Dossier for Central Committee, 18–19 October 1986, IMG Papers, Warwick, File 230.
43 I-CL Membership List, n.d. – probably early 1980, AWL Papers, File AWL/1/9.
44 State of the Organisation for National Committee, 9/10 December 1978, Steve Jefferys Papers, File 244/2/1/2.
45 News Line Circulation Report, 9 September 1985, WRP Papers, Box 135.
46 The Split in the League for the Fifth International 2007, www.permanentrevolution.net/entry/1356, accessed 10 July 2016.
47 Other examples of splits leading to a net loss of members include the breakup of the Workers Fight – Workers Power group in 1976; the I-CL and WSL split in 1983; and the Socialist League splits in 1985 and 1988.
48 I-CL, National Committee Minutes, 9 May 1976, AWL Papers, File AWL/1/5.
49 AWL, National Committee Minutes, 7 January 1995, AWL Papers, File AWL/1/33/3.
50 Western Europe is defined here as the former EU 15 plus Cyprus, Norway and Switzerland.
51 The defunct groups and their international affiliations, names in English, are as follows: Belgium: International Socialist Organization (Fourth International 1993); Finland: Socialist League (International Socialist Tendency IST); France: Class Struggle (Workers International to Rebuild the Fourth International), Internationalist Group (League for the Fourth International), What Is to Be Done? (IST) and Workers Power (League for the Fifth International); Germany: Communist Organization for the Fourth International – Germany (COFI); Ireland: Fightback (International Marxist Tendency

IMT); Italy: Communism from Below (IST), Reds Association (None); Norway: International Socialists (IST); Portugal: Movement for Socialism (International Workers Unity – Fourth International), Revolutionary Socialism (Committee for a Workers International); Spain: The Struggle (IST); Sweden: Communist League (SWP Pathfinder Tendency), International Socialists (IST); Switzerland: The Spark (IMT), Revolutionary Socialist Organization (RSO).

52 The new groups, their names in English, are as follows: Austria: Revolutionary Communist Organization for Liberation (Revolutionary Communist International Tendency); Belgium: Workers Struggle (Lutte Ouvrière); France: Socialist Equality Party (International Committee of the Fourth International – SEP); Germany: Revolutionary Communist International Tendency Germany (RCIT); Italy: Anticapitalist Left and International Solidarity (both Fourth International 1938), Internationalist Nucleus of Italy (League for the Fourth International).

53 www.verfassungsschutz.de/en/fields-of-work/left-wing-extremism/figures-and-facts-left-wing-extremism/left-wing-extremists-efforts-2015, accessed 15 December 2016.

7

PARTY ELECTORAL PERFORMANCE

The first election fought by British Trotskyists was at Neath, South Wales in May 1945, a by-election in a safe Labour seat. In line with the wartime electoral truce, the Conservatives and Liberals declined to stand so the Revolutionary Communist Party (RCP) General Secretary Jock Haston took on the Labour Party and Plaid Cymru, obtaining 1,781 votes (4.58 per cent of votes cast). It would be another 24 years before Trotskyists fought an election but from February 1974 at least one Trotskyist group has stood in every general election as well as in elections for the European Parliament, the London and Welsh Assemblies and local councils.[1] Since the late 1990s elections have been fought both by individual Trotskyist groups as well as by electoral coalitions involving Trotskyist and Communist groups as well as the Rail, Maritime and Transport Union. It is true that electoral activity is far less important for Trotskyist organizations than for mainstream political parties yet the regularity of their participation shows the electoral arena has become far more important since the turn of the century. The first part of this chapter sets out the general approach of Trotskyist groups to electoral participation, drawing particularly on the ideas of Lenin. The second part examines their results in a range of British elections before exploring explanations for their generally poor performance. The final section examines the responses of Trotskyist groups to their own poor electoral results.

The long-term decline of communist parties in Europe from the middle of the twentieth century, accelerated by the collapse of the Soviet Union in 1991, and the rightward shift of social democratic parties as they began to adopt neoliberal policies (and more recently, austerity policies) opened up an electoral space on the left. Parties such as Die Linke in Germany obtained more than 10 per cent of the vote in the 2009 election (falling back a little in 2013) whilst the Left Bloc in Portugal scored approximately 10 per cent in both the 2009 and 2015 elections (see the Appendix to this chapter). The Greek party Syriza (Coalition of the Radical Left) won the January and September 2015 elections with approximately 36 per cent of the vote (although its austerity policies have disappointed many supporters). Radical left parties, often including Trotskyist factions, have performed well in countries with high unemployment; popular antagonism to the European Union and to economic austerity policies; where many voters hold 'post-materialist' values; competitor parties, such as the Greens, are weak; and where proportional representation means the threshold for securing representation in the legislature is low (Hobolt and Tilley 2016; March 2011: 200). The continuing decline in the membership of mainstream parties (Scarrow 2007) and the rising incidence of anti-austerity and anti-capitalist protests and demonstrations, often involving, if not organized by, the radical left, might also point to reasonable electoral prospects for candidates of the far left (Rucht 2007).

Elections, parliament and the state

The general approach of Trotskyist organizations to elections and electoral participation is mainly derived from the writings of Marx, Engels and Lenin rather than Trotsky himself. The 1938 Transitional Programme assumed that contemporary capitalism was ripe for revolution but this outcome was hindered principally by the absence of a revolutionary working-class leadership (Trotsky 1938). Given that world view, and in the context of fascist regimes across Europe, it is understandable that Trotsky showed little interest in electoral issues. Among contemporary Trotskyists there are two main elements in their approach to elections: on the one hand, there is a highly critical theoretical tradition in which the state is analysed as an instrument of class rule that cannot be used to achieve socialism. On the other hand, there is a tactical view that revolutionary socialists must use every opportunity to promote their ideas, including participation in elections.

The critical tradition dates back to the statement in the Communist Manifesto that 'The executive of the modern state is but a committee for managing the common affairs of the whole bourgeoisie' (Marx and Engels 1848: 44). A few years later, in a famous essay on France, Marx castigated those politicians who believed that class power resided in parliament as victims of what he dismissively called 'parliamentary cretinism', a phrase that now enjoys widespread currency on the revolutionary left (Marx 1852). In 1871 he wrote a highly influential analysis of the Paris Commune, a working-class insurrection in which the participants began to construct their own rudimentary and embryonic state, before the uprising was brutally suppressed by French troops. The Paris Commune, declared Marx, showed that 'the working class cannot simply lay hold of the ready-made state machinery, and wield it for its own purposes' (Marx 1871). The reason, as Lenin later wrote, is that the state is *necessarily* an instrument of class rule, consisting at its core of 'special bodies of armed men, prisons etc.'. The presence of periodic elections is of little consequence because these events merely allow workers, 'To decide once every few years which member of the ruling class is to repress and crush the people through parliament – this is the real essence of bourgeois parliamentarism' (Lenin 1916: 56). Lenin therefore concluded that the state apparatus, including parliament, had to be 'smashed' and replaced by soviets, or workers' councils, bodies elected in workplaces and neighbourhoods whose members would be regularly accountable to their constituents and which were supposed to encourage higher levels of political participation than bureaucratic and elitist parliaments (Lih 2014: 66).

In the wake of the 1917 Russian Revolution some communists took this line of argument to imply that parliamentary institutions and elections were an irrelevance that revolutionaries could ignore, concentrating instead on extra-parliamentary class struggles. Lenin's response articulated what was to become the second strand in Trotskyist thought, insisting that revolutionaries *must* use the opportunity presented by elections to stand candidates and disseminate socialist propaganda and was scathing about 'ultra-left' activists who thought otherwise (Lenin 1920). Whilst the Bolshevik Party had occasionally boycotted parliamentary elections, for example during the 1905 wave of strikes and protests, he was adamant that so long as large numbers of workers were attached to parliament then revolutionaries had to contest elections and, if successful, work within parliament.

Most contemporary Trotskyists have combined these two views. Callinicos of the SWP reiterated Lenin's argument that the state is an oppressive 'instrument of class rule' and that parliament 'has little effective control over what the government does' (Callinicos 1983a: 22, 26; and Choonara and Kimber 2011). The military overthrow in September 1973 of the democratically elected leftist government of Salvador Allende in Chile is frequently cited as proof that socialism cannot be achieved through parliament and that the state must be 'smashed' (see for example Callinicos 1983b; Harman 2007: 37; Mandel 1978: 182–83; Sell 2006: 65). At the same time, SWP founder Tony Cliff also noted that, 'for so long as workers and their revolutionary organizations are not strong enough to overthrow parliament, said Lenin, it can be used as a platform for revolutionary socialist propaganda' (Cliff 1987: 7).

Shortly after the IS/SWP entered the electoral arena, in a series of mid-1970s by-elections, its Central Committee wrote that the aim was 'to establish our electoral hegemony to the left of Labour'. In addition the party aimed to recruit members, build up sales of its newspaper and establish trade union and labour movement contacts.[2]

The Socialist Party holds a more optimistic view of the value of elections, dating back to its success as an entrist organization in the Labour Party during the 1980s. Operating as the Militant Tendency, it was a leading force in the Liverpool Labour Party when it gained control of the city council in the 1983 local election. Making up in organization what it lacked in numbers – only 16 of the 51 Labour councillors belonged to Militant – it began to mount a serious challenge to central Conservative government spending restrictions, mobilizing local people in a six-year campaign of defiance (Crick 2016: 237; Taaffe and Mulhearn 1988). By 1987 there were three Militant Tendency MPs: Dave Nellist in Coventry, Terry Fields in Liverpool and Pat Wall in Bradford. Consequently the Socialist Party looks sympathetically on workers or community campaigners standing as 'anti-cuts candidates' in order to gain support for socialist ideas (Sell 2006: 82–83). Indeed the Socialist

Party has even argued that 'in a country like Britain it would be possible for an entirely peaceful socialist transformation of society to be carried out', a position argued occasionally by Marx and Engels, but never by Lenin or Trotsky (Socialist Party 2008: 27; and on Marx and Engels see Callinicos 1983b: 160–62). Socialist Resistance, the British affiliate of the Mainstream Fourth International, also strongly favours electoral participation: 'Election results might not be as important for anti-capitalist parties, who emphasize extra-parliamentary struggles, as for mainstream parties. Nonetheless, it is our only, albeit very problematic, parameter for measuring the broader public support these parties have' (Videt 2011: 15).

One final piece of evidence suggesting Trotskyist organizations take elections seriously is the efforts they have devoted to building electoral coalitions, including the Socialist Alliance (early 1990s–2005), the Respect Coalition (2004–2008), No2EU; Yes to Democracy (created 2009) and the Trade Unionist and Socialist Coalition (TUSC) (created 2010) (Burton-Cartledge 2014; Clive Heemskerk interview; and see also Chapter 4).

Electoral participation has been shaped by three factors: political constraints, economic resources and political tactics. Between the late 1940s and the mid-1960s all Trotskyist groups worked inside the Labour Party (see Chapter 3). An open electoral challenge by an independent Trotskyist against an official Labour candidate is a breach of Labour Party rules and would have quickly led to expulsion, ending the group's entrist activity. Given their small size the Trotskyist groups could ill-afford to become independent organizations outside the Labour Party. Once the majority of Trotskyist groups had ceased to work inside the Labour Party, from the late 1960s, the political constraint of Labour rules was replaced by the economic constraint of finance. Although Trotskyist organizations are remarkably effective at fund-raising (see Chapter 8), electoral participation is expensive. At the time of writing (2017) each candidate in a UK parliamentary election must submit a deposit of £500, refundable only if he/she obtains at least 5 per cent of the votes cast (and Trotskyist candidates rarely achieve anything like that figure). A candidate in a European Parliamentary election must submit a deposit of £5,000, refundable on obtaining at least 2.5 per cent of the vote. Local council elections, in contrast, require no deposit. This means that the 138 candidates who fought the 2015 general election had to raise £69,000 simply for their deposits, not to mention the additional funding required for campaign material and room bookings. Consequently the very small Trotskyist groups such as the AWL, Communist League, SEP, Workers Fight and Workers Power, either abstain from elections or contest only a handful of seats (Anna Hunt interview).

Third, as Cliff wrote: 'Marxists do not insist either on participation in elections or abstention from them. For us it is a tactical question, and not an especially important one' (Cliff 2000: 139). IS/SWP participated in a number of parliamentary by-elections in the late 1970s, before abandoning electoral work for over 20 years, because 'there was very little evidence that it provided lasting organizational gains for the Party' (Charlie Kimber interview). In contrast, other organizations such as the WRP have adopted a different tactic, standing candidates in every general election since February 1974.

Trotskyist electoral performance in the UK 1974–2017

Table 7.1 provides a summary of the results for all Trotskyist organizations in the 12 general elections since February 1974, excluding members of the Militant Tendency/RSL who stood as Labour candidates.[3] The table records median votes and vote share, expressed as a percentage of all votes cast in each constituency, ignoring spoilt and invalid papers. Results are shown for England and Wales only on the grounds that the Scottish and Northern Ireland party and electoral systems are significantly different from those in the rest of the UK. The table shows median figures because occasionally a candidate has secured an unusually large vote share, and such outlying results distort the mean though not the median, for example Dave Nellist in Coventry. Respect candidates have been included in the 2005 results because although the *de facto* coalition leader George Galloway is not a Trotskyist, the organization at that time was dominated by the SWP and many of its candidates were SWP members. Following the split with the SWP in 2007,

TABLE 7.1 Trotskyist general election results, England and Wales 1974–2017

Election date	Median (mean) vote	Median (mean) vote share	Candidates	Parties and candidate numbers
1974 Feb	309 (476)	0.88 (1.04)	10	WRP 8, IMG 2
1974 Oct	359 (340)	0.85 (0.87)	10	WRP 10
1979	192 (236)	0.55 (0.64)	66	WRP 54, SU 10, WP2
1983	176 (186)	0.38 (0.46)	25	WRP 19, RCP 4, WP 2
1987	205 (208)	0.45 (0.48)	23	RCP 13, WRP 10
1992	104 (1,016)	0.29 (2.63)	18	RCP 8, M/IL 3, ICP 3, WRP 2, CL 2
1997	239 (379)	0.63 (0.89)	32	SP 21, WRP 8, SEP 3
2001	465 (557)	1.25 (1.61)	108	SA (SP, SWP, AWL, WPo) 98, WRP 6, SAlt 2, LA 1, MP 1
2005	447 (1,318)	1.22 (3.43)	63	Res (SWP) 26, SP 17, WRP 10, AGS 5, DSA 2, SU 2, CL 1
2010	184 (300)	0.45 (0.67)	44	TUSC (SWP, SP, SR) 28, WRP 7, SAlt 4, SEP 2, AWL 1, CL 1, WPo 1
2015	213 (259)	0.45 (0.59)	138	TUSC (SWP, SP) 119, LU 9, WRP 7, CL 2, SEP 1
2017	86 (115)	0.16 (0.24)	7	WRP 5, CL 2

Key: AGS Alliance for Green Socialism; AWL Alliance for Workers Liberty; CL Communist League; DSA Democratic Socialist Alliance; ICP International Communist Party; IMG International Marxist Group; LA Left Alliance; LU Left Unity; MP Marxist Party; M/IL Militant/Independent Labour; RCP Revolutionary Communist Party; Res Respect; SA Socialist Alliance; SEP Socialist Equality Party; SAlt/SP Socialist Party; SR Socialist Resistance; SU Socialist Unity (IMG and Big Flame); SWP Socialist Workers Party; TUSC Trade Unionist and Socialist Coalition; WP Workers Party; WPo Workers Power; WRP Workers Revolutionary Party.

Sources: Craig (1975, 1984, 1989); Rallings et al. (1993, 1998); House of Commons, http://research briefings.parliament.uk/ResearchBriefing/Summary/RP01-54, accessed 9 August 2016; Electoral Commission.

Respect could no longer be classified as a Trotskyist organization and its 2010 and 2015 results have been excluded from Table 7.1 (Leplat 2008).

The most striking feature of the results is how poorly Trotskyist candidates have performed. Their median vote share is normally less than 1 per cent and has only twice exceeded that figure, in the New Labour years 2001 (1.25 per cent) and 2005 (1.22 per cent), before falling back to less than half of 1 per cent in 2010, 2015 and 2017.[4] There is some variation over time: vote share was especially poor in the years of the Thatcher and Major Conservative governments – 1983, 1987 and 1992 – and picked up under New Labour – 1997, 2001 and 2005 – only to decline thereafter. Vote share tends to be significantly higher in elections won by Labour compared to Conservatives, 0.97 per cent vs 0.39 per cent, but this is a small difference between two small numbers. The 2005 election was probably the highpoint of Trotskyist success, coming just two years after the mass mobilizations against the Iraq War, coordinated by the SWP-led Stop the War Coalition. In that election the main Trotskyist challenge came from the Respect coalition in which the SWP was the key grouping. Ex-Labour MP George Galloway won the Bethnal Green and Bow constituency but lesser known candidates also achieved high vote shares, particularly in areas with high proportions of Muslim voters: Birmingham Sparkbrook 27.9 per cent, East Ham 20.7 per cent, West Ham 19.5 per cent and Poplar and Canning Town 16.9 per cent. In addition a further 11 candidates obtained more than 1,000 votes, a figure achieved by only two of the 138 candidates who participated in the 2015 general election (in Coventry North West and Tottenham).

The picture is little better for parliamentary by-elections and despite some modest results in the late 1990s and early 2000s, the results are still very poor (Table 7.2). Although vote shares are somewhat higher than for general elections, this is most likely the result of a relatively stable Trotskyist vote combined with low voter turnout.

TABLE 7.2 Trotskyist by-election results, England and Wales since 1945

Government and PM	Seats contested	Median vote share
Coalition Churchill 1940–1945	1	4.58
Labour Wilson 1966–1970	1	1.10
Labour Callaghan 1976–1979	9	1.30
Conservative Thatcher I 1979–1983	1	0.13
Conservative Thatcher II 1983–1987	2	1.21
Conservative Thatcher III 1987–1990	1	0.61
Conservative Major 1990–1997	2	3.51
Labour Blair I 1997–2001	3	3.96
Labour Blair II 2001–2005	6	1.78
Labour Blair III 2005–2008	0	n/a
Labour Brown 2008–2010	2	0.98
Conservative and Liberal Democrat Cameron I 2010–2015	4	1.31
Conservative Cameron II 2015–2016	0	n/a
Conservative May 2016–2017	0	n/a

Sources: Craig (1975, 1987); www.parliament.uk/mps-lords-and-offices/offices/commons/hcio/by-elections-2010/; Electoral Commission.

The poverty of these results is underlined when we consider the process of seat selection by Trotskyist groups. In smaller organizations the decision is made centrally but in larger organizations such as the Socialist Party or the SWP, national leaders will either encourage particular branches to consider an electoral contest or will solicit expressions of interest from local branches (Charlie Kimber interview). Key factors in the final decision will include the record of local activity and the financial resources of the branch so Trotskyists are often fighting seats where they have some roots (Clive Heemskerk interview). Not surprisingly many Trotskyist branches operate in traditional Labour seats: of the 234 different seats contested by Trotskyists between 1974 and 2017, Labour won 84 per cent of them.

Before considering explanations for this poor electoral performance, it is worth examining local election results given the tradition of left-wing councillors stretching back to the early years of the twentieth century and briefly maintained by the Communist Party. In 1945–1946, with a total membership of just over 42,000 the CP emerged with 215 seats in local council elections, the zenith of its influence in local government (Branson 1997: 114–15). Second, a range of minor parties has constructed local bases of support and won council seats, including the BNP and UKIP on the far right and the Greens and Respect on the left. Third, because financial deposits are not required in local elections, finance is no longer a barrier to participation. Finally, low turnouts mean that small parties with strong mobilizing capacity can often do well.

The Socialist Party has fought local elections more consistently than any other Trotskyist group but its achievements have proved to be limited and fragile. In Coventry, home of former MP Dave Nellist and one of the party strongholds, SP councillors were elected in 1998, 2004 and 2006 giving it three seats on Coventry City Council by 2006 (including Dave Nellist). Yet by 2012 all three seats had been lost. Two SP councillors were elected to Lewisham Borough Council (London) in 2002 and 2003 respectively but both seats were soon lost (in 2006

TABLE 7.3 Trade Unionist and Socialist Coalition local election results, England and Wales 2011–2017

Election	Candidates	Median vote share (%)	Council seats won and (lost)
2011	174	3.0	0 (3)
2012	134	4.6	2 (0)
2013	120	1.9	0 (0)
2014	554	2.7	1 (0)
2015	617	2.0	1 (0)
2016	302	2.8	1 (2)
2017	59	2.2	0 (0)

Sources: TUSC 2011, 2012, 2013, 2014, 2015, 2016, 2017 local election results all at www.tusc.org.uk/ candidate, accessed 9 June 2017. The table excludes mayoral, town council and parish council elections but includes small numbers of non-TUSC candidates that were nonetheless endorsed by TUSC, for example anti-cuts independents in Southampton and the Democratic Labour Party in Walsall.

and in 2010). An SP councillor was elected in Huddersfield in 2006 but lost in 2010. With other gains and losses in more recent years the upshot is by 2017 the party has just three councillors, including two Labour defectors and an anti-cuts campaigner, in Southampton. The SWP record in local government is even thinner: Liverpool academic Michael Lavalette was elected to Preston council in 2004 but after his resignation in 2014 for family reasons, the seat was retaken by Labour. These results need to be seen in the context of a relatively large number of electoral contests fought in recent years as Table 7.3 reveals.

In addition Trotskyists have fought 18 mayoral contests between 2002 and 2017 and despite the occasional strong showing – 12.7 per cent in Hackney 2002 and 21.6 per cent in Newham 2006 – the median vote share is just 2.35 per cent.[5] It is clear that the vote share for Trotskyist candidates in local elections is somewhat higher than in general elections but it is also clear that the TUSC vote is spread very thinly: in 2014 for example only one of TUSC's 554 candidates won a seat and only four of them managed second place.

Explaining poor electoral performance

In order to throw light on these results there are three factors that need to be examined: the electoral system, the degree of electoral competition and the electoral strategy of Trotskyist organizations (Gallagher et al. 2011).

The electoral system

According to one veteran activist, 'first past the post is a very, very major impediment' for leftist parties because the vote share required for electoral success is so high (Alan Thornett interview). In contrast, parties in the more proportional electoral systems of Western Europe can secure parliamentary seats with around 4–5 per cent of the popular vote (Gallagher et al. 2011: 378–79). Yet the obstacles posed by majoritarian systems for small parties are not insuperable as shown by the electoral victories for George Galloway (Respect) and Caroline Lucas (Green Party). One way of testing the electoral system effect is to examine Trotskyist vote shares in those UK elections that are based on proportional representation, that is, the European Parliament from 1999 and the London and Welsh Assemblies. Low turnout in European elections might suggest many voters are indifferent to the European Parliament but low turnout can also favour smaller parties with high mobilizing capacity. For instance, the Green Party has performed well in recent European elections and in 2014 won three seats. However, there has been no such effect for Trotskyist candidates as their median vote share in these elections has been just as bad as in general elections, only once rising above 1 per cent (Table 7.4). It is true that the median vote share has been fractionally higher since the introduction of proportional representation – an average of 0.81 per cent compared to a pre-1999 average of 0.62 per cent – but the difference is trivial and both numbers are abysmal. Elections to the London and Welsh Assemblies have yielded similar results:

TABLE 7.4 Trotskyist UK European election results 1979–2014

Election*	Median vote share %	Number of candidates
1979	0.93	1
1989	0.35	3
1994	0.57	2
1999	0.85	1
2004	1.11	11 candidates in all 10 constituencies
2009	0.98	10 candidates, 1 in each constituency
2014	0.31	7 candidates in 6 out of 10 constituencies

Sources: House of Commons Library; Electoral Commission.

* Elections in 1979, 1989 and 1994 were conducted under the first past the post system with voting in 73 English and Welsh constituencies; elections from 1999 were conducted under proportional representation with votes cast in ten English and Welsh constituencies. Trotskyists did not contest the 1984 European Parliamentary election.

London top-up results between 2000 and 2012 ranged from 0.8 to 4.6 per cent with a median score of 2.0 per cent and Welsh results 1999–2016 ranged between 0.3 and 2.1 per cent with a median result of just 1.4 per cent.[6]

Electoral competition

Trotskyist groups not only compete with social democratic parties such as Labour in the UK and the SPD in Germany, but also face competition from other leftist organizations such as Communist and Green parties. Competition from the Communist Party has steadily declined since its electoral peak of 1945 when it secured a second MP. By the 1970s, despite a membership of around 25,000 and a large trade union base, it was still polling only fractionally better than the far smaller Trotskyist parties. In the 1974 elections, for example, its candidates obtained median vote shares of 1.20 (February) and 1.05 (October) but in every subsequent election, however, Communist vote share was less than 1 per cent.[7] Although some doubt whether the Greens can be classified as a left party, the Comparative Manifesto data places them firmly on the left in many European countries, including Austria, Finland, the Netherlands, Sweden and Switzerland (Budge et al. 2001: 37–45). From the early 1980s the Greens began to field more candidates and have posed an increasing threat ever since, with 53 candidates in 1979 and 457 in 2017. Prior to 1992 no Green candidate in the seats also fought by Trotskyists had ever obtained more than 1,000 votes but in the 2015 general election 83.8 per cent of Green candidates in such contests (104 out of 124) exceeded 1,000 votes. The advance of the Greens does appear to have squeezed the already small Trotskyist vote in 2015 still further, a dismal outcome for the largest ever Trotskyist electoral challenge (Laker-Mansfield 2015). For a brief period, the left-wing Socialist Labour Party (SLP) stood in many of the seats also

TABLE 7.5 Trotskyist parliamentary candidates and electoral competition, England and Wales 1974–2017

Year	Seats contested by Trotskyists	Seats with other left candidates (incl. Greens)	Seats with at least three left candidates	Main left competitors and candidate numbers
1974 (Feb)	9	3	0	CPGB 1
1974 (Oct)	10	3	0	CPGB 2
1979	60	16	1	CPGB 7
1983	25	10	3	CPGB 8, Green 6
1987	23	10	1	Green 9
1992	17	11	2	Green 11
1997	29	12	6	SLP 9, Green 8
2001	102	61	16	SLP 40, Green 38
2005	59	37	9	Green 35, SLP 9
2010	42	31	3	Green 31, SLP 4
2015	133	126	21	Green 123
2017	7	7	0	Green 7

Key: CPGB: Communist Party of Great Britain; SLP: Socialist Labour Party.

Sources: As for Table 7.1.

contested by Trotskyists. Created in 1996 by former mining union leader Arthur Scargill, the SLP stood 65 candidates in the 1997 election, and 114 in the 2001 election, but its electoral presence fell dramatically in the 2000s and was down to just three candidates in 2017, a similar number to George Galloway's Respect Party. Finally, Left Unity, formed in 2013, contested nine seats in the 2015 general election (although six of these were joint Left Unity-TUSC candidates).[8] Table 7.5 (above) shows that a rising proportion of seats contested by Trotskyists is also being fought by other left parties.

Electoral strategy

Electoral strategy entails decisions about whether to stand as part of an electoral coalition or as an independent group, how many candidates to stand and which seats to contest. Electoral coalitions avoid direct competition between Trotskyist organizations and pool resources, permitting economies of scale in canvassing and in the production of election materials. The first Trotskyist electoral coalition was Socialist Unity in 1979 and subsequent elections have involved various combinations of groups in a variety of coalitions: Socialist Alliance (2001), Respect (2005) and the Trade Unionist and Socialist Coalition TUSC (2010 and 2015). Coalitions have generally performed better than independent Trotskyist candidates (Table 7.6) and this was especially true of the Respect Coalition in 2005 which almost certainly capitalized on opposition to Labour support for the 2003 war in Iraq (Borisyuk et al. 2007).

TABLE 7.6 Electoral performance by Trotskyist coalitions and single parties, England and Wales 1979–2015*

Election	Coalition	Median vote for coalition candidates	Median vote for single party candidates
1979	Socialist Unity	0.85	0.55
2001	Socialist Alliance	1.28	0.44
2005	Respect	2.87	0.64
2010	Trade Unionist and Socialist Coalition	0.54	0.22
2015	Trade Unionist and Socialist Coalition	0.49	0.20

Sources: As for Table 7.1.

* TUSC did not contest the 2017 general election.

Nonetheless we cannot infer a causal connection between coalition formation and higher vote share because the organizations that decline to participate in electoral coalitions are the more sectarian Trotskyist groups such as the WRP and the SEP, whose vote shares have always been relatively low.

The number of candidates in each general election has varied between 7 and 138 but the scale of the Trotskyist challenge bears no relation to median vote share (Spearman's rho = +0.34 which is not statistically significant). Equally irrelevant is the celebrity status of the candidate. In the February 1974 general election the IMG's Tariq Ali, famous for his role in the Vietnam protests of the late 1960s, obtained just 424 votes (0.89 per cent) in Sheffield Attercliffe. The actress Vanessa Redgrave fought three elections in the late 1970s for the WRP but performed only fractionally better than unknown Trotskyists in other seats. In Newham North East she polled 760 votes (1.71 per cent) in February 1974 and 572 votes (1.46 per cent) in the same constituency in October 1974. In the Manchester Moss Side by-election in July 1978 she received 394 votes (1.46 per cent).[9]

With regard to seat choice, 544 Trotskyist candidates contested a total of 234 different seats in the 12 elections between February 1974 and June 2017. The seat number takes into account seat abolition, seat merger and subsequent name changes, which altogether affected 54 seats. For example, the Peckham constituency was abolished in 1997 and largely absorbed into the new seat of Camberwell and Peckham so electoral contests in Peckham pre-1997 and in Camberwell and Peckham from 1997 onwards have been considered as contests in the same seat. Almost half these seats – 106 (45.3 per cent) – have been fought on just one occasion and no seats have been contested on all 12 occasions (Vauxhall in south London comes close with 11 contests).[10] Only 11 seats have been contested in a majority of the 12 general elections between 1974 and 2017 and six of those are in London, consistent with the high proportion of Trotskyist party members living in the capital (and two are in the former Militant Tendency strongholds of Coventry and Liverpool, Table 7.7). Shifting focus to the one organization that has fought every election since February 1974, the WRP, we find a similar absence of sustained and consistent electoral activity.

TABLE 7.7 Seats contested on multiple occasions by Trotskyist candidates, England and Wales 1974–2017 (12 elections)

11 contests
Vauxhall (includes Lambeth Central)
8 contests
Camberwell and Peckham (includes Peckham)
Coventry North East (includes Coventry South East)
Hackney South and Shoreditch (includes Hackney Central)
Holborn and St Pancras (includes St Pancras North)
Sheffield Central (includes Sheffield Park)
7 contests
Bethnal Green and Bow (includes Bow and Poplar; Stepney and Poplar)
Bristol South
Liverpool Riverside (includes Liverpool Toxteth)
Manchester Gorton
Tottenham

Source: As for Table 7.1.

However, TUSC has displayed somewhat more consistency between its first and second electoral contests, in 2010 and 2015. Of the 32 seats contested in 2010 (28 by TUSC and four by the Socialist Party under the label Socialist Alternative) around two-thirds (23 seats) were also fought in 2015. On the other hand the character of TUSC as an electoral coalition means that it lacks any enduring infrastructure and is therefore completely invisible between elections. That fact in turn is rooted in the desire of SWP and Socialist Party leaders to preserve their separate organizations, rendering TUSC a weak and secondary organization that will inevitably struggle to achieve an electoral breakthrough. Overall therefore, Trotskyist electoral activity has displayed little evidence of any strategic planning.

One reason is Trotskyist groups experience high levels of membership turnover which means party branches will contract significantly or even disappear, depleting the human resources available to fight an election campaign in a particular area. The resource issue, however, is somewhat more complicated than simple numbers of party members. As the SWP National Secretary Charlie Kimber pointed out,

> People in the SWP haven't really joined the organisation to stand in elections, that's the truth. It's not what motivates people so it's often quite a hard argument actually for quite good reasons, people are suspicious of the whole process, they think well that's rubbish really.
>
> *(Charlie Kimber interview)*

Equally important is the way in which the two main organizations, the Socialist Party and the SWP, determine seat choice. According to the SWP National Secretary,

> I will ring people up and say have you thought about standing or people will say to me we're thinking of standing, what do you think? And those decisions are . . . based very much on what people think on a local level but they also depend on the agreement of the Central Committee about whether you stand or not.
>
> *(Charlie Kimber interview)*

A similar point about bottom–up nomination was made by the Socialist Party whose election agent noted that 'TUSC . . . has only ever turned down two applications' (Clive Heemskerk interview). In part this willingness to contest many seats reflects the strategic aim of the Socialist Party, 'to consolidate the Trade Unionist and Socialist Coalition and to spread the arguments inside the trade union movement . . . that the working class needs an independent political voice' (Clive Heemskerk interview).

In contrast, the SWP has tended to the view that 'it's better to concentrate on a few places where you're relatively strong and you can get a decent vote' (Alex Callinicos interview). Strategically, that means you are 'able to go to other people, trade unionists and say look we're a credible force' (Charlie Kimber interview).

Local activist influence over the pattern of electoral contests is a key part of the explanation for the relatively low degree of consistency in the choice of electoral battlegrounds and for the low vote share in most seats. Although low vote totals can be discounted by appealing to the view that parliament is irrelevant and ultimately has little power, low votes do create potential problems, even for revolutionary organizations, and it is to those problems we now turn.

Dealing with electoral 'failure'[11]

Poor electoral performance creates a significant dilemma for Trotskyist party leaders. On the one hand, an open acknowledgement of an extremely poor vote could imply there is very little support for their policies, calling into question the policies themselves, the commitment of party activists and key elements of Trotskyist doctrine. On the other hand, the denial of poor electoral performance or indeed claims that it constitutes some form of success, potentially threatens the credibility and authority of party leaders.

In the 2010 general election eight Trotskyist organizations from five party families stood candidates and their newspapers, magazines and websites carried considerable amounts of election coverage. The organizations and their publications were as follows: AWL (*Solidarity*), Communist League (*The Militant*), Socialist Party (*The Socialist*), Socialist Resistance (*Socialist Resistance*), SWP (*Socialist Worker*), SEP (World Socialist Web Site), Workers Power (*Workers Power*) and the WRP (*The News Line*). The Socialist Party, Socialist Resistance and the SWP joined forces in TUSC. Only four organizations produced a definitive post-election analysis yet the themes that comprised party discourse about electoral performance were often prefigured in pre-election articles, particularly in *The Socialist* and *Socialist Worker*.

Publications and websites from these eight organizations were therefore examined over a time span starting 6 April 2010 – the date the election was called – and ending 31 May, over three weeks after the 6 May election, an exercise that yielded 54 articles. Their analysis revealed a number of significant themes that together comprised what we may describe as 'the discursive reconstruction of electoral failure'. Since this analysis was originally produced in 2014 the evidence has been updated with material from the 2015 general election, which featured seven of the eight participants from 2010 (Workers Power was the 2015 absentee).

We should recall that in 2010 the 44 Trotskyist candidates received a median vote share of just 0.45 per cent (with a median vote of 184) and in 2015 the largest ever field of Trotskyist candidates – 138 in England and Wales – achieved an identical median vote share (0.45) but a fractionally higher median vote of 213. Trotskyist press coverage of the general elections acknowledged their vote shares were very unimpressive, although the language employed was somewhat euphemistic. The results were never abysmal or dreadful, they were 'poor' (*Solidarity* 7 May 2010 and 13 May 2015), 'disappointing' (*Socialist Worker* 8 May 2010) or 'modest' (*The Socialist* 7 May 2010). One senior interviewee acknowledged that 'we never made the kind of breakthrough that we were hoping' (Alex Callinicos interview). Yet these observations were typically surrounded by three more positive claims: that the Trotskyist vote share underestimated the level of popular support for Trotskyist ideas and policies; that the campaigns generated many positive outcomes such as high levels of newspaper sales; and finally, it was sometimes suggested the Trotskyist vote share was not too bad given that many electors were driven reluctantly to vote Labour through fear of the Conservatives. *The News Line*, paper of the WRP, normally doesn't even mention the party's dismal vote shares, but former party leader Gerry Healy apparently took an optimistic view of their results. When WRP candidate Gerry Downing obtained just 290 votes (0.76 per cent) in Brent East at the 1979 general election he reported his disappointment to Healy only to be told, 'No Gerry, you didn't get 290 votes, you got 290 *revolutionary socialist* votes!' (Gerry Downing interview).

The vote underestimates our level of support

The most conspicuous theme in the 2010 Trotskyist texts, present in 67 per cent of the 54 articles examined, was that the level of support for their policies was far higher than indicated by vote shares. The most subtle variant of this theme is captured in the statement that 'The Trade Unionist and Socialist Coalition (TUSC) campaign has won the argument in Cardiff Central even if we have not won the election . . . where people have been able to hear the arguments, we are the winners' (*The Socialist* 28 April 2010). This claim bolsters the idea that Socialist Party policies are popular but hints at one possible reason for the low vote share, namely lack of resources. Contacting voters so they can 'hear the arguments', on the streets or in door-to-door canvassing, is enormously resource-intensive. The Socialist Party at the time of the 2010 election had fewer than 2,000 members, distributed across the whole of England and Wales. The numbers who could be deployed in each of 32 election campaigns (28 candidates stood as TUSC and four as the 'Socialist Alternative') was therefore very limited. Resources were stretched even more thinly in 2015 when the party's 2,500 members campaigned for 125 TUSC candidates. Yet whilst small numbers are clearly disadvantageous from the standpoint of electoral resources, they become advantageous as a means of explaining poor election results.

Other organizations offered a more subtle variant of this theme, referring to the 'good hearing' (*Socialist Worker* 1 May 2010), the 'warm response' (*Workers Power* 9 May 2010) and the 'good response' (*Solidarity* 13 May 2015) their candidates and supporters received from voters. This terminology is both positive and ambiguous: positive because it conveys claims about party support, but ambiguous because it *implies* popular support without offering hard evidence. Furthermore, the notion of a 'sympathetic hearing' can help undermine the threatening idea that Trotskyist arguments attracted so few votes because people rejected them out of hand; on the contrary, they attracted 'widespread support' (*Socialist Worker* 1 May 2010).

Allied to this argument is the theme that votes are a poor measure of attitudes. According to the SEP vote share 'is not the only, or even the best measure of the political importance of the campaign the party waged' (Marsden and Hyland 2010), and their hard left critique of Labour policies was 'shared by millions of working people' (Socialist Equality Party 2010). This phrase is a particularly interesting rhetorical device because it deals with low vote share, not by avoiding any reference to numbers, but rather by juxtaposing a far more impressive number, the 'millions' who allegedly shared the party's viewpoint. In similar vein, SWP texts often asserted a huge discrepancy between votes and attitudes: the numbers who sympathize with Trotskyist rejection of public spending cuts is 'far greater' than the number who voted for Trotskyist candidates (*Socialist Worker* 15 May 2010). Likewise in 2015, the strong support for the Scottish National Party's anti-austerity message was often used to argue that the low votes for Trotskyist anti-austerity candidates were a misleading indicator of antipathy to austerity (*The Socialist* 13 May 2015; *Socialist Worker* 16 May 2015; *Workers Power* June 2015).

Opposition to austerity policy is significant because as several texts asserted 'Getting representatives into parliament is important. But real change comes when millions of ordinary people say "Enough is enough"' (League for the Fifth International/Workers Power 2010a; and *Solidarity* 13 May 2015). The effect of this type of discourse is to redirect the reader's attention away from the paucity of votes, the election and the parliamentary process and onto a different and more appealing terrain, that of working-class mobilization for collective action. Such action is more familiar to left activists than the rhythms of parliamentary politics and represents a terrain in which their own efforts often yield tangible results, in the form of meetings and demonstrations. The reference to collective action therefore appeals both to a sense of agency (we can control our environment) and to a sense of efficacy (we can make a difference).

Votes matter, but there are other, positive features of the election campaigns

The second component of Trotskyist election discourse switches focus towards positive outcomes. A pervasive theme was the self-congratulatory idea that the election campaigns and the candidates were 'excellent', and 'lively' (*The Socialist* 12 May 2010; *Socialist Worker* 15 May 2010; League for the Fifth International/ Workers Power 2010b; *The Militant* 1 June 2015) because activists had 'explained basic socialist ideas to thousands of people' (*Solidarity* 7 May 2010) and 'leafleted over 80 per cent of the constituency' (*Socialist Worker* 8 May 2010). In similar vein, '260 copies' of a key book were sold (*The Militant* 19 April 2010); '440 papers' were sold and '25 people have applied to join' (*The Socialist* 12 May 2010); and 'many new recruits were made' (*The News Line* 26 April 2010). The message here is that many thousands of people have been exposed to socialist ideas so in due course these seeds will bear fruit yet there is an element of risk in this discursive move. If so many people received party literature and were addressed, then why was the vote so poor?

Another significant outcome was improved organizational capacity. Party activists built 'links with local trade unionists' (*The Socialist* 12 May 2010) and helped create 'networks of resistance and solidarity' (*Socialist Worker* 10 April 2010) so we will be 'better . . . able to resist the cuts that are coming' (*Solidarity* 7 May 2010). The theme of capacity points to outcomes other than votes and therefore reinforces the discursive strategy of backgrounding poor electoral performance. It also helps in this aim by alluding to the prospects of greater political success thanks to higher membership and to links with other activists and campaigning organizations, key elements in the underlying ideology of class struggle as a key factor in social change.

The vote was not that bad under the circumstances

The third major theme in the election texts recapitulates the argument that votes do not necessarily reflect attitudes. According to the Socialist Party, many more people 'would have voted for us' but the threat of a Conservative election victory led them to 'vote New Labour in order to stop the Tories' (*The Socialist* 7 May 2010 and *Socialist Worker* 16 May 2015). The language used in these and other texts portrays powerful emotions at work. Even though workers may have given Trotskyist ideas a 'sympathetic hearing', the prospect of another Conservative government 'alarmed' and 'terrified' them (*The Socialist* 7 May 2010); it triggered a 'gut hatred' of Conservatism (*Socialist Worker* 8 May 2010). The language used is critical in reconstructing group boundaries, creating an affinity between workers and the Trotskyist parties ('us'), because both share a deep and powerful antipathy to a common Conservative enemy ('them'). In addition the two largest organizations both declared that 'all capitalist parties [were] losers' (*The Socialist* 7 May 2010), that it was the election 'where everyone lost' (*Socialist Worker* 15 May 2010) because the Conservatives failed to obtain a majority of seats and Labour and the Liberal Democrats both lost seats. This claim seeks to undermine the notion that parties with small vote shares (in particular, the Trotskyist parties) are 'losers' whereas those with large vote shares – Conservative, Labour, Liberal Democrat – are 'winners'. The binary divide between winners and losers is submerged in the theme that 'everyone lost', albeit in different ways.

Taken as a whole the thrust of Trotskyist discourse around the 2010 and 2015 general elections was to downplay the potentially unsettling and threatening reality of dismal vote totals by constructing a complex, alternative discourse. It aimed to uncouple votes and popularity, stressed evidence of the popularity of far left policies and outlined a range of positive outcomes beyond votes. Poor electoral performance was not denied as such, but was reconfigured within a discourse that provided an optimistic message for party activists and sympathizers.[12]

Conclusions

Trotskyist organizations do not take elections as seriously as mainstream political parties because of their belief that parliament is a branch of the capitalist state, an institution that must be destroyed through a seizure of power led by a revolutionary vanguard party. However, they also recognize that elections and parliament can be used as platforms from which to disseminate socialist propaganda. The balance between these views has shifted over time so that the larger organizations, the Socialist Party and the SWP, as well as smaller groups such as Socialist Resistance, now routinely participate in general and local elections, whereas their participation in the 1970s was far more sporadic. The main results of electoral participation, however, have been almost uniformly dismal. Vote shares have rarely exceeded 1 per cent, in general and European elections as well as in parliamentary by-elections and Assembly elections. Local election results have been somewhat better and several Trotskyist councillors have been elected in various parts of the country yet their numbers remain tiny and they have rarely held their seats for more than a few years.

Electoral performance has been as poor under proportional representation as under the 'first past the post' system; it has also remained low whether Trotskyists stood alone or in coalition with other groups; and it is unrelated to the number of seats contested. Vote share has probably been depressed by the absence of a consistent electoral presence in successive elections and of local work in between elections. It has also been depressed by increased electoral competition. The steady rise of the Green Party; the continuation of Respect as a non-Trotskyist organization from 2008; the rise and fall of the Socialist Labour Party; the emergence of Left Unity in 2013 and of Corbyn's Labour Party from 2015 have all served to increase congestion in the left electoral space and squeeze the already limited Trotskyist vote.

We noted in Chapter 1 that poor electoral performance typically elicits one or more of five changes from political parties, in electoral institutions, policies, organizational structures, target constituencies and relations with other parties. Leaving aside electoral institutions, change in the other four areas is extremely difficult because of the constraints of Trotskyist doctrine. Party policies in election manifestos are driven by profound antagonism to the capitalist system, limiting the scope for significant modification. Where parties have focused on more immediate demands in their manifestos and downplayed revolutionary goals, this shift brings them closer to the programmes of the Greens or Labour (particularly in 2017), placing them at a major competitive disadvantage. The structure of the typical Trotskyist organization is equally resistant to change because it is rooted in a key element of doctrine, the necessity for a democratic centralist, vanguard party. The same is true of their target constituency, which remains the working class and its class interests. Finally there is no prospect of accommodating to the policies of more successful rivals, such as Labour or the Greens, because they are by definition reformist not revolutionary organizations and accommodation would therefore entail an impermissible violation of the core commitment to revolution. In short, Trotskyist doctrine renders the normal mechanisms of adjustment to electoral failure inoperable. Trotskyist responses to poor electoral performance have therefore been discursive, centring on a variety of self-serving claims, that their policies were far more popular than suggested by their vote share, which wasn't too bad under the circumstances and that in any case the election campaigns generated multiple, positive outcomes such as increased membership and newspaper sales. This type of election discourse is a rationalization, an organizationally 'positive' reconfiguration of the electoral outcome, providing party activists with an account that challenges the debilitating ideas of electoral failure and unpopularity. On the other hand, the backgrounding of low vote share discourages any more critical reflection on why organizations that claim to represent the 'working class' as a whole are unable to secure more than 1 per cent of the popular vote.

Appendix: Trotskyist electoral performance in Western Europe

British Trotskyists often point to the success of other West European parties as evidence of what can be achieved by revolutionaries, particularly under proportional systems of representation. Continental Europe is also a reference point in attempts to show the widespread and growing influence of the Trotskyist movement in anti-austerity protests, strikes and demonstrations. Finally because many British organizations belong to a Fourth International, links to their sister organizations across Western Europe form a key element in their claims to represent an international movement.

Trotskyist electoral performance in Western Europe[13] since the onset of the economic crisis in 2008 has been highly variable with countries falling into three groups: first, there are five countries without any Trotskyist electoral participation, Cyprus, Finland, the Netherlands, Norway and Switzerland. Three of these countries have only one Trotskyist organization (Finland, Norway and Switzerland) and Cyprus has just two, so the Trotskyist movement in those countries is almost certainly very weak. In contrast, 'radical left parties' have secured significant vote shares in elections held between 2008 and 2015: the Cypriot party AKEL has averaged 32.7 per cent, the

Finnish Left Alliance 7.6 per cent, the Dutch Socialist Party 9.8 per cent and the Norwegian Socialist Left Party 5.2 per cent (March 2016: 40, 42).[14] There are clearly small leftist constituencies in these countries but they have not been mobilized by the tiny Trotskyist groups.

In a second set of countries – Austria, Belgium, Italy and Sweden – Trotskyists have mounted independent electoral challenges but as in the UK they have proved largely ineffectual (see Table 7.8). Vote shares for a variety of Trotskyist groups, some affiliated to British-based internationals such as the Committee for a Workers International and the League for the Fifth International, have never exceeded 1 per cent, even where parties have chosen to fight only in those districts where they possess some degree of local organization. It is also important to note that these four countries operate highly proportional electoral systems with 'disproportionality indexes' ranging from 1.9 in Sweden to 4.7 in Italy compared to a score of 16.5 for the UK majoritarian parliamentary electoral system (Gallagher et al. 2011: 391). Moreover Trotskyist presence in these countries is not insignificant, as we established in Chapter 6. Austria and Italy each have eight

TABLE 7.8 Trotskyist election results in Austria, Belgium, Italy and Sweden 2008–2014

Country and election date	Party (international affiliation)	Mean vote share	Constituencies contested
Austria			
28 Sept 2008	Socialist Left Party (CWI) and League for the Socialist Revolution (L5I) as part of Left (Far left coalition)	0.08	5 out of 9
29 Sept 2013	Socialist Left Party (CWI)	0.12	1 out of 9
Belgium			
13 June 2010	Party of Socialist Struggle (CWI)	0.20	4 out of 11
	Party of Socialist Struggle (CWI) and Revolutionary Communist League (FI 1938) as part of Left Front (Far left coalition)	0.75	6 out of 11
25 May 2014	Workers Struggle (ICU)	0.48	1
Italy			
13/14 Apr 2008	Workers Communist Party (CCRFI)	0.57	All constituencies
	Critical Left (FI 1938)	0.46	All constituencies
	Communist Alternative Party (IWL–FI)	0.06	1
24/5 Feb 2013	Workers Communist Party (CCRFI)	0.26	All constituencies
	Communist Alternative Party (IWL–FI)	0.01	All constituencies
Sweden			
19 Sept 2010	Socialist Justice Party (CWI)	0.03	All constituencies
	Communist League (SWP-PT)	0.00	8 out of 29
14 Sept 2014	Socialist Justice Party (CWI)	0.01	23 out of 29

Sources: Austria: Ministry of the Interior; Belgium: National Elections Authority; Italy: Ministry of the Interior; Sweden: Official Elections Authority.

organizations, Belgium has five and Sweden four, all of which are currently affiliated to an International and many of which produce newspapers and magazines (see Table 6.3). In light of this organizational presence, the vote shares at recent elections must be considered derisory.

Finally, there is a substantial group of eight countries where Trotskyists have claimed vicarious electoral success because of their factional presence in relatively large and influential 'radical left parties' such as Die Linke in Germany and Syriza in Greece (for example Bensaid et al. 2011; Bouma 2016).[15] Table 7.9 shows the results for these parties at the most recent election compared with results from the last pre-crisis election, that is, prior to 2008. In fact with the exception of France, Greece and Spain, their performance has generally been unimpressive. In France the Trotskyist vote in the 2007 French parliamentary election was just 3.41 per cent whereas in 2017 the radical left coalition La France Insoumise (incorporating Ensemble, part of the Mainstream Fourth International: see Escalona and Vieira 2016: 122) secured 11.03 per cent and 15 parliamentary seats.[16] French presidential election results showed a similar trajectory.[17]

In Greece, Syriza (Coalition of the Radical Left) achieved a dramatic increase in its vote share from 3.26 per cent in 2004, the year of its formation, to 36.34 per cent in January 2015 when it emerged as the largest party in the Greek parliament and formed a government. Pledged to oppose the austerity policies implemented from 2008 by both conservative and social democratic governments, the Syriza project immediately attracted the support of several Trotskyist groups: the Internationalist Workers Left (part of the Mainstream Fourth International), Marxist Voice (International Marxist Tendency) and the Socialist Internationalist Organization (Committee for a Workers International). Not surprisingly, one Trotskyist group – the SWP, affiliated to the International Socialist Tendency – joined a rival coalition, Antarsya (Front of the Greek Anti-Capitalist Left) whilst another refused to join either coalition and continued to contest elections as a separate organization (Workers Revolutionary Party). Between 2004 and 2015 Syriza became more of an 'office seeking' party, willing to compromise on key policies to secure power and to negotiate further loans from the European Troika (Eleftheriou 2016). Disillusioned with the willingness of the Syriza government to continue with austerity, the three Trotskyist groups decamped prior to the September 2015 election and helped formed a new coalition, Popular Unity. Its fate was similar to that of its more radical rival, Antarsya and other independent Trotskyist groups, with a vote share of less than 3 per cent (the threshold required for parliamentary representation) whilst the Syriza vote share fell by less than one percentage point despite the betrayal of its core anti-austerity policy (Table 7.9).

The Spanish electoral coalition Podemos was formed in January 2014 and the Trotskyist group Anti-Capitalist Left (part of the Mainstream Fourth International) was a key player in its genesis (Ramiro 2016). It secured almost 8 per cent of the vote in the May 2014 European parliamentary election, just two points behind the

TABLE 7.9 Radical left and Trotskyist election results in eight West European countries 2012–2017

Country and election dates	Party (international affiliation)	Vote share (pre-2008 vote)	Deputies elected/total in chamber
Denmark			
18 June 2015 (13 Nov 2007)	Socialist Workers Party (FI 1938) as part of Red-Green Alliance (far left and left coalition)	7.70 (2.15)	14/175
France*			
10/17 June 2012 (10/17 June 2007)	Anti-Capitalist Left (FI 1938) (as part of Left Front, left and far left coalition)	6.91 (3.41)	10/577
	Workers Struggle	0.98	0
2017	Workers Struggle	0.77	0
Germany			
22 Sept 2013 (18 Sept 2005)	Marx 21 (IST) and Socialist Alternative constituency (CWI) (as part of Die Linke) party list	8.22 (7.98) (constituency) 8.59 (8.71) (party list)	64/631
	Party for Social Equality (ICFI) party list	0.01 (0.03)	0
Greece			
25 Jan 2015 (16 Sept 2007)	Internationalist Workers Left (FI 1938), Marxist Voice (IMT) and Socialist Internationalist Organization (CWI) (as part of Syriza)	36.34 (5.04)	149/300
	Socialist Workers Party (IST) (as part of the Front of the Anti-Capitalist Left)	0.64	0
	Workers Revolutionary Party (CCRFI)	0.06**	0
	Organization of Internationalist Communists of Greece-Spartacus (FI 1938)	0.03	0
20 Sept 2015	Internationalist Workers Left (FI 1938), Marxist Voice (IMT) and Socialist Internationalist Organization (CWI) (as part of Popular Unity)	2.86	0
	Socialist Workers Party (IST) (as part of the Front of the Anti-Capitalist Left) and Workers Revolutionary Party (CCRFI)	0.85	0
	Organization of Internationalist Communists of Greece-Spartacus (FI 1938)	0.04	0

Ireland

26 Feb 2016 (24 May 2007)	Socialist Party (CWI) and Socialist Workers Party (IST) as Anti-Austerity Alliance-People Before Profit	3.95*** (7.91/3.69)	6/158

Luxembourg

20 Oct 2013 (13 June 2004)	Revolutionary Socialist Party (as part of The Left, far left and left coalition)	4.94 (2.01)	2/60

Portugal

4 Oct 2015 (20 Feb 2005)	Revolutionary Socialist Party (FI 1938) (as part of Left Bloc, a far left coalition)	10.22 (6.54)	19/230
	Socialist Alternative Movement (IWL-FI)	0.38	0

Spain

20 June 2016 (14 Mar 2004)	Anti-Capitalist Left and Revolutionary Workers Party (both FI 1938) (as part of Unidos Podemos)	21.10 (4.96)	71/350

Sources: Denmark: Statistics Denmark; France: Ministry of the Interior; Germany: Federal Returning Officer; Greece: Ministry of Interior; Ireland: Government website (Houses of the Oireachtas); Luxembourg: Official Elections Authority; Portugal: National Elections Commission; Spain: Ministry of the Interior.

* First round vote share.
** Fought 23 out of 56 constituencies.
*** Fought 31 out of 40 constituencies.

communist-led leftist coalition United Left (which included the Revolutionary Workers' Party, another affiliate of the Mainstream Fourth International). In the December 2015 general election Podemos made huge gains as its vote share rose to 20.68 per cent (and United Left fell back to just 3.67 per cent, the worst result in its 30-year history). However, at a snap election called in June 2016 Podemos failed to maintain its upward momentum, despite (or perhaps because of) an electoral coalition with United Left: the 21.1 per cent vote share of Unidos Podemos was more than three points lower than the combined vote share of its component parts just six months earlier.

Elsewhere radical left party gains during the economic recession have been modest or non-existent. Vote shares have risen in Denmark (up 5.55 points to 7.7 per cent), Portugal (up 3.68 points to 10.72 per cent) and Luxembourg (up 2.93 points to 4.94 per cent) although the Portuguese Left Bloc has simply recovered its 2009 vote share after a collapse in 2011 (Freire and Lisi 2016) and the German party Die Linke lost ground slightly between 2005 and 2013 (from 8.71 per cent to 8.59 per cent). The Left Bloc has offered support to the minority

Socialist administration but radical left party support for social democratic govern-ments in Denmark, Finland, Norway and Sweden in the 1990s and 2000s almost invariably led to radical left vote losses at the ensuing elections (March 2016: 42).

Finally, the Irish case has also been mentioned frequently because a Trotskyist electoral coalition won six seats in 2016 following its leadership of a prolonged and popular campaign against the introduction of charges for water consump-tion (Dunphy 2016). Yet the presence of a record number of Trotskyist deputies in the Irish parliament needs to be set in the context of the Irish recession. At the February 2011 election three far left groups secured the election of five deputies – the Socialist Party, People before Profit (led by the SWP) and the United Left Alliance (including Workers and Unemployed Action, the Socialist Party and the SWP). Socialist Party candidates obtained 6.93 per cent of the vote in the eight constituencies they contested and the SWP figure was 4.81 per cent in nine constituencies. Following five more years of austerity, the two par-ties combined forces for the February 2016 election, to form the Anti-Austerity Alliance-People before Profit coalition. It contested far more constituencies than in 2011 (31 out of 40) but made a net gain of just one seat, taking its total to six, and recorded a lower vote share of 3.95 per cent. Overall therefore the Trotskyist left in Ireland has not advanced significantly between 2011 and 2016 (Dunphy 2016).

The period 2008–2016 was one of almost unprecedented turmoil in the advanced capitalist world, characterized by an exceptionally long and profound economic recession, the continuation of neo-liberal austerity policies and an his-toric decline in living standards. These conditions ought to have been highly propitious for the growth of the Trotskyist left, particularly in the relatively pro-portional electoral systems of Western Europe. Yet its achievements ranged from mixed to minimal, even in countries such as France, where the Marxist left has tra-ditionally been strong, or in the countries of Southern Europe that have witnessed large-scale protests, demonstrations and general strikes against austerity (Hamann et al. 2013). The failure of the Trotskyist left to capitalize on these protests and to challenge effectively the conditions that gave rise to them is an intriguing issue that will be addressed in the concluding chapter.

Notes

1 The distinction is significant because members of the Socialist Review Group contested a number of general elections as Labour candidates. There was one candidate in 1959, two in 1964, two in 1966 and one member of the International Socialists who stood as a Labour candidate in 1970 (Rudge 2017).
2 Socialist Workers Party Central Committee, Election Strategy, SWP Pre-Conference Bulletin No. 2, May 1978, Nigel Clark Papers, File 489/8; IS Central Committee, Parliamentary Candidates: By-Election Campaigns – How We Expect To Build, International Socialists Internal Bulletin, September 1976, Will Fancy Papers, Box 23/4.
3 There were three Militant/RSL candidates in England and Wales 1979 (none elected), five in 1983 (two elected) and four in 1987 (three elected) (see Crick 2016: 327–30; Taaffe 1995: 300).

4 The 2017 result is slightly anomalous because abstention by TUSC left only a handful of candidates, five from the Orthodox WRP, which has always performed very badly, and two from the tiny Communist League whose lack of resources were clear from their vote totals of 27 and 7 respectively (in Manchester Gorton and Islington North, Jeremy Corbyn's constituency).

5 See the sources for Table 7.3.

6 Data from the Electoral Commission.

7 The CPGB dissolved itself in 1991 but the Communist Party of Britain, 'refounded' in 1987, has obtained equally poor vote shares of around 0.5 per cent for its 5–6 candidates in elections between 1997 and 2015.

8 The joint candidates were run in five seats: Bermondsey and Old Southwark, Bethnal Green and Bow, Camberwell and Peckham, Ellesmere Port and Neston, Exeter and Leigh.

9 The only possible exception to this rule is the performance of George Galloway who won Bethnal Green and Bow in 2005 as a candidate for the Respect Coalition, but since Galloway himself was not a Trotskyist the result tells us nothing about the attractive power of Trotskyism.

10 Vauxhall includes the former seat of Lambeth Central, incorporated into the constituency in 1983.

11 Much of this section is adapted from Kelly (2016). The article contains more details on the methods and sources of evidence.

12 The classic study of how fundamentalist religious groups respond to the failure of their predictions or expectations is Festinger et al. (2008). First published in 1956, it established the ways in which group members 'reconfigured' events to reduce the 'cognitive dissonance' between doctrine and reality.

13 Western Europe is defined here as 18 countries comprising the former EU 15 (Austria, Belgium, Denmark, Finland, France, Germany, Greece, Ireland, Italy, Luxembourg, Netherlands, Portugal, Spain, Sweden and the UK) plus Cyprus, Norway and Switzerland. The six very small countries (Andorra, Iceland, Liechtenstein, Malta, Monaco and San Marino) are excluded because there is no evidence of Trotskyist activity with the exception of Iceland in the 1970s and 1980s (Alexander 1991a: 514–15).

14 On the Cypriot Progressive Party of Working People (AKEL) see Ioannou and Charalambous (2016); on the Finnish Left Alliance see Dunphy (2004: 139–47); and on the Dutch Socialist Party see Keith (2016).

15 Working as a faction inside larger leftist parties is not without its risks: in the Netherlands the Socialist Alternative group (affiliated to the Committee for a Workers International) was expelled from the Socialist Party in 2009 for factional activity (Keith 2016: 162).

16 In contrast Lutte Ouvrière obtained less than 1 per cent of the vote.

17 In 2007 the main Trotskyist Presidential candidate Olivier Besancenot from the Fourth International's Revolutionary Communist League (RCL) obtained 4.08 per cent in round one, compared to 1.33 per cent for Lutte Ouvrière's perennial candidate Arlette Laguiller and just 0.34 per cent for the Workers Party (leading group in the Lambertist Fourth International). In 2017 Jean Mélenchon of France Insoumise scored an impressive 19.58 per cent in round one but votes for other Trotskyist candidates were derisory: 1.09 per cent for the New Anti-Capitalist Party, successor to the RCL, and just 0.64 per cent for Lutte Ouvrière, its worst ever presidential election result.

8

ORGANIZATIONAL RESOURCES

Previous chapters have demonstrated some of the persistent weaknesses of the Trotskyist movement in Britain, above all its strict attachment to the core elements of Trotskyist doctrine and the resulting hostility between different Trotskyist families and organizations. It is true that the presence of both attributes is uneven across the movement: there is for example a significant difference between the novelty of the 'eco-socialist and feminist' perspective of the Mainstream Socialist Resistance and the programmatic rigidity of the Orthodox WRP. Nevertheless every Trotskyist group today is significantly smaller than 20 years ago and the movement as a whole is less than half the size it achieved in the mid-1980s. It is also more fragmented than at any time in its history with no less than 22 organizations – many of them miniscule – competing for members and supporters. The entry of Trotskyist parties into the electoral arena has failed to improve their standing and dismal electoral performance continues to be the norm. After many years of austerity and recession the prospects of a revolutionary assault on capitalist state power by Britain's small and divided Trotskyist groups seem utterly remote.

Yet despite these weaknesses and failings, the Trotskyist movement displays a remarkable degree of resilience, both in Britain and elsewhere. Its placards and newspaper vendors are a familiar sight on picket lines and demonstrations; it has an organized presence on dozens of university campuses (Chapter 6); and at the time of writing (2017) it is the subject of a media hue and cry about its allegedly baleful and growing influence in the Labour Party.[1] For some Trotskyists their persistence is easily explained: Trotskyism is the 'Marxism of the twenty-first century', a body of ideas 'whose time has come'. We can, and should, reject such accounts not least because they have been proclaimed by Trotskyists every year for the past 80 years or more, in complete disregard of any evidence. Moreover they are often to be found embedded in teleological arguments which echo Lenin's famous and simplistic refrain that 'The Marxist doctrine is omnipotent because it is true' (1913).

More useful insights are to be gained by analysing the acquisition and deployment of a variety of organizational resources. Human resources comprise members and their willingness to work for the organization; the key material resource, for social movements and political parties alike, is money; social-organizational resources consist of the structures designed by groups to organize and motivate members, to formulate policies and to decide on forms of collective action; finally, the most common cultural resource for many social movements and parties is a publication such as a newspaper or magazine, whether hard copy or online (Edwards and McCarthy 2004). The argument of this chapter will be that one key element in the resilience of Trotskyist organizations is their exceptional efficiency in the acquisition and deployment of such resources. We have already examined membership induction and control in Chapter 5 and membership recruitment in Chapter 6 so after a brief discussion of membership activity levels this chapter concentrates on material, social-organizational and cultural resources.

Membership resources

We established in Chapter 6 that Trotskyist groups have experienced increasing difficulty in recruiting and retaining members. That fact alone places a premium on building high levels of commitment amongst the membership and securing high levels of participation in organizational activities. One former WRP activist recalled that in the early 1980s there was, 'this enormous work ethic – people worked, worked, worked on the basis that the crisis was around the corner' (Bob Archer interview). Another activist from the same period recalled a daily drive to Glasgow railway station to collect copies of the *News Line* and distribute them around the city: bundles of papers to individual party members for paper sales, individual papers to subscribers at their home addresses and a bundle to a local bookshop (Informal conversation with Terry Brotherstone). The same organization issued a short pamphlet in the early 1970s (reprinted many times) that set out a typical week's programme for a Young Socialist branch combining political and social activity: on Sunday there would be a swimming gala; Tuesday evening was spent recruiting at a local college; Wednesday was assigned for visiting new members; Thursday was the branch meeting; Saturday was a dance; and Sunday was a football match between local YS branches.[2]

The Orthodox WRP did have a reputation for promoting unusually frenetic activity but it was not alone in this regard: a longstanding member of Workers Fight talked about getting up at 4 a.m. for a newspaper sale to early shift workers at King's Cross station (Anna Hunt interview). The Radical Trotskyists of Workers Power also set high standards of membership activity:

> There was a very strong expectation of everyone who was physically able-bodied to be an active participant in all aspects of the group's life. There was an expectation of attendance at branch meetings. There was an expectation of attendance at regional events.
>
> *(George Binette interview)*

In the words of a current member of the group, 'to join Workers Power you've got to be pretty serious about what you're doing' (Workers Power interview). The Mainstream International Group (now Socialist Resistance) reported in 1988 that its work was organized by nine separate 'commissions', each involving between five and ten of its fewer than 300 members. In addition to their commission work members were also expected to attend a range of demonstrations and meetings on a wide range of issues such as the Gulf War, anti-trade union laws, lesbian and gay rights and Latin America.[3]

Smaller organizations are obviously limited in their range of activities but this hardly applies to the two largest organizations, the SWP and the Socialist Party.

An insight into the wide range of activities of SWP members can be gleaned from its weekly bulletin Party Notes which both catalogues recent and upcoming events and issues instructions to members. The 1 August 2016 issue is typical, despite the mid-summer date when one might expect a lull in political activity. It began with a list of ten Corbyn campaign meetings over the coming week and provided links to a leaflet, model motion, petition and placard as well as details of a new edition of a pamphlet on Corbyn and the Labour Party; members were urged to register for the Stand up to Racism conference on 8 October; they were asked to attend Mark Duggan protests on 5 and 6 August and a Black Lives Matter meeting on 9 August; there were details of a demonstration at the Conservative Party conference in Birmingham on 2 October ('Unwelcome the Tories'); four upcoming Pride events were listed and members were urged to attend with placards and leaflets as well as collecting tins for the 'Pink Bus to Calais' (for refugees); there were details of six industrial disputes with contact addresses for messages of solidarity and details of solidarity demonstrations or pickets; there was a request to register for the Unite the Resistance national conference on 12 November and another request to help with crowdfunding the party bookshop and publisher Bookmarks; finally there was a reminder about an International Socialism Dayschool on 'Marxism and Nature' on 15 October.

The Socialist Party website offers activities on an equally wide range of issues including the workplace, the environment, housing, racism, anti-war protests and the health service. It also promotes sections of the party dealing with particular issues and identities such as students, women and LGBT as well as its various front organizations, Youth Against Racism in Europe, Youth Fight for Jobs, the National Shop Stewards Network and the Trade Unionist and Socialist Coalition.[4] An active membership is clearly a key resource for Trotskyist organizations, but it turns out the members are also the chief source of income.

Raising money: the income of Trotskyist organizations

Mainstream leftist political parties charge relatively modest annual membership fees and raise only modest sums through fund-raising drives. In 2014 full Labour Party membership cost £47.04 per annum whilst the Green Party charged £31 and both offered lower fees for categories such as students, retired people and low-wage workers.[5] Taking into account these differential membership fees as well as the high propensity of retired people to join political parties and ineffi-ciencies in dues collection, we would expect the membership income per capita for such parties to be significantly lower than the standard rates of £47 and £31 respectively and that is exactly what we find (Table 8.1). When we include figures for other leftist parties with parliamentary representation in 2014 – Plaid Cymru, the Scottish National Party and George Galloway's Respect Party – we see that Labour was the most successful in raising income from members with a figure of £30.82 per capita. However, when we include the AWL we find that this small Trotskyist group raised over *11 times* the income per capita of the Labour Party, an astonishing £332 per member. All of these figures have been audited and all were submitted to the Electoral Commission and met their reporting guidelines so they are unlikely to be the result of data distortion. If we turn to another Marxist, but non-Trotskyist organization, the Communist Party of Britain, we find that it too raised significantly more income per head than Labour – slightly over £100 – which suggests there may be features of revolutionary parties that facilitate hyper-efficient fund raising. Electoral Commission data for the AWL between 2009 and 2013 shows that the 2014 figure (the last one available) was no flash in the pan because the average per capita annual membership income for that five year period was £360.90.

There is no standardized party financial data prior to the creation of the Electoral Commission in 2001 and there is no data for the two largest groups, the SWP and the Socialist Party because they file very limited information through their electoral organization, the Trade Unionist and Socialist Coalition. Two other parties have regularly filed accounts with the Commission, the SEP and the WRP and there is financial data available in the archives of several Trotskyist organizations and individuals covering a range of years from the 1960s to the 1980s (Table 8.2). This data was collated by organizational members in charge of finance and presented in internal reports to leading committees so although unaudited, its internal character reduces the likelihood of data distortion. Membership income, for example, was

TABLE 8.1 Membership income, UK left political parties 2014

Political party	Membership income (£)	Individual membership	Membership income per capita (£)
Alliance for Workers Liberty	43,205	130	332.35
Labour Party	5,971,000	193,754	30.82
Scottish National Party	1,330,465	93,045	14.30
Green Party	431,411	30,900	13.96
Plaid Cymru	135,274	7,965	16.98
Respect	13,095	612	21.40
Socialist Labour Party	5,180	385	13.45
Communist Party of Britain	94,853	917	103.44

Source: Electoral Commission 2014, accessed 17 August 2016.

TABLE 8.2 Historic membership income, UK Trotskyist organizations 1967–1987

Organization	Year	Membership income (£)	Individual membership	Membership income per capita 2016 prices (old prices) (£)
International Marxist Group	1971–72	4,182	315	169.50 (13.28)
	1976	21,823	662	249.74 (32.79)
	1979	39,608	664	309.32 (59.65)
Militant Tendency	1971–72	6,343	217	373.14 (29.23)
	1987	624,000	8,000	206.43 (78.00)
IS/Socialist	1967	1,940	383	85.23 (5.07)
Workers Party	1978	81,604	4,200	109.12 (19.43)

Sources: IMG Financial Statement 28 May 1972: June 1971 to May 1972, Tony Whelan Papers, File/1/1/1; IMG Party Builder Bulletin No. 9, July 1978, IMG Papers Warwick, File 171; IMG Finance Report 1980, IMG Papers Warwick, File 168; Militant Tendency Finance Statement 1 April 1971 – 31 March 1972, Socialist Party Papers, File 601/C/5/2/5; Beishon, J., Finance, Members Bulletin 16 March 1996, Socialist Party Papers, File 601/D/1/2/2; IS Financial Balance Sheet 1967, Will Fancy Papers, Box 16/1; SWP Finance Report January 1979, Steve Jefferys Papers, File 244/2/1/2.

money actually received rather than money owed, anticipated or budgeted. In order to make the data comparable with the 2014 figures and to assist their interpretation they have all been adjusted to current (2016) values using the 'This is Money' website.[6] All three organizations – the IMG, the IS/SWP and the Militant Tendency – raised income per head well in excess of the Labour Party's £30 and Militant was particularly effective. Despite its patchiness this evidence suggests that the exceptional fund raising capacity of Trotskyist groups suggested by the AWL data is neither peculiar to the AWL nor a recent phenomenon.

Money is raised from members (and sympathizers) through four main channels: subscriptions (sometimes called membership dues), fund-raising drives, collections at rallies and publications.[7] Table 8.3 shows the available data on current and historic subscription rates for the main Trotskyist groups and demonstrates that they are currently well in excess of mainstream party rates and have been for many years. Obviously we cannot assume that all members will pay subs at their appropriate rate or even pay subs at all. Some people classified as 'members' may no longer belong to the organization and Trotskyist groups vary significantly in the efficiency of their dues–collection systems. For example in 2013 the SWP reported that only 51 per cent of their claimed membership of 7,180 had paid dues that year.[8]

Second, the larger Trotskyist groups frequently organize major fund-raising drives, which invariably generate substantial sums: in 2015 five of the largest Trotskyist groups raised over £365,500 (Table 8.4). Historical data (Table 8.5) suggests that the amounts raised in recent years are comparable to monies raised in the 1970s and 1980s. Little is known about the contributors to these fund drives but as they are mainly publicized in party newspapers and websites whose main readers are almost certainly party members then it follows that a large proportion of these funds are probably contributed by those members. Evidence for this supposition is limited but data for the IMG provides some support. Of the £18,500 raised during their 1978–1979

TABLE 8.3 Trotskyist organizations' subscription rates 1972–2016

Organization	Subscription (£) (waged workers)	Annual rate (£) (2016 prices)
Socialist Workers Party	10–30 pcm 2016	120–360
Socialist Party	0.50–20 pw 2016	26–1,040
Counterfire	25 pcm 2016	300
International Marxist Group	36 pa 1974	393
Militant Tendency	31.20 pa minimum 1972	398
Socialist Workers Party	18 pa 1977	117
Socialist Charter	4% gross income 1980	229
Workers Socialist League	1.5% net income 1982	312
Workers Power	10% gross income 2000	1,800

Key: pcm: per calendar month, pw: per week, pa: per annum

Sources: SWP, Socialist Party and Counterfire websites, accessed 17 August 2016; IMG National Committee Minutes 26–27 January 1974, IMG Papers Warwick, File 82; Militant Tendency National Committee Minutes 8/9 April 1972, Socialist Party Papers, File 601/C/5/2/5; SWP Membership Card 1978, Nigel Clark Papers, File 489/7; What Is the Socialist Charter? PC and MD (Mike Davis) June 80 in Socialist Charter Annual Conference 1980, Christ Taylor Papers, File 406/6/1/4; WSL Dues, n.d. – probably early 1982, AWL Papers, File AWL 1/21; Workers Power, George Binette interview.

Development Fund Drive, £8,500 came in the form of donations (almost certainly by members), £7,000 was collected at national rallies (where attendees will be members and sympathizers) and £1,400 was collected by youth members and supporters.[9]

Third, there are collections at rallies and large public meetings and although the sums raised comprise a relatively small proportion of total annual income they do indicate the willingness of party members – the main attendees at these events – to make additional contributions over and above their subscriptions. For example, the Socialist Party holds an annual festival of meetings and debates, with dozens of workshops and seminars on a wide range of topics. The final rally at Socialism 2015, attended by almost 1,000 people, raised an astonishing £30,000, an average of £30 per head (*The Socialist* 11 November 2015). On a smaller scale the AWL's comparable event that year, the annual Ideas for Freedom Summer School, was attended by 'over 200 people' and the collection at its closing rally raised

TABLE 8.4 Major Trotskyist fund-raising drives 2015

Organization	Fund	Amount raised (£)	Membership	Income per capita (£)
Socialist Party	Fighting Fund	123,000	2,500	49.20
SWP	Socialist Worker Appeal	106,264	5,886	18.05
WRP	News Line Monthly Fund	96,000	125	768.00
Socialist Appeal	Fighting Fund	25,000	300	83.33
AWL	Annual Fund	15,245	140	108.89

Sources: *The Socialist* 6 January 2016; *Socialist Worker* 9 January 2016; *The News Line* various issues; *Socialist Appeal* February 2016; *Solidarity* 11 November 2015.

TABLE 8.5 Historic Trotskyist fund-raising drives 1979–1993

Organization	Membership	Fund and Year	Target (raised) ($£K$)	Target in 2016 prices ($£$)
IMG/Socialist	715	Development Fund 1978–79	20 (18.5)	112,000
League	504	Building Fund Drive 1984	50 (27.2)	152,000
Socialist Party	1,900	Fighting Fund 2010	100 (105)	121,000
WRP	2,495	Trotsky Centenary 1979	30 (30)	156,000
	2,495	General Election 1979	100 (94)	487,000
	2,614	Party Expansion 1980	50 (54)	247,000
	2,614	News Line Anniversary 1980	11 (11.6)	53,000
	2,755	Party Development 1981	60 (60)	244,000
WRP (News Line)	2,000	Party Press Fund 1986–88	250 (220)	410,000

Sources: IMG Finance Report 1980, IMG Papers Warwick, File 128; *Socialist Action* 27 April 1984 and 26 April 1985; *The Socialist* 12 January 2011; WRP Special Funds, WRP Papers, Box 375; *The News Line* 1 February 1986 and 30 June 1988.

£2,534 (£12.67 per head) (*Solidarity* 15 July 2015). The WRP holds a News Line Anniversary Rally each November and in 2013 the 200 people present contributed £1,214 to a collection, just over £6 per head (*The News Line* 19 November 2013; no more recent figures are available).

Finally, income is obtained from members through their purchase of party publications, and these fall into two categories: first, those produced by the party itself, such as the regular newspaper and magazine as well as books and pamphlets by leading party figures. In the case of the Socialist Party for example there is the weekly *Socialist* newspaper, the monthly magazine *Socialism Today* and books and pamphlets by party leaders such as Peter Taaffe and Hannah Sell. Socialist Appeal offers the eponymous fortnightly newspaper, the quarterly magazine *In Defence of Marxism* and numerous books by current leader Alan Woods and the late Ted Grant. Second, there are reprints of classical Marxist literature either issued by the party itself under its own imprint or purchased wholesale from the original publisher and resold to members. Many of Trotsky's works for example are published by the American company Pathfinder Press (linked to the US Socialist Workers Party and the UK Communist League) and resold through the websites of organizations such as the Socialist Party and Socialist Appeal. Pathfinder titles include the 14-volume *Writings of Leon Trotsky 1929–40* as well as classics such as *The Revolution Betrayed*, *The History of the Russian Revolution* and the three-volume collection *The Challenge of the Left Opposition*. In the UK many of Trotsky's classic works were also published by the WRP publisher New Park, including *Lessons of October*, *The First Five Years of the Communist International* (two volumes), *Writings on Britain* (three volumes), *Platform of the Joint Opposition* and *In Defence of Marxism*. Indeed shortly before its implosion in 1985 the WRP had planned a new English edition of Trotsky's works in 24 volumes.[10] Needless to say the project was still-born and no volumes were ever issued.

Since booksellers will expect to receive up to 50 per cent of the cover price for each sale this is a potentially lucrative revenue stream but one on which there is little available evidence. Only a handful of Trotskyist publishing firms are registered at Companies House, namely Socialist Publications (Socialist Party), WL Publications (AWL) and Mehring Books (SEP). Second, even when accounts exist there are problems of interpretation so for instance, it is hard to establish whether an annual operating loss represents a real loss on trading, that is, production and distribution costs exceeded total sales income or whether it reflects a purely paper loss because company profits were being used to cross-subsidise the Trotskyist parent group. For example, the accounts of Mehring Books show annual 'administrative expenses' ranging between £70,819 (2006) and £1,253 (2013), yet it seems unlikely that the costs of office administration fell by 95 per cent in this period! Third, changes in company law mean that before 2006, and since 2011, some small companies (including many Trotskyist groups) have been exempt from reporting income, expenditure and turnover.

However, the available figures reveal that the Socialist Party publishing firm Socialist Publications increased its turnover from £116,972 in 2007–2008 to £189,230 by 2010–2011. That makes sense because its membership rose over the same period from 1,600–1,700 to almost 2,000. As membership continued to increase until 2015, reaching 2,500, it is a reasonable assumption that turnover also continued to grow. Assuming it grew at its historic rate of approximately £18,000 per annum then projecting forward to 2014–2015 would suggest an annual turnover of around £260,000 in 2014–2015, approximately twice the amount raised in the 2015 Fighting Fund of £123,000. In contrast, the AWL publishing arm WL Publications showed a slow but steady decline in turnover between 1994 and 2007

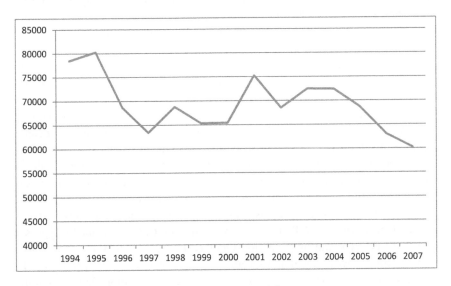

FIGURE 8.1 WL Publications turnover 1994–2007 (£)

Source: Companies House.

(Figure 8.1) and that too makes sense because AWL membership slowly declined over the same period from a little under 160 to approximately 100.

In addition to membership income some Trotskyist groups enjoy other revenue streams such as commercial printing contracts using their own printing equipment. In 1974 the IS printshop reported an annual turnover of £40,000, equivalent to £2.73 million in 2016 prices. That's a somewhat misleading comparison because it does not take into account the dramatic reduction in printing costs arising from new technology since the 1980s but nevertheless it underlines the potential of using an organization's own capital to generate revenue. Bookshops have provided another source of revenue although this is now much reduced in scale as the number of small, independent bookshops has declined. The WRP once owned six (three in London plus one each in Glasgow, Liverpool and Norwich) but four closed in 1988 and the remaining two in the early 1990s.[11] There are no detailed accounts for the bookshops although we know that their combined income in 1984 was £316,000 (just under £1 million in 2016 prices) and they were often profitable (Informal conversation with Terry Brotherstone).[12] The IMG ran two bookshops in the 1980s (in London and Birmingham) but both were closed by 1990.[13] There is no financial information on the latter but the London bookshop was certainly profitable in 1978 and 1979.[14] The only Trotskyist bookshop still remaining is Bookmarks, first opened in 1974 in north London and still in existence in 2017 in a central London location.

Financial precariousness

Trotskyist organizations are clearly very efficient in obtaining money from members yet one of their paradoxical features is that they are frequently wracked by major financial crises, marked by a significant excess of expenditure over income. In 1988 Socialist Organiser (now the AWL) was spending about £8,250 per month but its income was £7,900, making a monthly shortfall of £350, or 4.4 per cent of income.[15] In December 1996 its monthly expenditure exceeded income by 12.9 per cent and by the following September the deficit had grown to 14.3 per cent.[16] Similar reports of excess expenditure can be found throughout the same organization's history, in 1973, 1986, 1987, 1995, 2004, 2005 and 2006.[17] The IMG in the 12 months 1971–1972 recorded a 32 per cent shortfall of income against expenditure despite a 25 per cent increase in membership. One year later it was experiencing an expenditure gap over income of 17 per cent but the following year this rose to an unsustainable 27 per cent.[18] By 1982 its finances had almost stabilized but the following year, after a period of steady membership decline and escalating factional struggle, it was back into serious financial difficulty.[19] It is a similar story for the IS/SWP: in 1964 expenditure outstripped income by approximately 17 per cent and in the period October–December 1978, after substantial membership growth, expenditure again exceeded income by 17 per cent![20] In between times, organizational finances do recover and occasionally yield significant surpluses, for example the Militant Tendency 1970–1971, ISG (now Socialist Resistance) 1988–1989 and the AWL 1999.[21]

These crises reflect three features of Trotskyist organizations: first, whilst many items of expenditure are relatively fixed and predictable – staff wages, office rent and printing costs, for example – many sources of income are relatively unpredictable. Membership numbers, the proportion of members who pay dues, the amount of dues paid and the proportion of newspapers actually sold all fluctuate significantly. Second, financial planning in Trotskyist organizations appears for many years to have been at best rudimentary and at worst non-existent. This is partly due to lack of expertise but also reflects a 'voluntarist' organizational culture in which financial problems can always be resolved by more effort, in effect, squeezing more money from the membership, through fund-raising drives or special appeals.

Third, every Trotskyist group aspires to produce a regular newspaper but the perennial state of Trotskyist newspaper finances is one of deficit. In the first place they carry no paid advertising, an income source that comprised 50 per cent of the revenue of UK national newspapers in 2008 (OECD 2010: 59). Second, they hardly ever achieve the print runs required for significant economies of scale, and finally their paid sales often fall well short of total print runs. Table 8.6 shows that a succession of newspapers published by a range of Trotskyist organizations over a lengthy period of time has regularly lost money, and often very substantial sums. The losses are typically offset by monies raised from members so that, in effect,

TABLE 8.6 Trotskyist newspaper losses 1966–1998

Organization	Newspaper and date	Monthly Loss (£)	Monthly loss in 2016 prices (£)
IMG	*Red Weekly* 1973	520	6,200
	Socialist Challenge 1981	1,600	6,200
Socialist League	*Socialist Action* 1984	1,600	4,878
International Socialists	*Labour Worker* 1966	23	402
SWP	*Socialist Worker* 1978	572	3,212
Militant Tendency	*Militant* 1969–70	5.18	77
WRP	*Workers Press* 1976	6,400	48,489
	The News Line 1977	304	1,977
	The News Line 1978	5,136	28,844
	The News Line 1980	10,000	45,729
WSL	*Socialist Organiser* 1981	400	1,550
AWL	*Workers Liberty* 1998	400–500	660–820

Sources: Estimated Income and Expenditure for IMG 8 May 1973, Tony Whelan Papers, File 1/1/5; The Finances of Socialist Challenge, n.d. – probably early 1981, MRC IMG Papers, File 196; 1984 Conference Delegates Kit, MRC IMG Papers, File 206; Secretary's Report September 1966, Steve Jefferys Papers, File 244/2/1/1; Finance Report January 1979, Steve Jefferys Papers, File 244/2/1/2; Militant Tendency Internal Bulletin June 1970, Socialist Party Papers, File 601/C/5/1/2; Minutes of the Political Committee 26 November 1976, WRP Papers, Box 56; Letter from Healy to All CC Members and Alternates 10 October 1977, WRP Papers, Box 177; Increases Over the Past Year 4 May 1978, WRP Papers, Box 326; News Line Finance and Sales Letter to CC Members 19 September 1980, WRP Papers, Box 719; Financial Report 16 March 1981, AWL Papers, File AWL/1/9; Draft Resolution for Executive Committee 13 February 1998, AWL Papers, File AWL/1/34/1.

the organization subsidizes its own newspaper. The losses incurred by the WRP are exceptionally high but it should be recalled the WRP is the only Trotskyist group to have launched a *daily* newspaper. Even if the reported losses have been exaggerated in order to cajole members into selling more papers it is obvious that an organization of a few thousand members simply cannot sustain a daily paper. The WRP leadership's solution to this problem was twofold: first, to shut down *Workers Press* in late 1976 and quickly launch a new paper – *The News Line* – printed outside London and using advanced technology to cut costs; second, to secure external sources of funding, which are examined shortly.

One reason for the parlous finances of Trotskyist newspapers is the relatively large number of papers that are printed and ordered by party branches but remain unsold. Data on paper sales in relation to print runs and orders dates from the 1960s–1980s and is patchy but consistent. *Socialist Worker* sales as a proportion of print runs fluctuated between lows of 50–55 per cent (1973, 1976–1978) and highs of around 70–75 per cent (1965, 1974). The IMG was receiving between 52 and 63 per cent of the revenue expected from branch orders of its weekly paper *Red Mole* in 1971. In 1979–1980 it was a similar picture for *Socialist Challenge*: branches returned between 53 and 78 per cent of the revenue owed for their newspaper orders although by 1984 the Socialist League (formerly IMG), recouped 82 per cent of the sales income for copies of *Socialist Action*.[22] Very occasionally organizations would enjoy a period of high sales, but these were unusual: 'We sold so many *Socialist Workers* during the miner's strike that it transformed our finances, but that's exceptional' (Alex Callinicos interview).

Figures for 'paid sales' may, however, be misleading and inflate the number of newspapers actually handed over in exchange for money. WRP interviewees reported strong central pressure to pay for all papers ordered, even if they had not actually been sold.[23] Such was the relentless pressure to 'sell the paper' that members sometimes rebelled. Dave Douglass, an ex-member of the Posadist RWP in the 1970s, relates the story in his memoirs of a good friend, an SLL coal miner, whose appetite for paper sales had clearly expired. As told in his Newcastle dialect,

> He was the only dissident member of the SLL I had ever met, picking up his armfuls of *Newsletters*, the sale of which was an act of faith and devotion as strang as Sunday communion. What the hell, I wondered, was he ganna dey we them as we heeded oot ower the Swing Bridge . . .? The question was soon answered as he hoyed the bundles of revolutionary gospel ower the bridge and into the Tyne with a roar of irreverent laughter. I wondered how many other bundles of the revolutionary words of wisdom . . . from the steely Healyite cadre ended their days in the drink.
>
> *(Douglass 2008: 258)*

The peculiar finances of the WRP

In the late 1960s the SLL began to cultivate good relations in the Middle East, initially with the Palestine Liberation Organization (PLO) and from the mid-1970s with the Gaddafi regime in Libya. In 1976 *News Line* editor Alex Mitchell negotiated an agreement to print Libyan pamphlets and newspapers, thus providing a 'healthy revenue stream' for the WRP daily paper (Mitchell 2011: 331). However, the full details of Middle Eastern funding of the WRP only came to light after the 1985 split when the anti-Healy WRP instructed two members, from Germany and the USA respectively, to examine the finances of the organization. They inspected receipts, invoices, bills and cheques in order to provide an accurate summary of the main income and expenditure flows of the WRP and Table 8.7 presents their findings.

The WRP had been heavily funded by foreign governments, in particular the Libyan regime, to the tune of over 1 million pounds (over 5 million pounds in 2016 prices). Payments began in 1976, peaked in 1979 with a figure of £347,755 (£1.8 million in 2016 prices) and ended in 1983. Moreover there was documentary evidence that Healy had deliberately concealed these transactions from other members of the WRP's International Committee of the Fourth International (ICFI).[24] In some cases the rounded figures suggest the investigators provided estimates so there is clearly a question mark about their reliability. The transfers from the other national affiliates of the ICFI are difficult to interpret because all national sections of a Fourth International will pay dues to support international congresses, staff and publications. The ICFI held four congresses between 1977 and 1985 but does not appear to have employed any dedicated staff. By 1975 its 'quarterly' journal *Fourth International* was appearing with diminishing frequency and over the next ten years only two issues appeared (in 1979 and 1982) (North 1986: 3). The limited cost of running the ICFI between 1975 and 1985 suggests that some portion of the half million pounds paid by national affiliates was almost certainly used illegitimately to cover national WRP expenditure.

Despite these substantial income flows the WRP by 1985 was in financial meltdown. One reason is the growing divergence between the costs of producing the daily *News Line* and the revenue generated. According to the International

TABLE 8.7 WRP overseas funding, sources and amounts 1975–1985

Middle Eastern governments and organizations 1977–1983 (£)		International Committee of the Fourth International, overseas sections 1975–1985 (£)	
Libya	542,267	USA	288,977
Kuwait	156,500	Australia	122,195
Qatar	50,000	Germany	69,557
Abu Dhabi	25,000	Others*	16,045
PLO	19,997		
Iraq	19,697		
Other	261,163		
Total	1,074,624	Total	496,774

Source: WRP (Workers Press) International Committee, Commission Interim Report 16 December 1985, WRP Papers, Box 97.

* According to *The News Line* 1 May 1976 there were also ICFI sections in Greece, Ireland and Portugal whilst a meeting of the ICFI the following year claimed there were 12 sections (ICFI 1977).

report, SLL/WRP total newspaper revenue rose from 1969 (when *Workers Press* was launched as a daily) until 1981, but paid sales of the paper then declined dramatically from a weekly average of 90,162 in 1980–1981 to 50,449 by 1984–1985. This is an extraordinary outturn in light of the 1984–1985 miners' strike, which should have boosted sales, and against the background of rising WRP membership, from a little over 2,500 in 1980 to a claimed figure of over 8,000 in early 1985. The second factor in the WRP financial crisis was excessive and uncontrolled expenditure: by mid-1985 the organization owned its own printing press (purchased for £686,802, at historic prices), an educational college (£74,000), seven youth training centres (£207,762), five trucks (£55,399) and a fleet of motor bikes (£32,000) and employed 91 staff.[25]

Staffing and organizational resources

With the exception of the WRP, the buoyant finances of many Trotskyist groups allow them to transcend the limitations of small and/or volatile membership levels by employing full or part-time staff to perform many of the key functions of a political organization: running an office, recruiting and mobilizing members and producing and distributing publications. Table 8.8 compares the 2015 staffing levels of the main Trotskyist groups with those of mainstream leftist parties. What emerges is that the ratio of Trotskyist full-timers to members is far in excess of their social democratic and Green rivals.

TABLE 8.8 Staff numbers employed by Trotskyist organizations and mainstream left parties 2015

Organization	Individual membership	Staff numbers (FTEs)	Number of members per staffer
Socialist Party	2,500	45	56
Socialist Workers Party	5,886	32.5	181
Socialist Appeal	300	6	50
Alliance for Workers Liberty	140	4	35
Counterfire	250	1.5	167
Socialist Resistance	95	1.5	63
rs21	250	1	250
Labour Party*	388,262	293.5	1,323
Green Party	63,219	45.6	1,386
Plaid Cymru*	8,015	13	617

Sources: Interviews with Clive Heemskerk (SP), Charlie Kimber (SWP), Rob Sewell (Socialist Appeal), Martin Thomas (AWL), John Rees (Counterfire), Alan Thornett (Socialist Resistance) and Anindya Bhattacharyya (rs21); Other parties: Electoral Commission, Party Accounts 2015.

* Labour Party staffing in 2015 was reported as 247 full-timers and 93 part-timers; the Plaid Cymru figures were 11 full-timers and 4 part-timers. In the absence of data about the hours worked by the part-time staff I have assumed each part-timer worked half-time and counted each one as 0.5 FTE

The SWP, for example, employed a total of 23.5 full-time equivalents: five administrative staff in its National Office, seven staff on the weekly *Socialist Worker*, four student organizers, three in the Industrial Department, 2.5 staff on the monthly *Socialist Review* and two on a subscription drive. The Socialist Party's weekly paper was staffed by eight people and it also employed eleven regional organizers. In the mid-1970s the WRP was able to produce a daily paper with just 20 staff including printers because it used modern printing equipment and direct input from journalists (Mitchell 2011: 290–91). We also have historic data on the staffing levels of various Trotskyist groups, between 1969 and 1990 which shows that a relatively high ratio of staff to members is not a peculiarity of recent years or of any particular organization but a longstanding feature of all Trotskyist groups (Table 8.9). The evidence is taken entirely from internal group documents, often reports to central or national committees, and so the figures are likely to be reliable.

One of the main drivers of high staffing levels is the pursuit of a number of activities that are largely absent from mainstream parties. Trotskyist groups produce newspapers and magazines; they attempt to organize and mobilize workers in industry and services; they mobilize for demonstrations and protests; and they are pro-active in recruitment because of their small size and high membership turnover. One additional factor that permits high staffing levels is low levels of staff pay.

TABLE 8.9 Historic staffing levels of Trotskyist organizations 1969–1990

Organization	Year	Membership	Staff (FTEs)	Number of members per staffer
International Group	1986	160	3	53
International Marxist Group	1969	80	1	80
	1973	550	14	40
International Socialists	1974	3,405	21.5	158
Militant Tendency	1974	517	20	26
	1978	1,433	53	27
	1987	8,000	250	32
Socialist Labour	1973	3,000	80	38
League/WRP	1985	8,913	91	98
Workers Socialist League	1978	150	2	75
Workers Power	c. 1990	120	2.5	48

Sources: IG: Minutes of Central Committee 19/20 July 1986, Dani Ahrens Papers, File 1/1/1/; IMG: Petersen, P., 'Aspects of the History of the International Marxist Group', IMG/SL Fusion Conference, Pre-Conference Internal Bulletin No. 3, February 1972, IMG Papers Warwick, File 92; Estimated Income and Expenditure for IMG 8 May 1973, Tony Whelan Papers, File 1/1/5; IS: Finance Report May 1974, Nigel Clark Papers, File 489/4; Militant Tendency: International Bulletin March/April 1974, Socialist Party Papers, File 601/C/5/1/5; How We Have Developed, n.d. – probably 1983, Socialist Party Papers, File 601/C/2/2/7; Beishon, J., Finance Members Bulletin No. 16 March 1996, File 601/D/1/2/2; SLL/WRP: Harding (2005: 3); Notes from C. Slaughter for the 8th Congress WRP (Workers Press) Internal Bulletin 7 January 1986, WRP Papers, Box 77; WSL: WSL: Problems and Tasks for 1979, Pre-Conference Discussion Bulletin, n.d. – probably December 1978/January 1979, Alan Clinton Papers Warwick, File 539/2/2/40; Workers Power: Workers Power interviewee.

In 1981 the WSL was spending £270 per month on the wages of each of its full-time workers when gross average earnings in the UK were approximately £580 per month.[26] In 1983 an internal document by IMG staff reported that their current gross pay was just one-third of gross average earnings in the UK, down from half average earnings in the 1970s.[27] A former WRP employee reported that hours were long and that even when staff were paid union rates for their jobs, for example in printing, they were expected to repay a substantial proportion of the money back to the organization (Harding 2005: 189; Hillary Horrocks interview).[28] More recently the ageing leadership of many Trotskyist groups has resulted in a supply of free labour from retired members living on pensions, for example in Socialist Fight, Socialist Resistance, Workers Power and the WRP.

The second major organizational resource of the Trotskyist movement is a large decision-making structure that generates participation by a relatively high percentage of party members whilst the content and frequency of meetings is likely to secure relatively high levels of membership commitment. The most common structure vests supreme authority in a national delegate or member conference that normally meets annually and is the supreme policymaking body of the organization. The IMG, RSL, Socialist Party, SWP and WRP all hold, or held annual National Conferences attended by delegates from branches; the AWL in contrast expects that all of its members attend annual conferences whilst the Socialist Resistance conference is biennial.[29] Each conference elects a National Committee which is often a relatively large body: the SWP National Committee has 52 members and meets quarterly whilst its smaller Central Committee meets weekly. IMG's Central Committee in 1981 had 55 members and the Militant Tendency's leading committee had 44 members in 1986.[30]

In addition to its decision-making structures Trotskyist groups often create an additional layer of *ad hoc* groups to handle particular issues and once again these provide additional routes for membership engagement. In 1983 for instance the WSL (now AWL) involved significant numbers of its 178 members in no less than 13 separate commissions (working groups) on a range of issues including Ireland, black workers, women, party programme, Eastern Europe and Stalinism and CND.[31] In January 1972 the IS was operating with 11 subcommittees of its executive covering issues such as industrial work, education and publications, finance, youth, women, Irish work and tenants as well as the *Socialist Worker* editorial board.[32] The Socialist Party today (2016) has separate sections of the organization for women, black and Asian members, students and LGBT members. The SWP and the Socialist Party have also created discrete, single-issue organizations in many of which they exercise a commanding influence. These will be examined in Chapter 10 but for now we can simply note that Youth for Jobs and Education and Youth Against Racism in Europe were both initiated and are largely controlled by the Socialist Party whilst Stand up to Racism, Unite Against Fascism and Unite the Resistance were the initiatives of the SWP.[33] These committees, groups and organizations help augment member participation and loyalty and bring a wide range of expertise to organizational debates and decisions.

Cultural resources

Turning from organizational resources to cultural resources, it is clear that Trotskyists produce an array of publications that is astonishing for a movement with fewer than 10,000 members. As of May 2017 there were 8 newspapers and 18 magazines of which 11 appeared regularly (Table 8.10). The newspaper cover price is low, mostly £1 (the *Guardian* is £2) but the typical Trotskyist paper – a 16-page tabloid - means the price per page is high. Unlike the Communist Party daily *The Morning Star*, Trotskyist papers are not carried by any newsagents or supermarkets and so distribution is conducted entirely by party members. The magazines are well produced in an A4 format with colour printing and retail between £2 and £3 for anywhere between 26 and 48 pages. Additionally eight organizations have since around 2012 or thereabouts begun to issue free electronic bulletins to subscribers, varying in frequency from several times per week through to monthly, viz. Counterfire, Marxist World, RCITB, rs21, Socialist Action, Socialist Appeal, Socialist Resistance and Workers Power (and during the general election campaign Counterfire issued a very informative daily election briefing). Finally, many Trotskyist organizations have publishing companies that issue Trotsky's works as well as books and pamphlets by Marx, Engels and Lenin.

Two factors have facilitated this plethora of publications: the economics of magazine production and the minimal costs of online production. The cost of printing 500 copies of an A4, 36-page, glossy paper, colour magazine is no more than around £500, that is, £1 per issue for a magazine that would normally retail at £2–3. The cost of producing 1,000 copies in the same format can be as low as

TABLE 8.10 The British Trotskyist press July 2017

Newspapers = 8	*Magazines (regular) = 11*	*Magazines (irregular) = 7*
The News Line (d) WRP	*Socialist Review* (m) SWP	*Fifth International* WP
The Socialist (w) SP	*Socialism Today* (m) SP	*In Defence of Trotskyism* SF
Socialist Worker (w) SWP	*The Red Flag* (m) WP	*Marxist Revival* AWL
Solidarity (w) AWL	*Workers Fight* (m) WF	*Marxist World* MW
The Militant (w) CL	*Marxist Review* (bi-m) WRP	*Socialist Fight* SF
Counterfire (m) CF	*Class Struggle* (q) WF	*Socialist Voice* ISL
Socialist Appeal (f) SA*	*In Defence of Marxism* (q) SA	*The Truth* (*La Vérité*) FI
Workers Hammer (q) SLB	*International Socialism Journal* (q) SWP	
	rs21 (q) rs21**	
	1917 (ann) IBT	
	The Spartacist (ann) ICL (FI)	

Sources: Organizational websites, accessed 8 July 2017.

Key: d: daily; w: weekly; f: fortnightly; m: monthly; bi-m: bi-monthly; q: quarterly; ann: annually.

* Fortnightly from late March 2017.

** Described as quarterly but is actually produced three times per annum.

Socialist Resistance (q) ceased publication with No. 82 Winter 2016.

TABLE 8.11 British Trotskyist organizations and their publishing companies

Organization	Publisher	Titles available August 2016
Communist League	Pathfinder Press	378*
Socialist Equality Party	Mehring Books	258*
Socialist Workers Party	Bookmarks	215
Socialist Party	Socialist Publications	101
Workers Revolutionary Party	Revolutionary Books	47
Socialist Resistance	Resistance Books	35
Socialist Appeal	Wellred Books	19

Sources: Online catalogues, accessed 26 August 2016.

* Catalogue includes books from other publishers and multiple editions of single titles, for example paperback, hardback, e-book.

£750, that is, 75p per issue.[34] In other words what industrial economists refer to as the 'barriers to entry' for new competitors are very low. Individuals or groups disaffected with their own organization can produce a rival magazine at very low cost, even on very low print runs and this fact is one part of the explanation for the large number of Trotskyist organizations currently in existence. Second, most Trotskyist magazines and newspapers are now available online, free of charge, and whilst this availability does nothing to defray production costs and is likely to cut sales revenue, it does help increase readership. Impressive as this range of Trotskyist publications might appear, its impact is somewhat diminished when we consider the print runs of Trotskyist newspapers as a way of gauging the reach of the Trotskyist press (Table 8.12). The two largest organizations, the Socialist Party and the SWP print 20,000 copies of their weekly papers although on past evidence from these and other Trotskyist organizations, paid sales will be significantly lower, perhaps 15,000. On the other hand the papers are freely available on the organizations' websites, a fact that will depress hard copy sales. These figures are well below the peak print runs from the 1970s and 1980s but that is true of all mainstream newspapers. For comparison, the *Guardian*'s paid circulation in 2015 was 164,000 (down from 306,000 in 1976). Magazine print runs are even smaller: the Socialist Party's monthly *Socialism Today* prints 2,000 copies; rs21 between 500 and 1,000.[35] Small groups have even smaller print runs, so for example the Socialist Party breakaway Marxist World printed just 200 copies of its eponymous magazine.[36] In contrast, mainstream left-wing political magazines have significantly higher paid circulations: in 2015 the Audit Bureau of Circulation reported the *New Statesman* figure as 33,395 and *Prospect* at 32,123.[37] Older data for the bi-monthlies *New Left Review* and *Red Pepper* suggest paid circulations of 8,500 and 7,000 respectively in 2004.[38]

Trotskyist publications are clearly an important resource for their own members, many of whom will read the newspaper and some of whom will read the more theoretical magazines. Small numbers of sympathizers and larger numbers on demonstrations and protests will also encounter Trotskyist literature but overall the 'reach' of the Trotskyist press is very limited.

TABLE 8.12 Trotskyist newspaper print runs 2016

Organization	Newspaper and frequency	Print run 2016	Previous peak print run
SWP	*Socialist Worker* w	20,000	31,000 (1974)
Socialist Party	*The Socialist* w	10,000	c. 25,000 (1986)
AWL	*Solidarity* w	2,000	9,000 (1995)
Counterfire	*Counterfire* m	2,000*	n/a
Socialist Appeal	*Socialist Appeal* f	2,000	n/a
Workers Power	*The Red Flag* m	1,000	n/a
Spartacist League	*Workers Hammer* q	n/a	c. 1,000 (1981)
Socialist Resistance	n/a	n/a	6,000 (1981)**
WRP	*The News Line* d	n/a	15,000 (1980–81)***
CPB	*The Morning Star* d	13,000 (2015)	50,000 (***)

Sources: 2016 print runs: Charlie Kimber interview 11 February 2016; Clive Heemskerk interview 1 March 2016; Counterfire, 'The fight is on – help us hit our campaign target', 14 July 2016, www. counterfire.org/news/18419-the-fight-is-on-help-us-hit-our-campaign-target, accessed 15 September 2016; Rob Sewell interview 3 May 2016; Anon, email re *Red Flag* 15 June 2016. Previous print runs: IS: Birchall (1981: 18–19); Crick (2016: 149) reports a paid sale of around 20,000 suggesting a print run of about 25,000; AWL National Committee Minutes 7 January 1995, AWL Papers, File AWL/1/33/3; SL/B Subs and sales figures 8 August 1981, MRC IMG Papers, File 258; Circulation figures for *Socialist Challenge* February 1981, MRC IMG Papers, File 196; WRP (WP) International Committee Commission Interim Report 16 December 1985, WRP Papers, Box 97; 'Inside the *Morning Star*, Britain's last Communist newspaper', *New Statesman* 4 August 2015, www.newstatesman. com/2015/07/red-all-over-article, accessed 15 September 2016.

* Readership figure of 10,000 used to infer a print run of 2,000.
** Figure is for the IMG newspaper *Socialist Challenge*
*** Paid average daily sales.

Conclusions

Trotskyist groups are sometimes portrayed as small and ineffectual organizations but they have adapted to their small size and become remarkably effective and efficient at the acquisition and deployment of organizational resources. Their memberships may be small, sometimes miniscule, but Trotskyist groups are built on high levels of commitment and activism. This is particularly true in smaller groups, such as the AWL or Workers Power, whose periods of probationary membership and strict organizational rules weed out all but the most dedicated revolutionaries. The maintenance of high and sustained levels of activism is difficult in larger organizations which lack the cohesion generated amongst small, close-knit groups of local activists. Yet if members are not always willing or able to supply time to their chosen organization they more than compensate through finance. Trotskyist groups are exceptionally effective in raising funds from members and their income levels per capita are up to ten times greater than those of mainstream parties. Through subscriptions, donations to fund-raising drives, collections at meetings and rallies and literature sales, Trotskyist activists contribute impressive amounts of money in order to fund revolutionary politics. It is true that many Trotskyist organizations appear to be locked in near-permanent financial crisis but this financial precariousness reflects the impact of two major items of expenditure: staffing levels and newspapers. Trotskyist groups have a very high ratio of full-time staff to members, well in excess of mainstream parties. At the peak of its membership and influence in the mid-late 1980s the 8,000-strong Militant Tendency employed more staff than the Labour Party, whose membership then stood at around 300,000 (McGuinness 2012). High staffing levels raise the mobilizing capacity of Trotskyist groups in comparison to their mainstream rivals, but they simultaneously raise the likelihood of financial crises as organizations struggle to maintain staff numbers in the face of fluctuating and uncertain income flows.

These pressures are magnified by the priority assigned to the production of a regular newspaper, a venture that entails high fixed costs – staffing, printing and distribution – but highly uncertain revenues. The upshot is that party newspapers almost invariably lose money and end up being subsidized by the party, that is, by the members. Yet the party newspaper continues to be produced because it is one of the main channels through which Trotskyist groups disseminate their views to a wider audience, beyond the limited ranks of their own membership. At the same time, and in conjunction with magazines, pamphlets and books, it also plays a vital role as a cultural resource, educating the membership on party policy, reinforcing their commitment and ensuring the resilience of the organization.

Notes

1 Letter, Tom Watson to Jeremy Corbyn 10 August 2016, available at http://labourlist.org/2016/08/tom-watson-sends-corbyn-dossier-as-proof-of-far-left-entryism-into-labour/, accessed 14 September 2016.
2 SLL, How to Build Young Socialists, n.d. – early 1970s, WRP Papers, Box 405.
3 On the commissions see Minutes of Central Committee, 23/24 September 1988, Dani Ahrens Papers, File 1/1/2; and on activities see National Mailing 19 March 1991, Dani Ahrens Papers, File 401 3/6.
4 www.socialistparty.org.uk/main/Socialist_Party_campaigns, accessed 18 August 2016.
5 Information taken from party websites 18 August 2016.
6 www.thisismoney.co.uk/money/bills/article-1633409/Historic-inflation-calculator-value-money-changed-1900.html, accessed 10 May 2016.
7 Gregor Gall has pointed out that money may also be secured from legacies, wills and redundancy payments although there is simply no systematic data on these income sources: e-mail 8 July 2017.
8 SWP Central Committee, Money Matters, SWP Pre-Conference Bulletin No. 3, November 2013.
9 IMG, Finance Report 1980, IMG Papers, Warwick, File 128.
10 New Park Publications, *New Books Autumn 1984*, London: New Park.
11 www.leftontheshelfbooks.co.uk/images/doc/Radical-Bookshops-Listing.pdf, accessed 22 August 2016.
12 Bookshop Income 1984 and 1985, WRP Papers, Box 177.
13 www.leftontheshelfbooks.co.uk/images/doc/Radical-Bookshops-Listing.pdf, accessed 22 August 2016.
14 IMG, Finance Report 1980, IMG Papers, Warwick, File 128.
15 Report on Money, 5 August 1988, AWL Papers, File AWL 1/28.
16 Finance Report, 17 September 1997, AWL Papers, File AWL/1/34/2.
17 National Committee Minutes, 13 January 1973, AWL Papers, File AWL1/2; Executive Committee Minutes, 28 August 1986 and 20 August 1987, AWL Papers, File AWL/1/29/1;

Executive Committee Minutes, 8 February 1995, AWL Papers, File AWL/1/33/3; Secretariat Minutes, 3 February 2004, AWL Papers, File AWL1/46/1; Executive Committee Minutes, 11 February 2005, AWL Papers, File AWL1/47/1; Executive Committee Minutes, 27 January 2006, AWL Papers, File AWL/1/48.

18 Financial Statement: June 1971 to May 1972, 28 May 1972, Tony Whelan Papers, File/1/1/1; Estimated Income and Expenditure for IMG, 8 May 1973, Tony Whelan Papers, File 1/1/5; Finance Breakdown, National Committee Minutes, 26–27 January 1974, IMG Papers, Warwick, File 82.

19 Accounts for 1982, IMG Papers, LSE, File 212; Proposals on Re-organising the Apparatus and Leadership, n.d. – probably late 1983, IMG Papers, LSE, File 225.

20 Financial Balance Sheet 1964, Tony Cliff Papers, File 459/4/1; Finance Report, January 1979, Steve Jefferys Papers, File 244/2/1/2.

21 Financial Statement 1 May 1970 – 30 April 1971, Socialist Party Papers, File 601/C/2/1/1; ISG, Statement of Accounts December 1988, January 1989, February 1989, Dani Ahrens Papers, File 1/1/2; Cash Flow 6 July 1999, AWL Papers, File AWL1/35/3.

22 IS Bulletin No. 1: 31 April 1965, Colin Barker Papers, File 152/1/1/1; Perspectives for IS, 12 September 1968, Richard Hyman Papers, File 84/3; Socialist Worker Sales, n.d. – probably 1977, Nigel Clark Papers, File 489/7; State of the Organisation for National Advisory Committee, 9/10 December 1978, Steve Jefferys Papers, File 244/2/1/2; Report on the Red Mole, 20 June 1971, Tony Whelan Papers, File/1/1/1; Addendum to 1980 Conference Finance Report, IMG Papers, Warwick, File 205; Socialist Action, Finance Dossier for Central Committee, 18/19 October 1986, IMG Papers, Warwick, File 230.

23 Informal conversation with Terry Brotherstone; Hillary Horrocks interview.

24 WRP (Workers Press), International Committee, Commission Interim Report, 16 December 1985, p. 2, WRP Papers, Box 97.

25 WRP (Workers Press), International Committee, Commission Interim Report, 16 December 1985, p. 2, WRP Papers, Box 97; and Notes from C. Slaughter for the 8th Congress, WRP Internal Bulletin, 7 January 1986, WRP Papers, Box 77.

26 Broad Groups and I-CL Accounts: Rough Monthly Averages, n.d. – probably June 1981, AWL Papers, File AWL/1/9.

27 A Cry from Below the Poverty Line, n.d. – c. 1983, IMG Papers, Warwick, File 247.

28 The Communist Party paper, the *Morning Star*, reportedly used the same practice in order to avoid the embarrassing charge of failing to comply with trade union negotiated pay rates.

29 The Alliance for Workers Liberty, Our Constitution, www.workersliberty.org/story/2006/04/15/join-awl#j4, accessed 25 August 2016; Constitution of the International Marxist Group 1971, Chris Bambery Papers, File 419/1/4; Constitution of the Revolutionary Socialist League 1969, Socialist Party Papers, File 601/C/1/1; Socialist Resistance, Alan Thornett interview; SWP, Conference Democracy, https://socialistworker.co.uk/art/41965/Message+from+SWP+conference+-+build+up+the+movement+that+helped+Jeremy+Corbyn+win, accessed 25 August 2016; Workers Revolutionary Party Constitution 1974, WRP Papers, Box 54.

30 SWP:, Conference Democracy, https://socialistworker.co.uk/art/41965/Message+from+SWP+conference+-+build+up+the+movement+that+helped+Jeremy+Corbyn+win, accessed 25 August 2016; IMG: Tasks, Orientation and Slogans of the IMG, Resolution passed at 1981 conference, IMG Papers, Warwick, File 239; Militant Tendency: Crick (2016: 332).

31 British Supporters of TILC (Trotskyist International Liaison Committee), Internal Bulletin No. 4, June 1983, Richardson/Higgins Papers, Box 28, File 1.

32 Report of the National Committee to Conference 1972, IS Bulletin, February 1972, Will Fancy Papers, Box 23/3.

33 Information from SP and SWP websites, 26 August 2016.

34 Quotes from 1–2 Print, www.1-2-print.co.uk/gb_en/catalog/category/view/s/saddle-stitch-stapled/id/89/?gclid=CI654JiOoM8CFQ8W0wodeMULIA, accessed 21 September 2016.

35 Clive Heemskerk interview; Anindya Bhattacharyya interview.
36 Editorial introduction, *Marxist World*, No. 2, p. 2, 2016.
37 www.pressgazette.co.uk/full-2015-mag-abcs-breakdown-cosmopolitan-bucks-trend-uk-magazines-decline-average-4-cent/, accessed 15 September 2016.
38 www.independent.co.uk/news/media/if-circulation-is-low-have-a-row-just-ask-cristina-and-peter-how-749994.html, accessed 15 September 2016.

9

WORKING IN THE TRADE UNIONS

Trotskyists have always attached enormous importance to work inside the trade union movement because of the belief that it represents the most organized and class conscious section of the working class. It was Marx and Engels (1848) who first identified the working class as the only social force that possessed an objective interest in the destruction of capitalist exploitation and the only group that could acquire the power to meet that objective, through collective organization and collective action. Their enthusiastic description of trade unions as 'schools of war' was eventually superseded by a more nuanced view in which classical Marxists such as Lenin, Luxemburg, Gramsci and Trotsky recognized the contradictions and limitations as well as the strengths of trade unionism (Hyman 1971; Kelly 1988). Nevertheless all Trotskyist groups have required their members to join a trade union (if it is available) and to work with fellow party members to promote militant collective action.

The first section of the chapter briefly rehearses the theoretical rationale for trade union activity and the expectations of Trotskyists about their engagement in workers' struggles against employers and the state before describing the parameters of Trotskyist activity and influence within the contemporary trade union movement. The bulk of the chapter then draws on the party/sect/social movement framework to identify and analyse two major contradictions inherent in Trotskyist trade union work. On the one hand effective collective action by unions can often best be organized around specific bargaining demands such as higher wages or shorter hours but on the other hand Trotskyist groups also wish to develop revolutionary class consciousness, a process that may require the promotion of more radical demands. For example, in the midst of a pay campaign in a clearing bank, the Trotskyist call for nationalization of the banking and finance sector may antagonize some employees, undermine their support for the campaign and weaken the union's collective action. Second, in any kind of trade union struggle the logic of working-class unity pushes Trotskyist groups into various forms of cooperation within the trade union movement against the class enemy but the sectarian logic of competing Trotskyist groups continually erodes such unity as militants strive to recruit workers into their own particular organization because of its alleged superiority over other Trotskyist rivals.[1] The logic of action of a social movement pulls one way; the logic of the revolutionary party and its Trotskyist doctrine often pulls in a different direction.

It is also important to note one major constraint on the effectiveness of Trotskyist union activity. Whilst the larger organizations often possess the critical mass of activists required to maintain some presence in a trade union over an extended period, this is not true of smaller groups. Their activity in a particular union is often sustained by one or two individuals and their resignation from the group or their geographical relocation can swiftly eliminate the group's presence in a particular union or workplace.

Revolutionary politics and the trade unions

The basic principles of Trotskyist political activity in the trade unions can be summarized fairly easily; it is the precise application of the principles in concrete circumstances that has often led to divergences both between and sometimes within the groups themselves. The core proposition, about class struggle and class consciousness, was well expressed by the SWP in its 1984 Perspectives document:

> We understand that workers will only be won to revolutionary socialism through their own experience of struggle. Consequently revolutionaries have themselves to orient on workers in struggle . . . Hence the stress laid by Marxists on the trade unions.
>
> We seek to break down the reformist division between trade unionism and electoral politics, to lead workers in using their collective strength for the political struggle against capitalism.[2]

The reasoning here is that the hegemony of bourgeois ideas – about the neutrality of the state, the role of parliament and the prospects for reforms, for example – will begin to fracture when workers' picket lines are attacked by police, their strike action is denounced by Labour MPs and their employer threatens to move jobs offshore unless workers comply with demands for wage cuts and work intensification. In this unsettling period, with people's beliefs in a state of flux, revolutionaries can intervene and hopefully find a more receptive audience for Trotskyist ideas (cf. Mandel 1977a).

Second, in addition to promoting strikes in particular workplaces or sectors, Trotskyists have always sought to promote solidarity with striking workers and have often aspired to promote the 'general strike' as the 'highest' form of solidaristic strike activity. Drawing on Luxemburg's analysis of what she called the 'mass strike', Trotskyists have often held that in a pre-revolutionary or revolutionary situation a large-scale strike by millions of workers from different industries can become a 'political demonstration' as state intervention on the side of employers poses questions about political power (Luxemburg 1970: 170). Contemporary Trotskyist groups vary in their approach to this issue: the Socialist Party, the SWP and Workers Power have been pushing for an anti-austerity general strike for some years (for example Socialist Party 2013: 22; Vernell et al. 2012) whilst the WRP has been issuing the same call since the early 1970s and at regular intervals ever since (Westwell 2015).[3] Socialist Resistance, on the other hand, has expressed some ambivalence whilst the AWL has been highly critical of what it sees as an attempt to short-circuit the arduous work of building opposition to austerity and rebuilding trade unions.[4]

Third, 'trade unions are dialectically both an opposition to capitalism and a component of it' (Anderson 1967: 264) and the key agency that oversees the integration of trade unions is its full-time leadership, the trade union bureaucracy. There is a vast Trotskyist literature devoted to explicating the precise parameters of the 'bureaucracy' and to analysing the roots of its allegedly conservative behaviour, although much of it is repetitive and tendentious (for an older discussion and critique see Kelly 1988). In essence, the argument is that union officials become attached to the capitalist system and to the process of securing reforms because of their high rates of pay, considerable job security, frequent interaction with employers and limited accountability to the union membership. Their role as negotiators leads them to value compromise settlements with capital and the state as the pinnacle of their ambitions (for example Callinicos 1995; Darlington 2014; Sewell 2015; Workers Power 1978).

From this analysis there is a small set of demands shared by all Trotskyists groups, past and present, overlaid with a diversity of strategic orientations. All agree that full-time union officials should be paid the average wage in their industry; that union members should be able to recall and hold them to account; and that collective agreements should only be signed after ratification by the membership (for example Sewell 2015; Socialist Organiser 1980; Socialist Party 2013; Workers Power 2014). Strategically the IS/SWP argued in the 1970s and 1980s for the creation of rank and file groups within unions that would argue for militant campaigns around the major issues then facing workers – pay freezes and redundancies. According to their 1984 Perspectives document,

> Our aim is to lead workers in struggle so that through their own experience they will break politically with reformism. Differentiating ourselves especially from the left bureaucracy is therefore crucial to winning people to our politics . . .
>   . . . we constantly seek to highlight the antagonism between the bureaucracy and the rank and file, and to warn of the dangers of relying on the full-time officials.[5]

This perspective was sharply counterposed to the Communist Party strategy of building 'broad lefts', coalitions of CP and Labour stewards and members that would contest union positions and seek to challenge and eventually usurp 'right-wing' officials, despite the fact that Trotsky himself had urged the replacement of

right-wing union officials by revolutionary militants. In the CP view it is the ideological division between left and right officials that constitutes the main cleavage in
trade unions, not the social divide between bureaucracy and rank and file (Roberts
1976a; Seifert and Sibley 2012: 110–18).

As for trade union goals, Tony Cliff's best-selling book on productivity deals
concluded with a set of demands around issues such as labour mobility, job evalu-
ation and pay systems that made no reference either to socialism or to transitional
demands. Indeed a few years later he claimed that 'Inflation plus unemployment
bring the class struggle to the centre of political life' (Cliff 1975: 157 and see also
Cliff and Barker 1966 for similar themes). The idea that economic struggle led by
Trotskyist shop stewards would engender far-reaching working-class politiciza-
tion was sharply criticized by rival Trotskyist groups and families. For the Radical
Trotskyists of Workers Power, a rank and file orientation necessarily entailed a
set of transitional demands, 'stemming from today's conditions and from today's
consciousness of wide layers of the working class and unalterably leading to one
final conclusion: the conquest of power by the proletariat' (Trotsky 1938: 7).
When brought together into a coherent programme they would help transcend
the inevitable limitations of trade union militancy (Workers Power 1978, 2014).[6]
The Orthodox SLL/WRP was equally scornful of what it variously described as
the IS/SWP's 'economism' and 'syndicalism', firmly insisting as early as 1966 that,

> Revolutionary work in the trade unions means a struggle against the trade
> union bureaucracy and against the political tendencies which reflect and
> sustain it. The Stalinists and the social democrats must be defeated, and revo-
> lutionary cadres trained in this struggle as the centre of our trade union work.[7]

To that end it argued for the construction of networks of SLL/WRP militants
coordinated through a multi-union body firmly under the direct control of the party
(Banda 1972: 5). Although the WRP sometimes employed the language of transitional demands, critics such as Alan Thornett's (1979) Workers Socialist League
(WSL) alleged that this terminological orthodoxy concealed a familiar division
between short- and long-term demands (or the minimum and the maximum programmes). The critique of trade union bureaucracy has been taken one step further
by the Orthodox SEP which argues that since the 1980s the trade unions 'have been
fully integrated into the apparatus of corporate management and the state'. Workers
should therefore abandon the idea of union rank and file groups and 'break with
these corrupt organisations' to build new organizations such as factory committees
(International Communist Party 1990: 103; Socialist Equality Party 2011: 140–41).

What remains unclear in these different perspectives is whether Trotskyists
should contest elected positions in the trade union bureaucracy, such as General
Secretary, and whether it is permissible to apply for appointed full-time posts. The
pitfalls of joining the union bureaucracy and the danger of 'broad lefts' degen-
erating into electoral machines, out of touch with the 'rank and file', had led
many Trotskyist organizations to shun full-time officer posts and to supplement

the strength of rank and file groups only with lay positions such as seats on union National Executives. In the early 1980s the SWP even stressed the need to avoid full-time steward/convener positions on 50 or 100 per cent facility time because they sucked activists 'into the lower echelons of the bureaucracy'.[8] Yet the IS position was more nuanced than it appears because its National Committee affirmed in 1974 that a full-time officer post *could* be pursued provided there was rank and file pressure behind the candidate *and* so long as the National Committee had given its blessing.[9] More recently it has authorized members to take up full-time *organizing* posts in the Bakers' Union but this is an exception to its general reluctance to become part of the union bureaucracy (Charlie Kimber interview 2016).

The Militant Tendency/Socialist Party has always drawn a radically different strategic conclusion from the conventional analysis of bureaucratic conservatism. Provided union officials receive the average wage of those they represent and that members have the right to recall them and to ratify collective agreements, then it follows that Trotskyist officials would behave very differently from their reformist counterparts (Militant 1980, 1981b; Socialist Party 2013). Consequently the Militant Tendency began to contest the most senior positions in the union bureaucracy from the late 1970s and has continued to the present day. Tendency member Joe Marino was elected General Secretary of the Bakers Union in 1979; Socialist Party member Chris Baugh is currently (2017) Assistant General Secretary of the Public and Commercial Services Union (PCS); and fellow party member Martin Powell-Davies is a London regional official with the National Union of Teachers (NUT).

Contrary to some claims, the SWP has never denied the existence of differences of view within the trade union bureaucracy. Rather it has taken the line that whilst these differences may occasionally prove significant and should be exploited as appropriate, they are subordinate to the common interests of the bureaucracy as a whole (Callinicos 1995: 20–22; Darlington 2014). However the SWP orientation to union officialdom has shifted significantly since around 2010–2011 as noted in Chapter 5 and annual conferences of Unite the Resistance are now routinely addressed by union General Secretaries. Darlington (2014) somewhat downplays the shift in position, arguing that in an era of falling union membership and historically low strike levels left officials can play a significant role in promoting working-class militancy. Consequently he claims that UtR is neither a rank and file group nor a CP-style broad left but rather is a classical 'united front' between revolutionaries and reformists.

Finally, all Trotskyist groups emphasize that one of the key criteria by which to judge the success of union activity is recruitment to the party so according to the Militant Tendency for example,

> At work and in the unions each individual Marxist is an ambassador for this organisation. Their task is to build our support and to recruit new members . . . Recruitment should be the main criteria [sic] by which we judge our success in all areas of our trade union and industrial work. It should not be left to chance.[10]

Trotskyism and contemporary British trade unionism

Trotskyists have made significant inroads into the executive committees (EC) of a number of trade unions and have a presence in many others with a combined total of 56 EC members in 2016 (Table 9.1). That number is divided fairly evenly between the SWP and the Socialist Party with major concentrations in the University and College Union UCU (SWP), PCS (SP), Unison and NUT (both SWP and SP). These numbers also include Trotskyists holding senior full-time official positions, such as Chris Baugh, PCS and Joe Simpson, Assistant General Secretary at the POA as well as John McInally, PCS Vice-President on full-time facility release. To those officials one might add several others with a background in, and continuing sympathy for Trotskyism, namely Mark Serwotka, PCS General Secretary, formerly a member of the AWL and Matt Wrack, Fire Brigades Union General Secretary and ex-member of Militant Labour (McIlroy and Daniels 2009: 150).

Unions not shown in Table 9.1 had no Trotskyist presence on their executives and they include several large unions where the left has traditionally been weak, such as the Association of Teachers and Lecturers (ATL), the General, Municipal and Boilermakers Union (GMB), the National Association of Teachers/Union of Women Teachers (NASUWT) and the scientific and technical union Prospect. They also include unions where the left, either communist or Trotskyist, has exerted some influence in the past, notably the Communication Workers Union (CWU) and the builders' union UCATT (see below). Beneath the executive level, Trotskyist presence can also be found in delegations to union annual conferences and amongst the

TABLE 9.1 Trotskyists on trade union executive committees 2016

Union	Total	SWP	Socialist Party	Others	Size of EC
UCU	15	15*	–	–	64
Unison	10	4	6	–	65
PCS	10	3	7	–	37
NUT	9	3	4	2 (AWL)	45
TUC	2	–	1	1 (AWL)	59
Unite	2	–	1	1 (Counterfire)	62
ASLEF	1	–	1	–	8
BFAWU	1	–	1	–	19
EIS	1	1	–	–	125
NAPO	1	–	1	–	34
NUJ	1	1	–	–	23
POA	1	–	1	–	10
RMT	1	–	1	–	20
USDAW	1	–	1	–	16
Totals	56	27	25**	4	–

Sources: Clive Heemskerk, Charlie Kimber and Martin Thomas interviews.

* All 15 belong to UCU Left, an SWP-controlled faction and most, though not all, are SWP members.
** The April 2017 figure was 19 according to *The Socialist* 12 April 2017.

ranks of workplace union representatives and union branch officers. We have no reliable data on the numbers of Trotskyist lay representatives but we do have figures for attendance at cross-union conferences and rallies organized by the SWP and the Socialist Party respectively. Unite the Resistance was created in 2011 and is largely controlled by the SWP, which dominates its steering committee.[11] It holds national meetings and maintains a lively and regularly updated website with information on a wide range of industrial disputes. According to the organizers, its October 2013 annual conference was attended by 'more than 500', its November 2014 event by 'more than 550' and in November 2015 'up to 500' were reported to be present.[12] Many of these participants are likely to be SWP members but they are also local activists from a diverse set of unions. The Socialist Party's National Shop Stewards' Network also attracts hundreds of union activists to its annual meetings, with its June 2013 meeting described as '400 strong' and 'over three hundred' present at its July 2014 event.[13]

Trotskyist success in recruiting and mobilizing activists and winning union positions is often based on many years of patient and meticulous work in union branches, regional committees and national conferences. An indication of the extensive planning and preparation involved was revealed in a Militant Tendency report on its CPSA caucus in the late 1970s:

> Comrades had been allocated the topics on which to move resolutions. The main points to raise in the resolutions were also suggested . . . From this work we had a spread of resolutions across the whole agenda . . . At the nightly caucus the paper and pamphlet selling was allocated . . . and contacts discussed . . . The most important work of the caucus though was preparing in detail for the next day . . . The main points were discussed and comrades wrote down the points, then if one comrade failed to get into speak other comrades with the same points might succeed . . . This was a little tedious at times but it paid dividends in that all the comrades were confident to come in and speak.[14]

Trotskyist union factions rarely issue regular bulletins or newsletters nowadays but tend to rely on websites, most of which are open, regularly updated and user friendly, for example UCU Left, PCS Left Unity and Unison Action Broad Left.[15] Some organizations issue simultaneous online and hard copies of rank and file bulletins such as the Socialist Party publication *The Activist: Bulletin of Socialist Party Members in USDAW* (Union of Shop, Distributive and Allied Workers; latest issue No. 65 December 2016).[16] Other organizations produce occasional bulletins for specific groups, normally one or two page documents, such as the AWL's *Tubeworker* (latest issue 3 June 2017) and *Lewisham Hospital Worker* (issue No. 55 appeared in May 2015) and *London Underground* and *Postal Workers Bulletins*, both issued by Workers Power.[17] The tiny organization Workers Fight (an affiliate of the Internationalist Communist Union) produces an eponymous fortnightly bulletin with detailed reports, written by its members, of developments inside Kings

Cross railway station, the Royal Mail sorting office at Mount Pleasant in north London and the BMW Cowley plant. Many organizations also produce bulletins during trade union conferences, such as the AWL's *Workers Liberty Teachers* and the UCU Left's Conference Bulletins.

Taken as a whole, the Trotskyist movement appears to have a position of some significance in sections of the contemporary trade union movement. It has a substantially greater number of union activists compared to the dog days of the 1950s but comparisons with more recent times are hampered by lack of hard evidence. Neither the SWP nor the WRP occupied any leading national trade union posts in the 1980s: in the case of the SWP this was the result of its effective prohibition on members joining the 'bureaucracy' whilst the WRP's sectarian politics had undermined its few union strongholds in television, theatre and the car industry (McIlroy 1999a: 266, 269 and see below). The Militant Tendency as the largest and most rapidly growing Trotskyist group in the 1980s had begun to make inroads into the leaderships of several trade unions, including the Bakers Union and the CPSA, as well as the National Executives of the Transport and General Workers Union (TGWU now Unite) and the Post Office Engineering Union (POEU now CWU) (McIlroy 1999a: 263). The national profile of the Trotskyist movement with 56 Executive Committee members in 2016 is undoubtedly greater than at any time in the past.

In contrast, a comparison between the Trotskyist movement and its historic rival the Communist Party of Great Britain casts the former in a far less flattering light. At the zenith of CP influence, shortly after the Second World War, the party could boast of many individual factories in which its membership was counted in hundreds, such as Napier's in London, the Austin Aero factory in Longbridge, Birmingham and the Metro Vickers plant in Trafford Park, Manchester, to name only a few. In these and many other factories the CP had recruited literally thousands of shop stewards. In the Amalgamated Engineering Union (AEU), the CP held 'two out of seven Executive seats and constituted two out of three National Organisers and three of the seven Regional Officers for the Executive Division' (Callaghan 2003: 228). There were nine CP members on the 34-person TGWU Executive and party members held the General Secretaryships in the mining and electrical unions (NUM and ETU) (Callaghan 2003: 229 and see also Fishman 1995: 331–33, 352–54).

The impact of Trotskyist activists on union policy and action is hard to disentangle from the myriad other influences that shape trade union behaviour: product markets, labour markets, government policy, rank and file pressure and the influence of CP and other left union leaders. Nevertheless there are several points that can be made. In the first place Trotskyist militants have built and sustained a number of local workplace organizations and promoted militant collective action with Alan Thornett's WRP/WSL group at BL's Cowley plant in Oxford being one of the best-known examples. Second, Trotskyist groups have played a key role in opposition to 'moderate' and right-wing Labour factions in quite a few unions, forcing debates on bargaining objectives and collective action and challenging overly close relations with government and employers. This has been particularly the case in

Equity in the 1970s, CPSA and NUT in the 1980s, PCS in the early 2000s and NALGO/Unison and USDAW more recently. The PCS case is especially significant because a leftist leadership was consolidated in 2002 with the election of Mark Serwotka (an ex-member of Socialist Organiser) as General Secretary and through the influence of the Socialist Party on the National Executive and amongst senior officials. Within a short period the union had become a firm critic of Labour government policy and a staunch advocate of industrial action in support of its members' terms and conditions of employment (McIlroy and Daniels 2009: 154–55). Writing of the period 1964–1979, McIlroy's judgement seems equally apt for the more recent period if perhaps a little generous: 'In many workplaces and unions, the presence of Trotskyists, their exemplary action as trade unionists, the regular bulletins they produced, ensured socialist arguments were heard, democratic tendencies in trade unionism were strengthened, militancy was sustained' (McIlroy 1999a: 283).

The logic of sectarian competition

Present day competition

Yet Trotskyist influence in the trade unions, both now and in the past, has been limited and undermined by the fraught relations between the various Trotskyist groups, rooted in their differing interpretations of core elements of Trotskyist doctrine. These differences do not preclude agreement on a wide range of other issues such as the need to combat the far right across Europe and nor do they necessarily hinder cooperation in specific movements such as the Stop the War Coalition, supported by all but a handful of sectarian Trotskyist organizations (see Chapter 10). But the historical and contemporary evidence reviewed in Chapter 5 suggests that the logic of competition between Trotskyist organizations and families is powerful, profound and enduring. We begin with a survey of rank and file and broad left groups both inside and across the trade unions before turning to the historical record.

The most significant Trotskyist presence is to be found in those unions where they have made significant inroads at national level, viz. NUT, PCS, UCU, Unison and Unite. In only one of these unions – Unison – is there any degree of unity, around the Unison Action Broad Left grouping, which is currently (2017) backed by the SWP and the Socialist Party. Even that initiative is precarious, emerging as it did after many years of disunity and conflict between those two organizations. Moreover whilst the left was able to agree a slate of candidates for the NEC elections in 2015, it was unable to agree on a candidate to defeat the incumbent Dave Prentis in the 2015 General Secretary election. Prentis was eventually challenged by three candidates including two Trotskyists, John Burgess, supported by the SWP, AWL and rs21 and Roger Bannister, a longstanding Socialist Party member and union activist, backed by his own party. The PCS left is dominated by Left Unity with the support of the Socialist Party, the major force in that union, along with the SWP. But the AWL leads a separate organization (which also has its own website) called Independent Left and contests executive elections although so far without success.[18] In NUT, the far left is even more fragmented: the SWP and Socialist Resistance are part of the Socialist Teachers Alliance (STA), a group that can trace its ancestry back to the 1970s; the Socialist Party and the AWL operate through the Local Associations National Action Campaign (LANAC); and the Workers Power group maintains its own teachers' fraction.[19] The two big groups compete in national elections and in 2016 the SWP held three seats on the National Executive whilst LANAC candidates held six (four Socialist Party and two AWL members).[20] The predictable result of these divisions emerged in the 2015 General Secretary election when the SWP and Counterfire urged support for the left-leaning incumbent Christine Blower whilst the Socialist Party, the AWL and rs21 campaigned (unsuccessfully) for Socialist Party member Martin Powell-Davies.[21]

The Unite left grouping split in 2013 with the relaunch of Grassroots Left in opposition to the United Left, a division that emerged from disagreements over candidates in the 2013 General Secretary election.[22] The Socialist Party, AWL and Socialist Appeal called (successfully) on union members to re-elect the left-leaning incumbent Len McCluskey. In contrast, the SWP along with Socialist Fight, Socialist Resistance and Workers Power, campaigned for the rank and file militant Jerry Hicks.[23] Similar divisions appeared in the 2017 election when seven Trotskyist groups backed McCluskey (AWL, Counterfire, Socialist Action, Socialist Appeal, Socialist Party, Socialist Resistance and Workers Power) whilst five groups backed the rank and file candidate Ian Allinson (Marxist World, rs21, RCITB, Socialist Fight and the SWP). Finally, in the higher and further education sector, UCU is dominated by UCU Left a largely SWP-led organization whilst the Socialist Party retains its own independent union fraction, cooperating (or competing) with the SWP on an issue-by-issue basis (Dave Beale interview). Counterposed to these groups is the Independent Broad Left, a coalition of CPB and Labour activists.[24]

Overlaying these divisions *within* unions is a variety of multi-union, anti-austerity organizations, each rooted in a particular Trotskyist grouping. In 2007 the RMT union, in cooperation with the Socialist Party, launched the National Shop Stewards Network (NSSN) to try to revive the structures and traditions of workplace union organization that had atrophied since the 1980s.[25] A few years later the SWP revived its 1970s Right to Work campaign, a body wound up in 1982 as the SWP retrenched in the 'downturn' (Birchall 2011: 408, 457). Right to Work ran some high-profile campaigns around precarious work and workfare in 2010 but it was already competing with yet another organization, the Coalition of Resistance (CoR). This too was created in 2010 by a mixture of left-wing MPs including Jeremy Corbyn and John McDonnell, union general secretaries such as Bob Crow (RMT) and Mark Serwotka (PCS) and left-wing organizations including Counterfire, Socialist Resistance, the CPB and the Greens. Although the SWP was conspicuous by its absence, a group of leading members expelled (or resigned) earlier in the year, notably John Rees and Lindsey German, took a more positive view of the CoR initative.[26] Rees and German had quickly created a new organization, Counterfire, which played an important role in mobilizing 1,000 people for the first CoR convention in November 2010, building on their experiences in the Stop the War and Respect coalitions (see Chapter 10).[27]

In 2011 the annual meeting of NSSN debated a sensible proposal to create a unified anti-cuts organization but by now both the SWP and the Socialist Party each controlled an organization capable of mobilizing hundreds of trade union militants. The NSSN website, for instance, notes the support of PCS as well as other unions on whose Executives there is currently Socialist Party representation – the Bakers Union, the probation officers (NAPO), the POA and the RMT (as well as CWU, FBU, the National Union of Journalists NUJ and the NUM). Although both the Socialist Party and SWP have always supported demonstrations organized by the CoR and its 2013 successor organization, the People's Assembly, neither group was prepared to risk losing ground to the other. The SWP effectively walked out of NSSN and transformed Right to Work into Unite the Resistance, an organization now officially backed by the SWP's union strongholds such as NUT, PCS, Unison and UCU. Within the space of 12 months 2010–2011, a succession of competitive party manoeuvres solidified the existence of three competing Trotskyist-led anti-cuts organizations. Whilst leaders of the different groups have expressed regrets over the division and a preference for a unified body, none seems disposed to make the first move towards organizational unity (Alex Callinicos and John Rees interviews).[28]

Historical competition

Competition between Trotskyist groups within the trade union movement is not a recent phenomenon but can be traced back to the 1960s and the struggle to achieve hegemony on the revolutionary left. At various times in the 1970s all of the major groups aspired to create a 'revolutionary alternative' to 'Stalinism' and to displace the Communist Party as the leading force in industry. Indeed, by 1987 the Militant Tendency was openly boasting that 'we have supplanted the CP as the Left opposition in the British trade union movement'.[29] Competition was particularly fierce in those sections of industry deemed to be critical in the class struggles of the 1970s – coal mining, docks, engineering, motor vehicles and railways – and in those parts of the public sector that came to employ relatively large numbers of Trotskyists – central and local government, education and health.

The NUM was difficult territory for Trotskyists because the union was dominated by strong pro-Labour traditions and by the Communist Party although the CP was always stronger in the union hierarchy than in the pits (Allen 1981; McIlroy 1999b: 228–30, 238). Nevertheless, defectors from the CP helped to build small pockets of SLL supporters in the 1960s and vigorous recruitment by the Posadists (Revolutionary Workers' Party, notably Dave Douglass) and later by IS, particularly around the 1972 and 1974 strikes, helped to create further pockets of Trotskyist militants in particular coalfields.[30] By the aftermath of the 1984–1985 strike, coal miners were to be found in no less than seven Trotskyist groups (or miners' 'fractions') between whom there was little or no cooperation: International

Communist Party (now SEP), Militant Tendency (with its paper *Militant Miner*), Socialist Action, SWP, Workers Power (with its own paper *The Red Miner* and see also Workers Power 1984b), WRP (News Line) (see Temple 1983) and WRP (Workers Press).[31] In the docks, Trotskyists also faced a well-entrenched CP apparatus and, as in coal mining, it was the SLL that first made inroads, winning a few recruits in the early 1950s, most notably Harry Constable (Hunter 1998: 285 ff.; Ratner 1994: 162–70). By the early 1970s IS had recruited a few leading activists in London, notably Micky Fenn and Eddie Prevost, and its rank and file paper *Dockworker*, with a 1974 print run of 5,000 copies, almost certainly outsold *The Hook*, an irregular publication issued by Workers Fight.[32]

Ongoing employment contraction, both in docks and coal mining, hindered Trotskyist access to these industries but the strike-prone engineering and motor vehicles industries were still recruiting labour in the 1970s. The SLL had a presence among engineering workers as early as 1964 and published a few issues of an *Engineering Workers Bulletin* in the 1960s.[33] In the following decade six Trotskyist rivals also became active in the engineering union but given the size and diversity of the industry their activities and bulletins were often localized: the IS produced bulletins for GEC and Ferranti factories; the International-Communist League (now AWL) issued a bulletin for a few years at the Lansing Bagnall plant in Basingstoke; there was an IMG fraction in TASS, the CP-dominated white collar section of the AEU (McIlroy 1999b: 232–33); by the early 1980s the Militant Tendency was producing occasional issues of the *Militant Engineer* as well as a pamphlet setting out its programme for the union (Militant 1980); and the Workers League organized a small group of stewards in the Lucas plants in Birmingham following their expulsion from IS (Thornett 1998: 115).[34]

In the car industry, competition between Trotskyist groups was particularly fierce given the strike-proneness of carworkers and the concentration of car plants in a small number of locations, principally Birmingham, Liverpool, London and Oxford. The SLL had recruited significant numbers of shop stewards at the British Motor Corporation's plants in the Oxford suburb of Cowley in the 1960s and in 1975 published the first issue of the ATUA carworkers' bulletin, *The Track* (Thornett 1987: 74–82; Thornett 2011: 17, 24).[35] In the 1970s competition intensified as other Trotskyist groups created car industry fractions and bulletins in the fight to recruit militant car plant stewards and by the end of the decade there were no less than *ten* Trotskyist groups with varying numbers of members and bulletins:[36] the I-CL produced Ford Dagenham and Longbridge bulletins; IMG produced two bulletins, *Red Rover* and *The Organiser* and had a small group of members at the BMC Cowley plant; there was an IS/SWP rank and file paper *Carworker* as well as Ford Dagenham and Longbridge factory bulletins; the Militant Tendency had members at the Rover plant in Solihull (Mullins 2016: 6); the Revolutionary Workers' Party (Posadists) had a few members; the Spartacist League/Britain had recruited a few workers in the BL Longbridge plant; Workers Fight issued fortnightly bulletins at the Ford Dagenham and Austin Rover Cowley plants; Workers Power produced a *Ford's Bulletin*; and the WRP was strong in BL's Cowley plant until the expulsion of Alan Thornett and his supporters in 1974 who then launched the Workers Socialist League and produced regular factory bulletins.[37]

Finally the rail industry, both London Underground and British Rail, provided yet another arena in which the rival heirs to the Trotskyist tradition fought for supremacy. In the 1970s there were three contestants: the SLL/WRP and the Militant Tendency each organized a Rails fraction whilst the IS rail group also produced a paper called *Platform*. In the 1980s they were joined by the Socialist League (formerly IMG) rail fraction, the WSL (later AWL) and its 1990s bulletin *Tubeworker*, the Workers Fight group with its Kings Cross bulletin, *Workers Platform* and the Workers Power group which had a handful of members working for London Underground.[38]

A similar picture emerged in the fast-growing public sector unions, particularly NALGO, CPSA and the NUT. IS launched the NALGO Action Group in 1969 with a regular bulletin *NAG News* and two years later created an IS NALGO fraction. The Militant Tendency had developed a small NALGO 'caucus' in 1972, as had the IMG, and in the 1980s began production of an irregular bulletin, *NALGO Militant*. By 1993 Militant Labour boasted 37 delegates at the union's annual conference, making it the group's second most significant union stronghold behind the CPSA. In the 1980s both the WSL (now AWL) and the WRP also created NALGO fractions.[39] Civil service rank and file activity can be traced back to 1973 when both the Militant Tendency and IS were already building fractions in the Civil and Public Services Association (CPSA), now merged into PCS.[40] They were joined in the1970s by the IMG and in the 1980s by the WSL (later AWL).[41] Militant influence first peaked in 1986 when Tendency member John McCreadie was elected General Secretary of CPSA until a legal challenge forced a rerun of the election in which he was then defeated. The following year he successfully contested the Deputy General Secretary position in the union, reinforcing the Tendency's influence in the union where it held nine seats on the National Executive by the mid-1980s (Crick 2016: 280: Taaffe 1995: 292–93). An internal Militant Labour report claimed three full-time officers and two NEC members in the CPSA as well as 69 members as delegates at the union's 1993 annual conference.[42]

It was the education sector, however, that undoubtedly witnessed the most intense rivalry on the far left. IS was first into action when Duncan Hallas helped create the Rank and File Teachers' group in 1967 and its eponymous publication.[43] Two years later the Militant Tendency produced the first issue of *Militant Teacher*, which was published without any substantial breaks until at least 1990.[44] By the mid-1970s Workers Fight (now the AWL), the IMG and the WRP all had teachers' 'fractions', groups of party members who met regularly to coordinate their union activities and Workers Power developed a teachers' group sometime in the 1980s.[45] Following the WRP split in 1985, several of its splinter groups reconstructed 'fractions' within the NUT, for example the SEP and the WRP (Workers Press).[46]

If we turn to initiatives at the level of the trade union movement as a whole we find a similar story of actions by single organizations designed to enhance their own membership and influence at the expense of their rivals. In 1968 the SLL created an industrial arm, the All Trades Unions Alliance, whose main activity was convening national rallies, often attended in the 1970s by over 1,000 people, many of whom were non-party rank and file trade union militants. The principal aim of the Alliance was to recruit workers into the SLL/WRP but it did not aspire to build rank and file groups in particular unions or workplaces. In only two areas of the economy did it organize significant numbers of workers: the entertainment unions ACTT and Equity where its leadership included the director Roy Battersby and the actors Vanessa and Corin Redgrave and the BMC Cowley car plant where its key activists were Alan Thornett and Tony Richardson (Thornett 1998). Elsewhere its industrial base comprised very small pockets of membership, sometimes just one or two people, in large workplaces (McIlroy 1999a: 265–66; Mitchell 2011: 265). The SLL/WRP's unremitting hostility to other Trotskyist groups extended to rallies of the ATUA as delegations from the IS or IMG were never invited.

By 1974 the IS had built an industrial base around a cluster of rank and file organizations in a range of unions and sectors (see above) and believed the time was now ripe to launch the modern equivalent of the CP Rank and File Minority Movement of the 1920s, particularly given the continued erosion of CP workplace organization (on which see Hinton and Hyman 1975). The National Rank and File Movement was launched in 1974 (and relaunched in 1977) but as the strike wave of 1968–1974 receded and the organization was shunned by most CP militants, it was effectively 'stillborn' (Callinicos 1982: 22, 29). In 1984 the Militant Tendency, then growing rapidly with fractions in a number of large unions, announced the formation of the Broad Left Organising Committee (BLOC) to coordinate the work of revolutionary socialists inside the various rank and file and Broad Left groups. However, just as the ATUA was dominated by the SLL and the NRFM by the IS/SWP, so BLOC was largely under the control of the Militant Tendency. Many of the spokespeople at its first conference were all Militant 'supporters': Phil Holt (POEU), Joe Marino (Bakers Union), John McCreadie (CPSA), Kevin Roddy (CPSA) and George Williamson (USDAW) with Holt and Williamson holding the posts of Secretary and Organizing Secretary respectively (Mullins 2014).[47] Yet by summer 1985 one of its leading activists, Kevin Roddy, had already noted the emergence of serious problems, owing to the defeat of the miners' strike, the hostility of the CP and the inadequate functioning of BLOC's National Committee.[48] By the late 1980s, an accumulation of problems, including the continued decline in trade union membership and strike rates, led Militant to dissolve the organization it had worked so hard to create (Mullins 2014).

Limitations and achievements of trade union work

One of the perennial issues facing Trotskyist militants is how to frame the objectives of trade union campaigns. Demands that are precise and achievable, such as a strike for an above-inflation pay rise, may well elicit broad support from workers. On the other hand they may not raise any deeper issues about capitalist profitability and state power, and may lead to charges of 'economism', the belief that economic struggle alone can develop revolutionary class consciousness. Radical demands that avoid the charge of 'economism', such as a general strike to bring down the government and prepare the way for workers' power, may be too radical and achieve little support. Trotskyists in the late 1960s and early 1970s appeared to err on the side of the former as in Cliff's (1970) book on productivity deals which set out an extensive programme of concrete bargaining demands but without clearly specifying how their pursuit or achievement would develop class consciousness. The focus on concrete demands was also maintained in the IS/SWP rank and file bodies such as the NALGO Action Group. It's 1975 document 'What We Stand For' covered low pay, union democracy, trade union rights, opposition to wage restraint, more public services and solidarity with other workers but made no reference to socialism![49] The IMG 1973 statement of aims for its 'Revolutionary Left Caucus' in TASS covered a similar range of basic trade union issues: 'independence of the trade unions from the state; active solidarity with any section of the working class in struggle; no to any form of incomes policy . . .; full trade union democracy'.[50] In contrast, the Orthodox SLL's trade union arm, the All Trades Unions Alliance issued a Charter of Basic Rights in 1970 stipulating the right of every worker to a job, to strike and organize, to a higher standard of living, welfare benefits, decent housing and a vote on the Common Market. These were clearly intended to be classic transitional demands:

> Every one of these elementary demands raises the question: is it the will of the ruling class to defend its dying system which shall prevail? Or is the working class to impose its will on the economy, through the conquest of power?[51]

The SLL's commitment to party building was also manifest in Healy's decision in the early 1970s that party members should focus on sales of *Workers Press* rather than the rank and file paper *The Miner*.[52] In similar vein Militant Tendency was warning in 1975 about the dangers of rank and file papers purely focused on an industry or workplace: 'We need to broaden the horizons of the workers and must not pander to syndicalist moods'.[53] Consequently the Militant Tendency pamphlets produced for specific industries comprised a mixture of immediate demands, on pay, redundancies or working time for instance, alongside the 'maximum' programme of nationalization of the leading monopolies under workers' control (for example Militant 1980, 1981b). Nonetheless one of the Socialist Party's UCU activists noted that 'It was easy to get drawn into day to day work and lose sight of the bigger political perspective' (Dave Beale interview).

If we turn to contemporary left groups within unions we find the same emphasis on concrete issues. The statement of purpose from the SWP-dominated UCU Left declares it is committed to building a democratic, accountable campaigning union which aims to mobilise and involve members in defending and improving our pay and conditions and defending progressive principles of education.

We fight for better funding and to defend academic freedom and civil liberties . . . We stand for the principle of free universal education under democratic control of education workers, local communities and learners at all levels.

We oppose oppression of all kinds and will fight to ensure that equality work is central to the union.[54]

For SWP activists this set of demands reflects a *political* trade unionism, combining both 'bread and butter issues . . . and political issues such as Palestine, and the wider issues of education' (Jane Hardy interview). References to socialism are more conspicuous in the Socialist Party-dominated PCS Left Unity faction whose website declares:

Our aim: to build a fighting, democratic union and to drive forward a socialist agenda in the TUC.

As socialists, we stand for an independent and democratic union that puts up a determined fight for its members and a union that participates in the wider struggle for political and social change for working people . . . We . . . campaign for a socialist society that provides for the needs of the many, not the greed of a few.[55]

Yet the day to day reality of PCS activity is governed by the same kinds of bargaining demands that can be found on the websites of any major trade union such as job losses, outsourcing and living wage campaigns.[56] It is true that PCS has a relatively high strike rate compared to other unions in central and local government and that it vigorously promotes militant, independent trade unionism, a reflection in part of the presence of the Socialist Party as a major force in the union's national and local leaderships (Hodder et al. 2017).

Trotskyists' own estimates of their achievements in the unions are generally quite positive, not unlike their self-assessments of electoral activity (Chapter 7). Problems and limitations are sometimes mentioned, and they have been referred to in this chapter, but they rarely disturb the self-congratulatory tenor of Trotskyist self-appraisal. According to the WRP in 1976, 'The defeat of the right wing in Equity by our Party shows that workers everywhere will respond to our leadership'.[57]

The differences between unions and workers are of no real consequence; the achievement in one union can be replicated in every other union. In 1981 the SWP noted that 150 party members had been elected as delegates to a total of 20 trade union conferences, including 30 at NALGO, 25 NUT and 15 CPSA.[58] These numbers represent potentially critical masses of Trotskyist militants but such reports never indicate their relative weight, that is, what proportion of all delegates do these numbers represent? Reports of strike interventions are also hard to interpret as with this example from the AWL in 2002:

> Our Tube worker comrades . . . did good work in the very important battle against Tube privatisation, and fought honourably and hard against the eventual sell-out. Our comrades played a big part in the extraordinary victory of the left in the PCS general secretary election . . . secured a quarter of the vote for a rank-and-file class struggle candidate in the CWU deputy general secretary poll.[59]

These are all significant achievements and there is no reason to doubt the dedication and efforts of AWL members such as Maria Exall in the CWU or Janine Booth in the RMT (Gall 2017). But in 2002 the organization's total membership was approximately 100, employed in a range of occupations and sectors across 15 different geographical branches, so the number active in any single union would be miniscule. Praise from credible authorities, although rare, provides another source of satisfaction particularly when it is accompanied by denigration of Trotskyist rivals. According to the WRP, miners' leader Arthur Scargill, 'considered the WRP political conclusions of the strike to be "spot on". He praised the *News Line* coverage during the strike . . . Other political organisations were "way off beam", like the SWP'.[60]

Yet despite regular and intense involvement in many industrial disputes, the organizational results have often proved disappointing:

> The excellent and necessary work around the Myton's dispute has brought us nothing beyond friendly acknowledgement from the builders involved. Not one member or any significant increase in sales of Labour Worker. (IS, building industry 1968.)[61]

> Jones made contact with a few stewards, produced a pamphlet on an upcoming dispute over wages, sold 200 copies and argued for a strike. This helped produce better TU militants . . . All fine, but no real work to pull militants towards IMG. (IMG, British Oxygen 1971.)[62]

> Leading comrades in Manchester are active in their unions but not really pushing Workers Fight. They say it's hard to raise revolutionary politics in their unions. (Workers Fight, 1972.)[63]

> Trade union militants are generally very wary of involvement with revolutionary groups. (I-CL, 1976.)[64]

> Our national trade union fractions perform . . . very badly when it comes to recruiting workers to our ranks . . . the central *raison d'etre* of the fraction. (AWL, 1995.)[65]

One constraint on party recruitment through rank and file or left union groups is the weakness of these bodies, a problem compounded by job quits and party membership resignations. In 1966 the London area of the SLL noted that, 'trade union factions have not functioned very well under the leadership of the Area Committee . . . Changing of jobs and trades, and other individualistic actions must cease'.[66]

By 1978 the SWP's enthusiasm for rank and file papers and bulletins was replaced with a more sober assessment: 'Factory bulletins often don't get beyond two issues as the response is poor'.[67] In 1979 the I–CL noted that its Acton Rails bulletin had ceased to exist because their only member at the workplace had resigned from the League and its Fords bulletin had also vanished because it no longer had any contacts inside the plant.[68] Indeed by 1984 the same organization (now the WSL) noted that 'Regular workplace bulletins, already in decline last year, have now disappeared completely from our work', and NUT fraction work 'now depends on one comrade'.[69] In 1986 the WRP (Workers Press) noted that in the pre-split WRP the production, distribution and sales of its loss-making daily paper *The News Line*, had become a millstone round the party's neck, diverting resources and leading 'to the abandonment of trade union work'.[70] A few years later a WRP (Workers Press) NATFHE activist noted that whilst there were a number of party members in the union 'we have no agreed approach to the work and each tends to do their own thing'.[71] In 2002 AWL trade union work was 'damaged by the withdrawal of one central London colleague' and a few months later its Executive ruefully noted that its 'Unions Fightback initiative has dwindled into nothingness . . . [owing to] too few people'.[72] The influence of Workers Power in the RMT hinged on just 'a few Underground drivers' (George Binette interview). Socialist Action's NUM fraction comprised just 13 members in June 1986 but by September it had fallen to just five and was clearly on the verge of collapse.[73] A few years later, after a series of debilitating splits, followed by a merger with Alan Thornett's Socialist Group, the newly formed ISG reported that, 'The problem of our trade union work remains largely unresolved and a balance sheet of the past year is largely negative . . . A few c[omra]des hold TU positions but that's the exception'.[74]

These problems in turn are compounded by the weaknesses of union workplace organizations themselves: falling union density, poorly attended meetings and shop steward and branch committee roles that go uncontested mean that becoming a shop steward can be a mixed blessing. As the AWL noted in 1995:

> The vast majority of our TU comrades are shop stewards and/or BEC [com-mittee] members . . . Unfortunately, in many cases, the comrades *walked* into these positions and did not have to *fight* for them.

> This . . . means that a substantial section of our *comrades* spend a large part of their time "holding together" TU organisations that could otherwise col-lapse without us.[75]

But even when Trotskyists do fight for senior positions, their attitude towards union elections is deeply ambivalent, as is clear from a brief history of the IS Rank and File Teacher group, written in the late 1970s:

> We don't want to run the union because we understand the role of trade union leaderships in capitalist society. We don't want to be sucked into a

role that involves policing the membership . . . We fight for positions on the NUT Executive mainly to provide a platform for our ideas, and we know we can never be more than a minority.[76]

One consequence of these problems in Trotskyist trade union work is that the period from the early 1970s through to the early 1990s is littered with an extraordinary number of ephemeral Trotskyist fractions, caucuses and bulletins.

However the problems of Trotskyist trade union work are not simply organizational but are rooted in an impoverished theory of class consciousness. According to Cliff, 'while workers are trying to defend themselves, they change themselves, and become capable of creating a new society', a tradition often described as 'socialism from below' (Cliff 1975: 154). There is no indication here of any sophistication or complexity but only a crude model of rank and file participation in struggle leading to radical change in ideas or consciousness. There is no analysis of different types of collective action, the significance of different types of demand or the relevance of the outcome of struggles. Nor is there any attempt to transcend the familiar dichotomy of reformist vs revolutionary consciousness and to think more carefully about different forms of class consciousness. Gramsci famously distinguished between the sectional consciousness of an occupation or trade, the corporate consciousness of the working class as a whole in opposition to a particular state policy and hegemonic or revolutionary consciousness (Kelly 1988: 66–67) but most Trotskyist organizations remain trapped within the confines of Trotsky's reform vs revolution dichotomy.

Conclusions

The trade union movement is an obvious and attractive arena for Trotskyist activity because of its proximity to class exploitation and class struggle and Trotskyists have been actively engaged in trade union work since the 1930s. The larger organizations eventually acquired a relatively substantial trade union base during the Golden Age of the 1970s and by 2016 there were Trotskyist militants on the national executives of 13 trade unions with strong concentrations in the NUT, PCS, UCU and Unison. Trotskyists have been assiduous in the production of rank and file bulletins, magazines and pamphlets focused on workplace issues around pay and jobs. They have promoted ambitious bargaining demands, frequently called for strike action in their pursuit and campaigned tirelessly against the trade union bureaucracy. They have on occasion framed their demands in a broader context of capitalist profitmaking and its consequences for workers but without an adequate theory of the conditions under which participation in economic struggles will result in the development of revolutionary class consciousness.

Yet the trade union arena has also revealed the tensions that invariably arise between the social movement logic of unity and cooperation and the sectarian logic of competition. From time to time Trotskyist groups have cooperated in rank and file bodies within trade unions, in unions like Unite and Unison, and have also engaged in joint campaigns behind particular candidates for office. But far more often it is the sectarian logic of competition with Trotskyist rivals that has taken precedence. In the most heavily unionized parts of the public and private sectors Trotskyists have not only campaigned against 'conservative' officials and against the employer, they have also competed against each other. In industries such as coalmining there were no less than seven Trotskyist groups active in the mid-1980s and similar numbers were found in education, engineering, local government and rail. It was in motor vehicles, one of the most strike-prone industrial sectors in the 1970s and early 1980s, that Trotskyist competition was at its most intense and at one period in the early 1980s an astonishing ten groups organized their own union fractions, leaflets and bulletins. Across the movement as a whole it is a similar picture where the presence of three anti-austerity organizations is testimony to the superior weight of the competitive logic of sectarianism as against the rival logic of social movement unity and cooperation.

Notes

1 In his writings on trade unionism Trotsky himself was somewhat disparaging about what he called the 'fetish of trade union unity' (Trotsky 1929b: 44).
2 Perspectives SWP Conference 1984, Discussion Bulletin No. 1, p. 8, Nigel Clark Papers, File 489/14.
3 http://uniteresist.org/2013/01/model-motion-for-trade-union-branches-tuc-general-strike-consultation/, accessed 18 October 2016; *Workers Power*, October 2012 and on the WRP see for example *Workers Press* 6 May 1974, *The News Line* 23 June 1988, 27 June 1990 and 9 October 1995.
4 http://socialistresistance.org/political-challenges-today-perspectives-and-tasks-for-sr/7237; www.workersliberty.org/story/2012/09/18/general-strike-what-does-it-mean, both accessed 18 October 2016.
5 Perspectives SWP Conference 1984, Discussion Bulletin No. 1, Nigel Clark Papers, File 489/14.
6 The I-CL argued a similar position in the late 1970s (see I-CL 1977) and its successor organization also emphasizes the role of political ideas in the building of a rank and file movement: www.workersliberty.org/10reasons, accessed 19 October 2016.
7 Draft Resolution on Work in the Trade Unions from the PC for 8th Annual Conference 1967, SLL International Discussion Bulletin No. 1, 1 September 1966, Alan Clinton Papers, Warwick, File MSS.539/1/1.
8 Perspectives SWP Conference 1984, Discussion Bulletin No. 1, p. 8, Nigel Clark Papers, File 489/14.
9 National Committee Report, IS Internal Bulletin, May 1974, Nigel Clark Papers, File 489/4.
10 Building in the Work Places and the Trade Unions: National Policy Statement, April 1991, Socialist Party Papers, File 601/C/3/2/6.
11 Dewar, J., 'SWP Line in Unite the Resistance: Carry on Regardless', 25 January 2012 www.workerspower.co.uk/2013/01/swp-line-in-unite-the-resistance-carry-on-regardless/, accessed 16 October 2016.
12 *Socialist Worker* 22 October 2013, 18 November 2014 and 21 November 2015.
13 *The Socialist* 3 July 2013 and 9 July 2014.
14 Militant Tendency, Internal Bulletin, July 1977, Socialist Party Papers, File 601/C/2/2/4.

15 http://uculeft.org/, www.leftunity.org.uk/, http://unisonaction-broadleft.co.uk/, accessed 16 October 2016.

16 www.socialistparty.org.uk/txt/456.pdf, accessed 16 June 2017.

17 www.workersliberty.org/system/files/Tubeworker%20-%20June%202017.pdf; www.workersliberty.org/node/25171; www.workerspower.co.uk/category/unions/rmt/; www.workerspower.co.uk/category/unions/cwu/, all accessed 16 June 2017.

18 https://pcsindependentleft.com/front-page/, accessed 16 October 2016.

19 www.socialistteacher.org/about-us; https://letsactnetwork.wordpress.com/, accessed 16 October 2016; George Binette interview 11 April 2014.

20 There is also an older electoral grouping, the Campaign for a Democratic and Fighting Union, based around Labour Party and CP activists; Owen, R., 'NUT Election: Why We Should Vote for the Radical Left', 16 June 2014, https://rs21.org.uk/2014/06/16/nut-why-we-should-vote-for-the-radical-left/, accessed 16 October 2016.

21 *Socialist Worker* 3 June 2014; Baisley, A., Why I'm Voting for Christine Blower for NUT General Secretary', 6 June 2014, www.counterfire.org/articles/opinion/17254-why-im-voting-for-christine-blower-for-nut-general-secretary, accessed 16 October 2016; *The Socialist* 2 July 2014; *Solidarity* 11 June 2014; Owen, R., 'NUT Election: Why We Should Vote for the Radical Left', 16 June 2014, https://rs21.org.uk/2014/06/16/nut-why-we-should-vote-for-the-radical-left/, accessed 16 October 2016.

22 www.grassrootsleft.org/; http://unitedleft.org.uk/?Name=Value; accessed 16 October 2016.

23 *The Socialist* 9 January 2013; www.workersliberty.org/story/2013/01/17/workers-liberty-statement-unite-general-secretary-election, accessed 17 October 2016; *Socialist Appeal* February 2013; *Socialist Worker* 12 January 2013; *Socialist Fight* No. 12, 2012–2013; http://socialistresistance.org/support-jerry-hicks-for-unite-general-secretary/4775, accessed 17 October 2016; *Workers Power* February 2013.

24 http://uculeft.org/; https://ucuindependentbroadleftnetwork.org/about/, accessed 24 October 2016.

25 http://shopstewards.net/about-the-nssn/, accessed 17 October 2016.

26 www.theguardian.com/commentisfree/2010/aug/04/time-to-organise-resistance-now, accessed 17 October 2016.

27 Coalition of Resistance, Conference Represents a Good Start, 28 November 2010, www.permanentrevolution.net/entry/3210, accessed 17 October 2016.

28 For the sake of completeness we should add the WRP's All Trades Unions Alliance, a grouping of WRP members and sympathizers which also holds the occasional national meeting although it is now a pale shadow of the original body. In May 1973 its annual conference reportedly attracted 2,200 people and even in the early months of 1985, shortly before the split, its meeting was attended by 'over 2,000'. Yet by May 2000 attendance had dwindled to just 300 and by 2017 it was down to about 150: *Workers Press* 14 May 1973; *Young Socialist* 9 February 1985; *Young Socialist* 27 May 2000; *The News Line* 13 February 2017.

29 Industrial Work – General Summary, 1987 Conference Report, Socialist Party Papers, File 601/C/3/2/5.

30 SLL, A Political Letter to All Members, 28 December 1961, Richardson/Higgins Papers, Box 220, File 3; Posadists: *Red Flag* 10 March 1968; Organisation Conclusions of the 4th Conference of the British Section, 29 January 1974, Posadist Tendency Papers, Box 8, File 1; and see also Douglass (2008: 296 ff.; 2009: 243 ff.); Charlton, J., 'IS Miners' Fraction: Report and Perspectives', n.d. – probably October 1972, Colin Barker Papers, File 152/1/1/7.

31 Militant: National Miners Broad Left, 2 October 1986, Socialist Party Papers, File 601/C/3/2/5; Socialist Action: NUM Fraction Report, September 1986, IMG Papers, Warwick, File MSS 128; SEP: *International Worker* July–August 1986; SWP: Perspectives SWP Conference 1984, Discussion Bulletin No. 1, Nigel Clark Papers, File 489/14; Workers Power: Interview with George Binette 11 April 2014; WRP (News Line):

Temple (1983); WRP (Workers Press): Minutes of Central Committee, 20 June 1988, WRP Papers, Box 77.

32 IS Industrial Report 1973/74, Internal Bulletin Pre-Conference issue, n.d. – probably June 1974, Nigel Clark Papers, File 489/4; Perspectives, Workers Fight Aggregate, 27/28 May 1972, Richardson/Higgins Papers, Box 28, File 3.

33 Political Committee Resolution on Work in the Trade Unions for 1964 Conference, 14–16 March 1964, WRP Papers, Boxes 682, 683.

34 IS Industrial Bulletin No.1, n.d. – probably 1972, Colin Barker Papers, File 152/1/1/7; I-CL, Letter to National Committee Members and Branch Organisers, 24 July 1977, AWL Papers, File AWL 1/6 Pt 2; I-CL, Steering Committee Minutes, 20 September 1979, AWL Papers, File AWL/1/8; I-CL Internal Bulletin No. 28, May 1979, Richardson/Higgins Papers, Box 260, File 2; IMG, Draft Statement of Aims for the Revolutionary Left Caucus in TASS, 24 January 1973, Tony Whelan Papers, File 1/1/5; *Militant Engineer*, Socialist Party Papers, File 601/C/5/7/7.

35 *The Track* No. 1, March 1975, WRP Papers, Box 584.

36 In addition the libertarian socialist group Big Flame had a group of members at the Ford Halewood plant in Merseyside (Big Flame 1973).

37 I-CL, Letter to National Committee Members and Branch Organisers, 24 July 1977, AWL Papers, File AWL 1/6 Pt 2; IC-L, Steering Committee Minutes, 20 September 1979 and I-CL Internal Bulletin No. 28, May 1979 both in Richardson/Higgins Papers, Box 260, File 2; IMG, *The Organizer*, IMG Papers, Warwick, File 28; IS Industrial Bulletin No. 1, n.d. – probably 1972, Colin Barker Papers, File 152/1/1/7; IS, Industrial Report 1973/4, Internal Bulletin Pre-conference Issue, n.d. – probably June 1974, Nigel Clark Papers, File 489/4; Various SWP Car Factory Bulletins, Alan Thornett Papers, File 5/P/5; *Red Flag* 10 March 1968; Spartacist League/Britain, Central Committee Minutes, 4 June 1980, IMG Papers, Warwick, File 258; Workers Fight, Ford Dagenham Bulletins and Austin Rover Cowley Bulletins, Richardson/Higgins Papers, Boxes 234 and 235; WSL Bulletins, Alan Thornett Papers, File 5/P/6.

38 SLL/WRP, ATUA Rails Section, Meetings *Workers Press*, various issues 1972–1975; Militant Internal Bulletin, December 1975, Socialist Party Papers, File 601/C/5/1/6 and also Militant (1981b); IS, Industrial Report, 1973/74, Internal Bulletin Pre-conference Issue, n.d. – probably June 1974, Nigel Clark Papers, File 489/4; Socialist League, Party Tasks in Rail, 8 September 1985, IMG Papers Warwick, File 230; WSL, Organising Committee Minutes, 13 August 1981, AWL Papers, File AWL /1/13; Executive Committee Minutes, 31 January 1982, AWL Papers, File AWL/1/14; Organisation Report, WSL Internal Bulletin No. 116, June 1984, Richardson/Higgins Papers, Box 100, File 3; AWL, Executive Committee Minutes, 27 March 1992, AWL Papers, File AWL/1/32; Workers Fight *Workers Platform*, Richardson/Higgins Papers, Box 234; Workers Power: Interview with George Binette.

39 NALGO Action Group Chronology, Industrial Bulletin No. 2, April 1970, Will Fancy Papers, Box 12/5; IMG, Trade Union Sub-committee Minutes, 26 May 1973, Tony Whelan Papers, File 1/1/5; IMG, Quarterly Budget for Trade Union Activities, 27 January 1976, IMG Papers, Warwick File 103; ISG, Internal Information Bulletin No. 1 (new series), February 1988, Dani Ahrens Papers, File 401/3//3; Militant Tendency: Internal Bulletin, July 1972, Socialist Party Papers, File 601/C/5/1/4; Internal Bulletin, December 1975, Socialist Party Papers, File 601/C/5/1/6; Internal Bulletin, July 1977, Socialist Party Papers, File 601/C/2/2/4; WSL: Organisation Report, WSL Internal Bulletin No. 116, June 1984, Richardson/Higgins Papers, Box 110, File 3; WRP: *The News Line* 9 February 1990, 10 May 1990.

40 Militant Tendency Internal Bulletin, March/April 1973, Socialist Party Papers, File 601/C/5/1/4; Industrial Report 1973/4, IS Internal Bulletin Pre-conference Issue, n.d. – probably June 1974, Nigel Clark Papers, File 489/4.

41 Information for Workers League on IMG Trade Union and Industrial Fractions, n.d. – probably September 1978, IMG Papers Warwick, File 254; WSL, Organisation Report, Internal Bulletin No. 116, June 1984, Richardson/Higgins Papers, Box 110, File 3.

42 Report to EC on Industrial Work, n.d. – probably April 1993; National Industrial Bureau Report 3 July 1993, Socialist Party Papers, File 601/D/2/4/2.

43 ISG, Bulletin No. 1, February 1967, Colin Barker Papers, File 152/1/1/2; IS Bulletin, July 1971, Nigel Clark Papers, File 489/1.

44 File 601/C/5/7/13, Socialist Party Papers.

45 Workers Fight, Standing Committee Minutes, 13 August 1973 and 3 November 1974, AWL Papers, File AWL/1/2; AWL/1/2/; National Editorial Board Minutes, 12–13 December 1987, AWL Papers, File AWL/1/36/6; IMG, Trade Union Sub-committee Minutes, 26 May 1973, Tony Whelan Papers, File 1/1/5; *Workers Press*, various issues in September 1972; Workers Power: Interview with George Binette 11 April 2014.

46 SEP: *International Worker*, No. 5, December 1986, p. 16; Minutes of WRP (Workers Press) Teachers Fraction, 11 June 1986, WRP Papers, Box 429.

47 BLOC National Industrial Bureau, 7–8 February 1987, Socialist Party Papers, File 601/C/3/2/5.

48 Letter from Kevin Roddy to BLOC National Committee, n.d. – probably August 1985, Socialist Party Papers, File 601/C/3/2/2.

49 NALGO Action Group, What We Stand For, 1975, Will Fancy Papers, Box 9/1.

50 Draft Statement of Aims for the Revolutionary Left Caucus in TASS, 24 January 1973, Tony Whelan Papers, File 1/1/5.

51 ATUA, Draft Manifesto National Conference, 6 November 1971, WRP Papers, Box 535; ATUA, The Way Forward for All Trade Unionists, Statement Adopted at 5th Annual ATUA Conference, Birmingham, 22 October 1972, Alan Clinton Papers, Warwick, File 539/1/5.

52 Cliff Slaughter email 8 April 2014.

53 Militant Tendency Industrial Bulletin, September 1975, Socialist Party Papers, File 601/C/5/1/6.

54 http://uculeft.org/about/, accessed 21 October 2016.

55 www.leftunity.org.uk/who-are-lu/, accessed 21 October 2016.

56 www.pcs.org.uk/en/news_and_events/pcs_comment/pcs_comment.cfm, accessed 21 October 2016.

57 London Area WRP Weekly Political Letter, 12 November 1976, WRP Papers, Box 676.

58 Intervention at the Union Conferences, SWP Internal Bulletin No. 4, 1981, Will Fancy Papers, Box 13/1.

59 AWL, National Committee Minutes, 19 January 2002, AWL Papers, File AWL/1/44/2.

60 WRP, Report of Meeting with Arthur Scargill, 16 March 1985, Sheffield, WRP Papers, Box 459.

61 ISG, Secretary's Report, 6 January 1968, Colin Barker Papers, File 152/1/1/3.

62 Jones, A. and Howard, C., 'Perspectives for the Fourth International in Britain', 23 February 1972, Tony Whelan Papers, File/1/1/1/.

63 Workers Fight, National Committee Minutes, 29 September 1972, AWL Papers, File AWL1/1/.

64 I-CL, National Committee Minutes, 9 May 1976, AWL Papers, File AWL/1/5.

65 AWL, National Committee Minutes, 14 October 1995, AWL Papers, File AWL/1/41/1.

66 SLL Internal Document, n.d. – probably 1966 for London Area Conference, Alan Clinton Papers, Warwick, File 539/1/1.

67 State of the Organisation for National Advisory Committee, 9/10 December 1978, Steve Jefferys Papers, File 244/2/1/2.

68 I-CL, National Committee Minutes, 6 June 1979, AWL Papers, File AWL/1/9.

69 Organisation Report, WSL Internal Bulletin No. 116, June 1984, Richardson/Higgins Papers, Box 110, File 3.

70 WRP (WP), Draft Resolution for London District Conference, 19 January 1986, WRP Papers, Box 610.

71 Letter from Geoff Barr to Jim Bevan, 9 March 1989, WRP Papers, Box 98.

72 AWL, National Committee Minutes, 22 June 2002; Executive Committee Minutes, 8 October 2002, AWL Papers, File AWL/1/44/1.
73 Socialist Action, NUM Fraction Report, September 1986, IMG Papers, Warwick, File MSS 128.
74 ISG, Central Committee Minutes, 13 May 1989, Dani Ahrens Papers, File 401/1/1/3.
75 AWL, National Committee Minutes, 14 October 1995, AWL Papers, File AWL/1/41/1.
76 Hyson, M., 'Rank and File: Its History', n.d. – probably 1979, Will Fancy Papers, File 6/2.

10

SOCIAL MOVEMENTS AND FRONT ORGANIZATIONS

In addition to their trade union work, Trotskyist groups have played a key role in creating some of the most successful social movements of recent times. The Anti-Nazi League (1977) and the Anti-Poll Tax Federation (1989) were both coalitions of left-wing political activists in which Trotskyists played a key role. In contrast, Trotskyist groups have struggled to make an impact in the environmental movement and have experienced particular difficulty in relating to movements around women's rights and sexuality (Bruley 2014; Willett 2014). This chapter begins by classifying the rich variety of social movements into a number of specific domains and further subdivides them according to the relationships between their Trotskyist and non-Trotskyist components. The next section then examines some of the most successful social movements before looking in turn at those which have proved less successful and those in which Trotskyists have exerted relatively little influence. Finally we consider the terrain of gender and sexual politics where Trotskyists have faced a series of more far-reaching challenges and problems.

Varieties of social movement and varieties of engagement

Snow et al. (2004: 12) classify the major social movements into six categories: labour movement, anti-war and peace, ethnic and nationalist, women, environmental and religious. We can discount religious and nationalist movements because Trotskyists, in common with almost all Marxists, are confirmed atheists and internationalists, but we should add another category that has proved especially important for Trotskyist groups, anti-imperialism. Anti-war movements sometimes frame their analyses and slogans in the language of anti-imperialism and conversely anti-imperialist campaigns have often emerged in the midst of conflict, for example the Nicaragua Solidarity Campaign (1978). Nonetheless there is a sufficiently long history of campaigns of solidarity with anti-imperialist movements and governments, such as the Anti-Apartheid Movement (AAM), that it seems appropriate to consider them as a separate category. The labour movement is conventionally taken to comprise trade unions but in this chapter the category will be used more broadly to encompass campaigns around the workplace that involve service consumers as well as workers, such as school, college or university students in the case of education. Finally, the category of 'women's movement' will be broadened to include issues of sexuality as well as gender.

Social movements can be further sub-divided according to the relationships between Trotskyists and non-Trotskyists (Table 10.1). At one end of a continuum there are broad social movements created by non-Trotskyist groups in which Trotskyists are active, usually as junior partners, for example the Anti-Apartheid Movement (1959/60) and the Palestine Solidarity Campaign (1969). Second, there are social movements created by Trotskyists and others in which Trotskyists wielded a significant, sometimes a dominant, influence, for example the Anti-Nazi League (1977). Third, there are organizations created and exclusively controlled by a single Trotskyist group and which function, in effect, as a 'front' organization for the group, for example Hands off Venezuela (Socialist Appeal). In some cases this outcome may have been intended, as with the SEP's NHS Fightback campaign because the SEP has repeatedly derided every other section of the Trotskyist, social democratic and communist left. In other cases, social movements have simply failed to attract wider support and have therefore remained *de facto* front organizations, for example the AWL's Welfare State Network (Table 10.2).[1]

TABLE 10.1 Trotskyists and contemporary social movements

	Broad social movements	Social movements initiated and led by Trotskyists	Trotskyist front organizations
Labour movement	Campaign for Trade Union Freedom NSSN (SP)	UtR (SWP) People's Assembly (Counterfire, SR) NCAFC (AWL, SWP Soc Action, WP)	NHS Fightback (SEP)
Anti-war	Campaign for Nuclear Disarmament	StW (Counterfire SWP, SR)	–
Ethnic	–	STUR (SWP) UAF (SWP)	–
Women and sexuality	–	Campaign Against Domestic Violence (SP)	–
Environmental	Campaign Against Climate Change	–	–
Anti-imperialist	Palestine Solidarity Campaign	Solidarity with anti-Fascist Resistance in Ukraine (CF, WP, Socialist Fight)	Hands off Venezuela (Socialist Appeal) Pakistan Trade Union Defence (Socialist Appeal)

Sources: Organizational websites, accessed 5–6 April 2017.

TABLE 10.2 Trotskyists and defunct social movements

	Broad social movements	Trotskyist-initiated broad social movements	Trotskyist front organizations
Labour movement	–	Anti-Poll Tax Federation (MT) Globalize Resistance (SWP) Campaign for Free Education (AWL, SWP)	NRFM (IS) RtW (IS) Welfare State Network (AWL) Unions Fightback (AWL)
Anti-war	–	–	Campaign Against Militarism (RCP)
Ethnic	–	ANL (SWP)	ELWAR (RCP) AFA (Red Action) Stand up to UKIP (SWP) Socialist Campaign to Stop Tories and Fascists (AWL)
Women and sexuality	–	Working Women's Charter (IMG) NAC (IMG)	–
Environmental	–	–	–
Anti-imperialist	AAM	VSC (IMG) Anti-Internment League (IS) TOM (IS, IMG)	Smash the PTA (RCP) Irish Freedom Movement (RCP)

Sources: Organizational archives (see Bibliography); Birchall (2011); Callaghan (1984); Fieldhouse (2005); Taaffe (1995); Tate (2014).

Finally, no examination of social movements is complete without consideration of the difficult issue of the meaning of the term 'successful' and the criteria to be deployed in gauging 'success' (cf. Doherty 2009). Social movements aim to mobilize large numbers of people in collective action designed to resist initiatives from powerful groups or to enforce demands on them. The first two criteria of success that flow from this definition are therefore the scale of mobilization, measured by the size of marches and rallies and the degree of unity amongst the protestors, and the degree to which its opponents become disorganized and divided (Tarrow 1994). As social movements are engaged in a power struggle we can also utilize Lukes' (2005) three-level conceptualization of power to analyse their success. According to Lukes, power is manifested in the outcomes of conflicts, in control of the agenda of debate and at the deepest level in the beliefs or ideologies which underpin debates and shape the ways people think about the social world. Each of these dimensions generates its own criteria of success.

Successful Trotskyist-led social movements

Measured by some or all of these criteria for success, there are five examples of successful Trotskyist-led social movements in the UK: the Vietnam Solidarity

Campaign (created 1966), the Anti-Nazi League (1977), the Anti-Poll Tax Federation (1989), the Stop the War Coalition (2001) and the People's Assembly (2013). VSC was created by the International Group, forerunner of the IMG, and although there was involvement from IS members and support from Labour Party and trade union branches, it was firmly in the hands of the IMG (Tate 2014: 85, 97).[2] A succession of demonstrations against the Vietnam War, including a violent protest outside the American Embassy in October 1967, drew increasingly large numbers and culminated in the famous demonstration in October 1968 when an estimated 100,000 people marched to Trafalgar Square (Tate 2014: 241–42, 263–69). The 1968 march was one of the largest post-war demonstrations and clearly succeeded in mobilizing large numbers. Unlike other organizations that called for peace in Vietnam or an end to the war, the VSC was uncompromisingly in favour of victory for the National Liberation Front (Ali 1987: 160, 228). Some Labour MPs did respond to the growing anti-war sentiment and pressured Prime Minister Harold Wilson to take a tougher line with the Americans, but to no avail. Nonetheless the Vietnam War protests did create disillusion with Labour, especially among young people and the Party's membership fell by almost 100,000 over the next few years in the run-up to its 1970 election defeat (McGuinness 2012; Pimlott 1992: 459–65, 556). IMG meanwhile experienced modest if significant membership growth (from 25 members in 1966 to 210 in 1970) but so too did the rest of the Trotskyist left.

The Anti-Nazi League was an initiative of the SWP and its national organizer was Paul Holborow, assisted by Jerry Fitzpatrick and Nigel Harris, all of whom were in the SWP (Renton 2006: 34, 77). Yet the breadth of the organization is reflected in the fact that it was initially led by a troika comprising Holborow, Labour Party member Peter Hain and Ernie Roberts, a senior official with the engineering union AUEW. Although the ANL attracted support from other Trotskyist groups such as the IMG, they did not participate in its leadership (John Rees interview; Alex Callinicos interview). It was launched at the House of Commons and the steering committee, elected at its first meeting, included four Labour MPs (Renton 2006: 77). The first conference, in 1978, attracted 800 delegates and by the following year it claimed a membership of between 40,000 and 50,000 in 250 branches (Renton 2006: 175). Its single-issue focus was the far-right National Front, which it branded as a Nazi organization, and its conferences rejected attempts to broaden its remit and embrace the struggle in Ireland. When conference passed a motion opposing all immigration controls this was not transformed into a condition of membership because of worries about deterring Labour Party activists (Renton 2006: 104). In contrast, Orthodox organizations such as the Revolutionary Communist Group (1979) were highly critical of the League's decision to eschew a more comprehensive anti-racist and anti-imperialist stance.

Over the period 1977–1979 the National Front vote share in local elections suffered a significant decline and in the 1979 general election none of its 330 candidates obtained more than 5 per cent of the vote. It is true, as Virdee (2014) notes, that some NF supporters may have voted Conservative because of its more aggressive right-wing policies under new leader Margaret Thatcher. Yet it seems likely that ANL propaganda and demonstrations may have helped delegitimize the NF and this was certainly the view of one of its key officials, Martin Webster (Widgery 1986: 111).

The Anti-Poll Tax Federation began in 1989 in response to the Community Charge, or poll tax as it was popularly known, which was enacted in 1988, first rolled out in Scotland in 1989 and subsequently introduced in England and Wales from 1990. The Trotskyist left was divided on how to respond: the SWP argued that unions should campaign for their local authority members to refuse tax collection or the processing of tax payments (Birchall 2011: 505–06). The Militant Tendency on the other hand, argued for a community campaign of non-payment and this proved ultimately to be a far more effective strategy, particularly in Scotland where it was led by the charismatic Tommy Sheridan (Gall 2012: 24–25). As the largest Trotskyist organization at the time with around 7,500 members compared to the SWP's 5,000, Militant was in a strong position to initiate and lead the anti-poll tax campaign. It called large delegate conferences in Scotland and later in England in order to create the Anti-Poll Tax Federation and through mobilization of its own supporters was able to secure 13 of the 16 seats on its National Executive committee (Burns 1992: 79). By 1990 there were approximately 1,500 local anti-poll tax unions and not even Militant had the resources to control that number of organizations so consequently its influence at local level never matched its degree of national control (Bagguley 1995). The year 1989 witnessed a growing number of local anti-poll tax demonstrations, even in traditionally Conservative towns such as Bath, Exeter and Plymouth, culminating in a national demonstration, estimated at 200,000 in March 1990 (Burns 1992: 84–87). Both the geographical spread of the protests and the riots at the London demonstration unnerved Conservative MPs and generated increasing divisions inside the government and the parliamentary Conservative party. In November 1990 MPs deposed Margaret Thatcher as Conservative Party leader and Prime Minister and replaced her with John Major who moved swiftly to announce the abolition of the poll tax (Campbell 2008: 558–60).

Ten years later the murderous Al Qaeda attacks against the USA on 11 September 2001 triggered not only the American 'war on terror' but the anti-war movement in Britain. The SWP moved quickly to organize a public meeting and chose to replicate the ANL model of a broad coalition with speakers from the Labour Party (Jeremy Corbyn), CND and the SWP (John Rees) as well as the writers and activists Tariq Ali and George Monbiot. The meeting was an overwhelming success with attendance estimated at around 2,000 and a follow-up organizing meeting attracted approximately 500 people, including senior Communist Party figure Andrew Murray as well as representatives of 'every small political sect in London' (Murray and German 2005: 48). The meeting chose to focus on just three campaign slogans – Stop the War, No to Racism and Defend Civil Liberties. In order to maintain a broad coalition, including the Muslim Association of Britain, the Green Party and Plaid Cymru, it explicitly rejected calls from the AWL, RCG and others to oppose imperialism and to condemn Muslim fundamentalism.[3] Its elected leadership reflected an unprecedented degree of cooperation between the Trotskyist movement and the Communist Party with Lindsey German (SWP) as convener and Andrew Murray (CPB) as Chair.[4] Over the next few years the Coalition organized a series of meetings and protests culminating in the largest demonstration ever seen in Britain, on 15 February 2003, attended by over 1.5 million, possibly 2 million people (and a protest shortly after the commencement of war mobilized an estimated 400,000) (Murray and German 2005: 163, 199; Whiteley 2009: 786).

On the most straightforward measure of success, StW failed in its key objective: the war in Iraq was not stopped, as the Vietnam War had not been halted by the VSC in the late 1960s. But the campaign probably did engage large numbers of young people and Muslims and like VSC probably contributed to the erosion of Labour's membership and electoral base, both of which had been declining since 1998 (McGuinness 2012; Whiteley 2009: 782–83). It may also have helped to push the issue of the Iraq War higher up the political agenda and shifted public opinion, constraining the ability of later British governments to engage in foreign wars of intervention in Libya and Syria (Murray and German (2005: 274). It may also have played some part in the genesis of the Chilcott Inquiry into the war, established by the Labour government in 2009 and finally reporting in 2016. The Coalition has also demonstrated an unusual degree of resilience: in May 2017 its website lists 58 local branches in England and Wales.[5] In common with the ANL, the Stop the War Coalition has made compromises that have attracted criticism, both externally and internally: rallies in Muslim areas have been interrupted, by agreement, so that local imams could issue a call to prayer and others have segregated men and women in compliance with Islamic tradition (Murray and German 2005: 62).

Finally we consider the People's Assembly, a relatively new anti-austerity grouping that has organized a series of large demonstrations against Conservative government economic policy. Its origins lie in the Coalition of Resistance, an anti-austerity organization founded in 2010 following a call by Labour MPs, trade union leaders and two Trotskyist groups – Counterfire and Socialist Resistance.[6] Its opening conference was attended by around 1,000 people but was not without controversy given the existence of two other anti-austerity organizations, the Right to Work Campaign (controlled by the SWP) and the National Shop Stewards Network (led by the Socialist Party). CoR was effectively relaunched in 2013 and rebranded as the People's Assembly against Austerity with an equally wide range of backers and with a key role being played by Counterfire's John Rees. The Assembly began with a mass rally in central London on 22 June 2013 and has since organized several national and regional anti-austerity demonstrations, the two largest of which were the 20 June 2015 and 16 April 2016 protests (and it was also involved in the 4 March 2017 'Save Our NHS' demonstration). In common with StW it also claims a large number of local groups (88 in England and Wales, May 2017) and a wide range of supporters.[7] The impact of the Assembly, both at national and local level, is difficult to gauge, in part because its anti-austerity focus is both broad and diffuse, in contrast to say the Anti-Poll Tax campaign. It appears to have made no impact on either the Conservative-Liberal Democrat coalition or its Conservative successor government but it may have provided some of the support for the pro-Corbyn movement inside and outside the Labour Party between 2015 and 2017 and indirectly contributed to Labour's remarkable result in the June 2017 general election.[8] Compared to 2015 its vote share rose 9.6 percentage points (from 30.4 per cent to 40.0 per cent) and its total vote rose by an astonishing 3.5 million (from 9.34 million to 12.88 million).

These five social movements have all enjoyed some degree of success but how is that to be explained? First, their main *demands were clear, focused and achievable* within capitalism; they were neither revolutionary nor transitional in character. One of the leaders of Counterfire stressed the importance of fighting for such basic demands by quoting with approval the Labour MP Tony Benn:

> He received a letter from a constituent that said Dear Mr Benn, I've seen that the Russians have put a wheeled space vehicle on the Moon. Do you think there is any chance of a decent bus service in Bristol?
>
> *(John Rees interview)*

Second, the movements themselves embraced a *wide range of social forces*, many of whom were non-revolutionary. The range of groups involved in the Anti-Nazi League and the Stop the War Coalition suggested that its composition went well beyond the parameters of a classical united front and was close to the much-despised 'Popular Front'. Whilst this issue has worried Orthodox Trotskyist critics of both movements, it does not appear to have caused much concern amongst their SWP and Counterfire architects. Third, the movements were able to appeal to a *large constituency*, either because of the numbers of people affected by a particular policy such as the poll tax or austerity or because the issue had become highly salient in both national and international debates, such as the rise of the far right or the Vietnam and Iraq wars. Fourth, their Trotskyist instigators deliberately downplayed or set aside key elements of Trotskyist *doctrine* in the interests of building a broad and united social movement. References to imperialism and anti-imperialism were downgraded in the interests of coalition building. As an SWP interview noted: 'Our perspective changed with the anti-capitalist movement [after Seattle 1999] towards one where we stressed much more what we agreed with people about than what we disagreed about' (Charlie Kimber interview). Finally, these movements have all benefited from a significant input of *resources*, particularly people, finance and organizational infrastructure such as a network of party branches with mobilizing experience and capacity. In addition, the SWP placed its print shop at the disposal of the ANL and the VSC and Anti-Poll Tax Federation both benefitted from the presence of charismatic and inspiring orators, Tariq Ali and Tommy Sheridan respectively.

Less-successful Trotskyist-led social movements

Examination of the less successful social movements initiated by Trotskyists allows us to explore the relevance of these five factors. In the labour movement category we can identify a series of social movements, some extant, others short-lived and now-defunct, that remained under the control of a single Trotskyist group and for that reason failed to escape the widespread (and accurate) perception that they were 'front' organizations. This applies to the Right to Work and National Rank and File Movements of the 1970s (SWP), the Socialist Party's Youth for Jobs and Campaign for a New Workers Party, the AWL's Welfare State Network, Unions Fightback and Socialist Campaign to Stop the Tories and Fascists and the SEP's NHS Fightback. In the case of the AWL and the SEP, the small size of the groups has also hindered the potential success of their campaigns.

In the realm of anti-imperialist work, attempts to build Irish solidarity movements have proved largely fruitless, irrespective of whether they were controlled by a single Trotskyist organization or by a group of organizations because in neither case was there any substantial involvement from Labour Party or trade union branches or other non-Trotskyist groups. The former category includes the now-defunct RCP bodies Smash the Prevention of Terrorism Act and the Irish Freedom Movement as well as the IMG's Irish Solidarity Campaign; the latter includes the 1970s organizations, the Anti-Internment League (IS and others) and the Troops Out Movement (IS, IMG and others) and the more recently formed Irish Republican Prisoners Support Group (Socialist Fight and Workers Power). To this list one can add a variety of other contemporary solidarity campaigns that have remained under the tutelage of a single organization and have suffered accordingly, for example Hands off Venezuela and the Pakistan Trade Union Defence Campaign (Socialist Appeal) and Tamil Solidarity (Socialist Party). Irish solidarity movements almost certainly struggled to build a constituency because of the IRA's reckless decision to launch a bombing campaign in Britain in 1972 whilst the more recent international struggles, in Venezuela and elsewhere, have been eclipsed by the attention devoted to the wars in the Middle East and North Africa and have never achieved the international salience of events such as the Vietnam War (Callaghan 1984: 138–43). In the field of anti-racist and anti-war campaigning, the RCP was again prominent in the creation of bodies under its exclusive control – Workers Against Racism and the Campaign Against Militarism – and which therefore had limited support beyond the ranks of its own members and small periphery of sympathizers. Anti-racist campaigning was also affected by the competition between Trotskyist groups that has weakened its activities in the trade union movement and in the electoral arena. In the early 1990s the SWP relaunched the Anti-Nazi League, the Socialist Party created Youth Against Racism in Europe and Socialist Action was the driving force in the National Assembly Against Racism (Renton 2014: 250–51).

We can also identify a number of social movements in the past that enjoyed a broad base of support and appeared to resonate with a large constituency but which nonetheless failed to achieve any significant degree of success because they lacked clear-cut goals. In 1981 the left-wing Labour MP Tony Benn and supporters around the journal *New Left Review* helped launch the Socialist Society, an educational and research organization that aspired to achieve greater unity on the left, particularly between those working inside and outside the Labour Party (Thompson 2007: 117). Trotskyist supporters included the Socialist Organiser Alliance (now the AWL) and the International Socialist Group (now Socialist Resistance). Shortly after Labour's third successive election defeat in 1987, the Socialist Society and the leftist Campaign Group of Labour MPs launched the more broadly-based Socialist Movement at a conference in Chesterfield. Although attended by almost 2,000 activists, including Trotskyists from the RCP, SWP, the International Communist Party (predecessor of the SEP) and the Spartacist League amongst others, the movement suffered from an absence of clear, achievable goals, a huge problem for any developing social movement, and it expired in the early 1990s (Newman 2002: 305–07).

One other significant factor in the failure of some of these movements is their relative paucity of resources: RCP membership for most of the 1980s and early 1990s was 200–300 and that of the AWL 100–200 and both organizations were involved at any one time in several campaigns and movements. In the case of the AWL the effects of their resource poverty were sometimes magnified by compe- tition as their own social movements on welfare, trade unions and anti-fascism competed with much larger and more heavily resourced campaigns and NGOs, for example the SWP's Unite Against Fascism and in the field of welfare the Child Poverty Action Group and Low Pay Unit.

Non-Trotskyist social movements

There are three significant social movements in Britain which can claim some measure of success but in which Trotskyists have played only a minor role: the Campaign for Nuclear Disarmament (CND, founded in 1957 with its public launch in 1958), the Anti-Apartheid Movement (founded 1959 as the Boycott Movement and relaunched in 1960 as the AAM) and the Palestine Solidarity Campaign (PSC), launched in 1969 to campaign for an independent Palestinian state (Byrne 1988; Fieldhouse 2005; Kelemen 2012).[9] Whilst CND's principal goal has yet to be achieved, in Britain or elsewhere, it did organize some of the largest demonstrations of the 1980s in protest at the siting of Cruise nuclear weapons on American bases in Britain, peaking in 1982 with an estimated 400,000 strong march (Byrne 1988: 152). In contrast the AAM never organized marches on a compara- ble scale but did help contribute to the fall of the apartheid regime that began in 1990 with the release from jail of ANC leader Nelson Mandela and climaxed in 1994 with the first South African elections held under universal suffrage. PSC has become increasingly prominent following a succession of aggressive Israeli actions, including the 1982 and 2006 invasions of Lebanon, the wars in Gaza 2008, 2012 and 2014 and its suppression of the first and second Palestinian uprisings (1987 and 2000) (Kelemen 2012). In 2014 for instance it organized two demonstrations, in July and August, in protest at Israeli aggression against Gaza, each of which attracted at least 100,000 participants. All three movements proclaimed specific if ambitious goals; they were built by a wide range of social forces, including the Labour and Liberal parties, a number of trade unions, Middle Eastern and South African exiles and peace campaigners; and all three movements have been able to appeal to, and mobilize large constituencies (Byrne 1988; Fieldhouse 2005).

Yet in none of these movements did Trotskyists play a major role despite significant efforts at involvement. In 1962 both the SLL and the International Group (forerunner of the IMG) strongly urged their members to become active in CND and help it 'evolve to the left and adopt parts of the transitional programme'.[10] In 1981 the Socialist League (successor to the IMG) was still active in CND with members on local committees; in 1983 its heavy involvement in Youth CND, along with Socialist Organiser, led to the suspension of the section's leadership; and in 1986, despite reduced membership and a major organizational split, it retained an organized CND fraction (Byrne 1988: 84; Callaghan 1984: 154).[11] Both Socialist Action (successor to the Socialist League) and Socialist Organiser were active in the Anti-Apartheid Movement in the 1980s but their involvement was eclipsed by the Revolutionary Communist Group (RCG) whose control of the City of London branch allowed it in 1982 to initiate the famous non-stop picket of South Africa House in central London. Its direct action approach alone might have been tolerated by the rather conservative AAM but the RCG was more ambitious and over-reached itself. Its efforts to shift the movement towards a comprehensive, anti-imperialist programme led to several years of internal conflict, culminating in its expulsion from the AAM in 1985 (Fieldhouse 2005: 218–21).[12]

There were three main barriers to Trotskyist influence within these broad movements. In the first place they were initiated by a range of non–Trotskyist forces which were determined to retain the focus on a narrow range of clear and achievable goals. Attempts to broaden movement policy with elements of Trotskyist doctrine, such as opposition to US imperialism, threatened the involvement of Liberals and other non-socialists and therefore the size of constituency to which the movements could appeal. Second, whilst Trotskyists are often very experienced in factional struggles they found themselves up against the equally experienced activists of the Communist Party, who had become entrenched in AAM and CND in the 1960s and 1970s, notwithstanding the CP's initial doubts about CND (Callaghan 2003: 147; Fieldhouse 2005: 57). By the mid-1970s the intelligence services believed eight of the 15-person CND Executive Committee were CP members and by 2003 the organization's Chair, Kate Hudson, was a leading CP member (Andrew 2009: 673). Third, there was also substantial trade union involvement in these movements, particularly CND with its Trade Union Section, and that too constituted a potential source of opposition to Trotskyist influence.

Women and gay movements

Beyond these cases, it is in the field of identity politics, particularly around women and sexuality, that Trotskyists have encountered significant difficulties. Formally, all Trotskyist organizations condemned the oppression of women, gays and lesbians and as long ago as the early 1970s many had created working groups or commissions to examine the specific issues arising out of these forms of identity. Even groups with a poor record on women's issues and sexuality, such as the Militant Tendency, finally began to engage with identity politics and the Socialist Party now has both a Women's group as well as a Lesbian, Gay, Bisexual and Transgender group.[13] From time to time various groups including the IMG, the SWP, the Spartacist League and the AWL have issued separate women's magazines (*Socialist Woman, Women's Voice, Women and Revolution* and *Women's Fightback* respectively) although only the last of these still survives.

The most fundamental problem for Trotskyist groups is rooted in doctrine. Whereas the exploitation of labour by capital is self-evidently a product of the capitalist mode of production, the oppression of women and gays has existed for millennia, sanctified by the patriarchal and misogynistic values of Christianity and Islam, and its relationship to capitalist exploitation is therefore problematic and contentious (for an early account see Barrett 1980). Neither Trotsky nor Lenin wrote anything of substance on women and the Transitional Programme devoted only a few lines of its 43 pages to the subject.[14] It was Engels' *Origin of the Family, Private Property, and the State* which bequeathed to the Trotskyist movement its core proposition, that the contemporary oppression of women was intimately connected to the ownership of private property and to patrilineal inheritance. Consequently women's emancipation could only be achieved through socialist revolution and not through the campaigns of 'bourgeois feminism' on issues such as abortion or contraception (Bruley 2014: 157). There is now a vast literature on this subject, triggered in part by the first equal pay strike in modern times (the Ford sewing machinists' dispute in 1968), the passage in 1970 of the Equal Pay Act and the Women's Liberation Movement conference in Oxford, also in 1970. If the first two events reinforced the classical Marxist schema of women as *workers*, the Oxford conference and its four demands raised far wider and, for Trotskyists, more troubling issues. 'Equal pay' and 'Equal job and educational opportunities' were the first two demands but the others were 'Free contraception and abortion on demand' and 'Free 24 hour nurseries' (Bruley 2014: 158). In principle, none of these demands required the overthrow of capitalism and since they were neither fully revolutionary nor 'transitional' it was unclear how to accommodate them within core Trotskyist doctrine. The problem was even more acute in the case of the gay rights movement whose core demands revolved around sexuality and sexual freedom and whose place in the Trotskyist world view was even less clear and so even more problematic (Robinson 2007).

Nonetheless the leaders of both Mainstream and Third Camp Trotskyist groups (IMG and IS respectively) were sufficiently adroit to realize that women's oppression had emerged as a salient issue and responded with the creation of women's journals and women's sections. In contrast the Orthodox SLL and the Institutional Militant Tendency simply dismissed what Tendency leader Ted Grant later described as 'the nonsense of the petty bourgeois – women's lib, gay lib . . . – you name it!' (Woods 2013a: 275). Whilst women activists often welcomed the crea-tion of dedicated journals and sections, their production quickly generated fresh problems and tensions. The logic of a democratic centralist party structure is that a women's journal was in the final analysis a *party* publication: its editors were subject to the control of higher levels of the party and its content was required to reflect party policy. This logic, however, increasingly clashed with one of the emerging themes of identity politics, that oppressed groups such as women and gays required their own separate organizational space and autonomy within which to think through the politics of their oppression.

What also became increasingly clear through the 1970s is that party leader-ships held a strongly instrumental view of such specialist journals and sections. Tony Cliff complained in his autobiography, quoting SWP Women's Organizer Lindsey German, that the *Women's Voice* groups and campaigns 'could become a bridge out of the party rather than a means of recruitment' (Cliff 2000: 149). Consequently the SWP decided to shut down the groups in 1981 and the mag-azine in 1982, decisions which precipitated both resignations and expulsions (Bruley 2014: 165–66; Wandor 1990). The IMG had taken a more tolerant view of separate sections for women and gays but also became frustrated with the meagre fruits of its extensive involvement in movements such as the National Abortion Campaign and the Working Women's Charter (on the NAC see Byrne 1997: 113–19). According to Callaghan (1984: 155) 'the complaint was heard that this activity did nothing to build IMG but only consumed its resources'.

It was a similar story with gay rights where the IS gay group was shut down in 1973, relaunched in 1976 but gradually seems to have become absorbed into gen-eral industrial and trade union work from the early 1980s (Willett 2014: 181–86). Whilst active in campaigns against specific pieces of homophobic legislation, such as Clause 28 of the Local Government Bill (1987), the SWP in the late 1980s and 1990s maintained its hostility to 'separatism' and a tendency to prioritize class oppression and class struggle over gay oppression (Edge 1995; and see Choonara and Kimber 2011: 32–34). The SLL and the Militant Tendency both evinced a response to gay politics consistent with their attitude towards the women's move-ment, in other words it was dismissed as 'middle class' and 'bourgeois' (Robinson 2007: 100).

Some of the emerging tensions and problems at the interface between identity politics and Trotskyist politics were consolidated and elaborated in 1979 in the famous booklet *Beyond the Fragments* by Sheila Rowbotham (ex-IS), Lynne Segal ('libertarian left') and Hilary Wainwright (ex-IMG). They located the weaknesses of the revolutionary left not only in specific practices, such as democratic central-ism, but also in a flawed model of the development of political consciousness. For most Trotskyist organizations it is the intervention of the vanguard party in class struggles that is critical for the development of workers' revolutionary class con-sciousness. Rowbotham et al. set out to deconstruct this schema, raising profound questions about how an organization acquired vanguard status and how it grap-pled with, or even acknowledged, the complexities and contradictions of people's world views. Whilst the emphasis placed on 'lived experience' in the formation of people's thinking was not as alien to Trotskyism as the authors implied, their critique helped crystallize a growing disillusionment with the verities of Trotskyism that would soon engulf the movement in a shattering series of splits and ruptures.

The paradox of 'success'

The most successful social movements, measured by the achievement of their ostensible goals, by shifts in the political agenda and popular opinion or by scale of mobilization, have all involved strategic decisions by their Trotskyist instigators to delimit their goals and to downplay potentially relevant elements of Trotskyist doctrine, such as anti-imperialism, in the pursuit of a broad coalition. Yet the paradox of these campaigns is that their own success has rarely translated into any improvements in membership for their Trotskyist creators; indeed in three cases, the ANL, the Anti-Poll Tax Federation and the Stop the War Coalition, membership of their Trotskyist instigators actually fell during the highpoint of protests and demonstrations (Table 10.3). Table 10.3 is based on membership figures presented in Chapter 3 whilst the social movements are dated from their formation to a point just beyond their peak, thereby allowing time for membership gains (or losses) to filter through into party membership records. The main VSC protests occurred in 1967 and 1968; the ANL campaigns began to wind down after the Conservative election victory in May 1979; the abolition of the poll tax was announced in 1991; the main Stop the War mobilizations ran from 2001 until late 2003; and the People's Assembly data has been curtailed at 2015 because Corbyn's election that year as Labour Party leader had a significant effect on Trotskyist party membership that could therefore confound the impact of social movement activity.

TABLE 10.3 Membership gains and losses associated with Trotskyist-led social movements

Social movement	Membership change in the lead group	Membership change in other Trotskyist groups
VSC 1966–1969	IG +115	SLL +666
		IS +564
		MT +85
ANL 1977–1979	SWP –500	SLL –1714
		IMG –63
		MT +428
APTF 1989–1991	MT –1000	SWP +800
StW 2001–2004	SWP –2880	SP –60
PA 2010–2015	CF +210	SP +600
		SWP –701
PA 2013–2015	CF +50	SP +300
		SWP –1294

Sources: See Appendix 2.

Looking at each movement in turn, it is clear that whilst the International Group (predecessor of the IMG) recorded membership gains over the period of VSC activity, they were dwarfed by the membership increases achieved by the IS as it turned to industry and by the SLL despite its sectarian hostility to VSC. Even if the International Group's leadership of VSC did help to boost the Group's membership it is clear that in the early years of the 'Golden Age' of Trotskyism this was one of the least effective roads to growth. The case of the ANL is even more intriguing because over the two years of its intense and wide-ranging activities, and a dramatic growth in its membership, the SWP parent body actually shrank, recording a net loss of around 500 members. As a senior SWP figure at the time observed, 'The problem with the ANL is . . . because we were running it we weren't also using it as a means of recruiting to the party' (Ian Birchall interview).

It is true that other groups also lost members as the 1970s strike wave abated during the latter years of the Labour government-trade union Social Contract, although the Militant Tendency escaped these trends as it capitalized on the growth of the Labour Party left. Ten years later, however, it was Militant's turn to experience the paradox of building a successful social movement and watching its own membership decline. This outcome was doubly ironic because its longstanding rival the SWP gained almost as many members as Militant lost despite its strong opposition to the ultimately successful strategy of non-payment of the poll tax.

By the early 2000s, the Trotskyist movement was reaching the end of a long period of disintegration, splits and decline but even the creation of the SWP-led Stop the War Coalition in 2001 was unable to halt these trends. SWP membership had been declining since the late 1990s and only began to recover in 2005, four years after the creation of StW and two years after its million-strong anti-Iraq War demonstration in February 2003. According to interviews with John Rees (Counterfire) and Alex Callinicos (SWP) both organizations recruited from the large numbers of protesters who have participated in the cycle of anti-war demonstrations that began in the early 2000s and has continued to the present, with protests around the invasion of Iraq, Western involvement in Libya and Syria and the Israeli assault on Gaza in 2014. The largest protests have drawn over 1 million people whilst the Gaza marches drew hundreds of thousands so it would be surprising if recruits had not been made.[15] On the other hand the net membership losses suffered by the SWP since 2013 suggest that any recruitment arising out of StW mobilizations has been insufficient to offset the damaging impact of its 2013–2014 splits.

It is true that other Trotskyist groups were also losing members in the 2000s (for example Socialist Resistance, Workers Power, WRP) or failing to grow (AWL) but this was surely no consolation for the SWP after its prodigious investment of resources in the anti-war movement (see for instance Murray and German 2005). Finally, and most recently the People's Assembly anti-austerity protests and demonstrations do appear to have helped boost the membership of the newly-created Counterfire organization, and perhaps too of the Socialist Party, and this is true whether the results are measured from 2010 – the launch of the Coalition of Resistance – or 2013 and its relaunch as the People's Assembly. (The recent SWP losses should perhaps be discounted because they arose from a prolonged and acrimonious internal dispute over sexual harassment and rape allegations which triggered major waves of resignations.)

If we turn to the smaller scale social movements, we find a similar pattern in which the investment of Trotskyist resources has repeatedly failed to translate into membership growth. The AWL for example has been particularly assiduous in such movement activity: Welfare State Network (formed 1994), Campaign for Free Trade Unions (1997), No Sweat (c. 2000), Iraq Union Solidarity (2004) and the Socialist Campaign to Stop Tories and Fascists (2010) to name only a few. The Welfare State Network simply did not take off and the AWL National Committee noted one year after its creation, 'at the current time it is extremely difficult to build broad local campaigns that involve significant forces other than ourselves'.[16]

There are three reasons why successful social movements have often been associated with a net shrinkage of Trotskyist organizations or at best, very limited growth. In the first place, the conditions for movement success – specific and achievable goals, the downplaying of doctrine and a broad coalition of social forces – call into question the necessity for a fundamental challenge to capitalism. For example, the erosion of far right vote share in the 1970s and the repeal of poll tax legislation in the 1990s demonstrated that neither was integral to the British party political system or to the British capitalist economy. In principle any number of theories, non-Marxist as well as Marxist, could account for the rise and fall of the far right and the initiation and demise of the poll tax. Consequently the *modus operandi* of these social movements creates hardly any incentives for participants to join a Trotskyist party. Second, the short-term success of social movements, whether measured by substantive outcomes or by the scale of mobilization, provides a marked contrast to the long haul and the meagre fruits of the normal routines of Trotskyist activity, paper selling, leafleting, branch meetings and the like. That is perhaps one reason for any reverse flow of members, out of Trotskyist groups and into social movements. Third, when Trotskyist groups throw themselves wholeheartedly into social movement campaigns, the normal organizational routines may atrophy. Branch meetings and branch education programmes may wither as the scarce time of activists is diverted into anti-poll tax or anti-fascist campaigning. Insofar as branch activity has a control function, helping maintain the involvement of less committed members, it is these people who may drift away from the organization during its most vibrant social movement campaigns.

Conclusions

Trotskyist involvement in social movements has contributed significantly to their standing and reputation. The creation of the Vietnam Solidarity Campaign and the Anti-Nazi League, the coordination of opposition to the poll tax and the articulation of anti-war and anti-austerity sentiment have all provided mechanisms through which their Trotskyist architects have influenced contemporary politics. That influence can be measured in different ways: the achievement of their ostensible goals, alteration in the political agenda or public opinion, mobilization of supporters and disorganization of the opposition. It is true that over this same period Trotskyists have also created many unsuccessful social movements but that fact should not detract from their achievements. The difference between success and failure turns on several factors and the most successful movements have pursued clear, specific and achievable goals that have helped to create broad coalitions able to appeal to, and mobilize, a large constituency. Organizational success has undoubtedly been facilitated by the substantial resources of Trotskyist organizations (see Chapter 8) but has required core elements of Trotskyist doctrine to be firmly downplayed.

Paradoxically, social movement success has rarely translated into Trotskyist organizational success and indeed it is more common to find an inverse relationship between the two: during the heyday of the ANL and the Anti-Poll Tax Federation their respective creators (the SWP and the Militant Tendency) both suffered significant erosion of membership. The reasons for this are not entirely clear but several explanations suggest themselves. In the first place, organizations may lose members as they are drawn to the greater attractions of working in a vibrant and successful social movement compared to the heavy personal and financial demands of working in a small revolutionary group in non-revolutionary times. Second, the parent organization will be devoting most of its resources to building the successful social movement and therefore diverting resources from the usual routines of party recruitment, induction and member education. Finally, the downplaying of doctrine that has proved essential for social movement success obscures the relevance of Trotskyist ideas and the perceived necessity for a Trotskyist organization.

Notes

1 'Front' organizations often lack the range of support and influence of larger social movements but they still conform to the definition of a social movement in Chapter 1.
2 Petersen, P., 'Aspects of the History of the International Marxist Group', IMG/Spartacus League Fusion Conference, Pre-Conference Internal Bulletin No. 3, February 1972, IMG Papers, Warwick, File 92. Tariq Ali's own account is in Ali (1987). Ian Birchall, Chris Harman and Paul Foot were all involved according to Tate (2014: 253).
3 Consequently the Spartacist League attacked the Coalition as a 'popular front' (Len Michelson and Mick Connor interview).
4 Socialist Party activists were also involved (Murray and German 2005: 54).
5 www.stopwar.org.uk/index.php, accessed 12 May 2017.
6 www.theguardian.com/commentisfree/2010/aug/04/time-to-organise-resistance-now, accessed 12 May 2017.
7 www.thepeoplesassembly.org.uk/local-groups, accessed 12 May 2017.
8 Seymour's (2016) account of Corbyn's rise to power mentions several social movements, such as Occupy, but does not refer to the Coalition of Resistance or the People's Assembly.
9 We could also add movements such as UK Uncut and Occupy but there is no academic literature on either of these bodies.
10 International Group Circular 28 February 1962, Chris Arthur Papers, File 711/A/5/1. On the SLL see Political Letter No. 5, 15 August 1962, David Spencer Papers, File 164/1/A/1.
11 An appeal from the Mansfield/Bolsover branch, n.d. – probably 1981, IMG Papers, Warwick, File 155; Socialist League, National Mailing No. 14, 2 July 1986, Dani Ahrens

Papers, File 401/3/4. On the WSL, see British Supporters of Trotskyist International Liaison Committee, WSL Internal Bulletin No. 3, May 1983, Richardson/Higgins Papers, Box 28, File 1.

12 As noted in Chapter 4, the RCG had begun to evolve away from Trotskyism in the 1980s.

13 www.socialistparty.org.uk/main/Socialist_Party_campaigns, accessed 16 May 2017.

14 The edited collections of both men comprise short articles and speeches that are of little or no theoretical significance: Lenin (1974), Trotsky (1970).

15 The following 13 Trotskyist groups were present and selling literature at either or both of the Gaza demonstrations on 19 July 2014 and 9 August 2014: AWL, Communist League, Counterfire, IBT, rs21, Socialist Appeal, Socialist Fight, Socialist Party, Socialist Resistance, SWP, Spartacist League, Workers Power and the WRP (Source: Author observation).

16 AWL, National Committee Minutes, 11 November 1995, AWL Papers, File AWL/1/41/2.

11

THE PROLIFERATION OF TROTSKYIST INTERNATIONALS

On 3 September 1938 delegates from 11 countries attended the founding congress of the Fourth International: World Party of Socialist Revolution and endorsed Trotsky's main document, *The Death Agony of Capitalism and the Tasks of the Fourth International*, more commonly known as the Transitional Programme (Trotsky 1938). Almost 80 years later the world Trotskyist movement now comprises an astonishing 23 Fourth Internationals, the product of repeated organizational splits, and one of the main aims of this chapter is to analyse the mechanisms behind this dramatic metamorphosis. It begins with a discussion of what constitutes an 'International', briefly recaps the framework employed earlier to make sense of the fissiparous character of the British Trotskyist movement and then maps the contemporary world of Trotskyist Internationals.

Framework

The policy of splitting an existing organization to establish a new, more ideologically orthodox body has been an integral component of the twentieth-century world communist movement. In January 1919 the Russian Bolsheviks issued an invitation to revolutionaries around the world to split the parties of the Second International and participate in the first congress of the new Third International (or Comintern) (Hessel 1980b: xv). In July 1933 Trotsky claimed that the failure of the Comintern to prevent Hitler's accession to power proved it had now ceased to be a revolutionary organization, necessitating the formation of a new, Fourth International (Trotsky 1933a). Over the next few years he often remarked that in each country mass, revolutionary

Trotskyist parties would most likely emerge through a succession of 'splits and fusions' as they struggled against a variety of ideological deviations such as social democracy, Stalinism, syndicalism and centrism.[1] We established in Chapters 3 and 4 that the proclivity for splits has always outstripped any interest in fusions primarily because of the doctrinairism and sectarianism associated with each of the different Trotskyist families and with the individual members of those families. As noted earlier, these tendencies have been reinforced by two additional factors: first, the low barriers to entry into the Trotskyist world which means the costs of producing and distributing a newspaper or magazine and maintaining a website are so low that a mere handful of people can create a Trotskyist group. Second, the presence and power of dominant leaders has also reinforced the tendency to maintain a separate organization or in some cases to split an existing organization. However, fragmentation of national Trotskyist groups has been partially checked by pressures emanating from the party and social movement faces of these organizations. Disunity has repeatedly hindered both effective electoral participation and influence within trade unions and other social movements and realization of those facts has on occasion led to the creation of electoral coalitions, to united leftist factions within trade unions and to joint participation in social movements. On the international level, doctrinaire and sectarian pressures are likely to be at least as strong as those found within national environments but incentives for cooperation are almost entirely absent because of the paucity of cross-national Trotskyist activity.

The definition of an International is far from straightforward not least because many Trotskyist leaders often claim their own organization is the only 'true' International and that other, small bodies have no organizational reality. A Trotskyist International will be defined here as an organization with the following attributes: it describes itself as Trotskyist or locates itself in the Trotskyist tradition; it has a name; it has a website and web updates within the past six months; it has publications, either online, hard copy or both, regular or irregular; and it has affiliates in more than one country.[2] Very few organizations actually describe themselves as 'the International', but more modestly designate themselves as a 'Committee', 'League' or 'Tendency' whose aim is to 'rebuild', 'reconstruct' or 'reforge' the Fourth International. Some organizations have an international structure, such as an Executive Committee or Secretariat and some have regular congresses but many function as networks of like-minded groups, rather like the Communist Correspondence Societies established by Marx and Engels in 1846 as a means of disseminating ideas and information and organizing debates (Nimtz 2016). The six largest Internationals, each of which has at least 14 national affiliates, have been designated major internationals, with the rest designated as minor. The division is somewhat arbitrary but it is clear from Table 11.1 (below) that some organizations are clearly far more significant than others.

TABLE 11.1 The 23 Trotskyist Internationals 2017

Name, formation year, HQ	Total affiliates actual (claimed)	British affiliate	National affiliates
Major internationals – 6			
Committee for a Workers International, 1974, London	30 (37)	Socialist Party	Australia, Austria, Belgium, Brazil, Canada, Chile, China, Cyprus, France, Germany, Greece, India, Ireland, Israel, Italy, Malaysia, Mexico, Netherlands, Nigeria, Romania, Scotland, South Africa, Spain, Sri Lanka, Sweden, Tunisia, Turkey, UK, USA, Venezuela
United Secretariat of the Fourth International, 1938, Paris	26 (34)	Socialist Resistance	Argentina, Australia, Austria, Belgium, Brazil, Canada, Denmark, France, Germany, Greece, India, Ireland, Italy, Japan, Mexico, Netherlands, Philippines, Portugal, Russia, South Africa, Spain, Sweden, Switzerland, Turkey, UK, USA
International Marxist Tendency, 1992, London	26 (31)	Socialist Appeal	Argentina, Austria, Belgium, Bolivia, Brazil, Canada, Denmark, El Salvador, France, Germany, Greece, Indonesia, Italy, Mexico, Netherlands, New Zealand, Pakistan, Russia, Serbia, South Africa, Spain, Sweden, Switzerland, UK, USA, Venezuela
Fourth International (La Vérité), 1993, Paris	15 (na)	FI Britain	Algeria, Bangladesh, Brazil, France, Germany, Haiti, Mexico, Pakistan, Portugal, South Africa, Spain, Tunisia, UK, USA, Venezuela
International Workers League (Fourth International), 1982, Buenos Aires	15 (24)	International Socialist League	Argentina, Belgium, Brazil, Chile, Colombia, Costa Rica, Ecuador, Honduras, Italy, Peru, Portugal, Spain, UK, Uruguay, USA

International Socialist Tendency, c. 1979, London	14 (30)	Socialist Workers Party	Australia, Austria, Canada, Cyprus, Czech Republic, Denmark, Germany, Greece, Ireland, Netherlands, Pakistan, Poland, South Korea, UK

Minor internationals – 17

ICL (FI)*, 1974, New York	10 (13)	Spartacist League/ Britain	Australia, Canada, France, Germany, Greece, Japan, Mexico, South Africa, UK, USA
ICU (T), 1976, Paris	10 (11)	Workers Fight	Belgium, Caribbean, France, Germany, Italy, Ivory Coast, Spain, Turkey, UK, USA
RCIT, 2011, Vienna	8 (14)	RCIT Britain	Austria, Brazil, Germany, Israel/Palestine, Mexico, New Zealand, Turkey, UK
ICFI (SEP), 1985, Oak Park, Michigan	7 (8)	Socialist Equality Party	Australia, France, Germany, New Zealand, Sri Lanka, UK, USA
IWU (FI), 1997, Buenos Aires	6 (14)	None	Argentina, Brazil, France, Spain, Turkey, USA
SWP PT, 1990, New York	6 (6)	Communist League	Australia, Canada, France, New Zealand, UK, USA
CCRFI, 2004, Buenos Aires	5 (10)	None	Argentina, Finland, Greece, Italy, Uruguay
IBT, 1990, Oakland, California	5 (5)	International Bolshevik Tendency	Canada, Germany, New Zealand, UK, USA
L5I, 1984, London	5 (9)	Workers Power	Austria, Brazil, Germany, Sweden, UK
L4I, 1998, New York	5 (5)	None	Brazil, Germany, Italy, Mexico, USA
ICWL, 1987, London	4 (4)	Alliance for Workers Liberty	Australia, Iran, Turkey, UK
LCFI, 2011, London	4 (4)	Socialist Fight	Argentina, Brazil, UK, USA
ICFI (WRP), 1953, London	3 (5)	Workers Revolutionary Party	Greece, Russia, UK
RSO, 2007, Vienna	3 (4)	None	Austria, France, Germany
TF – FI, 1993, Buenos Aires	3 (10)	None	Argentina, Germany, Spain
WIRFI, 1990, London	3 (4)	WIRFI	Namibia, South Africa, UK
PRC, 2002, Paris	2 (2)	None	Austria, France

Sources: The websites of each International and the websites of each of their claimed national affiliates. Accessed 10 May 2017.

* For full names see Abbreviations.

The Trotskyist International archipelago

Table 11.1 presents key details of the 23 current Internationals, viz. their date of formation, national affiliates in 2017, the name of their British affiliate (if any) and the location of their headquarters, whilst Figure 11.1 charts the numbers of Internationals since 1938. The table provides both the number of actual, national affiliates as well as the number claimed on organizational websites. The latter figure is often fictitious because Internationals sometimes claim affiliates whose websites no longer exist (which almost invariably means the organization is defunct) as well as affiliates in places that are not independent countries such as Corsica, Hong Kong, Puerto Rico and Quebec. Very few Internationals have significant numbers of national affiliates and many are, in effect, national organizations with small groups of followers in other countries. For example, one of the two organizations known as the International Committee of the Fourth International (ICFI) is now, and always has been, controlled by its largest section, the British WRP. Since the implosion of that group in 1985 it is now even more clearly a British organization with two small outposts in Greece and Russia. The Socialist Workers Party Pathfinder Tendency, a minor International with just six small affiliates, is effectively controlled by its US creator, the SWP. However, many of the Internationals do hold regular congresses and produce regular publications, usually a magazine. All of the major Internationals hold regular international meetings and so too do seven of the minor Internationals including the London-based League for the Fifth International.[3]

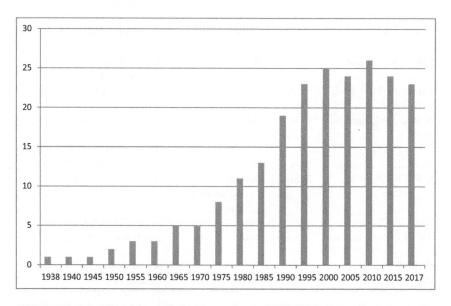

FIGURE 11.1 Numbers of Trotskyist Internationals 1938–2017

Source: As for Table 11.1.

Table 11.1 also shows the geographical concentration of world Trotskyism, with the six major internationals headquartered in just three cities, London (with three organizations, the Committee for a Workers International (CWI), the International Marxist Tendency (IMT) and the International Socialist Tendency (IST)), Paris (with two organizations both calling themselves the Fourth International) and Buenos Aires.[4] The inclusion of the minor internationals shows that no less than eight Trotskyist Internationals are headquartered in London, with four each in Buenos Aires and Paris and three in New York. The entire continents of Africa, Asia and Oceania are conspicuous by their absence.[5] A closer look at the geographical spread of the Internationals' affiliates reveals a pronounced European dominance (Table 11.2). Almost half the national affiliates of the major internationals are European and a similar picture emerges from the minor Internationals (43 out of 89 affiliates). The CWI, the IMT and the Mainstream USFI count approximately half their affiliates in Europe whilst the IST is becoming a *de facto* European organization as ten of its 14 actual affiliates are located in Europe. The International Workers League-Fourth International (IWL-FI), headquartered in Argentina, is the only exception to this Eurocentric tendency as the majority of its affiliates are drawn from South and Central America. Competition between Internationals *within* countries is intense. In the UK, for example, the 22 Trotskyist groups are divided among no less than 17 different Internationals (five groups are not affiliated to any International) and elsewhere in Western Europe the position is the same: Germany's 15 groups belong to 13 different Internationals; the 13 Trotskyist groups in France are divided between 11 different Internationals; and Spain's 11 groups are attached to seven Internationals. In the USA, a total of 13 Internationals have national sections in that country and if we turn to Latin America we find 11 Internationals competing for members in Brazil and seven each in Argentina and Mexico.

TABLE 11.2 The geographical spread of the major Trotskyist Internationals 2017

| International | *Numbers of affiliates by continent* | | | | | |
	Europe	*Latin America*	*Asia**	*Africa*	*North America*	*Total*
CWI	14	4	7	3	2	30
USFI	14	3	6	1	2	26
IMT	13	6	4	1	2	26
IST	10	0	3	0	1	14
FI (1993)	5	4	2	3	1	15
IWL–FI	5	9	0	0	1	15
Totals	61	26	22	8	9	126

Sources: As for Table 11.1.

* Asia here includes Israel, Palestine, Russia and Turkey as well as Australia and New Zealand.

We established in Chapters 3 and 4 that there is a high rate of births and deaths of Trotskyist groups and the same holds true on the International plane. Since 1970 a total of 36 Internationals have been created and 18 have disappeared and amongst the latter are the London-based Trotskyist International Liaison Committee (associated with Alan Thornett) in 1984, Michel Pablo's International Revolutionary Marxist Tendency in 1994 and the Posadist Fourth International in 2015. Within particular Internationals there is also a remarkable degree of turnover as national groups disappear, resign or face expulsion. Between 2011 and 2016, the CWI lost eight affiliates, including sections in Argentina, Bolivia and Portugal and gained two new groups, in South Africa and Tunisia. The USFI lost sections in four countries (Algeria, Croatia, Indonesia and Sri Lanka), but gained only one new section (India) whilst the IMT has a similar record of four losses (Australia, Iran, Ireland and Peru) and just one new affiliate (South Africa).

The most far-reaching losses have affected the IST and the three largest Latin America-based Internationals. On the basis of claimed affiliates from its website, the IST has haemorrhaged 16 members since 2011 including sections in France, Italy, Nigeria, Pakistan, South Africa and Uruguay, reducing the Tendency to just 14 national groups. Equally dramatic is the shrinkage of the IWL-FI which now comprises 15 affiliates after losing 10 in five years, mainly in its Latin American homeland, for example Mexico, Panama and Peru. Far from gaining at the IWL's expense, its smaller Latin American rivals, some swearing allegiance to Nahuel Moreno and all headquartered in Buenos Aires, have also suffered significant losses, suggesting a serious retrenchment of Trotskyism in that part of the world. The Trotskyist Fraction-Fourth International (TF-FI), founded in 1993, now comprises only three affiliates after losing six Latin American sections in the past few years; International Workers Unity (Fourth International) (IWU(FI)), founded 1997, now consists of just six sections after losses in Bolivia, Colombia, Peru and Venezuela; the Coordinating Committee for the Refoundation of the Fourth International (CCRFI) has also been halved in size after losing five sections, three in Latin America; and most dramatic of all, the idiosyncratic and cultist Fourth International of Juan Posadas is now defunct after peaking at 17 affiliates in 1971, including nine in Latin America.[6] There has been some growth amongst the major Internationals, with expansion in South Africa and Turkey for example, but otherwise growth has occurred amongst the minor Internationals. For example, the League for the Fourth International has recruited a handful of followers in Italy and the ICFI, led from the USA by David North, recently announced small, new Socialist Equality Parties in France and New Zealand.[7]

What these developments imply for total membership is unclear because the vast majority of Internationals decline to publish membership figures but the available, fragmentary evidence suggests most Fourth Internationals are extremely small. In 1948 the Fourth International claimed a total of 7,220 members in 33 countries and over 40 years later, in 1991, the USFI claimed a membership only a little higher, at 8,290 (in 42 countries) with decline in Europe balanced out by growth in Latin America (Woolley 1999: 169–70).[8] In 2013 the largest section of the CWI was the Socialist Party of England and Wales with around 2,300 members but the next largest section (India) had just 500 members whilst the Greek section contained just 30 people, despite the huge wave of protests against austerity. Overall, the CWI at that time numbered approximately 6,000 (Steve Dobbs and Toby Harris interview). Turning to the minor Internationals, the WRP, British section of the ICFI, comprised almost 3,000 members in the early 1980s, dwarfing two of its 'large' sections in Australia (150 members, early 1980s) and the USA (100 members in 1985) and a small group of 36 members in Germany, giving the ICFI a grand total in the early 1980s of around 4,000 (Alexander 1991a: 79; Lotz and Feldman 1994: 303). The US Spartacist League was almost certainly the largest section of the International Communist League (Fourth Internationalist) (ICL (FI)) but even after a period of growth in the 1970s its membership was no more than 300 (Alexander 1991a: 922). Adding in the other sections of the League at that time would give a total world membership of no more than 500–600 but even that figure dwarfs the League for the Fifth International whose total membership in 2006 was reported by expelled members as approximately 110.[9]

If we turn to relations between the national affiliates, we find a pattern inscribed in the Fourth International from its foundation. In 1938 its American section was by far the largest and not surprisingly exerted much influence over its deliberations. Alexander (1991a: 271) reports that the US SWP provided 2,500 of the Fourth International's 5,400 members at that time. In common with the ICFI and the League for the Fifth International, the CWI from its formation has been dominated by its British section – the Militant Tendency – which in 1974 comprised over 770 members and dwarfed all of its other affiliates combined, such as the 30 members in Ireland and 28 in Sweden.[10] The USFI was for a period dominated by its French section, the League for the Communist Revolution, which claimed a membership in 1972 of almost 5,000 (Alexander 1991a: 392). Its French neighbour, the Lambertist Fourth International, has long been dominated by its French party, the POI (formerly the PCI and the OCI), whilst the Lutte Ouvrière International is dominated by its eponymous French affiliate (Alexander 1991a: 389, 402). It was a similar story for the IWL-FI whose Argentinian section in 1982 probably comprised several thousand members (Alexander 1991a: 50–51, 557).

Even without numerical dominance, national groups have dominated Internationals through long-serving, charismatic or authoritarian leaders whose ideas, publications and policies come to exercise immense influence within the organization. Examples include Jack Barnes (SWP Pathfinder Tendency and SWP National Secretary since 1972), Tony Cliff (key figure in the IST from its 1979 inception until the late 1990s), Ted Grant (CWI leader 1974–1992 and IMT leader 1992–2006), Alan Woods (IMT leader 1992–present), Gerry Healy (ICFI-WRP leader 1950–1987), Pierre Lambert (FI La Vérité leader early 1950s–late 1990s), David North (ICFI-SEP 1986–present) and Peter Taaffe (CWI 1974–present). For example, when the CWI split in 1992, Ted Grant and his supporters sought to rebuild supportive sections of their new organization around the world, based on Grant's reputation as a Marxist intellectual and political leader. As the IMT took shape and began to expand, some of its non-UK sections rapidly acquired more members than the 200 or so in the British Socialist Appeal group (in Pakistan and Spain for example). Nevertheless the IMT remained headquartered in London; its quarterly journal *In Defence of Marxism* is produced and edited there; and of the 44 articles in its first 19 issues (excluding reprints of Trotsky and Ted Grant) almost two-thirds (28) have been written by the two British group leaders, Alan Woods and Rob Sewell. Websites of the national sections of the IST often highlight and promote the works of the British IS/SWP leader Tony Cliff and the annual meetings of the Tendency are held in London (Cliff 2000: 205), whilst the websites of the Latin American Internationals often feature the writings of Nahuel Moreno.

The Trotskyist Internationals: sectarianism and unity

It was suggested earlier that in the international sphere the pressures towards organizational cooperation and unity were likely to be weak, allowing free rein for sectarian impulses rooted in the defence of particular versions of Trotskyist doctrine. Although there have been several attempts at international unity, the record of these initiatives is one of almost complete failure. There was a degree of reunification in 1963 but even that process simultaneously generated its own schism when Posadas and his followers broke away to form their own International. In the late 1960s and early 1970s there were several meetings between Lutte Ouvrière and the British International Socialists because of their shared orientation to workplace class struggles but the discussions failed to produce a rapprochement (Birchall 2011: 326; Cliff 2000: 203). Between 1973 and 1978 there was correspondence between the Lambertist International and the USFI but nothing came of it (Alexander 1991a: 635). Shortly afterwards Pierre Lambert was involved in an equally abortive round of talks with Nahuel Moreno before the latter broke off and formed his own International. In 1997 the CWI put out feelers to the USFI, the IST and the IWL-FI but according to CWI leader Peter Taaffe, 'the conclusions which most of these organisations drew from the new world situation confronting the working class and the Marxist movement were at variance with ours, and in some cases quite decisively so' (Taaffe 2004: 10).[11]

In the International sphere, it is the sectarian impulse towards differentiation that has proved far more prevalent and powerful than the feeble pressures towards unity. The record of international Trotskyism from 1938 to the present day (2017) amply confirms this proposition although there are significant variations in the degree of sectarianism across the different international organizations. In the first place, we have witnessed a proliferation of Internationals because new families of Trotskyism have emerged from a succession of splits, each with their particular doctrines, leaders and eventually traditions (Table 11.3). Second, there have also been splits *within* families so that, to take one example, we now have a plethora of Internationals claiming to uphold orthodoxy (and denouncing the heresies of their rivals). Finally, the sectarianism of the Internationals is also reflected in historical accounts of the evolution of the world movement. Taaffe's (2004) *History of the CWI* devoted 46 of its 88 pages to attacks on rival Internationals: the USFI (29 pages), the IST (15 pages) and the IWL (two pages). Pierre Frank's Mainstream history of Trotskyism allocated far less space to rival organizations but still managed to denigrate the Healy/Lambert ICFI as 'rigid' and 'sectarian' (Frank and Bensaid 2010: 91, 97). Ted Grant, the founder and intellectual leader of the IMT until his death in 2006, was always dismissive of other Trotskyist groups: 'The French Mandelites have abandoned the dictatorship of the proletariat . . . And naturally, they are splitting in pieces everywhere . . . the sects are in disarray' (Grant quoted in Woods 2013a: 275).

The Morenoite IWL-FI disingenuously states that it 'does not claim to be the revolutionary leadership of the world proletariat' but then implicitly denigrates every other International by declaring that 'at present, it constitutes the *only* demo-cratically centralised world organisation struggling for these aims' (*Socialist Voice* November 2011, p. 5, italics added).

It is the Orthodox and Radical Internationals that display the most consistent and virulent sectarianism. The chapter headings in the Workers Power history of the Fourth International perfectly express its general viewpoint: 'The epigones destroy Trotsky's International', 'The degenerate fragments of the Fourth International' and 'After the splits, the splinters'. The USFI is dismissed as a centrist organization; the Spartacist International is 'a Stalinophilic right-sectarian cult'; the Lambertist International is 'Stalinophobic' and both Lambert and Moreno are 'centrist' lead-ers of 'degenerate' organizations' (Workers Power and Irish Workers Group 1983: 56–57, 65, 79, 90). The Socialist Equality Parties' International Committee rou-tinely dismisses other Internationals, such as the USFI and the WRP's ICFI as 'opportunist' (Socialist Equality Party 2011: 136). The rest of the Trotskyist left are simply practitioners of 'middle-class, pseudo-left politics' but its own International (with its seven small affiliates and a total, global membership in the hundreds) is 'the revolutionary, global centre of opposition to imperialist war'.[12] Finally, the

TABLE 11.3 The seven Trotskyist families and their Internationals

Family	Internationals	Main UK representatives
Mainstream	USFI, SWP PT	Socialist Resistance
Third Camp	IST, ICWL	Socialist Workers Party
		Alliance for Workers Liberty
Orthodox	ICFI (WRP), FI (La Vérité), ICL	Workers Revolutionary Party
	(FI), ICFI (SEP), IBT, L4I, LCFI	Socialist Equality Party
		Spartacist League/Britain
Institutional	CWI, IMT	Socialist Party
		Socialist Appeal
Radical	L5I, WIRFI, PRC, RCIT	Workers Power/The Red Flag
Workerist	ICU (T), RSO	Workers Fight
Latin American	IWL-FI, TF-FI, IWU (FI), CCRFI	International Socialist League

Sources: As for Table 11.1.

Spartacist ICL (FI) has devoted substantial resources over many years to bitter polemics against rival groups, labelled OROs, 'ostensibly revolutionary organizations'. In a series of pamphlets it has denounced the USFI for its 'Menshevik amorphousness', the CWI because it 'capitulate[s] to the capitalist state [and] to imperialism', and branded David North's ICFI as 'counterfeit Trotskyists'.[13]

The antagonism at the international level is strongly reinforced by competition *within* countries and we observed earlier that within the UK, the USA and the three largest European countries the majority of Trotskyist groups are attached to separate Internationals. This is not a feature peculiar to large countries because the same phenomenon is found in smaller countries with fewer groups. Austria has eight Trotskyist groups, every one of which is affiliated to a different International, and the same is true for each of Belgium's five groups. In fact the overwhelming majority of Western Europe's Trotskyist groups, 100 out of 113, are affiliated to a Fourth International.[14]

Conclusions

Despite the oft-repeated references to growth via 'splits and fusions' the record of international Trotskyism, as with national groups in Britain, is that splits are common, fusions are rare. The result of these two processes, even allowing for the demise of 18 smaller Internationals since 1970, is a proliferation of 'Fourth Internationals'. The forces making for fragmentation and disunity are powerful and pervasive: first, there are doctrinal differences between families of Trotskyism that are genuinely hard to reconcile. The Third Camp view that the USSR was a state capitalist formation was fundamentally different from the Orthodox and Mainstream claim that the USSR was a 'degenerated workers' state' and the significance of the dispute became clear when Trotskyists took different positions in the 1950–1953 Korean War. But some of the most dramatic splits have also involved tactical disagreements or differing analyses of immediate events that have subsequently been reframed as 'doctrinal' disputes. In the case of Latin American Trotskyism it is difficult to read Moreno's lengthy essays and discover any *doctrinal* reasons for the existence of this particular Trotskyist family and the associated Internationals. One could also note the shared commitment of both the USFI and the CWI to the building of new, left workers' parties as one of the main strategic goals for Trotskyists in the current period and yet the prospect of collaboration, let alone unity, between these organizations seems utterly remote.

The third factor implicated in the creation of disunity is that many of the Internationals, in common with the national groups that lead them, are dominated by a small number of long-serving, strong, charismatic leaders such as Jack Barnes (SWP Pathfinder Tendency), David North (ICFI-SEP), Peter Taaffe (CWI) and Alan Woods (IMT). The relatively unfettered exercise of power is often a significant source of motivation and satisfaction that would likely be jeopardized by an organizational merger (and conversely could be facilitated by a timely organizational split). Fourth, the costs of creating a 'Fourth International' are now relatively low so that a small number of individuals can quickly design, establish and maintain a website; they can produce, print and disseminate a magazine for a few hundred pounds; and communications via Skype, video or telephone conferencing or even air travel, mean that international meetings, even with small numbers of people, are perfectly feasible (Gerry Downing interview). Fifth, whilst there are some incentives, albeit weak, to cooperate in *national* politics, for example in building social movements such as the Stop the War Coalition or in fighting elections (see Chapters 7 and 10), the incentives to cooperate at international level are nugatory.

Finally, each new International that emerges into the crowded Fourth International 'market' has to justify its existence, to explain to its own members, supporters and potential members, why the world needs yet another International. Tactical, personal or organizational power differences – which would hardly be sufficient to justify a split – are therefore 'reframed' as doctrinal differences, where a split appears more defensible and perhaps even necessary. New recruits will be inducted into the history of the organization and invariably provided with a narrative justifying its separate existence. Taaffe's (2004) history of the CWI, Frank and Bensaid's (2010) account of the USFI, the IMT's 'Brief History' (Anonymous 2006) and Sagra's (2011) history of the IWL are excellent examples of this self-serving genre and to that extent serve to solidify and perpetuate the existing divisions between the seven Trotskyist families and their many Internationals.

Notes

1 See for example, 'Centrism and the Fourth International' 23 February 1934; 'War and the Fourth International', 10 June 1934 in the Trotsky Internet Archive www.marxists.org/archive/trotsky/works/index.htm#a1934, accessed 10 July 2016.
2 On these criteria the New York-based Communist Organization for the Fourth International, associated with Sy Landy, no longer counts as an international because the disappearance of its German and Palestinian affiliates reduced the International to its American base (http://lrp-cofi.org/). Otherwise there are two exceptions to this set of rules. The Fourth International founded by the French Trotskyist Pierre Lambert in 1972 (and then re-proclaimed in 1993) does have a regular journal *La Vérité* (*The Truth*) but its website has not been updated since 2013. The organization is variously referred to as Fourth International (La Vérité, Lambertist or 1993). Second, the WRP's International Committee of the Fourth International (ICFI) does not have a website or a publication but does issue occasional statements by the ICFI Executive in the WRP bi-monthly journal *Marxist Review*, for example May–June 2011 as well as statements from its Greek and Russian sections, for example January 2010, May 2010, November–December 2010, July–August 2015.
3 The other organizations with regular meetings are the IBT, ICL (FI), IWU (FI), RCIT and the TFFI. In contrast, there are five minor Internationals which do not appear to hold regular congresses or issue a regular publication: ICFI (WRP), LCFI, IWLC, PRC and RSO.
4 These are the Mainstream United Secretariat of the Fourth International and the Lambertist Fourth International (see note 2).
5 The 18 defunct Fourth Internationals show a similar geographical spread with five headquartered in London, three in Buenos Aires and the rest mainly in Western Europe (six) and North America (two) with one in La Paz and one unknown. For a list see Appendix 4.
6 All information taken from the websites of the Internationals and their claimed national affiliates between 2011 and 2017. For web addresses see Bibliography.

7 On the League for the Fourth International's Italian section, see *The Internationalist* No. 43, May–June 2016; and on the Socialist Equality Parties see 'The International Committee of the Fourth International Founds Its French Section', 15 November 2016 and 'New Zealand: Socialist Equality Group Holds Public Meeting on US Election Outcome', 29 November 2016, www.wsws.org/, accessed 9 December 2016.

8 Green, J., 'Report from the 13th World Congress', 1991, Dani Ahrens Paper, File 401/3/11.

9 'The Split in the League for the Fifth International', 3 July 2006 www.permanentrevolution. net/entry/1356, accessed 12 December 2016.

10 CWI Bulletin No. 2, January 1975, AWL Papers, File AWL/12/8.

11 The IST did attempt to engage with the anti-globalization movements after the protests in 1999 against the World Trade Organization meeting in Seattle although there is no indication of any formal discussions with other Internationals. Information supplied by Gregor Gall, email correspondence 8 July 2017.

12 SEP (UK) 'For a New Socialist Movement Against Militarism, Austerity and War', November 2016, available at http://socialequality.org.uk/resolution-2016/#more-1264, accessed 8 December 2016.

13 *ICL Trotskyism vs. Mandelite "Left" Polish Nationalism* (1999: 19), *Militant Labour's Touching Faith in the Capitalist State* (1994: 20), *The International Bolshevik Tendency – What Is It?* (1995: 4), *Trotskyism: What It Isn't and What It Is!* (1990: 12), *Moreno Truth Kit* (1980: 30), *David North's ICFI: From Support to Capitalist Counterrevolution in the USSR to Great Russian Chauvinism* (1997: 16).

14 Austria, Belgium, Cyprus, Denmark, Finland, France, Germany, Greece, Iceland, Ireland, Italy, Luxembourg, Netherlands, Norway, Portugal, Spain, Sweden, Switzerland, UK.

12

THE ACHIEVEMENTS, LIMITATIONS AND WEAKNESSES OF TROTSKYISM

Although Trotskyist opposition to Stalin dates from the 1920s it was not until 1938 that Trotsky and his followers proclaimed the Fourth International as the one true descendant of the Bolshevik-Leninist tradition. Almost 80 years later the movement has increased its geographical reach and in some countries Trotskyist groups have eclipsed their erstwhile communist rivals as the principal voice of revolutionary Marxism. Yet this achievement is overshadowed by the complete absence of a *mass* Trotskyist party anywhere on the planet and by the failure of any Trotskyist group to have led a socialist revolution, successful or otherwise. In part these failings are both cause and effect of the extraordinarily fissiparous character of world Trotskyism. Tactical and strategic divisions were a pervasive feature of the nascent Trotskyist movement but since 1938 they have been overlaid by doctrinal disputes that have successively restructured and divided the movement, resulting in the emergence of seven discrete ideological families, each with its own particular interpretation of Trotskyist doctrine and its own set of Fourth Internationals. Further waves of *intra-family* divisions have engendered a situation in which there now exist 23 organizations with pretensions to being the authentic voice of contemporary international Trotskyism. That said, the Trotskyist movement does have a significant record of achievement in the field of social movements, to which we turn shortly, but the chapter begins by recapping the main features of the movement before proceeding to summarize its intrinsic weaknesses and limitations.

Development of the Trotskyist movement

Trotskyist organizations are hybrid bodies combining elements of the political party, the sect and the social movement. Like other political parties, they recruit members, participate in elections and seek power, albeit by revolutionary methods, in order to implement their policies. But unlike mainstream parties their attachments to office, votes and policy are almost invariably subordinated to a fourth objective, the preservation of doctrine. Notwithstanding differing interpretations of Trotsky's thought, it is possible to distil his rich and varied writings into a small number of elements that can be considered as the core of Trotskyist doctrine: the theory of permanent revolution, the tactic of the united front, transitional demands, the critical analysis of the Stalinist states, the necessity for a new revolutionary International, the necessity for a democratic centralist, revolutionary vanguard party, the construction of rank and file union groups to challenge the trade union bureaucracy, the idea of revolution as a seizure of power to create proletarian dictatorship and the idea of the imperialist epoch as one of wars and revolutions. Trotsky himself can be said to have originated only some of these propositions and the concepts of permanent revolution, the united front and transitional demands are most often regarded as quintessentially Trotskyist. Other elements were first developed and promoted by Lenin, such as the idea of the vanguard party and the concept of the imperialist epoch, but were later incorporated by Trotsky into his own world view as it developed through the Bolshevik party conflicts of the 1920s and 1930s.

Numerous disagreements have arisen over the significance of these individual elements, on their precise meaning and over the most appropriate forms of implementation. The first major schism in the Trotskyist movement was triggered by the Soviet invasions of Poland and Finland in late 1939 and by Trotsky's insistence that 'critical analysis of the Soviet Union' was wholly compatible with unconditional military defence of the USSR in its conflicts with capitalist states. Out of this dispute emerged the first traces of what would later become *Third Camp Trotskyism*, characterized by its abandonment of the 'degenerated workers' state' designation and its replacement by an analysis of the USSR as a new form of exploitative economy, state capitalist or bureaucratic collectivist in the most popular formulations. In Britain, Tony Cliff's Socialist Review Group (later IS and the SWP) was synonymous with Third Camp Trotskyism but was joined in the late 1980s by the Socialist Organiser group (now the AWL) which has undertaken the systematic recuperation of the Third Camp tradition, reprinting substantial amounts of 1940s material from Max Shachtman and others (Matgamna 1998, 2015).

The second major split in the movement occurred in the 1950s in response to the proposal from *Mainstream* Trotskyist leader Michel Pablo that Trotskyists acknowledge the strength of world communism and the concomitant weakness of Trotskyism and pursue a policy of deep entry into social democratic or communist parties. The policy was pursued for a short period and abandoned in the 1960s, but not before reaction to Pablo's ideas had crystallized into the formation of a new family of Trotskyism, committed to the preservation of *Orthodoxy*. In Britain it was led by Healy's organization (later the SLL and the WRP) with its trademark antipathy to what it called 'Pabloite revisionism', its antagonism to the 1963 reunification of international Trotskyism and its avoidance of all forms of collaboration with other Trotskyist groups. In the 1970s the Orthodox camp was joined by the

Spartacist League and the number of groups expanded still further in the 1980s following the disintegration of the WRP.

Hostility to the 1963 reunification was also shared by groups of Latin American Trotskyists such as Juan Posadas whose growing complaints about North American and European domination of the movement issued in a further schism and the emergence of *Latin American Trotskyism*. Eventually led by the Argentinian Nahuel Moreno, this particular family of Trotskyism has flourished (and split) in its regional birthplace but has no distinctive ideological or doctrinal motif. Developing in parallel with these four families was the RSL led by Ted Grant, a doctrinaire Marxist committed to a long-term policy of deep entry into the Labour Party and the use of parliament to introduce socialism. This overriding orientation to existing institutions provides this family with its leitmotif and under the leadership of Grant (and his successors in the Socialist Appeal group) the *Institutional* family acquired a strongly sectarian attitude to all of its Trotskyist rivals. The 1980s witnessed the emergence of *Radical Trotskyism*, a family that believed the international Trotskyist movement, in all its forms, had begun to degenerate almost immediately after its inception; hence the call to write off the Fourth Internationals and found a new, Fifth International. Finally, the French organization Lutte Ouvrière (and its small circle of followers in Britain known as Workers Fight), is the leading force in *Workerist Trotskyism*, a family with a near exclusive focus on workplace factory bulletins to stimulate class struggle between workers and their employers.

The delineation of these discrete families of Trotskyism is important because it underlines the resilience and rootedness of the divisions between Trotskyist groups and simultaneously throws light on the perennial failure of the unity proposals that surface at regular intervals. It also helps explain why the Trotskyist movement has become significantly more divided over time: in 1967 there were six Trotskyist groups in Britain and five Fourth Internationals but 50 years later there are 22 Trotskyist groups and 23 Fourth Internationals.

The history of the British movement can be divided into five phases: the period of Formation 1932–1949 was marked by the emergence of a series of small groups that steadily grew during the inter-war and wartime years before the 1944 unification created the Revolutionary Communist Party (RCP), an organization with around 500 members. The RCP survived only a few years before an acrimonious split as a result of which the movement went into rapid decline. At the beginning of the Bleak years, a period spanning 1950 to 1965, the movement comprised no more than 100 people in three small groups, all working inside the Labour Party but with almost no presence or influence inside the trade union movement. Membership growth was very slow until the mid-1960s and even the 1956 crisis in the Communist Party generated relatively few converts to Trotskyism, despite strenuous recruitment efforts by Healy's organization.

The period from 1966 to 1985 constituted the Golden Age of British Trotskyism, marked by exceptionally rapid and substantial membership growth and the development of a significant trade union base. By 1985 the WRP had reached almost 9,000 members, the Militant Tendency was close to 7,000 and the SWP had reached 4,000 members so that the movement as a whole had now overtaken the Communist Party (CP) in terms of overall size, an historic milestone in the fortunes of the two wings of the communist movement in Britain. All three organizations had achieved a significant presence in the trade union movement, rivalling and in some cases exceeding the weight and influence of the CP. The movement had also experienced a large number of splits and by 1985 comprised 15 organizations in 13 Fourth Internationals but nonetheless as the 1984–1985 miners' strike approached its climax, many Trotskyist groups had every reason to believe their influence would continue to grow. In fact the miners' defeat in 1985 triggered a major crisis within the Trotskyist movement, ushering in the period of Disintegration, from 1985 until 2004. Three of the largest groups, the WRP, the Socialist League (formerly the IMG) and the Militant Tendency, split into a myriad of fragments; another organization, the Revolutionary Communist Party disappeared; and most of the remainder experienced significant membership decline. Total membership in the Trotskyist movement fell by two-thirds, from a little over 20,000 in 1985 to less than 7,000 in 2004, notwithstanding the success of the Anti-Poll Tax Federation (1989–1991) and the impressive growth of the SWP in the mid-1990s.

The period since 2004 has been one of Stasis: membership has recovered a little and now stands at approximately 9,500 but in the context of British involvement in the illegal war in Iraq, New Labour's accommodation to neoliberalism, prolonged economic crisis and Conservative austerity, this is a disappointing, not to say, meagre achievement. When we consider the huge demonstrations organized by the Stop the War Coalition in the early 2000s and the People's Assembly in more recent years, the limited recuperation of Trotskyist membership and the persistence of organizational divisions must be even more disappointing for Trotskyist leaders. To these problems has been added the fresh dilemmas thrown up by the election of the left-wing Jeremy Corbyn as Labour Party leader in 2015 and his impressive electoral performance in 2017 which saw Labour's vote share rise almost ten percentage points to 40 per cent. On the one hand, the re-emergence of left-wing policies creates a political climate in which Trotskyist ideas may gain some traction. On the other hand, the centrality of the Labour Party to this leftist renaissance has encouraged thousands of people to join a large, left social democratic party rather than a small Trotskyist group, further depleting Trotskyist membership.

Achievements of the Trotskyist movement

The most striking achievements of the Trotskyist movement are to be found in the field of social movements. The Anti-Nazi League (ANL), initiated and led by the SWP, played a significant part in rolling back the electoral advance of the far right National Front in the late 1970s whilst the Anti-Poll Tax Federation (APTF) was even more successful, helping to destroy Margaret Thatcher's poll tax and at the same time contributing to her downfall as Prime Minister. Both the ANL and the APTF mobilized large numbers of people into social movement activity and membership, through local ANL branches and local Anti-Poll Tax unions and through several impressively large national demonstrations. Although the Vietnam Solidarity Campaign, Stop the War Coalition and People's Assembly failed to achieve their ostensible aims, they did succeed in organizing some of the largest demonstrations ever seen in Britain. In all these bodies, their Trotskyist instigators and leaders significantly downplayed core elements of Trotskyist doctrine and cooperated with rival Trotskyist groups, compromising on slogans and arguments in order to construct broad coalitions around clear, achievable and non-revolutionary demands. That doctrinal moderation and movement success are causally connected is clear from the large number of Trotskyist-led social movements that have departed from these precepts and remained small and ineffectual, if doctrinally impeccable, especially in the fields of anti-racism, anti-war and anti-imperialist activity.

A similar story can be told of the trade union movement where Trotskyists have maintained a significant presence in many unions for several decades, particularly the public sector teaching, civil service and local government unions. They have defended ambitious claims on issues such as pay, pensions, working conditions and staffing levels and generally promoted militant action in support of these claims. In unions with conservative, pro-social partnership leaders such as the shop workers union USDAW, they play an important oppositional role in holding the leadership to account. In the only union where they took control of the executive and key positions, the Public and Commercial Services Union PCS, they have transformed a previously quiescent organization into a more militant and activist body.

Second, the Trotskyist movement has played a significant role in introducing the ideas of classical Marxism to successive cohorts of young people, particularly university and college students. Approximately 40–50 per cent of Britain's universities have Trotskyist groups on campus, many of whom reprint and distribute classical texts from Marx and Engels, Lenin and Trotsky as well as by modern Marxists such as Callinicos and Mandel. The prevailing definition of the Marxist canon is somewhat selective as Trotskyist publishing houses produce very little material from Luxemburg, even less from Gramsci and nothing at all from those Marxists such as Bukharin and Kautsky who fell out of favour with Lenin and Trotsky. Trotskyist groups also organize educational programmes which provide basic introductions to Marxist and Trotskyist ideas as well as public meetings and conferences which host debates about their contemporary applications and relevance. Through their work in social movements and trade unions, Trotskyist groups also provide their members with a basic grounding in a variety of organizational skills, such as chairing meetings, promoting resolutions and caucusing against political opponents. Although many new recruits quickly resign from Trotskyist organizations, some remain active in left politics for many years. '[W]ith both the IMG and the SWP . . . ex-members pop up all over the place, organizing this and organizing that, and in the unions' (Alan Thornett interview). For instance, PCS General Secretary Mark Serwotka was formerly a member of Socialist Organiser, the journalist Paul Mason once belonged to Workers Power and there may well be many others who retain elements of their Marxist education even if they have jettisoned most elements of Trotskyist doctrine.

Third, Trotskyist intellectuals have made a contribution to the revival of interest in Marxist ideas that began in the 1960s and re-emerged in the 2000s after a hiatus in the wake of the Soviet and East European collapse. In political economy there are several outstanding figures: Andrew Glyn, member of the Militant Tendency from the late 1960s until the early 1980s and best known for *British Capitalism, Workers and the Profits Squeeze* (1972) and his critique of the left's Alternative Economic Strategy, *Capitalist Crisis: Tribune's 'Alternative Strategy' or Socialist Plan* (1979); Michael Kidron, IS/SWP member from the 1950s until the 1970s, author of *Western Capitalism Since the War* (1970); and the Mainstream Trotskyist leader Ernest Mandel, probably the most influential Marxist economist of the late twentieth century through books such as *The Formation of the Economic Thought of Karl Marx* (1971), *Late Capitalism* (1975a), *The Second Slump* (1980) and *Long Waves of Capitalist Development* (1995b). In social theory, SWP leader Alex Callinicos has written a number of widely cited and influential texts such as *Making History* (1989), *Against Postmodernism* (1990b) and *Social Theory* (1999) and in the field of Soviet studies Tony Cliff's *State Capitalism in Russia* (1974 and original edition 1948) was one of the seminal texts in the state capitalist tradition. We should also mention the independent Marxist journals, *New Left Review*, *Historical Materialism* and *Revolutionary History*, since Trotskyist intellectuals have played key roles in their editorial boards over many years. Finally, we should note the early writings of the historian and political theorist Perry Anderson as well as his role in editing *New Left Review* from 1962 to 1983 and again from 2000. Although Anderson never followed some of his NLR colleagues such as Robin Blackburn and Quintin Hoare into the IMG, it is clear from books such as *Considerations on Western Marxism* (1976 and revised edition 1984) that for many years he maintained a strong affinity with Trotskyist ideas and the Trotskyist movement.

Fourth, Trotskyist groups have played a role in opposing the right wing of the Labour Party and pushing for left-wing policies. Trotskyists backed the Bevanites in the 1950s; they were active in the Labour Party Young Socialists until their expulsion in the early 1960s; and they were active in supporting Tony Benn in the late 1970s and through the 1980s. Most famously, the Militant Tendency had by the late 1980s become the largest ever Trotskyist group in the Labour Party, controlling the Young Socialists and Liverpool City Council and counting three MPs in its ranks. This would all change as the Labour right fought back, expelling a growing number of Tendency members and precipitating a split in the organization as the majority voted to decamp from the increasingly hostile Labour environment. Following the election of Jeremy Corbyn as Labour leader in 2015 a number of Trotskyist groups either resumed entry work (Workers Power, now known as The Red Flag) or intensified their presence in the Labour Party (for example the AWL).

Finally, one of the hallmarks of Trotskyist groups is their resilience in the face of adversity, internal conflicts, limited political influence and their failure to build anything approaching a mass party. It is true that the history of British Trotskyism is littered with the corpses of many small breakaways and splinter groups but it is also true that the three groups which defined the movement in the 1950s – the Socialist Review Group, the RSL and the SLL – still exist today (as the SWP, the Socialist Party and the WRP respectively, whilst 11 of the remaining 19 groups are offshoots of these three). The resilience of the Trotskyist movement is grounded in particular interpretations of doctrine, defended and promulgated by oligarchic leaderships that remain in power for decades. The dominant figures in British Trotskyism led their respective organizations from 1950 until 1985 (in the case of Gerry Healy) and until the 1990s (Tony Cliff and Ted Grant). Leadership stability is a reflection of charismatic personality and of high levels of membership loyalty but also derives from the widespread use of the 'recommended list'. In this practice, first introduced by Lenin in 1921, the outgoing leadership submits to the party annual congress a list of its preferred candidates for election and re-election and invites delegates to vote *en bloc*, for or against (and mostly they vote in favour).

Resilience is also rooted in the capacity of Trotskyist groups to engender high levels of commitment amongst their members and to translate this into financial contributions. Trotskyist groups raise far more income per member than mainstream parties and in some cases up to ten times more, from higher subscriptions, donations to fighting funds, collections at meetings and literature sales. High levels of income, coupled with low staff wages, allow Trotskyist groups to hire disproportionately large numbers of staff compared to mainstream parties and enable them to commit substantial personnel and other resources to party activities, trade union work and social movements.

Limitations and weaknesses of the Trotskyist movement

We have already referred to one of the most striking failures of the world Trotskyist movement and that is the absence of any revolutionary struggle led by Trotskyist forces. Nor is this the result of an absence of revolutionary situations, defined in Leninist terms as the inability of the ruling class to rule by traditional means and the reluctance of the working class and other groups to continue being ruled in this way. Mandel (1979: 42) for example defends the relevance of Trotskyism by listing no less than 20 'revolutionary crises' between the late 1920s and 1978 (24 if you include the four crises in Eastern Europe between 1953 and 1968). For some writers the absence of revolution is explained quite simply by the absence of a mass revolutionary, that is, Trotskyist, party and this viewpoint leads to a characteristic form of 'alternative history'. In Britain for instance, SWP leader Tony Cliff wrote about the final wave of coal mine closures in 1992 despite large protest marches in London and elsewhere, and mused: 'Imagine if we had 15,000 members of the SWP and 30,000 supporters . . . socialists could have taken 40 or 50,000 people to parliament. If that had happened . . . the government would have collapsed' (Birchall 2011: 513).

Leaving aside the wishful thinking about government collapse, the quote encapsulates one of the most familiar themes in Trotskyist accounts of working class defeats and revolutionary failures: if only there had been a mass revolutionary party to thwart the reformists and Stalinists, undermine and divide the ruling class and establish a hegemonic position within the working class, *then* the outcome would have been entirely different. This counterfactual history has been applied to a host of struggles, from Spain in 1936 through France 1968, Greece and Portugal 1974, Spain 1976, the miners' strike 1984–1985 and up to the anti-austerity protests in Southern Europe from 2010 onwards (for example Callinicos and Simons 1985: 251–52). Yet this type of reasoning is completely unilluminating. In place of empirical and theoretical analysis of *why* existing Trotskyist organizations were unable to win support and gain influence in these struggles, we are offered retrospective speculation about what *could* have happened if only the party had become a mass organization. Instead of analysing the Trotskyist party as an integral component of a developing set of conflicts, an effect as well as a cause of complex social processes, the party is treated as a *deus ex machina* that will irrupt into the path of history, violently altering its trajectory in a revolutionary direction. Such wishful thinking lacks any grounding in concrete analyses of popular opinion, political struggle, party competition and the enduring and pervasive weaknesses of the Trotskyist movement (see for instance Slaughter 2016).

The main source of these persistent weaknesses of political intervention and theoretical analysis lies in the foundation stones of the Trotskyist movement, the core elements of doctrine that define the distinctiveness of the movement and demarcate it from an assortment of ideological rivals, in particular Stalinism, social democracy and anarchism. At the heart of Trotskyist doctrine is the necessity to build a vanguard party that will lead a revolutionary overthrow of capitalism and replace parliamentary democracy with a superior, socialist democracy. The theory of permanent revolution, the tactic of the united front, the construction of rank and file union groups and a programme of transitional demands are vital components of party political practice in a pre-revolutionary period. Yet as Anderson eloquently wrote, this perspective is deeply flawed, suffering from, 'too close an imaginative adherence to the paradigm of the October Revolution, made against the husk of a feudal monarchy, and too distant a theoretical concern with the contours of a capitalist democracy the Bolsheviks never had to confront' (Anderson 1983a: 79). Many Trotskyists would reject this claim but if we deploy their own criterion – the test of practice and experience – against their own doctrine then we are obliged to face two overwhelming facts about the Trotskyist movement. Neither in Britain nor in any other country have Trotskyists been able to move beyond small groups of militants and build a stable, mass party wielding substantial political influence. Allied to this failing is the fact that almost 80 years after the foundation of the Fourth International no Trotskyist group has ever led a revolutionary struggle for power in any country in the world. Yet in the centenary year of the Russian Revolution it is clear from the books, articles and lectures issued by the different Trotskyist families that 'imaginative adherence' to 1917 and the dream of a mass Trotskyist party are alive and well.

The role of doctrine within the Trotskyist movement has generated a second and equally parlous set of consequences, splintering the movement into seven discrete and enduring ideological families. Doctrinairism, an excessively strong attachment to the maintenance and defence of doctrine, is grounded in the view that it represents an unshakable guide to political analysis. Orthodox Trotskyists, such as the WRP, the Spartacist League and the SEP have proved, not surprisingly, to be the most vehement defenders of doctrine, where it takes the form of an unswerving loyalty to the classical Trotskyist texts, unsullied by post-Trotsky amendments, revisions or reinterpretations. Whilst the differences between Orthodoxy and the remaining families are dramatic, even the Orthodox family is divided between six different (and small) groups in Britain, each proclaiming that its version of Trotskyist doctrine is superior to those of its perfidious rivals. Nor should we assume that doctrinairism is the exclusive preserve of Orthodox Trotskyism because it can also be found amongst other Trotskyist families, such as the Third Camp AWL, the Institutional family led for many years by the Militant Tendency and the Radical Trotskyists of Workers Power. A powerful attachment to the timeless verities of doctrine has also crippled the capacity of the Trotskyist movement to engage in critical analysis and to learn from failures and mistakes, a fact that is clear from the abundance of uncritical eulogies of the Russian Revolution. The only exceptions to this stricture are the Mainstream International, which has undertaken several dramatic policy shifts including current support for radical left parties, and the Socialist Organiser group which formally abandoned Trotsky's analysis of the USSR and orthodox anti-imperialism in the late 1980s.

A strong commitment to doctrine, whether to orthodoxy or to a more heterodox variety of Trotskyism, has normally been associated with sectarianism, an unremitting hostility to those believed to be guilty of departures from doctrinal rectitude. The Trotskyist movement, in common with religious movements, has therefore developed an exceptionally rich vocabulary to assist in the detection and classification of the different forms of ideological deviation. The existence of terms such as 'centrism', 'economism', 'liquidationism', 'opportunism' and 'ultra-leftism' is testimony to the linguistic creativity of Trotskyism, whilst the frequency of their usage illustrates the importance attached to the demarcation of 'doctrinally correct positions' from deviation and apostasy. As a result of divisions between and within families, Britain now has 22 groups operating within a world movement comprising 23 Internationals. Nor is Britain's situation unique: there are 15 Trotskyist groups in Germany, 13 in France, 11 in Spain and eight each in Greece and Italy. In the non-European centres of Trotskyism, the USA has 13 groups, there are 11 in Brazil and seven each in Argentina, Australia, Canada and Mexico.

Trotskyist doctrine has also proved to be of limited value in the analysis and prognosis of political developments. It foregrounds class exploitation, class struggle, the building of a vanguard party and the battle between revolutionary and reformist politics. Trotskyist language about political action, in programmatic and perspectives documents, invariably centres on those abstract actors, the working class or the masses, occasionally accompanied by an ill-defined petty

bourgeoisie. More fine-grained analyses, differentiating for instance the professional middle class, the steadily employed working class, the precarious working
class and so on, are rare (see Wright 2015). Other forms of oppression, based
on gender, sexual orientation and ethnicity for example, have caused significant
problems for Trotskyist groups, resulting in procrustean efforts to force identity
issues into the unyielding mould of general class politics. Interwoven with these
multiple class locations and identities are varied forms of consciousness that have
proved equally difficult to compress into the simplistic schema of reformist vs
revolutionary consciousness.

One consequence of this lack of precision about the constituencies for Trotskyist
politics and the simplistic model of class consciousness is that electoral programmes
and manifestos have almost invariably generated derisory results, with the median
Trotskyist vote varying between 0.29 and 1.25 per cent in British general elections
between February 1974 and 2017. The suggestion that such low vote shares reflect
the distortions arising from the majoritarian ('first past the post') electoral system
is simply untrue. Trotskyist vote shares in elections based on proportional representation have been equally dismal: in European Parliament elections 1989–2014
vote shares ranged between 0.35 and 1.11 per cent and in Welsh Assembly elections 1999–2016 the Trotskyist vote ranged between 0.3 and 2.1 per cent. Across
Western Europe, where proportional electoral systems are ubiquitous, Trotskyist
vote shares in elections held since 2008 have rarely exceeded 1 per cent; the
only exceptions are France and Ireland where vote shares of up to 7.9 per cent
have been achieved. Further afield it is an equally dismal picture, with the only
exceptions being Argentina and Brazil where Trotskyist groups won a handful of
parliamentary seats in the 2014 general elections in both countries.

Mainstream Trotskyist groups have been active since the 1990s as factions
inside radical left parties and organizations, such as Die Linke (Germany), Left
Bloc (Portugal) and the Red-Green Alliance (Denmark) and the electoral performance of these parties has significantly exceeded the vote shares for independent
Trotskyist platforms, at between 5 and 10 per cent. But as in the case of social movements such as the ANL and APTF, success has been achieved by de-emphasizing
Trotskyist doctrine and focusing on specific, achievable reforms. Programmatic
moderation, however, throws up its own contradictions: Trotskyist electoral support for radical leftist organizations brings these parties closer to other left rivals,
such as the Greens and the social democrats, heightening the intensity of electoral
competition and therefore limiting the appeal of the radical left.

Factional work inside radical left parties, or external support for leftist parties
such as Corbyn's Labour Party, also raises a far more profound question, first aired
in the early 1950s debates about 'deep entrism'. If some Trotskyist policies and
demands can be successfully promoted through the medium of a radical left party,
then what is the point in building independent revolutionary parties? If some of
the reforms advocated by these parties are in principle achievable, such as higher
spending on public services or higher rates of top income tax, then surely those
outcomes call into question the widespread Trotskyist claim that the capitalist

system is historically exhausted and that no significant reforms are possible. Indeed if such reforms are infeasible, as Orthodox and doctrinaire Trotskyists have proclaimed for decades, then the resilience of social democracy is a genuine puzzle and one to which Trotskyists have advanced few satisfactory answers.

The dynamics of class consciousness is another, related topic on which Trotskyist doctrine has hindered the production of useful insights. The most common argument boils down to the claim that through participation in class struggle, 'fighting for a different kind of future' people 'can develop more radical ideas' (Choonara and Kimber 2011: 42, 56). Yet people can participate in collective action for a variety of reasons and in many different ways; they can hold a variety of views about tactics and strategies; hold different opinions about who is to blame for the injustice at which they are protesting; reach different conclusions about the outcomes of a particular campaign; and draw different inferences about future actions. For example, a victorious campaign may lead to demobilization because the main goal has been achieved; it could lead to empowerment and an enhanced willingness to engage in other, similar actions; or it could lead to a radical re-appraisal of one's previous ideas, about collective action, party politics and a host of related issues. Trotskyist thinking hardly begins to scratch the surface of these many and varied issues because it is heavily constrained by core elements of doctrine: politics as the struggle between labour and capital; the battle between reformism and revolution; and the overriding necessity to build the revolutionary vanguard party. These long-standing concepts are simply too crude and undifferentiated, too lacking in analytical power, to penetrate the complexities of mobilization and collective action.

One final weakness of the Trotskyist movement is a persistent inability to engage in critical self-reflection, a trait more obvious in some families than others. It is predictably most apparent in the Orthodox family where the WRP and the SEP, organizations with a combined membership of less than 200, each persists in its claim to be the only true, living link with Trotsky's Fourth International of 1938. It can also be seen in the self-congratulatory tone of publications by Institutional Trotskyists such as *Socialist Appeal* which claims to 'organize the most class conscious workers and youth around a Marxist programme to change society' (13 May 2017) yet has only 300 members. Peter Taaffe's (2017) 634-page history of Militant Labour and the Socialist Party, 1995–2007, is rich in description of the Party's many and varied achievements but is completely silent on why Party membership in 2007 was less than one-quarter of the Militant Tendency at its 8,000 strong peak. When it comes to elections, parties from across the range of Trotskyist families rarely admit their results were dismal and derisory, preferring instead to deploy euphemisms such as 'disappointing' or 'modest'. On occasion those parties most committed to electoral participation have struck quite a triumphant note, best captured in the Socialist Party headline about a 2010 contest in South Wales that 'We won the argument even if we lost the vote'.

In general, the Trotskyist movement embodies a paradoxical combination of exceptional levels of organizational resilience combined with persistent failure to achieve its major goals because of doctrinairism and sectarianism. Resilience derives from membership commitment and financial contributions but is also based on a track record of concrete achievements, particularly through the creation of social movements such as the Anti-Nazi League and the Anti-Poll Tax Federation. The paradox of those success stories is that they were achieved precisely because Trotskyist groups set aside core elements of Trotskyist doctrine and focused on building broad-based, single-issue campaigns around non-revolutionary goals. Trotskyist organizations will doubtless continue to instigate successful social movements and to promote a radical critique of capitalism and it is possible that a future 'cycle of protest' may help rejuvenate some of them (Tarrow 1994: 153 ff.). Yet they will still retain their pervasive and enduring weaknesses and chronic divisions, rooted in attachment to a rigid and unhelpful doctrine and its millenarian, revolutionary vision.

Appendix 1

BRITISH TROTSKYIST ORGANIZATIONS 1950–2017

Current organizations (N = 22)

Name and formation date	Split from?	Previous names	International affiliation
Workers Revolutionary Party 1947	None	The Club	International Committee of the Fourth International (WRP)
		Socialist Labour League	
Socialist Workers Party 1950	The Club	Socialist Review Group	International Socialist Tendency
		International Socialists	
Socialist Party 1950	The Club	Marxist Tendency	Committee for a Workers International
		International Socialist Group	
		Revolutionary Socialist League	
		Militant Tendency	
Socialist Action 1962	None	International Group	None
		International Marxist Group	
		Socialist League	

(continued)

(*continued*)

Name and formation date	Split from?	Previous names	International affiliation
Socialist Resistance 1962	Socialist League / Workers Socialist League	International Group / International Marxist Group / Socialist League / Socialist Group	Fourth International (1938)
Alliance for Workers Liberty 1966	Militant Tendency / International Socialists	Workers Fight / International-Communist League / Workers Socialist League / Socialist Organiser	Marxist Revival
Spartacist League/ Britain 1975	None	None	International Communist League (Fourth Internationalist)
Workers Power 1975	International Socialists	None	League for the Fifth International
International Bolshevik Tendency 1985	Spartacist League	None	International Bolshevik Tendency
Socialist Equality Party 1985	Workers Revolutionary Party	International Communist Party	International Committee of the Fourth International (SEP)
Workers Fight 1987	None	None	Internationalist Communist Union (Trotskyist)
Communist League 1988	Socialist League	None	Socialist Worker Pathfinder Tendency
International Socialist League 1988	Workers Revolutionary Party (Workers Press)	None	International Workers League-Fourth International
Workers International to Rebuild the Fourth International (WIRFI) 1990	Workers Revolutionary Party (Workers Press)	None	WIRFI
Socialist Appeal 1992	Militant Tendency	None	International Marxist Tendency

Socialist Fight 2009	Workers Revolutionary Party	None	Liaison Committee for the Fourth International
Counterfire 2010	Socialist Workers Party	None	None
Independent Socialist Network 2011	None	None	None
Marxist World 2014	Socialist Party	None	None
revolutionary socialism in the 21st century 2014	Socialist Workers Party	None	None
Fourth International (La Vérité) 2015	None	None	Fourth International (La Vérité)
Revolutionary Communist International Tendency in Britain 2015	None	None	Revolutionary Communist International Tendency

Defunct and ex-Trotskyist organizations (N = 31)

Name and dates	Split from?
Socialist Current 1956–1988	Revolutionary Socialist League
Revolutionary Workers' Party 1963–2011	Revolutionary Socialist League
Revolutionary Communist League 1969*	International Marxist Group
Spartacus League 1970–1971	None
Revolutionary Communist Group 1974*	International Socialists
Socialist Union (Internationalist) 1974–1981	Revolutionary Workers' Party
League for Socialist Action 1974–1982	International Marxist Group
Revolutionary Marxist Current 1975–1979	International Marxist Group
Socialist Labour Group 1975–1990	Workers Revolutionary Party
Intervention Collective 1976–1980	None
Marxist Worker Group 1976–1980	Workers Fight
Workers League 1976–1978	International Socialists
Revolutionary Communist Party 1977–1997	Revolutionary Communist Group
International Socialist Alliance 1978–1979	Socialist Workers Party
Workers Party 1979*	Workers Revolutionary Party
Red Action 1981–c. 2001	Socialist Workers Party
Workers News Group 1981–1982?	Workers Party
Revolutionary Democratic Group 1983–1996	Socialist Workers Party
Workers International League (1983) 1983–1984	Workers Socialist League

(continued)

(*continued*)

Name and dates	Split from?
Workers International Review Group 1984–1985	Workers International League (1983)
Workers Revolutionary Party (Workers Press) 1985–2000	Workers Revolutionary Party
Communist Forum 1986–1988	Workers Revolutionary Party (Workers Press)
Marxist Party 1987–2004	Workers Revolutionary Party (News Line)
Workers International League (1987) 1987–2006	Workers Revolutionary Party (News Line)
Revolutionary Internationalist League 1988–1995	Workers Revolutionary Party (Workers Press)
A World to Win* 1990–	Marxist Party
Trotskyist Group 1997–1998	Workers International League (1987)
Socialist Democracy Group 1998–2002	Socialist Party and International Socialist Group
Permanent Revolution Group 2006–2013	Workers Power
Anti-Capitalist Initiative 2012–2014	Workers Power
International Socialist Network 2013–2015	Socialist Workers Party

* Still in existence but ceased to be a Trotskyist organization.

Appendix 2

SOURCES FOR TROTSKYIST ORGANIZATIONAL MEMBERSHIP FIGURES

Only one of the 22 Trotskyist groups currently active in Britain regularly publishes membership figures (the SWP) so in the absence of public data there are four main sources of evidence on Trotskyist group membership. In descending order of utility, they are as follows: first, there is a substantial volume of internal bulletins and internal membership and financial reports in a variety of archives (see the Bibliography for a full list). In some cases these papers have been deposited in the names of specific organizations, for example the AWL Papers at the London School of Economics but in other cases they have been deposited by individuals who were members of one or more organizations, for example the Richardson/Higgins Papers at Senate House Library, London. Second, some interviewees have supplied figures for their organization, for example George Binette on Workers Power and its breakaway group, Permanent Revolution. Third, there is a variety of both academic and journalistic publications on the Trotskyist left, varying in quality from the highly rigorous studies of Alexander (1991a) and Callaghan (1984) to tendentious polemics such as Baker (1981) and Tomlinson (1981). Fourth, there are publications by members or ex-members of specific groups which contain membership figures for particular years, for example Birchall (2011) on IS and SWP, Pitt (2002) on the SLL and WRP and Taaffe (1995) on the Militant Tendency. Data supplied by members may be subject to bias and upward rounding whilst figures from ex-members and critics can be subject to downward bias, depending on the degree of hostility shown towards the writer's former organization. Detailed sources for the 22 current organizations are as follows:

Current organizations

Alliance for Workers Liberty (formerly Workers Fight, International-Communist League, Workers Socialist League, Socialist Organiser)
1967–1968: *International Communist* 2/3: 5; 1971–1988: Ideas on Organisation July 1988, AWL Papers, File 1/28; 1972: Workers Fight National Committee

Minutes January 1972, AWL Papers, File 1/1; 1972–1977: Membership 1977, AWL Papers, File 1/6 Part 2; 1975: WF National Committee Minutes April 1975, AWL Papers, File 1/3; 1977: I-CL Secretariat Minutes February, March, April, July, August, AWL Papers, File 1/6 Part 2; 1978: Organised Sympathisers January 1978, AWL Papers, File 1/7; 1979: I-CL National Committee Minutes September 1979, AWL Papers, File 1/8; 1980: Membership list, n.d. – early 1980, AWL Papers, File 1/9; 1981–1984: Organisation Report, WSL Internal Bulletin No. 116 June 1984, Richardson/Higgins Papers, Box 110, File 3; 1983: Membership Problems to Sort Out, n.d. – 1983, AWL Papers, File 1/23, Folder 3; 1985: Organisation, n.d. – probably late 1985, AWL Papers, File 1/25; 1986–1997: Organisation Report March 1997, AWL Papers, File 1/34/3; 1987–1989: Socialist Organiser EC Minutes September 1989, AWL Papers, File 1/29; 1997: Finance/Membership Report, n.d. – probably early 1997, AWL Papers, File 1/34/3; 2000: *Weekly Worker* 9 March 2000; 2002: *Weekly Worker* 14 March 2002; 2003: AWL National Committee Minutes April 2003, AWL Papers, File 1/45/3; 2004: *Weekly Worker* 14 October 2004; 2010–2011: Building the AWL, 2011 Conference Report www.workersliberty.org/awl-labour-and-left/awl/awl-conferences/awl-conference-2011, accessed 25 June 2016; 2012: Conference Report 2012 www.workersliberty.org/story/2012/11/21/awl-conference-2012-decisions-and-documents, accessed 25 June 2016; 2015: Martin Thomas interview.

Communist League
2007: *The Militant* 2 July 2007.

Counterfire
2010: *Weekly Worker* 1 April 2010; John Rees interview; 2013: Dave Renton email correspondence 3 April 2014; 2015: John Rees interview.

Fourth International (La Vérité)
1970–1985, 1991–1999 and 2015: Benoit Lahouze interview.

Independent Socialist Network
2011–2015: Estimate based on numbers of website posts.

International Bolshevik Tendency
1985–2015: Estimate based on (in)frequency of meetings and publications and number of magazine sellers on major demonstrations.

International Socialist League
1988–2015: Bob Archer interview; *International Worker* 27 February 1988.

Marxist World
2014–2015: Steve Dobbs and Toby Harris interview.

Revolutionary Communist Tendency in Britain
2015: RCIT, Reply to a Bitter Man, March 2015, www.thecommunists.net/rcit/reply-to-sf/, accessed 25 June 2016.

revolutionary socialism in the 21st century
2014: Socialist Party of Great Britain Post 13 May 2014; *Solidarity* 30 March 2014; 2015: International Socialist Network Final Meeting Minutes April 2015, http://international socialist network.org/, accessed 16 July 2016; Anindya Bhattacharyya interview.

Socialist Action
1986: SA Finance Dossier October 1986, MRC IMG Papers, File MSS 128.

Socialist Appeal
1992: Sewell (2002); 1999: Barberis et al. (2000: 161); 2015: Rob Sewell interview.

Socialist Equality Party (formerly International Communist Party)
1990: *International Worker* 15 December 1990.

Socialist Fight
2015: Reply to a Bitter Man March 2015, www.thecommunists.net/rcit/reply-to-sf/, accessed 25 June 2016.

Socialist Party (formerly Militant Tendency/Revolutionary Socialist League, Militant Labour)
1950: Woods (2013a: 112); 1964: McIlroy (1999a: 262); 1953–1965: Thayer (1965: 137); 1965: Woods (2013a: 163), Crick (2016: 340); 1966: Sewell (2002), Woods (2013a: 176); 1970: (Woods 2013a: 205); 1971–1986: Crick (2016: 340); 1972: How We Have Developed, n.d. – probably 1983, Socialist Party Papers, File 601/C/2/2/7; 1983–1986: MacGregor (1986: 68); 1984–1986: Andrew (2009: 681); 1987: Finance, Members' Bulletin No. 16, March 1996, Socialist Party Papers, File 601/D/1/2/2; 1988: Woods (2013a: 231), Taaffe (1995: 324); 1989: Sewell (2002); 1992: Gall (2012: 51), Sewell (2002), Anonymous (2006); 1993: Grant (1993), *Weekly Worker* 2 November 2000; 1990s: Hearse (2000), Taaffe (2017: 32); 2002: Taaffe (2002); 2011: Socialist Party 2011 Congress – A Party Growing in Strength, www.socialistparty.org.uk/articles/11270, accessed 25 June 2016; 2012: *The Socialist* 16–21 March 2012; 2013: Steve Dobbs and Toby Harris interview; 2015: *Weekly Worker* 12 November 2015.

Socialist Resistance (formerly International Group, International Marxist Group, Socialist League, International Group, International Socialist Group and also Workers Socialist League and Socialist Group)
1962: *Weekly Worker* 28 October 2010; 1965: Tate (2014: 24); 1966–1968: Tate (2014: 201, 257); 1968–1969: Aspects of the History of the International

Marxist Group, IMG/SL Fusion Conference, Pre-Conference Internal Bulletin No. 3, February 1972, MRC IMG Papers, File 92; 1971: Callaghan (1984: 131), Hennessy (2010: 132); 1972: Finances: Out of the Swamp, IMG Internal Bulletin New Series No. 4 September/October 1972, Bob Purdie Papers, File 59; McIlroy (1999a: 262); 1973: Estimated Income and Expenditure for IMG May 1973, Tony Whelan Papers, File 1/1/5; April 1978 Conference, MRC IMG Papers, File 205; 1974: IMG Internal Information Bulletin December 1974, Richardson/ Higgins Papers, Box 148, File 57; 1975–1976: April 1978 Conference, MRC IMG Papers, File 205; 1976 and 1978: Appendices to Finance Report November 1982, LSE IMG Papers, File 229; 1979: IMG Credentials Committee Report 1979, MRC IMG Papers, File 205; 1980: IMG Internal Information Bulletin No. 1 1980, MRC IMG Papers, File 205; 1981: IMG Internal Discussion Bulletin March 1982, LSE IMG Papers, File 1/21; 1982: National Conference 1982, LSE IMG Papers, File 218; 1983: 1983 Dues and Paper Sales Targets, LSE IMG Papers, File 212; 1984: Socialist League Conference Delegates Kit, MRC IMG Papers, File 206; 1985: Socialist League Internal Information Bulletin June 1985, MRC IMG Papers, File 208; 1986: Minutes of First National Conference of the Journal Group May 1986, Dani Ahrens Papers, File 1/9/1; 1988: Greetings from the Journal Group, n.d. – probably 1988, MRC IMG Papers, File 263; Conference Credentials Report 1988, Dani Ahrens Papers, File 401/3/8; Journal Group Central Committee Minutes December 1988, Dani Ahrens Papers, File 1/1/2; 1989: A Balance Sheet February 1989, Dani Ahrens Papers, File 1/1/2; 2003: *Weekly Worker* 1 May 2003; 2012: The Origins of Socialist Resistance, Regroupment Conference April 26 Bulletin No. 2; *Weekly Worker* 11 October 2012; 2014: The Origins of Socialist Resistance, Regroupment Conference April 26 Bulletin No. 2; 2015: Alan Thornett interview.

Socialist Workers Party (formerly Socialist Review Group and International Socialists)

1950: Alexander (1991a: 483); 1956: Shaw (1978: 103); 1958: Birchall (2011: 173); 1960: Cliff (2000: 63); 1962: Birchall (2011: 213); 1962–1966: IS Secretary's Report December 1966, Steve Jefferys Papers, File 244/2/1/1; 1963–1967: IS EC Minutes October 1963, January 1964, May 1964, January 1965, July 1965, April 1966, Colin Barker Papers, File 152/1/1/1; IS Secretary's Report mid-1967, Colin Barker Papers, File 152/1/1/2; 1968: Birchall (2011: 282), IS EC Minutes June 1968, Colin Barker Papers, File 152/1/1/3; IS Secretary's Report January 1968, Will Fancy Papers, Box 16/1; 1969: Hallas, Organisation of the IS Group, Colin Barker Papers, File 152/1/2/2; Subs Reports March–June 1969, July 1969– January 1970, Will Fancy Papers, Box 16/2; 1970: Birchall (1981: 19); 1971: IS Membership Report for 1971 Conference, Colin Barker Papers, File 152/1/2/4, IS Membership Report June 1971, Nigel Clark Papers; 1972–1977: Building the Periphery 1978, Nigel Clark Papers, File 489/8; 1972–1974: IS Internal Bulletin July 1974, Alastair Mutch Papers, File 284/1/1/1/; 1973: IS Membership Reports

March 1973 and August 1973 and IS National Committee Minutes July 1973, Colin Barker Papers, File 152/1/1/8; 1974: Birchall (2011: 372); 1975: The Crisis in IS 1975, Alastair Mutch Papers, File 284/1/1/1/; 1976: Birchall (2011: 413), Recruitment and Composition of Present Membership 1976, Stirling Smith Papers, File 205/1/6; 1977–1978: SWP Internal Bulletin No. 6, 1978, Will Fancy Papers, Box 13/1; 1979: Birchall (2011: 437); 1980: Birchall (2011: 457); 1981: SWP Internal Bulletin No. 5 1981, Nigel Clark Papers, File 489/11; 1982: Notes on Building Branches, SWP Internal Bulletin June 1982, Nigel Clark Papers, File 489/12; 1984: Birchall (2011: 457); 1986: Birchall (2011: 487); 1991: *Socialist Outlook* 23 November 1991; 1993: Taaffe (1995: 493); 1994: Birchall (2011: 517); 1995: SWP Party Notes 4 March 1995; 1998: Birchall (1998); 2003: *Weekly Worker* 6 November 2003; 2004: *Weekly Worker* 2 December 2004; 2007–2013: *Weekly Worker* 6 December 2007, 29 October 2009, 6 January 2011, 10 November 2011, 8 November 2012, 25 November 2013; 2014: SWP Internal Bulletin 2014; 2015: Charlie Kimber interview.

Spartacist League/Britain
1978: *Spartacist Britain* April 1978; 1981: Sullivan (2008: 6). Other years estimated from decline in the number of branches and frequency of publications.

Workers Fight
1987–2015: Anna Hunt interview.

Workers International to Rebuild the Fourth International
1990–2015: Bob Archer interview.

Workers Power
1975: George Binette interview; 1981: Baker (1981: 89); 1988, 1990, 1998: George Binette interview; 2003: *Weekly Worker* 1 May 2003; 2004: *Weekly Worker* 14 October 2004; 2006: The Split in the League for the Fifth International, July 2006, www.permanentrevolution.net/entry/851, accessed 25 June 2016; 2011: *Weekly Worker* 26 April 2011; 2013: George Binette interview; 2015: Workers Power interview.

Workers Revolutionary Party (formerly The Club, Socialist Labour League, WRP News Line)
1947, 1949: Pitt (2002: Chapter 2); 1950: Birchall (2011: 133); 1955: Pitt (2002: Chapter 4), McIlroy (2005); 1956: Callaghan (1987: 59); 1957: Pitt (2002: Chapter 4); 1957–1958: Thayer (1965: 131); 1959–1960: Pitt (2002: Chapter 5); 1960: Thayer (1965: 135); 1964: McIlroy (2005); 1964, 1966: Pitt (2002: Chapter 6); 1971: Hennessy (2010: 130); 1972: Tourish and Wohlforth (2000: 162); 1973: *Weekly Worker* 4 November 2010, Thornett (2011: 128); 1974: McIlroy (1999a: 262), Thornett (1998: 84); 1976: WRP Political Committee Minutes July, August,

September, October, November, WRP Papers, Box 56; 1978–1979: WRP Central Committee Minutes March 1979, WRP Political Committee Minutes April 1979, WRP Papers, Box 154; 1980: WRP Political Committee Minutes February and March 1980, WRP Papers, Box 347; Tomlinson (1981: 79); 1981: WRP Political Committee Minutes February, March 1981, WRP Papers, Box 570; WRP Political Committee Minutes, April 1981, WRP Papers, Box 348; Baker (1981: 12); 1982: Healy, Open Letter to All Members of the WRP January 1982, WRP Papers, Box 55; Note to CC Department and PC December 1982, WRP Papers, Box 716; 1983: WRP Political Committee Minutes March, April, May 1983, WRP Papers, Box 154; Letter to all CC Members June 1983, WRP Papers, Box 193; Letters to all CC Members, August, September and October 1983, WRP Papers, Box 26; 1984: WRP (1984b: 82), Healy, Letter to all CC Members and Alternates January, February, March 1984, WRP Papers, Box 26; Letters to all CC Members and Alternates September, October and December 1983, WRP Papers, Boxes 272, 270 and 325; WRP Central Committee Minutes April, June, July, August, WRP Papers, Box 236; 1985: Healy (1994: 334), WRP Political Committee Minutes February and April 1985, WRP Papers, Box 244; Monthly Questionnaire to all Districts February 1985, WRP Papers, Box 459; Healy, Letter to all CC Members and Alternates May 1985, WRP Papers, Box 135; 1986: *Weekly Worker* 4 November 2010, WRP (WP) 8th National Congress 1986, WRP Papers, Box 97; 1986–1987: Pitt (2002: Chapters 11 and 12).

Defunct and ex-Trotskyist organizations

A World to Win
1990–2004: Corinna Lotz interview.

Anti-Capitalist Initiative 2012–2014
2012: Statement on Resignations from the British Section of the League February 2012, www.fifthinternational.org/content/statement-resignations-british-section-league, accessed 25 June 2016.

Communist Forum 1986–1988
1986: Downing (1991: 35), WRP (Workers Press), A Political Letter to the Members of the WRP from PC August 1986, WRP Papers, Box 319.

International Socialist Alliance 1978–1979
1978: ISA Members/contacts, n.d. – probably early 1978, MRC IMG Papers, File 254; 1979: https://bigflameuk.wordpress.com/category/groups-which-joined-big-flame/, accessed 25 June 2016.

International Socialist Network 2013–2015
2014: D. Renton email 3 April 2014.

Intervention Collective 1976–1980
1979: B.J. Dayvie, 'What's Happening in the Intervention Collective?', *Intercorr*, 2(5) 1979, Chris Taylor Papers, File 406/3/1/3.

League for Socialist Action 1974–1982
1974: Anon, A Campaign of Gossip, n.d. – probably 1978, MRC IMG Papers, File 256.

Marxist Party 1987–2004
1987: Pitt (2002: Chapter 12); 1987, 1990: Corinna Lotz interview; 2002–2004: Electoral Commission.

Marxist Worker Group 1976–1980
Estimate based on its comprising one branch of Workers Fight in Bolton in the mid-1970s.

Movement for Socialism (formerly WRP Workers Press) 1985–2000
1985: Pitt (2002: Chapter 12), IG National Mailing No. 14 July 1986, Dani Ahrens Papers, File 401/3/4; WRP (WP) National Organiser's Report December 1985, WRP Papers, Box 153; 1987: Registration 1987, WRP Papers, Box 430; Minutes of WRP (WP) Central Committee May 1987, WRP Papers, Box 677; 1988: Financial Report April 1988–February 1989, WRP Papers, Box 271; 1989: WRP (WP) Finance Report 1989–1990, WRP Papers, Box 360.

Permanent Revolution Group 2006–2013
2006–2013: George Binette interview.

Revolutionary Communist Group 1974–1976
1980: Sullivan (2008: 6).

Revolutionary Communist League 1969–1980
1970: Letter, J. Robertson to Central Committee, Spartacist League November 1970, Richardson/Higgins Papers, Box 9, File 2; 1978: KES & BM, The Chartist: Towards an Analytical Review 1978, Chris Taylor Papers, File 406/6/1/4; 1980: GMB, Organising the Collective 1980, Chris Taylor Papers, File 406/6/1/3.

Revolutionary Communist Party (formerly Revolutionary Communist Tendency) 1977–1997
1980: Sullivan (2008: 7); 1990: D. Milligan, 'Radical Amnesia and the Revolutionary Communist Party', February 2008, www.donmilligan.net/index.php/articles/P12, accessed on 25 June 2016; 1991–1995: Frank Furedi email 9 April 2014.

Revolutionary Democratic Group 1983–1996
Estimate based on its comprising ex-members of the SWP from two locations.

Revolutionary Internationalist League 1988–1995
1988–1994: Gerry Downing email 28 April 2014.

Revolutionary Marxist Current 1975–1979
1977: Revolutionary Marxist Current https://bigflameuk.wordpress.com/2009/11/19/revolutionary-marxist-current/, accessed 25 June 2016.

Revolutionary Workers' Party 1963–2011
1963: Anon, Obituary Theodore Melville (1932–2010), *Revolutionary History*, 11(1): 193–95, 2013; 1965: Thayer (1965: 139); 1974: Organisation Conclusions of the 4th Conference of the British Section January 1974, Posadist Tendency Papers, Box 8, File 1; Douglass (2009: 259 ff.); 1980: Sullivan (2008: 7).

Socialist Current 1956–1988
1955–1964: Thayer (1965: 144).

Socialist Labour Group 1975–1990
1989: International Socialist Group Pre-Conference Discussion Bulletin No. 13 1990, Dani Ahrens Papers, File 401/3/9.

Socialist Union Internationalist 1974–1981
Douglass (2009: Chapter 16) and (2010: 17).

Spartacus League 1970–1971
C. Singh, Fusion. Notes for a Critique, 23 October 1971, for National Committee, Tony Whelan Papers, File 1/1/1.

Workers International League (1983) 1983–1984
1983–1984: Gard (1993); Anon, A Balance Sheet of the SLL, WSL & WIL, n.d. – probably 1985, Richardson/Higgins Papers, Box 28, File 1.

Workers International League (1987) 1987–2006
1987–2006: Richard Price email 7 March 2016.

Workers International Review Group 1984–1985
1984: Gard (1993); Anon, A Balance Sheet of the SLL, WSL & WIL, n.d. – probably 1985, Richardson/Higgins Papers, Box 28, File 1.

Workers League 1976–1978
1976: Baker (1981: 59); Higgins (1997: Chapter 13); 1978: Anon, A Report on the Workers League Aggregate 15–16 October 1978; Notes on the Workers League, n.d. – 1978 both in MRC IMG Papers, File 254.

Workers News Group 1981–1982
Estimate based on its comprising one branch in Rotherham.

Workers Party 1979–1980
1979: Leaflet, Where Is the WRP Going? n.d. – March 1979, MRC Alan Clinton Papers, File 539/2/2/22.

Workers Socialist League/Socialist Group 1974–1981; 1984–1987
1974: Barberis et al. (2000: 171); Thornett (1998: 87; 2011: 128–29); 1976: EC Resolution on Development of the WSL, 18 November 1976, MRC Alan Clinton Papers, File 539/2/1/2; 1979: WSL: Problems and Tasks for 1979, Pre-Conference Discussion Bulletin, n.d. – probably December 1978/January 1979, MRC Alan Clinton Papers, File 539/2/2/40; 1980: WSL Letter to all National Committee Members 5 June 1980, MRC Alan Clinton Papers, File 539/2/2/46; Letter to all WSL Branches 23 December 1980, Senate House Alan Clinton Papers, Box 7, File 12; 1986: Assessment of the First Conference of the Journal Group, Internal Discussion Bulletin No. 5 July 1986, Dani Ahrens Papers, File 3/2.

In general I have assigned first preference to internal organizational sources followed by informed external sources, for example serious academics and ex-members. Where there are multiple figures for a single year, I have taken the most reliable source and where there are multiple internal figures I have calculated and used the mean figure. Most Trotskyist organizations have not reported member-ship figures at a consistent time, for example the end of the financial year or annual conference and it has therefore proved impossible to construct a consistent time series for any organization. Averaging multiple figures over the course of a year therefore minimizes error due to fluctuations in the reliability of reporting. Where organizations report separate figures for total membership and paid up member-ship, I have taken the former in order to improve consistency over time and across organizations (total membership is the figure most frequently employed).

The absence of public data and of consistent time series means there are inevita-bly significant gaps in the membership data. I have therefore chosen to fill them by interpolation and decided the most straightforward approach is to assume a smooth and linear progression between the two figures either side of a gap. For example if we know that an organization had 200 members in 1980 but just 160 in 1984 then unless there is qualitative data, from internal or external sources, indicating a brief membership spike between 1980 and 1984, I have assumed a steady loss of membership over that period. A net loss of 40 over four years translates into an annual loss of ten so the interpolated 1981 figure would be 190, the 1982 figure 180 and so on. We know that membership trends are sometimes very uneven so this method of interpolation will probably smooth membership patterns over time; that is unfortunate but unavoidable. The full spreadsheet of membership figures is available on request from the author j.kelly@bbk.ac.uk.

Appendix 3

TROTSKYIST ORGANIZATIONS IN WESTERN EUROPE MAY 2017 (NAME AND INTERNATIONAL AFFILIATION)

AUSTRIA 8

Gruppe Klassenkampf (Class Struggle Group)	Permanent Revolution Collective
Liga der Sozialistischen Revolution (League for the Socialist Revolution)	League for the Fifth International
Linkswende (Left Turn)	International Socialist Tendency
Revolutionär-Kommunistischen Organisation zur Befreiung (Revolutionary Communist Organization for Liberation)	Revolutionary Communist International Tendency
Revolutionär Sozialistiche Organisation (Revolutionary Socialist Organization)	Revolutionary Socialist Organization
Sozialistische Alternative (Socialist Alternative)	The Fourth International (1938)
Sozialistiche Links Partei (Socialist Left Party)	Committee for a Workers International
Der Funke (The Spark)	International Marxist Tendency

BELGIUM 5

Ligue Communiste des Travailleurs (Communist Workers League)	International Workers League (Fourth International)
Ligue Communiste Révolutionnaire/ Socialistische Arbeiderspartij (Revolutionary Communist League/Socialist Workers Party)	The Fourth International (1938)
Linkse Socialistiche Partij/Parti Socialiste de Lutte (Socialist Left Party/Party of Socialist Struggle)	Committee for a Workers International
Vonk/L'Unité Socialiste (The Spark/Socialist Unity)	International Marxist Tendency
Lutte Ouvrière/Abeidersstrijd (Workers Struggle)	Internationalist Communist Union (Trotskyist)

CYPRUS 2

Neda (New Internationalist Left)	Committee for a Workers International
Ergatiki Dimokratia (Workers Democracy)	International Socialist Tendency

DENMARK 3

Internationale Socialister (International Socialists)	International Socialist Tendency
Socialistisk Standpunkt (Socialist Standpoint)	International Marxist Tendency
Socialistisk Arbejderparti (Socialist Workers Party)	The Fourth International (1938)

FINLAND 1

Marxilainen Työväenliitto (Marxist Workers League)	Coordinating Committee for the Refoundation of the Fourth International

FRANCE 13

Groupe Bolchevik (Bolshevik Group)	Permanent Revolution Collective
Comité pour la Construction du Parti Ouvrier Révolutionnaire (Committee for the Construction of the Revolutionary Workers Party)	None
Ligue Communiste (Communist League)	SWP Pathfinder Tendency
Parti Ouvrier Indépendant (Independent Workers Party)	The Fourth International (1993)
Groupe Socialiste Internationaliste (International Socialist Group)	International Workers League (Fourth International)
Nouveau Parti Anticapitaliste (New Anti-Capitalist Party)	The Fourth International (1938)
Révolution (Revolution) formerly La Riposte	International Marxist Tendency
Convergences Révolutionnaires (Revolutionary Convergence)	Revolutionary Socialist Organization
Gauche Révolutionnaire (Revolutionary Left)	Committee for a Workers International
Parti de l'Egalite Socialiste (Socialist Equality Party)	International Committee of the Fourth International (SEP)
Ensemble – Mouvement pour une Alternative de Gauche, Ecologiste et Solidaire (Together – Movement for a Left, Green and Solidary Alternative)	The Fourth International (1938)
Ligue Trotskyste de France (Trotskyist League of France)	International Communist League (Fourth Internationalist)
Lutte Ouvrière (Workers Struggle)	Internationalist Communist Union (Trotskyist)

(continued)

(continued)

GERMANY 15

Gruppe Internationaler Sozialistinnen (Group of International Socialists)	None
Internationale Bolschewistiche Tendenz (International Bolshevik Tendency)	International Bolshevik Tendency
Internationale Sozialistische Organization (International Socialist Organization)	The Fourth International (1938)
Internationale Sozialisten (International Socialists)	None
League for the Fourth International Germany	League for the Fourth International
Marx 21 (now part of Die Linke)	International Socialist Tendency
Partei für Soziale Gleichheit (Party for Social Equality)	International Committee of the Fourth International (SEP)
Revolutionär-Kommunistischen Internationalen Tendenz Deutschland (Revolutionary Communist International Tendency Germany)	Revolutionary Communist International Tendency
Revolutionären Internationalistischen Organisation (Revolutionary Internationalist Organization)	Trotskyist Fraction – Fourth International
Revolutionär Sozialistische Organisation (Revolutionary Socialist Organization)	Revolutionary Socialist Organization
Bund Revolutionärer Arbeiter (Revolutionary Workers Federation)	Internationalist Communist Union (Trotskyist)
Sozialistische Alternative (Socialist Alternative) (now part of Die Linke)	Committee for a Workers International
Der Funke (The Spark)	International Marxist Tendency
Spartakist-Arbeiterpartei Deutschlands (Spartacist League of Germany)	International Communist League (Fourth Internationalist)
Gruppe Arbeitermacht (Workers Power)	League for the Fifth International

GREECE 8

Diethnistiki Ergatiki Anistera (Internationalist Workers Left)	The Fourth International (1938)
Marxistiki Foni (Marxist Voice)	International Marxist Tendency
Organose Kommouniston Diethniston Ellados-Spartakos (Organization of Internationalist Communists of Greece – Spartacus)	The Fourth International (1938)
Epanastatiko Marxistiko Protathlima (Revolutionary Marxist League)	International Committee of the Fourth International (WRP)
Xekinima (Socialist Internationalist Organization)	Committee for a Workers International
Sosialistiko Ergatiko Komma (Socialist Workers Party)	International Socialist Tendency

Trotskyist Group of Greece	International Communist League (Fourth Internationalist)
Ergatiko Epanastatiko Komma (Workers Revolutionary Party)	Coordinating Committee for the Refoundation of the Fourth International

IRELAND 3

Socialist Democracy	The Fourth International (1938)
Socialist Party	Committee for a Workers International
Socialist Workers Party	International Socialist Tendency

ITALY 9

Sinistra Anticapitalista (Anti-Capitalist Left)	The Fourth International (1938)
Partito di Alternativa Comunista (Communist Alternative Party)	International Workers League (Fourth International)
Controcorrente (Countercurrent)	Committee for a Workers International
Solidarietà Internazionalista (International Solidarity)	The Fourth International (1938)
Nucleo Internazionalista d'Italia (Internationalist Nucleus of Italy)	League for the Fourth International
Sinistra Classe Rivoluzione (formerly Falce Martello, Sickle Hammer)	International Marxist Tendency
Lega Trotskista d'Italia (Trotskyist League of Italy)	International Communist League (Fourth Internationalist)
Partito Comunista del Lavoratori (Workers Communist Party)	Coordinating Committee for the Refoundation of the Fourth International
L'Internazionale (The International)	Internationalist Communist Union (Trotskyist)

LUXEMBOURG 1

Revolutionary Socialist Party (part of The Left)	None

NETHERLANDS 4

Internationale Socialisten (International Socialists)	International Socialist Tendency
Socialistisch Alternatief (Socialist Alternative)	Committee for a Workers International
Socialistische Alternatieve Politiek (Socialist Alternative Politics)	The Fourth International (1938)
Vonk (The Spark)	International Marxist Tendency

NORWAY 1

Forbundet Internasjonalen i Norge (Internationalist League of Norway)	None

(continued)

(continued)

PORTUGAL 3

Associação Política Socialista Revolucionária (Revolutionary Socialist Political Association)	The Fourth International (1938)
Movimento Alternativa Socialista (Socialist Alternative Movement)	International Workers League (Fourth International)
Partido Operário de Unidade Socialista (Workers Party of Socialist Unity)	The Fourth International (1993)

SPAIN 11

Izquierda Anticapitalista (Anticapitalist Left)	The Fourth International (1938)
Clase Contra Clase (Class Against Class)	Trotskyist Fraction – Fourth International
Lucha de Clases (Class Struggle)	International Marxist Tendency
Corriente Roja (Red Current)	International Workers League (Fourth International)
En Defensa del Marxismo (In Defence of Marxism)	None
Partido Obrero Socialista Internacionalista (International Socialist Workers Party)	The Fourth International (1993)
Lucha Internacionalista (Internationalist Struggle)	International Workers Unity (Fourth International)
Izquierda Revolucionaria (Revolutionary Left)	None
Socialismo Revolucionario (Revolutionary Socialism)	Committee for a Workers International
Partido Obrero Revolucionario (Revolutionary Workers' Party)	The Fourth International (1938)
Información Obrera (Workers Information)	None

SWEDEN 4

Revolution (Revolution)	International Marxist Tendency
Rattviseparteit Socialisterna (Socialist Justice Party)	Committee for a Workers International
Socialistika Parteit (Socialist Party)	The Fourth International (1938)
Arbetarmakt (Workers Power)	League for the Fifth International

SWITZERLAND 1

Gauche Anticapitaliste (Anticapitalist Left)	The Fourth International (1938)

Sources: http://marxists.org/history/etol/intl.htm; www.broadleft.org/ and individual organization websites, accessed between 15 July and 15 August 2016.

An organization is defined as a body that has all of the following attributes: a name; a website; web updates within the past six months; publications, either online, hard copy or both, regular or irregular; its own organization, that is, it is not simply a faction of a larger organization.

Appendix 4

DEFUNCT TROTSKYIST INTERNATIONALS 1965–2017 (N = 18)

Fourth International (Posadist) 1962–2015

International Revolutionary Marxist Tendency 1965–1994

Revolutionary Workers Ferment 1970s–1990?

Necessary International Initiative 1976–1981

Trotskyist International Liaison Committee 1979–1984

International Trotskyist Committee 1984–2004

International Committee of the Fourth International (Marxist Party) 1987–2004

Liaison Committee for the Reconstruction of the Fourth International 1988–1997?

Leninist-Trotskyist Tendency 1991–1997

Communist Organization for the Fourth International 1992–2013

Fifth International of Communists 1994–2005?

International Centre of Orthodox Trotskyism 1994–2008

Liaison Committee of Militants for a Revolutionary Communist International 1995–2004

Bolshevik Current for the Fourth International 1996–1999?

International Socialist League 2005–2010?

Revolutionary Internationalist Organization 2007–2011

International Liaison Committee 2009–2011?

Towards a New International Tendency 2010–2013?

Appendix 5

LIST OF INTERVIEWEES (24)

Anonymous	Workers Power/Red Flag 15 June 2016
Bob Archer	Workers International to Rebuild the Fourth International and ex-WRP 16 February 2016
Dave Beale	Socialist Party 10 May 2016
Anindya Bhattacharyya	revolutionary socialism in the 21st century 23 February 2016
George Binette	ex-Workers Power and Permanent Revolution Group 11 April 2014
Ian Birchall	ex-Socialist Workers Party 23 May 2016
Alex Callinicos	Socialist Workers Party 19 January 2016
Mick Connor	Spartacist League/Britain 7 March 2016
Clare Cowen	ex-WRP and WRP (Workers Press) 7 August 2015
Steve Dobbs	Marxist World 24 February 2016
Gerry Downing	Socialist Fight and ex-WRP 21 January 2016
Graham Durham	Socialist Labour 21 January 2016
Jane Hardy	Socialist Workers Party 14 April 2016
Toby Harris	Marxist World 24 February 2016
Clive Heemskerk	Socialist Party 10 February 2014 and 1 March 2016
Anna Hunt	Workers Fight 9 February 2016
Charlie Kimber	Socialist Workers Party 7 February 2014 and 11 February 2016
Benoit Lahouze	Fourth International (La Vérité) 14 December 2015
Corinna Lotz	A World to Win and ex-WRP 22 January 2016
Len Michelson	Spartacist League/Britain 7 March 2016
John Rees	Counterfire and ex-SWP 18 January 2016
Rob Sewell	Socialist Appeal 3 May 2016
Martin Thomas	Alliance for Workers Liberty 10 February 2016
Alan Thornett	Socialist Resistance 9 February 2016

Members and ex-members of the following organizations either did not respond to emails and letters, or promised to respond but failed to do so: the Communist League, International Bolshevik Tendency, International Socialist League, Revolutionary Workers' Party, Socialist Equality Party and the Workers Revolutionary Party.

BIBLIOGRAPHY

Private papers

Glasgow Caledonian University

Workers Revolutionary Party

London School of Economics and Political Science

Alliance for Workers Liberty

International-Communist League

International Marxist Group

Modern Records Centre, University of Warwick

Dani Ahrens

Chris Arthur

Chris Bambery

Colin Barker

Nick Clark

Tony Cliff

Alan Clinton

Richard Hyman

International Marxist Group/Socialist League

Steve Jefferys

Richard Kuper

Tim Lewis

Alistair Mutch

Bob Purdie

Stirling Smith

Socialist Party/Militant/Revolutionary Socialist League

Spartacist League

David Spencer

Ken Tarbuck

Chris Taylor

Alan Thornett

Tony Whelan

Senate House Library, University of London

Alan Clinton

Will Fancy

Jim Higgins and Al Richardson

Posadist Tendency

Theoretical journals and magazines: current (publisher)

1917 (International Bolshevik Tendency)

Class Struggle (Internationalist Communist Union)

Fifth International (League for the Fifth International)

In Defence of Marxism (International Marxist Tendency)

In Defence of Trotskyism (Socialist Fight)

International Socialism (Socialist Workers Party)

Labour News (Fourth International (1993))

Marxist Review (Workers Revolutionary Party)

Marxist Revival (Alliance for Workers Liberty and Revolutionary Marxists' Tendency, Iran)

Marxist World (Marxist World)

New International (Socialist Workers Party USA)

Revolutionary History

rs21 (revolutionary socialism in the 21st century)

Socialism Today (Socialist Party)

Socialist Fight (Socialist Fight)

Socialist Resistance (Socialist Resistance)

Socialist Review (Socialist Workers Party)

Socialist Voice (International Socialist League)

Spartacist (International Communist League (Fourth Internationalist)

The Truth/La Vérité (Fourth International (1993))

Workers Fight (Workers Fight)

Theoretical journals and magazines: defunct (publisher)

Confrontation (Revolutionary Communist Party 1977)

Fourth International (Socialist Labour League/Workers Revolutionary Party)

International Communist (International-Communist League)

Living Marxism (Revolutionary Communist Party 1977)

Militant International Review (Militant Tendency)

Revolutionary Communist (Revolutionary Communist Group)

Revolutionary Communist Papers (Revolutionary Communist Tendency/Party)

Socialist Action (Socialist Action 1988)

Trotskyist History (Revolutionary Internationalist League)

Workers' Liberty (Alliance for Workers Liberty)

Newspapers: current (publisher)

Counterfire (Counterfire)

Socialist Appeal (Socialist Appeal)

Socialist Worker (Socialist Workers Party)

Solidarity (Alliance for Workers Liberty)

The Militant (Socialist Workers Party USA/Communist League)

The News Line (Workers Revolutionary Party)

The Red Flag (Workers Power)

The Socialist (Socialist Party)

Weekly Worker (Communist Party of Great Britain)

Workers Hammer (Spartacist League/Britain)

Young Socialist (Workers Revolutionary Party)

Newspapers: defunct (publisher)

International Worker (International Communist Party)

Militant (Militant Tendency UK)

Red Flag (Revolutionary Workers' Party)

Red Weekly (International Marxist Group)

Socialist Action (Socialist League 1983–1988)

Socialist Challenge (International Marxist Group)

Socialist Organiser (Socialist Organiser)

Socialist Press (Workers Socialist League)

the next step (Revolutionary Communist Party 1977)

Workers Power (Workers Power)

Workers Press (Workers Revolutionary Party)

References

LCW: Lenin Collected Works in 40 volumes, Moscow: Progress Publishers, 4th edn, 1960–1970.
MECW: Marx and Engels Collected Works in 50 volumes, London: Lawrence and Wishart, 1975–2005.
Trotsky: For each work I have given two dates, that of first publication and that of the edition used in the text. The sequence consists of individual works, in order of first publication date, followed by collections.
(P): Pamphlet

Alexander, R.J. (1991a) *International Trotskyism 1929–1985: A Documented Analysis of the Movement*, Durham, NC: Duke University Press.
—— (1991b) 'Origins and Nature of International Trotskyism', in R.J. Alexander (ed.) *International Trotskyism 1929–1985: A Documented Analysis of the Movement*, Durham, NC: Duke University Press, pp. 1–32.

—— (2001) *Maoism in the Developed World*, Westport, CN: Praeger.

Ali, T. (1978) 'Revolutionary Politics: Ten Years After 1968', in R. Miliband and J. Saville (eds) *Socialist Register 1978*, London: Merlin Press, pp. 146–57.

—— (1987) *Street Fighting Years: An Autobiography of the Sixties*, London: Collins.

Allen, V.L. (1981) *The Militancy of British Miners*, Shipley: The Moor Press.

An Anonymous Author (1996) 'The Disunity of Theory and Practice: The Trotskyist Movement in Great Britain Since 1945', *Revolutionary History*, 6(2/3): 191–230.

Anderson, P. (1967) 'The Limits and Possibilities of Trade Union Action', in R. Blackburn and A. Cockburn (eds) *The Incompatibles: Trade Union Militancy and the Consensus*, Harmondsworth: Penguin, pp. 263–80.

—— (1983a) *In The Tracks of Historical Materialism*, London: Verso.

—— (1983b) 'Trotsky's Interpretation of Stalinism', *New Left Review*, 139: 49–58.

—— (1984) *Considerations on Western Marxism*, rev edn, London: Verso.

Andrew, C. (2009) *The Defence of the Realm: The Authorized History of MI5*, London: Allen Lane.

Andrews, G. (2004) *Endgames and New Times: The Final Years of British Communism 1964–1991*, London: Lawrence and Wishart.

——, Fishman, N. and Morgan, K. (eds) (1995) *Opening the Books: Essays on the Social and Cultural History of the British Communist Party*, London: Pluto Press.

Anonymous (1985) 'Healyism Implodes', *Spartacist*, 36–37, Winter.

Anonymous (2006) 'A Brief History of the IMT', www.marxist.com/history-marxist-tendency.htm, accessed 26 June 2016.

Athow, R. (2010) 'The International Committee of the Fourth International and the Struggle against Revisionism, Parts 2–4', *Marxist Review*, 25(2,3,5), February, March, May.

Bagguley, P. (2005) 'Protest, Poverty and Power: A Case Study of the Anti-Poll Tax Movement', *Sociological Review*, 43(4): 693–719.

Baker, B. (1981) *The Far Left: An Exposé of the Extreme Left in Britain*, London: Weidenfeld and Nicholson.

Banda, M. (1971) *The Theory and Practice of Revisionism: A Political Examination of IMG and 'Red Mole'*, London: Socialist Labour League (P).

—— (1972) *Marxism or Rank-and-File-ism? An Analysis of the Tactics and Strategy of the International Socialism Group*, London: Socialist Labour League (P).

—— (1975) *Whither Thornett? A Reply by Michael Banda to a Document Issued by A. Thornett*, London: Workers Revolutionary Party.

Barberis, P., McHugh, J. and Tyldesley, M. (2000) *Encyclopedia of British and Irish Political Organizations: Parties, Groups and Movements of the Twentieth Century*, London: Pinter.

Barnes, J. (1983) 'Their Trotsky and Ours: Communist Continuity Today', *New International*, 1: 9–89.

Barrett, D. (1996) *Sects, 'Cults' and Alternative Religions: A World Survey and Sourcebook*, London: Blandford.

Barrett, M. (1980) *Women's Oppression Today: Problems in Marxist Feminist Analysis*, London: Verso.

Beilharz, P. (1985) 'Trotsky as Historian', *History Workshop Journal*, 20(1): 36–55.

—— (1987) *Trotsky, Trotskyism and the Transition to Socialism*, London: Croom Helm.

Bensaid, D. (2009) *Strategies of Resistance and Who Are the Trotskyists?*, London: Resistance Books.

—— (2013) *An Impatient Life: A Memoir*, London: Verso.

——, Sousa, A. and Thornett, A. (eds) (2011) *New Parties of the Left: Experiences from Europe*, London: Resistance Books.

Berman, E. (2009) *Radical, Religious, and Violent: The New Economics of Terrorism*, Cambridge, MA: MIT Press.

Big Flame (1973) *Five Months of Struggle at Halewood*, Liverpool: Big Flame (P).

Birchall, I. (1981) *The Smallest Mass Party in the World: Building the Socialist Workers Party, 1951–1979*, London: Socialist Workers Party (P).

—— (1998) 'The Case for the SWP', *What Next? Marxist Discussion Journal*, 8.

—— (2011) *Tony Cliff: A Marxist for His Time*, London: Bookmarks.

—— (2014) 'Lenin Yes! Leninism No?', *rs21*, 1: 20–24.

Bird, F. (1993) 'Charisma and Leadership in New Religious Movements', *Religion and the Social Order*, 3A: 75–92.

Black, R. (1970) *Stalinism in Britain: A Trotskyist Analysis*, London: New Park.

Borisyuk, G., Thrasher, C., Rallings, M. and van den Kolk, H. (2007) 'Voter Support for Minor Parties: Assessing the Social and Political Context of Voting at the 2004 European Elections in Greater London', *Party Politics*, 13(6): 669–93.

Bornstein, S. and Richardson, A. (1986a) *Against the Stream: A History of the Trotskyist Movement in Britain 1924–38*, London: Socialist Platform.

Bornstein, S. and Richardson, A. (1986b) *War and the International: A History of the Trotskyist Movement in Britain 1937–1949*, London: Socialist Platform.

Bouma, A. (2016) 'Ideological Confirmation and Party Consolidation: Germany's Die Linke and the Financial and Refugee Crises', in L. March and D. Keith (eds) *Europe's Radical Left: From Marginality to the Mainstream?*, London: Rowman and Littlefield, pp. 133–54.

Branson, N. (1985) *History of the Communist Party of Great Britain 1927–1941*, London: Lawrence and Wishart.

—— (1997) *History of the Communist Party of Great Britain 1941–1951*, London: Lawrence and Wishart.

Brenner, R. (1996) *Trotsky: An Introduction*, London: Prinkipo Press.

Brinton, M. (1970) *The Bolsheviks and Workers' Control 1917–1921: The State and Counter-Revolution*, London: Solidarity.

Brotherstone, T. (1992) 'Trotsky's Future: An Essay in Conclusion', in T. Brotherstone and P. Dukes (eds) *The Trotsky Reappraisal*, Edinburgh: Edinburgh University Press, pp. 235–41.

Brown, A. (2009) *The Rise and Fall of Communism*, London: Bodley Head.

Bruley, S. (2014) 'Jam Tomorrow: Socialist Women and Women's Liberation, 1968–82. An Oral History Approach', in E. Smith and M. Worley (eds) *Against the Grain: The British Far Left from 1956*, Manchester: Manchester University Press, pp. 155–72.

Bryman, A. (1992) *Charisma and Leadership in Organizations*, London: Sage.

Budge, I., Klingemann, H-D., Volkens, A., Bara, J. and Tanenbaum, E. (2001) *Mapping Policy Preferences: Estimates for Parties, Electors, and Governments 1945–1998*, Oxford: Oxford University Press.

Burns, D. (1992) *Poll Tax Rebellion*, Stirling: AK Press.

Burton-Cartledge, P. (2014) 'Marching Separately, Seldom Together: The Political History of Two Principal Trends in British Trotskyism, 1945–2009', in E. Smith and M. Worley (eds) *Against the Grain: The British Far Left from 1956*, Manchester: Manchester University Press, pp. 80–97.

Byrne, P. (1988) *The Campaign for Nuclear Disarmament*, London: Croom Helm.

—— (1997) *Social Movements in Britain*, Abingdon: Routledge.

Callaghan, J. (1984) *British Trotskyism: Theory and Practice*, Oxford: Blackwell.

—— (1987) *The Far Left in British Politics*, Oxford: Blackwell.

—— (2003) *Cold War, Crisis and Conflict: The History of the Communist Party of Great Britain 1951–68*, London: Lawrence and Wishart.

Callinicos, A. (1982) 'The Rank-and-File Movement Today', *International Socialism*, 17: 1–38.

—— (1983a) *The Revolutionary Ideas of Karl Marx*, London: Bookmarks.

—— (1983b) *The Revolutionary Road to Socialism: What the Socialist Workers Party Stands For*, London: Socialist Workers Party.

—— (1989) *Making History: Agency, Structure and Change in Social Theory*, Cambridge: Polity Press.

—— (1990a) *Trotskyism*, Milton Keynes: Open University Press.

—— (1990b) *Against Postmodernism: A Marxist Critique*, Cambridge: Polity Press.

—— (1995) *Socialists in the Trade Unions*, London: Bookmarks.

—— (1999) *Social Theory: A Historical Introduction*, Cambridge: Polity Press.

—— (2003) *An Anti-Capitalist Manifesto*, Cambridge: Polity Press.

—— and Simons, M. (1985) *The Great Strike: The Miners' Strike of 1984–5 and Its Lessons*, London: Socialist Worker.

Campbell, J. (2008) *Margaret Thatcher, Volume 2: The Iron Lady*, London: Vintage.

Campbell, S. (2011) *A Rebel's Guide to Rosa Luxemburg*, London: Bookmarks.

Ceron, A. (2015) 'The Politics of Fission: An Analysis of Faction Breakaways among Italian Parties (1946–2011)', *British Journal of Political Science*, 45(1): 121–39.

Choonara, E. (2007) *A Rebel's Guide to Trotsky*, London: Bookmarks.

Choonara, J. and Kimber, C. (2011) *Arguments for Revolution: The Case for the Socialist Workers Party*, London: Socialist Workers Party.

Cliff, T. (1963) 'Permanent Revolution', *International Socialism*, 12: 15–22.

—— (1970) *The Employers' Offensive: Productivity Deals and How to Fight Them*, London: Pluto Press.

—— (1974) *State Capitalism in Russia*, London: Pluto Press (original edition 1948).

—— (1975) *The Crisis: Social Contract or Socialism*, London: Pluto Press.

—— (1983) *Rosa Luxemburg*, 2nd edn, London: Bookmarks (original edition 1959).

—— (1987) 'Introduction', in A.Y. Badayev, *Bolsheviks in the Tsarist Duma*, London: Bookmarks, pp. 7–15.

—— (1990) *Trotsky, Volume 2: The Sword of the Revolution 1917–1923*, London: Bookmarks.

—— (1993) *Trotsky, Volume 4: The Darker the Night, the Brighter the Star*, London: Bookmarks.

—— (1999) *Trotskyism after Trotsky: The Origins of the International Socialists*, London: Bookmarks.

—— (2000) *A World to Win: Life of a Revolutionary*, London: Bookmarks.

—— (2002) 'Factory Branches', in T. Cliff, *In the Thick of Workers' Struggles: Selected Writings, Volume 2*, London: Bookmarks, pp. 339–67.

—— and Barker, C. (1966) *Incomes Policy, Legislation and Shop Stewards*, London: London Industrial Shop Stewards Defence Committee.

—— and Gluckstein, D. (1988) *The Labour Party: A Marxist History*, London: Bookmarks.

Cohen, S.F. (1975) *Bukharin and the Bolshevik Revolution: A Political Biography, 1888–1938*, New York: Vintage Books.

—— (1985) *Rethinking the Soviet Experience: Politics and History since 1917*, New York: Oxford University Press.

Common Cause (1985) *The Far Left Guide: Directory of Organisations and Supporters*, London: Common Cause (P).

Communist League (1991) *The Split in the Marxist Party and the Struggle for Marxism*, London: Communist League.

Conger, J.A. (1990) 'The Dark Side of Leadership', *Organizational Dynamics*, 19(2): 44–55.

Cooper, L. and Hardy, S. (2012) *Beyond Capitalism? The Future of Radical Politics*, Winchester: Zero Books.

Cox, M. (1992) 'Trotsky and His Interpreters; Or, Will the Real Leon Trotsky Please Stand Up?', *The Russian Review*, 51(1): 84–102.

Craig, F.W.S (1975) *Minor Parties at British Parliamentary Elections 1885–1974*, London: Macmillan.

—— (1984) *British Parliamentary Election Results 1974–1983*, Chichester: Parliamentary Research Services.

—— (1987) *Chronology of British Parliamentary By-Elections 1833–1987*, Chichester: Parliamentary Research Services.

—— (1989) *Britain Votes 4: British Parliamentary Election Results 1983–1987*, Aldershot: Gower.

Crick, M. (2016) *Militant*, London: Biteback.

Croucher, R. (1982) *Engineers at War 1939–1945*, London: Merlin Press.

Darlington, R. (2013) *Radical Unionism: The Rise and Fall of Revolutionary Syndicalism*, Chicago, IL: Haymarket Books.

—— (2014) 'The Rank and File and the Trade Union Bureaucracy', *International Socialism*, 142: 57–82.

—— and Lyddon, D. (2001) *Glorious Summer: Class Struggle in Britain 1972*, London: Bookmarks.

Della Porta, D. (2015) *Social Movements in Times of Austerity*, Cambridge: Polity Press.

Department for Business, Innovation and Skills (2017) *Trade Union Membership 2016: Statistical Bulletin*, London: DBIS.

Deutscher, I. (1954) *The Prophet Armed: Trotsky: 1879–1921*, Oxford: Oxford University Press.

—— (1959) *The Prophet Unarmed: Trotsky: 1921–1929*, Oxford: Oxford University Press.

—— (1963) *The Prophet Outcast: Trotsky: 1929–1940*, Oxford: Oxford University Press.

Doherty, B. (2009) 'Protest', in M. Flinders, A. Gamble, C. Hay and M. Kenny (eds) *The Oxford Handbook of British Politics*, Oxford: Oxford University Press, pp. 719–34.

Douglass, D.J. (2008) *Geordies: Wa Mental*, Hastings: Read 'n' Noir.

—— (2009) *The Wheel's Still in Spin*, Hastings: Read 'n' Noir.

—— (2010) *Ghost Dancers: The Miners' Last Generation*, Hastings: Read 'n' Noir.

Downing, G. (1991) *W.R.P. Explosion: The Sabotage of an Opportunity to Regenerate Trotskyism 1985–1991*, London: Revolutionary Internationalist League (P).

Dunn, J. (1989) *Modern Revolutions: An Introduction to the Analysis of a Political Phenomenon*, 2nd edn, Cambridge: Cambridge University Press.

Dunphy, R. (2004) *Contesting Capitalism? Left Parties and European Integration*, Manchester: Manchester University Press.

—— (2016) 'Struggling for Coherence: Irish Radical Left and Nationalist Responses to the Austerity Crisis', in L. March and D. Keith (eds) *Europe's Radical Left: From Marginality to the Mainstream?*, London: Rowman and Littlefield, pp. 191–209.

Eagleton, T. (2001) *The Gatekeeper: A Memoir*, London: Allen Lane.

Edge, S. (1995) *With Friends Like These: Marxism and Gay Politics*, London: Cassell (P).

Edwards, B. and McCarthy, J.D. (2004) 'Resources and Social Movement Mobilization', in D.A. Snow, S.A. Soule and H. Kriesi (eds) *The Blackwell Companion to Social Movements*, Malden, MA: Blackwell, pp. 116–52.

Electoral Commission, www.electoralcommission.org.uk/party-finance/database-of-registers/statements-of-accounts/soa/lists/SoA_Index_(PDF)_-_22-03-2012.pdf.

Eleftheriou, C. (2016) 'Greek Radical Left Responses to the Crisis: Three Types of Political Mobilisation, One Winner', in L. March and D. Keith (eds) *Europe's Radical Left: From Marginality to the Mainstream?*, London: Rowman and Littlefield, pp. 289–309.

Engels, F. (1884) 'The Origin of the Family, Private Property and the State', MECW Vol. 26.

Escalona, F. and Vieira, M. (2016) 'The French Radical Left and the Crisis: "Business as Usual" Rather than "le Grand Soir", in L. March and D. Keith (eds) *Europe's Radical Left: From Marginality to the Mainstream?*, London: Rowman and Littlefield, pp. 115–32.

Evans, R. and Lewis, P. (2013) *Undercover: The True Story of Britain's Secret Police*, London: Faber and Faber.

Faulkner, N. (2017) *A People's History of the Russian Revolution*, London: Pluto Press.

Feldman, P. and Lotz, C. (2004) *A World to Win: A Rough Guide to a Future without Global Capitalism*, London: Lupus Books.

Festinger, L., Riecken, H.W and Schachter, S. (2008) *When Prophecy Fails*, London: Pinter and Martin (original edition 1956).

Fieldhouse, R. (2005) *Anti-Apartheid: A History of the Movement in Britain. A Study in Pressure Group Politics*, London: Merlin Press.

Figes, O. (1996) *A People's Tragedy: The Russian Revolution 1891–1924*, London: Pimlico.

Fishman, N. (1995) *The British Communist Party and the Trade Unions, 1933–45*, Aldershot: Scolar Press.

Fitzpatrick, S. (2008) *The Russian Revolution*, 3rd edn, Oxford: Oxford University Press.

Foot, P. (1990) *The Case for Socialism: What the Socialist Workers Party Stands For*, London: Socialist Workers Party.

Frank, P. and Bensaid, D. (2010) *The Long March of the Trotskyists: Contributions to the History of the Fourth International*, London: Resistance Books.

Freire, A. and Lisi, M. (2016) 'The Portuguese Radical Left and the Great Recession: Old Challenges and New Responses', in L. March and D. Keith (eds) *Europe's Radical Left: From Marginality to the Mainstream?*, London: Rowman and Littlefield, pp. 253–71.

Gall, G. (2012) *Tommy Sheridan: From Hero to Zero? A Political Biography*, Cardiff: Welsh Academic Press.

—— (2017) *Bob Crow: Socialist, Leader, Fighter*, Manchester: Manchester University Press.

Gallagher, M., Laver, N. and Mair, P. (2011) *Representative Government in Modern Europe*, 5th edn, Maidenhead: McGraw-Hill.

Gard, T. (1993) 'Whatever Happened to the Workers Socialist League?', *Trotskyist History*, 1, September.

Germain, E. (1974) 'Marxism vs. Ultraleftism', in J. Hansen (ed.) *Marxism vs Ultraleftism: The Record of Healy's Break with Trotskyism*, New York: Pathfinder Press, pp. 7–74.

Getzler, I. (1983) *Kronstadt 1919–1921: The Fate of a Soviet Democracy*, Cambridge: Cambridge University Press.

Glyn, A. (1979) *Capitalist Crisis: Tribune's 'Alternative Strategy' or Socialist Plan*, London: Militant (P).

—— (2006) *Capitalism Unleashed: Finance, Globalization, and Welfare*, Oxford: Oxford University Press.

—— and Sutcliffe, B. (1972) *British Capitalism, Workers and the Profits Squeeze*, Harmondsworth: Penguin.

Grant, T. (1959) *Problems of Entrism*, London: RSL, unpublished document, available at www.marxists.org/archive/grant/1959/03/entrism.htm, accessed 24 June 2016.

—— (1989a) 'Against the Theory of State Capitalism', in T. Grant, *The Unbroken Thread: The Development of Trotskyism over 40 Years*, London: Fortress Books (original edition 1949), pp. 197–246.

—— (1989b) 'Will There Be a Slump?', in T. Grant, *The Unbroken Thread: The Development of Trotskyism over 40 Years*, London: Fortress Books (original edition 1960), pp. 393–412.

—— (1989c) 'Britain in Crisis', in T. Grant, *The Unbroken Thread: The Development of Trotskyism over 40 Years*, London: Fortress Books (original edition 1977), pp. 480–524.

—— (1989d) 'Preparing for Power', in T. Grant *The Unbroken Thread: The Development of Trotskyism over 40 Years*, London: Fortress Books (original edition 1942), pp. 35–56.

—— (1993) 'Militant Labour Party; Alternative or Adventure?', *Socialist Appeal*, May.

—— (1997) *Russia: From Revolution to Counter-Revolution*, London: Wellred Publications.

Griffin, R. (2004) 'Introduction: God's Counterfeiters? Investigating the Triad of Fascism, Totalitarianism and (Political) Religion', *Totalitarian Movements and Political Religions*, 5(3): 291–325.

Groves, R. (1974) *The Balham Group: How British Trotskyism Began*, London: Pluto Press.

Hallas, D. (ed.) (1971) *The Origins of the International Socialists*, London: Pluto Press.

—— (1979) *Trotsky's Marxism*, London: Bookmarks.

Hamann, K., Johnston, A. and Kelly, J. (2013) 'Unions against Governments: General Strikes in Western Europe 1980–2006', *Comparative Political Studies*, 46(9): 1030–57.

Hansen, J. (ed.) (1974) *Marxism vs. Ultraleftism: The Record of Healy's Break with Trotskyism*, New York: Pathfinder Press.

Harding, Neil (1983) *Lenin's Political Thought: Theory and Practice in the Democratic and Socialist Revolutions*, London: Macmillan.

Harding, Norman (2005) *Staying Red: Why I Remain a Socialist*, London: Index Books.

Harman, C. (1969) *Russia: How the Revolution Was Lost*, London: Socialist Worker (P).

—— (1974) *Bureaucracy and Revolution in Eastern Europe*, London: Pluto Press.

—— (1997) *The Lost Revolution: Germany 1918 to 1923*, rev edn, London: Bookmarks.

—— (2001) 'Is It Propaganda? Or Do We Want Socialists Elected?', *Socialist Worker*, 24 February.

—— (2007) *Revolution in the 21st Century*, London: Bookmarks.

—— (2008) 'The Crisis in Respect', in F. Leplat (ed.) *Respect: Documents of the Crisis*, 2nd edn, London: Resistance Books, pp. 86–107.

Haslam, S.A., Reicher, S.D. and Platow, M.J. (2011) *The New Psychology of Leadership: Identity, Influence and Power*, Hove: Psychology Press.

Häusermann, S. and Kriesi, H. (2015) 'What Do Voters Want? Dimensions and Configurations in Individual-Level Preferences and Party Choice', in P. Beramendi, S. Häusermann, H. Kitschelt and H. Kriesi (eds) *The Politics of Advanced Capitalism*, New York: Cambridge University Press, pp. 202–30.

Hay, C. (1999) *The Political Economy of New Labour: Labouring under False Pretences*, Manchester: Manchester University Press.

Hayes, M. (2014) 'Red Action – Left-Wing Political Pariah: Some Observations Regarding Ideological Apostasy and the Discourse of Proletarian Resistance', in E. Smith and M. Worley (eds) *Against the Grain: The British Far Left from 1956*, Manchester: Manchester University Press, pp. 229–46.

Healy, G. (1990) *Materialist Dialectics and the Political Revolution*, London: Marxist Publishing Cooperative.

—— (1994) 'Interim Statement October 1985', in C. Lotz and P. Feldman, *Gerry Healy: A Revolutionary Life*, London: Lupus Books, pp. 334–38.

Hearse, P. (1978) *On Trotskyism and the Fourth International*, London: International Marxist Group (P).

—— (2000) 'Militant: What Went Wrong?', *Links: International Journal of Socialist Renewal*, http://links.org.au/node/149, accessed 28 July 2017.

Henn, M., Weinstein, M. and Forrest, S. (2005) 'Uninterested Youth? Young People's Attitudes towards Party Politics in Britain', *Political Studies*, 53(3): 556–78.

Hennessy, P. (2010) *The Secret State: Preparing for the Worst 1945–2010*, London: Penguin.

Hernandez, M. (2012) 'Some Reflections on "Morenism"', http://litci.org/en/some-reflections-on-morenism/, accessed 1 December 2016.

Hessel, B. (ed.) (1980a) *Theses, Resolutions and Manifestos of the First Four Congresses of the Third International*, London: Ink Links.

—— (1980b) 'Introduction', in B. Hessel (ed.) *Theses, Resolutions and Manifestos of the First Four Congresses of the Third International*, London: Ink Links, pp. xiii–xxxiv.

Higgins, J. (1997) *More Years for the Locust: The Origins of the SWP*, www.marxists.org/archive/higgins/1997/locust/index.htm, accessed 16 July 2016.

Hillebrand, R. and Irwin, G.A. (1999) 'Changing Strategies: The Dilemma of the Dutch Labour Party', in W.C. Müller and K. Strøm (eds) *Policy, Office, or Votes? How Political Parties in Western Europe Make Hard Decisions*, New York: Cambridge University Press, pp. 112–40.

Hinton, J. and Hyman, R. (1975) *Trade Unions and Revolution: The Industrial Politics of the Early British Communist Party*, London: Pluto Press.

Hobolt, S.B. and Tilley, J. (2016) 'Fleeing the Centre: The Rise of Challenger Parties in the Aftermath of the Euro Crisis', *West European Politics*, 39(5): 971–91.

Hodder, A., McCarthy, N. Williams, M. and Kelly, J. (2017) 'Does Strike Action Increase Trade Union Membership Growth?', *British Journal of Industrial Relations*, 55(1): 165–86.

Hodgson, G. (1975) *Trotsky and Fatalistic Marxism*, Nottingham: Spokesman Books.

Hollingsworth, M. and Fielding, N. (2000) *Defending the Realm: MI5 and the Shayler Affair*, London: Andre Deutsch.

Hosken, A. (2008) *Ken: The Ups and Downs of Ken Livingstone*, London: Arcadia Books.

Howard, M.C. and King, J.E. (1989) *A History of Marxian Economics, Volume 1: 1883–1929*, Basingstoke: Macmillan.

Howard, M.C. and King, J.E. (1992) *A History of Marxian Economics, Volume 2: 1929–1990*, Basingstoke: Macmillan.

Howe, I. (1978) *Trotsky*, Hassocks: Harvester Press.

Howell, J. (1981) 'Big Flame: Resituating Socialist Strategy and Organisation', in R. Miliband and J. Saville (eds) *The Socialist Register 1981*, London: Merlin Press, pp. 207–20.

Hughes, C. (2012) 'Young Socialist Men in 1960s Britain: Subjectivity and Sociability', *History Workshop Journal*, 73(1): 170–92.

Hunt, S.J. (2003) *Alternative Religions: A Sociological Introduction*, Aldershot: Ashgate.

Hunter, B. (1998) *Lifelong Apprenticeship: The Life and Times of a Revolutionary, Volume 1: 1920–1959*, 2nd edn, London: Porcupine Press.

Hyman, R. (1971) *Marxism and the Sociology of Trade Unionism*, London: Pluto Press (P).

Ibrahim, J. (2013) 'The Struggle for Symbolic Dominance in the British "Anti-Capitalist Movement Field"', *Social Movement Studies*, 12(1): 63–80.

Iannaccone, L.R. (1994) 'Why Strict Churches Are Strong', *American Journal of Sociology*, 99(5): 1180–211.

International Committee of the Fourth International (1973) *In Defence of Trotskyism*, London: Socialist Labour League (P).

—— (1977) *Manifesto of the 7th Congress of the International Committee of the Fourth International May 21–28 1977*, London: International Committee of the Fourth International (P).

—— (1986a) 'How the Workers Revolutionary Party Betrayed Trotskyism 1973–1985', *Fourth International*, 13(1).

—— (1986b) 'The ICFI Defends Trotskyism 1982–1986', *Fourth International*, 13(2).

International-Communist League (1977) *The Fight for Workers' Power: Manifesto of the International-Communist League*, London: International-Communist League (P).

International Communist League (Fourth Internationalist) (1990) *Trotskyism, What It Isn't and What It Is*, New York: ICL (FI) (P).

—— (1994) *Militant Labour's Touching Faith in the Capitalist State*, York: ICL (FI) (P).

—— (1995) *The International Bolshevik Tendency: What Is It?*, York: ICL (FI) (P).

—— (1998) 'Declaration of Principles and Some Elements of Program', *Spartacist*, 54: 9–23.

International Communist Party (1990) *The British Revolution and the Tasks of the International Communist Party*, Rotherham: International Communist Party (P).

International Marxist Tendency (2014) 'Perspectives for the World Revolution', *In Defence of Marxism*, 8: 3–22.

Internationalist Communist Union (1988) *Fifty Years after the Foundation of the Fourth International: What Perspectives for Internationalist Revolutionaries Today?*, Paris: Internationalist Communist Union (P).

Ioannou, G. and Charalambous, G. (2016) 'The Left and the Crisis in Cyprus: "In the Midst of Change They Were Not Changing"', in L. March and D. Keith (eds) *Europe's Radical Left: From Marginality to the Mainstream?*, London: Rowman and Littlefield, pp. 273–88.

Jeffries, P. (1973) *International Socialism Group: Falsifiers of Lenin*, London: Socialist Labour League (P).

Jenkins, P. (1977) *Where Trotskyism Got Lost: The Restoration of European Democracy after the Second World War*, Nottingham: Spokesman (P).

Johns, S. (1974) *Victimization at Cowley*, London: Workers Revolutionary Party (P).

Johnstone, M. (1968) 'Trotsky Part 1: His Ideas', *Cogito: Theoretical and Discussion Journal of the Young Communist League*, 1968.

—— (1977) 'Trotsky and World Revolution', *Cogito: Theoretical and Discussion Journal of the Young Communist League*, 1977.

—— (1991) *Trotsky Reassessed*, London: Socialist History Society, Our History Pamphlet 87 (P).

Kautsky, K. (1920) *Terrorism and Communism: A Contribution to the Natural History of Revolution*, London: National Labour Press (original edition 1919).

—— (1964) *The Dictatorship of the Proletariat*, Ann Arbor, MI: University of Michigan Press (original edition 1918).

Keen, R. and Audickas, L. (2016) *Membership of UK Political Parties*, London: House of Commons Library, Briefing Paper SN05125, 5 August.

Keep, J.L.H. (1976) *The Russian Revolution: A Study in Mass Mobilization*, London: Weidenfeld and Nicholson.

Keith, D. (2016) 'Failing to Capitalise on the Crisis: The Dutch Socialist Party', in L. March and D. Keith (eds) *Europe's Radical Left: From Marginality to the Mainstream?*, London: Rowman and Littlefield, pp. 155–72.

Kelemen, P. (2012) *The British Left and Zionism: History of a Divorce*, Manchester: Manchester University Press.

Kelly, J. (1988) *Trade Unions and Socialist Politics*, London: Verso.

—— (1998) *Rethinking Industrial Relations: Mobilization, Collectivism and Long Waves*, London: Routledge.

—— (2010) *Ethical Socialism and the Trade Unions: Allan Flanders and British Industrial Relations Reform*, New York: Routledge.

—— (2016) 'The Discursive Reconstruction of Poor Electoral Performance: The British Trotskyist Left and the 2010 General Election', *Journal of Political Ideologies*, 21(1): 78–98.

Kidron, M. (1961) 'Reform and Revolution: A Rejoinder to Left Reformism 11', *International Socialism*, 7: 15–21.

—— (1967) 'A Permanent Arms Economy', *International Socialism*, 28: 8–12.

—— (1970) *Western Capitalism since the War*, Harmondsworth: Penguin.

—— (1977) 'Two Insights Don't Make a Theory', *International Socialism*, 100: 4–9.

Kimber, C. (2016) *Jeremy Corbyn, Labour and the Fight for Socialism*, 2nd edn, London: Socialist Worker (P).

Kline, G. (1992) 'The Defence of Terrorism: Trotsky and His Major Critics', in T. Brotherstone and P. Dukes (eds) *The Trotsky Reappraisal*, Edinburgh: Edinburgh University Press, pp. 156–65.

Knei-Paz, B. (1978) *The Social and Political Thought of Leon Trotsky*, Oxford: Clarendon Press.

Kolakowski, L. (1978) *Main Currents of Marxism, Volume 3: The Breakdown*, Oxford: Oxford University Press.

Krasso, N. (1967) 'Trotsky's Marxism', *New Left Review*, 1/44: 64–86.

Laker-Mansfield, C. (2015) 'Is the Green Party a Real Alternative?', *Socialism Today*, 185, February.

Lalich, J. (2004) *Bounded Choice: True Believers and Charismatic Cults*, Berkeley and Los Angeles, CA: University of California Press.

Le Blanc, P. (2015) *Leon Trotsky*, London: Reaktion Books.

—— (2016) 'Introduction: Making Sense of October 1917', in F. Leplat and A. de Jong (eds) *October 1917: Workers in Power*, London: Merlin Press, pp. 1–23.

League for a Revolutionary Communist International (1989) *The Trotskyist Manifesto: A New Transitional Programme for World Socialist Revolution*, London: LRCI.

League for the Fifth International (2010) *From Resistance to Revolution: Manifesto for a Fifth International*, London: LFI.

League for the Fifth International/Workers Power (2010a) 'Anticapitalist-Workers Power Is Standing in British General Election', 26 April, www.fifthinternational.org/content/anticapitalist-workers-power-standing-british-general-election, accessed 9 August 2016.

—— (2010b) 'British General Election 2010: Workers Vote Labour to Stop Tories – Lib Dems Rush into Tory Talks', 9 May, www.fifthinternational.org/content/british-general-election-2010-workers-vote-labour-stop-tories-%E2%80%93-lib-dems-rush-tory-talks, accessed 9 August 2016.

Lenin, V.I. (1902) 'What Is to Be Done?', LCW Vol. 5.

—— (1904) 'One Step Forward, Two Steps Back', LCW Vol. 7.

—— (1913) 'The Three Sources and Three Component Parts of Marxism', LCW Vol. 19.

—— (1916) 'The State and Revolution', LCW. Vol. 25.

—— (1918) 'The Proletarian Revolution and the Renegade Kautsky', LCW Vol. 28.

—— (1920) '"Left-Wing" Communism: An Infantile Disorder', LCW Vol. 31.

—— (1921a) 'Preliminary Draft Resolution of the Tenth Congress of the R.C.P. on Party Unity', LCW Vol. 32.

—— (1921b) 'Preliminary Draft Resolution of the Tenth Congress of the R.C.P. on The Syndicalist and Anarchist Deviation in Our Party', LCW Vol. 32.

—— (1974) *On the Emancipation of Women*, rev edn, Moscow: Progress Publishers.

Leplat, F. (ed.) (2008) *Respect: Documents of the Crisis*, 2nd edn, London: Resistance Books.

Lih, L.T. (2011) *Lenin*, London: Reaktion Books.

—— (2014) 'Lenin and Bolshevism', in S.A. Smith (ed.) *The Oxford Handbook of the History of Communism*, Oxford: Oxford University Press, pp. 53–71.

Lloyd, C. and Brenner, R. (1994) 'Militant after Grant: The Unbroken Thread?', *Permanent Revolution*, 10: 100–39.

Lofland, J. (1977) '"Becoming a World-Saver" Revisited', *American Behavioral Scientist*, 20(6): 805–18.

Lotz, C. and Feldman, P. (1994) *Gerry Healy: A Revolutionary Life*, London: Lupus Books.

Lukes, S. (2005) *Power: A Radical View*, 2nd edn, Basingstoke: Palgrave Macmillan.

Luxemburg, R. (1961) *The Russian Revolution*, Ann Arbor, MI: University of Michigan Press (original edition 1918).

—— (1970) 'The Mass Strike, the Political Party and the Trade Unions', in M.A. Waters (ed.) *Rosa Luxemburg Speaks*, New York: Pathfinder Press (original edition 1906), pp. 223–70.

Lyddon, D. (2007) 'From Strike Wave to Strike Drought: The United Kingdom, 1968–2005', in S. van der Velden, H. Dribbusch, D. Lyddon and K. Vandaele (eds) *Strikes around the World, 1968–2005: Case Studies of 15 Countries*, Amsterdam: Aksant, pp. 339–65.

McCleary, R.M. (2011) 'The Economics of Religion as a Field of Inquiry', in R.M. McCleary (ed.) *The Economics of Religion*, Oxford: Oxford University Press, pp. 3–36.

McDonald, P. (2012) 'Workplace Sexual Harassment 30 Years On: A Review of the Literature', *International Journal of Management Reviews*, 14(1): 1–17.

MacGregor, S. (1986) 'The History and Politics of Militant', *International Socialism*, 33: 59–88.

McGuiness, F. (2012) *Membership of UK Political Parties*, London: House of Commons Library, Standard Note SN/SG/5125.

McIlroy, J. (1999a) '"Always Outnumbered, Always Outgunned": The Trotskyists and the Trade Unions', in J. McIlroy, N. Fishman and A. Campbell (eds) *British Trade Unions and Industrial Politics, Volume 2: The High Tide of Trade Unionism, 1964–79*, Aldershot: Ashgate, pp. 259–96.

—— (1999b) 'Notes on the Communist Party and Industrial Politics', in J. McIlroy, N. Fishman and A. Campbell (eds) *British Trade Unions and Industrial Politics, Volume 2: The High Tide of Trade Unionism, 1964–79*, Aldershot: Ashgate, pp. 216–58.

—— (2005) 'Gerry Healy', in K. Gildart and D. Howell (eds) *Dictionary of Labour Biography, Volume 12*, Houndmills: Palgrave Macmillan, pp. 136–46.

—— (2006) 'The Establishment of Intellectual Orthodoxy and the Stalinization of British Communism 1928–1933', *Past and Present*, 192: 187–226.

—— and Daniels, G. (2009) 'An Anatomy of British Trade Unionism since 1997: Organization, Structure and Factionalism', in G. Daniels and J. McIlroy (eds) *Trade Unions in a Neoliberal World: British Trade Unions under New Labour*, Abingdon: Routledge, pp. 127–64.

McShane, H. and Smith, J. (1978) *Harry McShane: No Mean Fighter*, London: Pluto Press.

Mair, P. and van Biezen, I. (2001) 'Party Membership in Twenty European Democracies, 1980–2000', *Party Politics*, 7(1): 5–21.

Mair, P., Müller, W.C. and Plasser, F. (2004) 'Introduction: Electoral Challenges and Party Responses', in P. Mair, W.C. Müller and F. Plasser (eds) *Political Parties and Electoral Change*, London: Sage, pp. 1–19.

Mandel, E. (1969) *The Inconsistencies of 'State Capitalism'*, London: International Marxist Group (P).

—— (1971) *The Formation of the Economic Thought of Karl Marx: 1843 to Capital*, London: New Left Books.

—— (1975a) *Late Capitalism*, London: New Left Books.

—— (1975b) *What Is Trotskyism?*, Dublin: Revolutionary Marxist Group (P).

—— (1977a) 'The Leninist Theory of Organisation', in R. Blackburn (ed.) *Revolution and Class Struggle*, London: Fontana, pp. 78–135.

—— (1977b) *From Class Society to Communism: An Introduction to Marxism*, London: Ink Links.

—— (1978) *From Stalinism to Eurocommunism: The Bitter Fruits of 'Socialism in One Country'*, London: New Left Books.

—— (1979) *Trotsky: A Study in the Dynamic of His Thought*, London: New Left Books.

—— (1980) *The Second Slump: A Marxist Analysis of Recession in the Seventies*, London: Verso.

—— (1990) 'A Theory Which Has Not Withstood the Test of Facts', *International Socialism*, 49: 43–64.

—— (1995a) *Trotsky as Alternative*, London: Verso.

—— (1995b) *Long Waves of Capitalist Development: A Marxist Interpretation*, rev edn, London: Verso.

—— (2016) 'October 1917: Coup d'État or Social Revolution?', in F. Leplat and A. de Jong (eds) *October 1917: Workers in Power*, London: Merlin Press (original edition 1992), pp. 34–117.

March, L. (2011) *Radical Left Parties in Europe*, Abingdon: Routledge.

—— (2016) 'Radical Left 'Success' before and after the Great Recession: Still Waiting for the Great Leap Forward?', in L. March and D. Keith (eds) *Europe's Radical Left: From Marginality to the Mainstream?*, London: Rowman and Littlefield, pp. 27–50.

Marglin, S.A. and Schor, J.B. (eds) (1990) *The Golden Age of Capitalism: Reinterpreting the Postwar Experience*, Oxford: Clarendon Press.

Marot, J.E. (2006) 'Trotsky, the Left Opposition and the Rise of Stalinism: Theory and Practice', *Historical Materialism*, 14(3): 175–206.

Marsden, C. and Hyland, J. (2010) 'Political Instability Follows Inconclusive British Elections', 8 May, www.wsws.org/en/articles/2010/05/elec-m08.html, accessed 9 August 2016.

Marx, K. (1852) 'The 18th Brumaire of Louis Bonaparte', MECW Vol. 11.

—— (1859) 'Preface to *A Contribution to the Critique of Political Economy*', MECW Vol. 29.

—— (1871) 'The Civil War in France', MECW Vol. 22.

—— and Engels, F. (1848) 'Manifesto of the Communist Party', MECW Vol. 6.

Matgamna, S. (1998) 'The Russian Revolution and Marxism', in S. Matgamna (ed.) *The Fate of the Russian Revolution: Lost Texts of Critical Marxism, Volume 1*, London: Phoenix Press, pp. 9–154.

—— (2006) 'What Does the AWL Do?', *Workers' Liberty*, 3(2): 46–48.

—— (2015) 'Introduction: The Two Trotskys', in S. Matgamna (ed.) *The Fate of the Russian Revolution, Volume 2: The Two Trotskyisms Confront Stalinism*, London: Workers' Liberty, pp. 3–113.

—— (2017) *The Left in Disarray*, London: Workers' Liberty.

Mavrakis, K. (1976) *On Trotskyism: Problems of Theory and History*, London: Routledge and Kegan Paul.

Medvedev, R. (1976) *Let History Judge: The Origins and Consequences of Stalinism*, Nottingham: Spokesman.

Meredith, S. (2008) *Labours Old and New: The Parliamentary Right of the British Labour Party 1970–79 and the Roots of New Labour*, Manchester: Manchester University Press.

Michail, L. (1977) *The Theory of Permanent Revolution: A Critique*, London: Communist Party of Great Britain, Trotskyism Study Group (P).

Miéville, C. (2017) *October: The Story of the Russian Revolution*, London: Verso.

Militant (1980) *AUEW: The Case for a Fighting Socialist Leadership*, London: Militant (P).

—— (1981a) *Militant: What We Stand For*, London: Militant (P).

—— (1981b) *A Fighting Programme for the NUR*, London: Militant (P).

Mitchell, A. (2011) *Come the Revolution: A Memoir*, Sydney: NewSouth Publishing.

Molyneux, J. (2012) *The Point Is to Change It: An Introduction to Marxist Philosophy*, London: Bookmarks.

Moreau, P. (2008) 'The PDS/Linkspartei.PDS and the Extreme Left: Decline and Renaissance of Communism in Germany', in U. Backes and P. Moreau (eds) *Communist and Post-Communist Parties in Europe*, Göttingen: Vandenhoeck and Ruprecht, pp. 39–85.

Moreno, N. (2014) *The Transitional Program Today*, Buenos Aires: Ediciones El Socialista (P) (original edition 1980).

Morrow, F. (1976) *Revolution and Counter-Revolution in Spain*, London: New Park (original edition 1938).

Mostyn, P. (2015) 'Introduction', in Socialist Resistance (ed.) *Unity and Strategy: Ideas for Revolution*, London: Resistance Books, pp. 7–14.

Müller, W.C. and Strøm, K. (eds) (1999) *Policy, Office, or Votes? How Political Parties in Western Europe Make Hard Decisions*, New York: Cambridge University Press.

Mullins, B. (2014) '30 Years Ago: The Broad Left Organising Committee's Huge Impact', 7 April, www.socialistparty.org.uk/articles/18411, accessed 13 October 2016.

—— (2016) *On the Track: An Account of Trade Union Struggles at British Leyland in the Turbulent 1970s*, London: Socialist Publications.

Murphy, K. (2007) *Revolution and Counter-Revolution: Class Struggle in a Moscow Metal Factory*, Chicago, IL: Haymarket.

Murray, A. and German, L. (2005) *Stop the War: The Story of Britain's Biggest Mass Movement*, London: Bookmarks.

Mutnick, B. (ed.) (1979) *Kronstadt by V.I. Lenin and Leon Trotsky*, New York: Pathfinder Press.

National Committee of the SWP (1953) 'The Open Letter of the Socialist Workers Party, November 16, 1953', in C. Slaughter (ed.) *Trotskyism versus Revisionism: A Documentary History, Volume 1*, London: New Park, 1974, pp. 298–313.

Newman, M. (2002) *Ralph Miliband and the Politics of the New Left*, London: Merlin.

News Line (1980) *Thornett's Clique Unmasked: The Case History of a Revisionist Provocation*, London: News Line.

Nimtz, A.H. (2016) 'Marx and Engels on the Revolutionary Party', in L. Panitch and G. Albo (eds) *Socialist Register 2017*, London: Merlin Press, pp. 247–64.

North, D. (1986) 'Editorial', *Fourth International: A Journal of International Marxism*, 13(1): 3.

—— (1988) *The Heritage We Defend: A Contribution to the History of the Fourth International*, Detroit, MI: Labor Publications.

—— (1991) *Gerry Healy and His Place in the History of the Fourth International*, Detroit, MI: Labor Publications.

—— (2013) *In Defense of Leon Trotsky*, 2nd edn, Oak Park, MI: Mehring Books.

OECD (2010) *News in the Internet Age: New Trends in News Publishing*, Paris: Organisation for Economic Cooperation and Development.

Olson, D.V.A. (2011) 'Toward Better Measures of Supply and Demand for Testing Theories of Religious Participation', in R.M. McCleary (ed.) *The Economics of Religion*, Oxford: Oxford University Press, pp. 135–49.

Pennington, B. (1977) *Revolutionary Socialism: Why and How*, London: International Marxist Group (P).

Pickard, J. (1989) 'Introduction', in T. Grant, *The Unbroken Thread: The Development of Trotskyism over 40 Years*, London: Fortress Books, pp. vii–xvi.

Pimlott, B. (1992) *Harold Wilson*, London: HarperCollins.

Pirani, S. (2008) *The Russian Revolution in Retreat, 1920–24*, Abingdon: Routledge.

—— (2013) 'The Break-up of the WRP: From the Horse's Mouth', http://libcom.org/history/break-wrp-horse%E2%80%99s-mouth-simon-pirani, accessed 2 April 2017.

Pitt, B. (2002) *The Rise and Fall of Gerry Healy*, www.whatnextjournal.org.uk/Pages/Healy/Contents.html, accessed 26 May 2015.

Pröbsting, M. (2012) 'What Sort of Fifth International Do We Need?', *Revolutionary Communism*, 2: 26–38.

Radice, H. and Dunn, B. (2006) 'Permanent Revolution: Results and Prospects 100 Years On', in B. Dunn and H. Radice (eds) *100 Years of Permanent Revolution: Results and Prospects*, London: Pluto Press, pp. 1–9.

Rallings, C., Thrasher, M. and Craig, F.W.S. (1993) *Britain Votes 5: British Parliamentary Election Results 1988–1992*, Aldershot: Gower.

Rallings, C., Thrasher, M. and Craig, F.W.S. (1998) *Britain Votes 6: British Parliamentary Election Results 1997*, Aldershot: Gower.

Ramiro, L. (2016) 'Riders on the Storm: United Left and Podemos during the 2008 Great Recession', in L. March and D. Keith (eds) *Europe's Radical Left: From Marginality to the Mainstream?*, London: Rowman and Littlefield, pp. 311–30.

Ratner, H. (1994) *Reluctant Revolutionary: Memoirs of a Trotskyist 1936–1960*, London: Socialist Platform.

Redfern, N. (2014) 'No Friends to the Left: The British Communist Party's Surveillance of the Far Left, c1932–1980', *Contemporary British History*, 28(3): 341–60.

Redgrave, V. (1991) *Vanessa Redgrave: An Autobiography*, London: Hutchinson.

Rees, J. (1991) 'In Defence of October', *International Socialism*, 52: 3–79.

—— (2002) 'The Broad Party, the Revolutionary Party and the United Front', *International Socialism*, 97, Winter.

—— (2010) *Strategy and Tactics: How the Left Can Organise to Transform Society*, London: Counterfire.

—— (2014) *The ABC of Socialism*, 2nd edn, London: Counterfire.

Reid, B. (1969) *Ultra-Leftism in Britain*, London: Communist Party of Great Britain (P).

Renton, D. (2006) *When We Touched the Sky: The Anti-Nazi League 1977–1981*, Cheltenham: New Clarion Press.

—— (2014) 'Anti-Fascism in Britain, 1997–2012', in E. Smith and M. Worley (eds) *Against the Grain: The British Far Left from 1956*, Manchester: Manchester University Press, pp. 247–63.

Revolutionary Communist Group (1979) *The Anti-Nazi League and the Struggle against Racism*, 2nd edn, London: RCG Publications (P).

—— (1984) *The Revolutionary Road to Communism in Britain: Manifesto of the Revolutionary Communist Group*, London: Larkin Publications.

Richards, F. (1975) 'The International Socialists and Centrism: The Re-Emergence of Economism', *Revolutionary Communist*, 1: 14–26.

Roberts, G. (1976a) 'The Strategy of Rank and Filism', *Marxism Today*, 20(12): 375–83.

—— (1976b) 'The Politics of the International Marxist Group: Aspects of a Critique', *Marxism Today*, 20(2): 46–55.

Roberts, J.P. (2007) *Lenin, Trotsky and the Theory of Permanent Revolution*, London: Wellred Books.

Robinson, L. (2007) *Gay Men and the Left in Post-War Britain: When the Personal Got Political*, Manchester: Manchester University Press.

Rowbotham, S., Segal, L. and Wainwright, H. (1979) *Beyond the Fragments: Feminism and the Making of Socialism*, Newcastle: Newcastle Socialist Centre and Islington Community Press.

Rubinstein, J. (2011) *Leon Trotsky: A Revolutionary's Life*, New Haven, CT: Yale University Press.

Rucht, D. (2007) 'The Spread of Protest Politics', in R.J. Dalton and H-D. Klingemann (eds) *The Oxford Handbook of Political Behavior*, Oxford: Oxford University Press, pp. 708–23.

Rudge, J. (2017) *Out for the Count: the SWP and UK Parliamentary Elections*, Unpublished MS.

Sagra, A. (2011) 'A Brief Outline of the History of the International Workers League - Fourth International (IWL-FI)', *Socialist Voice*, Special Edition, 6–16.

Samuel, R. (2006) *The Lost World of British Communism*, London: Verso.

Sartori, G. (2005) *Parties and Party Systems*, rev edn, Colchester: ECPR Press.

Scarrow, S.E. (2007) 'Political Activism and Party Members', in R.J. Dalton and H-D. Klingemann (eds) *The Oxford Handbook of Political Behavior*, Oxford: Oxford University Press, pp. 636–54.

Seifert, R. and Sibley, T. (2012) *Revolutionary Communist at Work: A Political Biography of Bert Ramelson*, London: Lawrence and Wishart.

Sell, H. (2006) *Socialism in the 21st Century: The Way Forward for Anti-Capitalism*, 2nd edn, London: Socialist Publications.

Senex (2013) 'Revolutionary Tactics in Spain', *Revolutionary History*, 11(1): 129–44.

Serge, V. (1967) *Memoirs of a Revolutionary 1901–1941*, Oxford: Oxford University Press.

Service, R. (2010a) *Trotsky: A Biography*, London: Pan.

—— (2010b) *Stalin: A Biography*, London: Pan.

Sewell, R. (2002) 'Postscript', in T. Grant *History of British Trotskyism*, London: Wellred Books.

—— (2015) *Trade Unions in the Age of Capitalist Crisis: The Need for a Revolutionary Policy*, London: Socialist Appeal/International Marxist Tendency (P).

—— (2017a) 'The Revolutionary Lessons of Lenin's *What Is to Be Done?*', *In Defence of Marxism*, 18: 22–27.

—— (2017b) 'Introduction: In Defence of the Russian Revolution', *In Defence of Marxism*, 18: 3.

Seyd, P. and Whiteley, P. (2004) 'British Party Members: An Overview', *Party Politics*, 10(4): 355–66.

Seymour, R. (2016) *Corbyn: The Strange Birth of Radical Politics*, London: Verso.

Shaw, Martin (1978) 'The Making of a Party? The International Socialists 1965–1976', in R. Miliband and J. Saville (eds) *Socialist Register 1978*, London: Merlin, pp. 100–45.

Shaw, Mickie (1983) *Robert Shaw: Fighter for Trotskyism 1917–1980*, London: New Park.

Sheppard, B. (2012) *The Party: The Socialist Workers Party 1960–1988, Volume 2: Interregnum, Decline and Collapse, 1973–1988. A Political Memoir*, London: Resistance Books.

Sherry, D. (2017) *1917: Revolutionary Russia and the Dream of a New World*, London: Bookmarks.

Shipley, P. (1976) *Revolutionaries in Modern Britain*, London: Bodley Head.

—— (1983) *The Militant Tendency: Trotskyism in the Labour Party*, Richmond: Foreign Affairs Publishing Company.

Slaughter, C. (1971) *Who Are the International Socialists?*, London: Workers Press (P).

—— (1972) *Why a Labour Government? A Reply to Some Centrist Critics*, London: Socialist Labour League (P).

—— (ed.) (1974) *Trotskyism versus Revisionism, Volumes 1–4*, London: New Park.

—— (ed.) (1975) *Trotskyism versus Revisionism, Volumes 5–6*, London: New Park.

—— (1996) *A New Party for Socialism: Why? How? When?*, London: Workers' Revolutionary Party (Workers' Press).

—— (ed.) (2016) *Against Capital: Experiences of Class Struggle and Rethinking Revolutionary Agency*, London: Zero Books.

Smith, E. and Worley, M. (eds) (2014) *Against the Grain: The British Far Left from 1956*, Manchester: Manchester University Press.

Smith, S.A. (ed.) (2014) *The Oxford Handbook of the History of Communism*, Oxford: Oxford University Press.

Snow, D.A. (2004) 'Framing Processes, Ideology, and Discursive Fields', in D.A. Snow, S.A. Soule and H. Kriesi (eds) *The Blackwell Companion to Social Movements*, Malden, MA: Blackwell, pp. 380–412.

——, Soule, S.A. and Kriesi, H. (2004) 'Mapping the Terrain', in D.A. Snow, S.A. Soule and H. Kriesi (eds) *The Blackwell Companion to Social Movements*, Malden, MA: Blackwell, pp. 3–16.

Socialist Action (2013) *Revolution and Counter-Revolution in the Middle East*, London: Socialist Action (P).

Socialist Challenge (1977) *The Politics of Militant*, London: Socialist Challenge (P).

Socialist Equality Party (2010) 'After the General Election: Where Is Britain Going?', 6 May, www.wsws.org/en/articles/2010/05/pers-m06.html, accessed 9 August 2016.

—— (2011) *The Historical and International Foundations of the Socialist Equality Party (Britain)*, Sheffield: Mehring Books.

—— (2016) *Jeremy Corbyn and the Labour Party: The Strategic Lessons*, Sheffield: Mehring Books (P).

Socialist Organiser (1980) *The Fight for Trade Union Democracy*, London: Socialist Organiser (P).

Socialist Party (2008) *Capitalism in Crisis: The Case for Socialism*, London: Socialist Books (P).

—— (2013) *The Case for Socialism: Why You Should Join*, London: Left Books (P).

Solano, W. and Iglesias, I. (2013) 'Trotsky and Spain: The POUM's Assessment', *Revolutionary History*, 11(1): 145–66.

Strøm, K. and Müller, W.C. (1999) 'Political Parties and Hard Choices', in W.C. Müller and K. Strøm (eds) *Policy, Office, or Votes? How Political Parties in Western Europe Make Hard Decisions*, New York: Cambridge University Press, pp. 1–35.

Stutje, J.W. (2009) *Ernest Mandel: A Rebel's Dream Deferred*, London: Verso.

Sullivan, J. (2008) *Go Fourth and Multiply and When This Pub Closes*, Coventry: New Interventions (1981 and 1988) (P).

Swain, G. (2006) *Trotsky*, Harlow: Pearson Education.

Taaffe, P. (1995) *The Rise of Militant: Militant's 30 Years*, London: Militant Publications.

—— (2002) 'Militant's Real History: In Reply to Ted Grant and Rob Sewell', www.socialistparty.org.uk/militant/reply/, accessed 25 June 2016.

—— (2004) *A Socialist World Is Possible: The History of the CWI*, London: Socialist Books.

—— (2008) *Socialism and Left Unity: A Critique of the Socialist Workers Party*, London: Socialist Publications.

—— (2013) *Marxism in Today's World*, 2nd edn, London: Socialist Publications.

—— (2017) *From Militant to the Socialist Party*, London: Socialist Books.

—— and Mulhearn, T. (1988) *Liverpool: A City That Dared to Fight*, London: Fortress Books.

—— and Sell, H. (2007) *1917: The Year That Changed the World*, London: Socialist Books (P).

Tarrow, S. (1994) *Power in Movement: Social Movements, Collective Action and Politics*, New York: Cambridge University Press.

Tate, E. (2014) *Revolutionary Activism in the 1950s and 60s, Volume 2: Britain 1965–1970*, London: Resistance Books.

Temple, D. (1983) *British Miners and the Capitalist Crisis*, London: Workers Revolutionary Party/All Trades Union Alliance (P).

Thatcher, I.D. (2003) *Trotsky*, Abingdon: Routledge.

Thayer, G. (1965) *The British Political Fringe: A Profile*, London: Anthony Blond.

Thompson, D. (2007) *Pessimism of the Intellect? A History of New Left Review*, Monmouth: Merlin Press.

Thompson, P. and Lewis, G. (1977) *The Revolution Unfinished? A Critique of Trotskyism*, Liverpool: Big Flame (P).

Thompson, W. (1992) *The Good Old Cause: British Communism 1920–1991*, London: Pluto Press.

Thornett, A. (1979) *The Battle for Trotskyism: Documents of the Opposition Expelled from the Workers Revolutionary Party in 1974*, 2nd edn, London: Folrose.

—— (1987) *From Militancy to Marxism: A Personal and Political Account of Organising Car Workers*, London: Left View Books.

—— (1998) *Inside Cowley: Trade Union Struggle in the 1970s: Who Really Opened the Door to the Tory Onslaught?*, London: Porcupine Press.

—— (2011) *Militant Years: Car Workers' Struggles in Britain in the 60s and 70s*, London: Resistance Books.

Ticktin, H. (1992) 'Trotsky's Political Economy of Capitalism', in T. Brotherstone and P. Dukes (eds) *The Trotsky Reappraisal*, Edinburgh: Edinburgh University Press, pp. 216–32.

Tilly, C. (1978) *From Mobilization to Revolution*, New York: McGraw-Hill.

Tomlinson, J. (1981) *Left-Right: The March of Political Extremism in Britain*, London: John Calder.

Tourish, D. (2011) 'Leadership and Cults', in A. Bryman, D. Collinson, K. Grint, B. Jackson and M. Uhl-Bien (eds) *The Sage Handbook of Leadership*, London: Sage, pp. 215–28.

—— and Wohlforth, D. (2000) *On the Edge: Political Cults Right and Left*, Armonk, NY: M.E. Sharpe.

Trotsky, L. (1903) *Report of the Siberian Delegation*, London: New Park, 1973.

—— (1904) *Our Political Tasks*, London: New Park, 1979.

—— (1906 and 1929) *The Permanent Revolution* and *Results and Prospects*, New York: Pathfinder Press, 1969.

—— (1920) *Terrorism and Communism: A Reply to Karl Kautsky*, London: Verso, 2007.

—— (1921) 'Report on the World Economic Crisis and the New Tasks of the Communist International', in L. Trotsky *The First Five Years of the Communist International, Volume 1*, London: New Park, 1973.

—— (1922) 'On the United Front', in L. Trotsky *The First Five Years of the Communist International, Volume 2*, London: New Park, 1974.

—— (1923) *Problems of Everyday Life and Other Writings on Culture and Science*, New York: Monad Press, 1973.

—— (1924a) *The New Course*, Ann Arbor, MI: University of Michigan Press, 1965.

—— (1924b) *Lessons of October*, London: New Park, 1971.

—— (1924c) *The First Five Years of the Communist International, Volume 1*, London: New Park, 1973.

—— (1924d) *The First Five Years of the Communist International, Volume 2*, London: New Park, 1974.

—— (1927) *The Platform of the Joint Opposition*, London: New Park, 1973.

—— (1929a) *The Third International after Lenin*, London: New Park, 1974.

—— (1929b) 'Communism and Syndicalism', in L. Trotsky, *Marxism and the Trade Unions*, London: New Park, 1972.

—— (1929c) 'The Errors in Principle of Syndicalism', in L. Trotsky, *Marxism and the Trade Unions*, London: New Park, 1972.

—— (1930) *My Life: An Attempt at an Autobiography*, Harmondsworth: Penguin, 1975.

—— (1931) 'Letter to the Conference of the French Communist League', in *Writings of Leon Trotsky 1930–31*, New York: Pathfinder Press, 1973.

—— (1931–1933) *The History of the Russian Revolution*, London: Pluto Press, 1977.

—— (1932) 'What Next? Vital Questions for the German Proletariat', in L. Trotsky, *The Struggle against Fascism in Germany*, Harmondsworth: Penguin, 1975.

—— (1933a) 'It Is Necessary to Build Communist Parties and an International Anew', in L. Trotsky, *The Struggle against Fascism in Germany*, Harmondsworth: Penguin, 1975.

—— (1933b) 'It Is Time to Stop', in *Writings of Leon Trotsky 1933–34*, New York: Pathfinder Press, 1975.

—— (1934) 'The State of the League and Its Tasks' in *Writings of Leon Trotsky 1934–35*, New York: Pathfinder Press, 1974.

—— (1936) *Whither France?*, London: New Park, 1974.

—— (1937) *The Revolution Betrayed: What Is the Soviet Union and Where Is It Going?*, New York: Pathfinder Press, 1972.

—— (1938) *The Death Agony of Capitalism and the Tasks of the Fourth International: The Transitional Program*, New York: Pathfinder Press, 1970.

—— (1939a) *Their Morals and Ours*, New York: Pathfinder Press, 1973.

—— (1939b) 'A Petty-Bourgeois Opposition in the Socialist Workers Party', in L. Trotsky, *In Defence of Marxism (Against the Petty Bourgeois Opposition)*, London: New Park, 1971.

—— (1940) 'From a Scratch – to the Danger of Gangrene', in L. Trotsky, *In Defence of Marxism (Against the Petty Bourgeois Opposition)*, London: New Park, 1971.

—— (1942) *In Defence of Marxism (Against the Petty Bourgeois Opposition)*, London: New Park, 1971.

—— (1947) *Stalin: An Appraisal of the Man and His Influence*, London: Hollis and Carter.

—— (1970) *Women and the Family*, New York: Pathfinder Press.

—— (1972) *Leon Trotsky on the Trade Unions*, London: New Park.

—— (1972–1979) *Writings of Leon Trotsky 1929–40*, 14 Volumes, New York: Pathfinder Press.

—— (1974a) *Trotsky's Writings on Britain, Volume 1*, London: New Park.

—— (1974b) *Trotsky's Writings on Britain, Volume 2*, London: New Park.

—— (1975) *The Struggle against Fascism in Germany*, Harmondsworth: Penguin.

—— (1980a) *The Challenge of the Left Opposition (1923–25)*, New York: Pathfinder Press.

—— (1980b) *The Challenge of the Left Opposition (1926–27)*, New York: Pathfinder Press.

Twiss, T. (2010) 'Trotsky's Analysis of Stalinism', *Critique*, 38(4): 543–63.

United Secretariat of the Fourth International (1977) *Socialist Democracy and the Dictatorship of the Proletariat*, Toronto: Vanguard Publications (P).

Van Biezen, I., Mair, P. and Poguntke, T. (2012) 'Going, Going . . . Gone? The Decline of Party Membership in Contemporary Europe', *European Journal of Political Research*, 51(1): 24–56.

Van der Linden, M. (2009) *Western Marxism and the Soviet Union: A Survey of Critical Theories and Debates since 1917*, Chicago, IL: Haymarket Books.

Vernadsky, P. (2017) *The Russian Revolution: When Workers Took Power*, London: Phoenix Press.

Vernell, S., Miles, L. and Renton, D. (2012) *Trade Unions and the Fight against Austerity*, London: Unite the Resistance (P).

Videt, B. (2011) 'Introduction', in D. Bensaid et al. (eds) *New Parties of the Left: Experiences from Europe*, London: Resistance Books, pp. 9–21.

Virdee, S. (2014) 'Anti-Racism and the Socialist Left, 1968–79', in E. Smith and M. Worley (eds) *Against the Grain: The British Far Left from 1956*, Manchester: Manchester University Press, pp. 209–28.

Vodslon, M. (2016) *Why We Must Rebuild the Fourth International*, London: Workers International to Rebuild the Fourth International (P).

Walker, D. (1985) *Quite Right Mr Trotsky! Some Trotsky Myths Debunked and How Trotskyists Today Hamper the Fight for Peace and Socialism*, London: Harney and Jones.

Wandor, M. (1990) *Once a Feminist: Stories of a Generation*, London: Virago.

Webb, P. (2002) 'Introduction: Political Parties in Advanced Industrial Democracies', in P. Webb, D. Farrell and I. Holliday (eds) *Political Parties in Advanced Industrial Democracies*, New York: Oxford University Press, pp. 1–15.

Westwell, W. (2015) 'Build Revolutionary Leadership', *Marxist Review*, 30(4): 2–3, July–August.

Whelan, T. (1970) *The Credibility Gap: The Politics of the S.L.L.*, London: International Marxist Group (P).

Whiteley, P. (2009) 'Participation and Social Capital', in M. Flinders, A. Gamble, C. Hay and M. Kenny (eds) *The Oxford Handbook of British Politics*, Oxford: Oxford University Press, pp. 773–97.

Wicks, H. (1992) *Keeping My Head: Memoirs of a British Bolshevik*, London: Socialist Platform.

Widgery, D. (ed.) (1976) *The Left in Britain 1956–68*, Harmondsworth: Penguin.

—— (1986) *Beating Time: Riot 'n' Race 'n' Rock 'n' Roll*, London: Chatto and Windus.

Willett, G. (2014) 'Something New Under the Sun: The Revolutionary Left and Gay Politics', in E. Smith and M. Worley (eds) *Against the Grain: The British Far Left from 1956*, Manchester: Manchester University Press, pp. 173–89.

Wilson, B.R. (1970) *Religious Sects: A Sociological Study*, London: Weidenfeld and Nicholson.

—— (1990) *The Social Dimensions of Sectarianism: Sects and New Religious Movements in Contemporary Society*, Oxford: Clarendon Press.

Wiltshire, D. (1995) *Lenin in 1917: A Study for Today*, London: Union Books (P).

Wohlforth, T. (1994) *The Prophet's Children: Travels on the American Left*, Atlantic Highlands, NJ: Humanities Press.

Woodhouse, M. and Pearce, B. (1975) *Essays on the History of Communism in Britain*, London: New Park.

Woods, A. (1997) 'Introduction', in T. Grant, *Russia: From Revolution to Counter-Revolution*, London: Wellred Publications, pp. 13–40.

—— (1999) *Bolshevism: The Road to Revolution. A History of the Bolshevik Party from the Early Beginnings to the October Revolution*, London: Wellred Books.

—— (2013a) *Ted Grant: The Permanent Revolutionary*, London: Wellred Books.

—— (2013b) '130 Years since the Death of Karl Marx', *In Defence of Marxism*, 4: 2–22.

—— and Grant, T. (1976) *Lenin and Trotsky: What They Really Stood For. A Reply to Monty Johnstone*, London: Militant.

Woolley, B.L. (1999) *Adherents of Permanent Revolution: A History of the Fourth (Trotskyist) International*, New York: University Press of America.

Workers Power (1978) 'The Rank and File Movement Today', *Workers Power*, 7/8: 43–49.

—— (1984a) *The Road to Working Class Power*, London: Workers Power (P).

—— (1984b) *Where Next for the N.U.M.?*, London: Workers Power (P).

—— (n.d., 1990?) *The Politics of the Socialist Workers Party: A Trotskyist Critique*, London: Workers Power (P).

—— (2014) *An Action Programme for Britain*, London: Workers Power (P).

—— and Irish Workers Group (1983) *The Death Agony of the Fourth International and the Tasks of Trotskyists Today*, London: Workers Power.

Workers Revolutionary Party (1983) *Documents and Resolutions of the Sixth Congress August 27–29 1983*, London: WRP.

—— (1984a) *The Miners and the Case for a General Strike*, London: New Park (P).

—— (1984b) *Resolutions Adopted by the Seventh Congress December 1–3 1984*, London: WRP.

—— (1985a) *Lessons from the Miners' Strike: The Struggle for Power*, London: New Park (P).

—— (1985b) *Manifesto May Day 1985*, London: New Park (P).

Wright, E.O. (2015) 'From Grand Paradigm Battles to Pragmatic Realism: Towards an Integrated Class Analysis', in E.O. Wright, *Understanding Class*, London: Verso, pp. 1–18.

Websites: UK Trotskyist organizations

Alliance for Workers Liberty www.workersliberty.org/

Communist League www.themilitant.com/index.shtm

Counterfire www.counterfire.org/

Independent Socialist Network www.socialistproject.org/

International Bolshevik Tendency www.bolshevik.org/

International Socialist League http://litci.org/en/

Marxist World http://marxistworld.net/

Revolutionary Communist International Tendency in Britain https://rcitbritain.wordpress.com/

revolutionary socialism in the 21st century http://rs21.org.uk/

Socialist Action www.socialistaction.net/

Socialist Appeal www.socialist.net/

Socialist Equality Party www.socialequality.org.uk/

Socialist Fight http://socialistfight.com/

Socialist Party www.socialistparty.org.uk

Socialist Resistance http://socialistresistance.org/

Socialist Workers Party www.swp.org.uk/

Spartacist League/Britain http://www.icl-fi.org/index.html

Workers Fight www.union-communiste.org/

Workers International to Rebuild the Fourth International http://workersinternational.info/

Workers Power www.workerspower.co.uk/ and www.redflagonline.org

Workers Revolutionary Party www.wrp.org.uk/

Websites: Trotskyist Internationals

Committee for a Workers International www.socialistworld.net

Coordinating Committee for the Refoundation of the Fourth International www.crfiweb.org/

Fourth International (1938) www.internationalviewpoint.org

International Bolshevik Tendency www.bolshevik.org/

International Committee for Workers' Liberty www.marxistrevival.com/?page_id=12

International Committee of the Fourth International (SEP) www.wsws.org/icfi.shtml

International Committee of the Fourth International (WRP) http://wrp.org.uk/modules.php?name=Content&pa=showpage&pid=5

International Communist League (Fourth Internationalist) www.icl-fi.org/

Internationalist Communist Union (Trotskyist) www.union-communiste.org/

International Marxist Tendency www.marxist.com/

International Socialist Tendency http://internationalsocialists.org/wordpress/

International Workers League – Fourth International (Liga Internacional de Los Trabajadores – Cuarta Internacional) http://litci.org/es/

International Workers Unity (Fourth International) (Unidad Internacional do Los Trabajadores (Cuarta Internacional) www.uit-ci.org/

League for the Fifth International www.fifthinternational.org/

League for the Fourth International www.internationalist.org/

Liaison Committee for the Fourth International http://socialistfight.com/

Permanent Revolution Collective www.revolucionpermanente.com/english/

Revolutionary Communist International Tendency www.thecommunists.net/

Revolutionary Socialist Organization www.sozialismus.net/

Socialist Workers Party USA/Pathfinder Tendency www.themilitant.com/

Trotskyist Fraction – Fourth International (Fracción Trotskista–Cuarta Internacional) www.ft-ci.org

Workers International to Rebuild the Fourth International http://workersinternational.info/

INDEX

Page numbers in *italics* refer to figures; those in **bold** refer to tables.

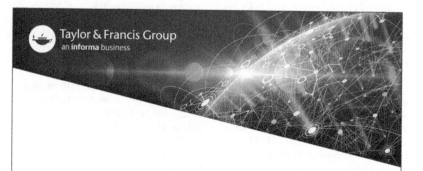